SAFE SANCTUARIES

For my Mum, and to the memory of my Dad

Let the love of our land's sacred rights
To the love of our people succeed
Let friendship and honour unite
And flourish on both sides the Tweed

Dick Gaughan

SAFE SANCTUARIES

Security and Defence in Anglo–Scottish
Border Churches 1290–1690

Christopher J. Brooke

JOHN DONALD
EDINBURGH

Published by John Donald,
an imprint of Birlinn Limited
8 Canongate Venture
5 New Street
Edinburgh EH8 8BH

www.birlinn.co.uk

ISBN 1 85976 535 0

British Library Cataloguing in Publication Data
A catalogue record for this book is available from the British Library

The publisher acknowledges subsidy from

English Heritage

CONTENTS

NOTE ON ACCESS TO
BUILDINGS AND SITES

The majority of churches and chapels described in this book are freely accessible to the general public. However, it is a sad reflection on our times that many now have to be kept locked, including those that were once secure, defensible buildings; keys are often available locally, but sometimes only by prior arrangement. Potential visitors are advised that some of the more remote and isolated churches may require a journey of some distance in order to procure a key.

Several of the features described in this work are located in upper chambers and towers which are not open to the normal visitor. *Bone fide* researchers will therefore need to make special arrangements beforehand in order to view these areas, and are warned that access is sometimes both restricted and difficult.

Whilst most churches are still in use for public worship, a few are now ruined, and several have no standing remains whatsoever. These ruins and sites are often located on private land, and visitors are reminded that they should seek the permission of the landowner before inspecting. Most of the larger monastic sites, and some ruined churches and tower-houses, are in the care of Historic Scotland or English Heritage, and these buildings are open to the public at times advertised.

PREFACE AND
ACKNOWLEDGEMENTS

This book was born out of a personal interest in three subjects: churches, castles, and the Anglo–Scottish borderland. A great deal has been written about all three, and much on the subject of churches and castles on the border individually. However, little has appeared in print on the seemingly paradoxical amalgamation of these two forms of architecture. It was over a decade ago, whilst preparing a series of lectures on the secular use of churches in the Middle Ages, that I became aware that only a handful of examples of fortified churches in this area appear in the literature. I considered it unlikely that this was the whole story, and so set about research for the present volume, venturing an examination of all standing churches, and many sites, within the six original Marches of the medieval frontier.

This is not an attempt to produce a definitive analysis of the churches in the region. A great deal of work remains to be done on individual buildings, and I have no doubt that more evidence remains to be discovered. This book is intended to cover the broad picture, insofar as the evidence allows, of a rare by-product of the perils and unrest of many centuries of warfare and violence: the defensible church.

Research of this nature, covering as it does, a wide geographical area, has called upon the generosity and expertise of many colleagues and individuals. My debt to them is great, and it is my hope that they will each gain some satisfaction from having helped to shed further light on a dark period in Anglo-Scottish Border history.

I am indebted to my sponsors who provided generous subvention towards the cost of this publication: Historic Scotland, English Heritage, and the John and Ruth Howard Charitable Trust.

A subject upon which little has previously been published inevitably generates weighty academic debate. This debate has assisted me in focusing upon specific issues, sites, and features, which may otherwise have received less attention than they deserve. For providing stimulating discussion, information on specific sites, and for assisting me in reducing the number of errors and misconceptions, I am especially grateful to Professor Rosemary Cramp,

Dr Philip Dixon, Dr Richard Fawcett, Professor Tony Goodman, Barbara Harbottle, Adrian Henstock, Dr Norman Macdougall, Thom Richardson, Peter
Ryder, David Sherlock, and Christopher Tabraham. For patiently reading the
draft of my manuscript (some parts more than once), and for their invaluable
advice, my particular thanks go to Professor John Beckett and Dr David Parsons.

Over the ten years it has taken to complete the fieldwork for this under-
taking, I have met with many kind people: priests, ministers, churchwardens,
elders, architects, and other church and lay officials, who have unselfishly
given of their time. I have been privileged to have been able to examine the
upper chambers of towers, chancels, porches, and turrets, to study roofs and
bellcotes, and visit other places to which the general public normally has no
access. To all those who made this possible, too numerous to list individually
here, I would like to express my most sincere thanks. I must however single out
two individuals for their specific help: Nigel Foxon and Ian Turnbull, from the
Newcastle and Carlisle Anglican Dioceses respectively, who were frequently
pestered by my telephone calls requesting the names of incumbents, churchwardens, or simply how to get hold of a ladder at some remote fellside church.
Their patience has been remarkable.

For his generous permission to examine Hulne Priory, I would like to thank
his Grace the Duke of Northumberland; for allowing me the free run of Carlisle Cathedral and Deanery, the Very Reverend Henry Stapleton; and for
getting me safely to the site of Memmerkirk, despite the perils of the deep
snow, I am indebted to Bob Smith. Others who deserve individual mention
for their especial help are: Robert Carmichael, Michael Holmes, the Reverend
Geraldine Hope, John Howliston, Joe Kent, Derek Thompson, and the Reverend Ian Wotherspoon. My thanks also extend to Mike Norris of the Wilton
Lodge Museum at Hawick for his help with the Wheel kirk, to Amanda Cum-
ming for the reconstruction drawing of Ladykirk church, and to Dr Fiona
Watson for being understanding about Appendix 2. Peter Ryder deserves a
second mention for his indispensable advice during the examination of a
number of churches in Northumberland, and for kindly creating Figure 3.

My father, the late Harold Brooke, assisted with some of my documentary
research in his capacity as Librarian and Archivist of Southwell Minster
Library, and I remember with deep gratitude his help and support. Donald
Fox has been a stalwart friend in assisting with the translation of some of
the more intractable medieval Latin texts, and I must thank another friend,
George Dawson, for his encyclopedic knowledge of bells. I would also like
to acknowledge the assistance given by the staff and IT services of Aberdeen,
Durham, Glasgow, Newcastle upon Tyne, Nottingham, and Oxford University
libraries.

Several plans are reproduced here by the very kind permission of Mike
Salter, and those of Holy Island and Tynemouth are the copyright of English
Heritage; these are individually acknowledged in the text. Figure 174 is repro-

duced by permission of Historic Scotland. I am grateful to Topic Records for their permission to reproduce the verse from Dick Gaughan's *Both Sides The Tweed*. At the business end, I am most grateful to all at John Donald who always seemed to make the big problems go away, and my thanks go to The Wheel in Edinburgh for creating the maps. All photographs, except where otherwise credited, are by the author.

Finally, I owe my greatest debt to my parents, Margaret and Harold Brooke who fostered my interest in northern British archaeology and history; they not only helped, unstintingly, with the extensive fieldwork, but offered me many timely words of wisdom, without which this project may never have reached completion.

C.J.B.

LIST OF FIGURES

LIST OF MAPS

The Anglo-Scottish Border showing principal towns and divisions of Marches in the sixteenth century

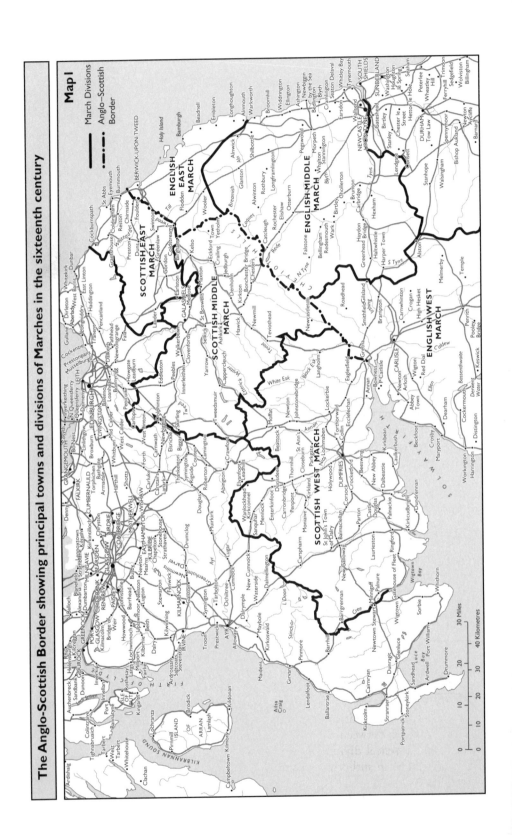

Map I

March Divisions

Anglo–Scottish Border

INTRODUCTION

For a period of four hundred years, from the close of the thirteenth century to the end of the seventeenth century, the people of the rugged country along the border between Scotland and England were subjected to repeated bouts of war and hostility. The political and social turmoil to which they were exposed meant they took matters of personal safety very seriously. Such was the need for defence and safe refuge from sudden raids, or more protracted incursions, that many parish churches were turned into secure havens, more suited to defence than the flimsily built homesteads of the common people. The use of the church as a physical refuge was certainly fitting, for in 1602 the inhabitants of the Scottish West March were described as 'void of the feir and knawledge of God and consequentlie of that dew reverence and obedience quhilk they aucht to his majestie and lawis' (Fraser 1894; Rae 1966, 67). This book is primarily concerned with one of the consequences of this instability, the construction or adaptation of churches for the purposes of providing local communities with safe refuges, and as repositories for valuables, during periods of unrest.

A rough border between England and Scotland was established in the early thirteenth century. Alexander II of Scotland's support of the northern English lords against King John provoked the English monarch's anger, and in the ensuing fighting the Scots lost their control over the northern counties of England, the border being drawn between the Solway Firth in the west and Berwick-upon-Tweed in the east. However, a century passed before this frontier was agreed by all parties at the Treaty of Northampton in 1328. To the north lay the Southern Uplands, with the fertile valleys of the Tweed and its tributaries, sandwiched between the great horseshoe shape of the Moorfoot and Lammermuir hills, and the long line of the Cheviots. In the west, the two great valleys of Eskdale and Liddesdale ran down to the Solway, and beyond Dumfries the land spilled out to form the Galloway peninsula. To the south the valleys of the Rede, Coquet, and Tyne stretched out eastwards from the hills and moors, whilst in Cumbria the valleys of the Eden, Wampool, and Waver softened the edges of the uplands as they ran quietly out into the Solway through the coastal marshes. Between the two countries, like guardian sentinels, rose the Cheviots: a physical dividing line without question, whose rugged presence was, and still is, an authority unchallenged.

Relations between the two countries had been generally peaceful in the twelfth century, although the Scottish King William the Lion laid waste to a large area of northern England during an uprising of 1173–74. According to an account by Reginald of Durham, the churches around Plumbland in Cumbria were used as refuges by the people of the area who brought with them all their possessions and turned Plumbland church itself into 'a kind of castle' (Reg. Mon. Dunelm., 275). Peace continued from the late 1170s more or less to the end of the thirteenth century, and the Borderland enjoyed comparative political stability. Monasteries were founded in the fertile valleys of the Tweed and Tyne, near the shores of the Solway, and in the foothills of the Cheviots. Numerous small parish churches and chapels were built. Religious establishments prospered here as, indeed, they did in much of Britain at this time.

The incident which provided a catalyst in the crucible of Anglo-Scottish politics took place on a wild, dark night in March 1286. Alexander III, the last of the Scottish Canmore kings, rode out of Edinburgh to join his new wife, Yolande de Dreux. On the journey he fell from his horse near Kinghorn and was killed. His first two sons had already died, and the heir to the throne was his granddaughter, Margaret the 'Maid of Norway'. Four years later, without ever seeing Scotland, she too was dead and the Canmore dynasty was ended. As fate would have it, the monarch on the English throne at this time was a strong, powerful king, Edward I, who wasted no time in seizing the opportunity to gain control by establishing as the new king, John Balliol, 'an ordinary man put into an impossible position by his arrogant overlord' (Mackie 1978, 68). Edward, forcing Balliol to rebel by his peremptory demands, drove the two nations into a bitter and bloody war, kindling in the Scots a strong patriotism and deep hatred of the English. That Edward was unable to subsume Scotland into his own kingdom was due mainly to the actions of two major players, William Wallace and Robert Bruce, who resisted the English king and his army, and forced him to make unrealistic economic claims on his nation, thus denying a successful, permanent invasion (Paterson 1996).

War continued on and off during the fourteenth century, with the balance of power regularly shifting between the two realms. The strong Scottish king, Robert Bruce, inflicted defeat on Edward II at Bannockburn in 1314, and achieved his nation's independence with the Treaty of Edinburgh in 1328. However, he was succeeded by the infant King David II at the same time as the ambitious Edward III, inheriting his grandfather's abilities as a leader, took control in London. Once more the two nations were plunged into bitter conflict. During the fifteenth century the majority of England's military efforts were directed across the Channel, but Scotland's continuing alliance with France ensured that cross-border hostilities would endure. Of the wars and battles which followed, much has been written, from the saga of Bannockburn, through the epic accounts of Otterburn, Neville's Cross, and Halidon Hill, to the tragedy which cost Scotland her king and army on Flodden Field in September of 1513.

Throughout these wars the Border was turned into a no-man's-land where armies rode without warning, and pillage and looting were commonplace. Although in the three hundred or so years of fighting there was more peacetime than war, the people became so hardened to the violence and rancour of the area that raiding, arson, murder, and extortion became a way of life, accepted as customary and normal. Of all the activities which took place against this backdrop of violence the most infamous was that of 'reiving', or raiding. It was not only cross-border raiding either, for clan and family feuds were frequent and stealing from one's 'enemie' might mean anyone outside the immediate family. Although forming an integral part of the lifestyle of the Border people, the activity of reiving became so widespread during the sixteenth century that the legal system of control, Border Law, all but fell apart. This system of provincial law was first introduced in the mid-thirteenth century to ratify the customs and practices which had long governed disputes between the two nations (Scott 1993; Neville 1998). The laws were strengthened by the monarchs of both countries following the Wars of Independence, a protracted power struggle between Scotland and England for the throne of the northern kingdom. Such laws were needed in order to regulate the unruly behaviour of the people, and by the fourteenth century to negotiate redress for military depredations committed during times of truce (Rae 1966).

The frontier between England and Scotland was divided into six territories known as 'Marches'. Three were on the Scottish side of the border and three on the English side, although the division into Middle and East Marches on the English side took place only midway through the sixteenth century (Lomas 1996a). Each of the Marches corresponds roughly to an area occupied by the confines of the old Scottish and English counties, prior to the reorganisation of the boundaries in 1974. The Marches were governed by a 'Warden', appointed originally by the monarch or Parliament, and later by Council (indeed members of both royal families held office as Wardens including John of Gaunt for England and Alexander, Duke of Albany, for Scotland). On the Scottish side, the position of Warden closely followed the social structure based on feudal tenure, and appointments were dominated by the principal families, notably Hume, Kerr, Douglas, and Maxwell. Up to a point this system worked, but it was often corrupt and brutal in its operation: 'Jethart Justice', derived in the Scottish Middle March town of Jedburgh, allowed a man to be hanged first and tried afterwards, and the infamous 'hot (or cold) trod' granted a victim the right to recover his stolen property by force up to six days after the offence had occurred. The machinery of Border justice was understandably flawed. Society as it existed was a relic of a social order older than feudalism, where families had been long accustomed to rely on self-help in the defence of their lives and property (Jones 1969).

The political administration of the Border continued to differ from that to the north or south of the region up until the Union of the Crowns in 1603. Even after the two nations became united under one monarch, James VI of

Scotland and I of England, some echoes of the previous difficulties continued, and as late as the third quarter of the seventeenth century the Register of the Privy Council records the setting up of special commissions to deal with Border troubles (Mitchison 1970).

Every part of society was caught up in the instability of these years. At the commencement of the Wars of Independence in 1296, the Scottish government ordered English clergy (on Scottish soil) to be ejected from their benefices (Young 1997). In the following year the English clergy reacted strongly to Wallace's Scottish invasion by issuing summonses to vote money for defence (Graham 1929). The clergy were themselves no strangers to bloodshed and war, indeed bishops and priests often led the way onto the field of battle (MacEwen 1913; Barrow 1962), and Bishop Kirkby of Carlisle led several military expeditions into Scotland in 1337 (Wilson 1901-5, ii). There are several surviving accounts which call on the Archbishop of York to array his clergy in defence against the Scots, for example in 1461 when Edward IV ordered the archbishop that 'ye do make open proclamacons that all yor clergie be redy upon a day warnyng, in moost defensable wyse, to goo forth for the resistence of oure auncienne ennemyes the Scottes' (Hexham Memorials, lxxviiii). The Scots on the other hand enjoyed a special status within the western church, as the *Ecclesia Scoticana* consisted of a group of bishoprics directly dependent on the papacy, a situation which was clearly intolerable to the English monarchy seeking a stake in the political control of the church (Barrow 1988). The fact that most Scottish bishops supported Robert I after 1306, despite the fact that he was under excommunication for the murder of John Comyn, his rival to the throne, illustrates the fierce patriotism and hatred of English domination which prevailed at the time (Grant 1984). Indeed, the relationship between church and monarchy was unusually close in Scotland, and the royal interest and control in ecclesiastical affairs probably exceeded that which Rome intended (Lynch 1992). The church of Durham did much to try to maintain the peace through diplomatic processes, and during the fourteenth century Bishops Hatfield and Skirlaw were heavily involved with political relations between the two nations (Dobson 1992).

Secularization of some aspects of church life was commonplace: to the medieval mind, God was almost a feudal lord, and fortification of a building, spiritual or temporal, was the outward and most visible sign of these lordly powers (Coulson 1982). The reivers and criminal elements of the borderland seem to have had little regard for religion or those representing its authority, and by the sixteenth century there appears to have been a high degree of corruption amongst the clerical ranks in the region. Fighting in churches and churchyards was commonplace, and excommunication was insufficient as a means of deterring this behaviour. The penalty was increased such that an offender 'not onely be deemed excommunicate . . . but also have one of his eares cutt of' (Durham Depositions, cccv).

During the later Middle Ages, a system of secular control of church lands in Scotland, which had begun in the late thirteenth century, resulted in the appointment of bailies and commendators whose job was the 'defence' of the church in its physical form, as well as from the usurpation of covetous men. These lay administrators had considerable power and influence (Sanderson 1982), and were not averse to using church buildings in the execution of their duties. Thus the bailie of Kilwinning Abbey, in Ayrshire, 'had the stepill [of the abbey] for a ward and prisoun to poneis and keip malefactouris and presowneres' (Murray 1995, 31). Furness Abbey, in Lancashire, apparently had a dungeon in the sixteenth century, the jailer for which was none other than the abbot himself (Wilson 1901–5, ii, 48). Even when direct administration was not a primary objective, secular interference in ecclesiastical affairs was commonplace; Lord Dacre referred to the abbot of Newminster as 'my monk' and was known to have seriously influenced the convent of Lanercost in their election decisions (Baskerville 1937, 51). The monarchy were however sometimes concerned with the level of outside intervention, and in the first Act of his first parliament, in 1424, King James I of Scotland declared the 'Freedom of Haly Kirk', intended to ensure the protection of the Church establishment against all encroachments upon its lands and possessions (Duke 1937, 112–3), a sentiment which echoed that which had been issued by Pope Alexander III in *c.* 1170 (Barrow 1992).

Monastic houses were no less vulnerable than parish churches, and during Edward III's great offensive against the Scots in 1335, the abbey of Newbattle near Edinburgh and the nunnery at Manuel further to the west near Linlithgow, were badly damaged by the invading army, despite, in the case of Newbattle, having received letters of protection (Nicholson 1965, 205). As repositories of precious objects such as liturgical vessels, gold and silver ornament, and fine linen, monasteries were often regarded as legitimate targets for plunder, especially during periods of war, and elements of security to safeguard such treasures were often introduced. Not surprisingly many Border abbeys have physical evidence of defence, such as the precinct walls surrounding Hulne and Sweetheart, the strong gatehouses at Alnwick and Wetheral, and the extreme example of fortification at Tynemouth where the gatehouse effectively became a castle in its own right.

In these unsettled circumstances it is no surprise to find the people of the Border region turning to the church for protection and, specifically, to the church building. Churches throughout the British Isles could be turned into 'castles' in response to social or political conditions (Kelland 1982). Some Anglo-Saxon towers show signs of having been built with defence in mind, such as that at Wickham in Berkshire, which has an external entrance 2.5 m (8 ft) above ground level (Fisher 1969; Audouy *et al* 1995, 92), although this may be a security feature which related to the use of the tower for domestic accommodation. The west façade of Lincoln Cathedral was furnished with machicolation slots above the entrance arcades, a feature later exploited by King Stephen during his siege, when he reportedly made a castle out of the church

Fig. 1. Bedale, North Yorkshire, entrance to tower stairway with portcullis slot above.

(Potter 1955, 47–8; Gem 1986). Also during the troubled years of Stephen's reign, churches throughout the realm were hurriedly fortified to provide a means of defence. Examples include Bampton, Oxfordshire (Brown 1976, 82), and Southwell Minster, Nottinghamshire (Cathcart King 1983, 382). Many churches on the border between England and Wales were first made defensible during the reign of Edward I, a trend which continued in later years, for example Old Radnor, Disserth, and Llanbister. Between 1200 and 1536, 135 Licences to Crenellate were issued for ecclesiastical buildings and related structures in England (Coulson 1982). Nor was this the end of the practice. In the Civil War of the seventeenth century, many churches were pressed into use as garrison posts and lookouts: at Alton, Hampshire, the parish church of St Laurence still bears the scars of the battle which took place there in December 1643, whilst the tower of Upton in Nottinghamshire was used as a lookout, the parish constable's accounts for the year 1645 recording that one Thomas Kirkin

Fig. 2. Dysart, St Serf's church, Fife, showing defensible tower of *c.* 1500 (after MacGibbon and Ross 1896–7).

was paid 8*d*. and tobacco and ale for the 'watch on the steeple' (Gill 1913). In other areas there are isolated examples of truly fortified churches, some with spectacular defences like the portcullis slot in front of the tower stairway at Bedale in North Yorkshire (Figure 1), the castle-like tower of Dysart kirk in Fife (Figure 2), and the former hoarding gallery to defend the tower of Newton Nottage on the Glamorgan coast. Churches on the fringes of the main theatre of Border warfare also suffered, and appropriate measures were taken: at Ripon Cathedral a battlemented wall formerly ran across the east end, and crenellations appear to have been added subsequent to fourteenth-century Scottish attacks (Forster *et al* 1993). So great was the impact of this conflict that the counties of Durham, North Yorkshire, Westmorland, the Lothians, Ayrshire and Lanarkshire, each have examples of ecclesiastical defence.

Monastic buildings were also fortified. The rebuilt abbey gatehouse at Bury St Edmunds, following the riots of 1327, was equipped with a portcullis and arrow slits, and 55 years later, after another riot, the abbot of Thornton in Lincolnshire obtained a licence to crenellate 'the new house over and about the gate' of the abbey (Platt 1990, 210). Quarr Abbey on the Isle of Wight had been fortified much earlier, in 1365 (Kightly 1979, 130).

However, these are individual examples. With the exception of the Welsh borderland, there are no other major groups of such churches in Britain. In addition, the defensible and fortified churches of the Anglo-Scottish Border region represent a relatively small group of such buildings at least compared to parts of continental Europe (Moulins 1857; Lemasson and Hanotaux 1938; Anghel 1982; Bonde 1994). The comparatively minor adaptations found in British churches hardly bear comparison with the impressive fortifications of the hybrid fortress-cathedrals and abbeys of France and eastern Europe, some of the latter being constructed for defensive purposes as late as the seventeenth century. An example is the heavily bastioned monastery of Jasna Gora near Czestochowa in Poland, which was fortified around 1650, and withstood a major artillery assault by Swedish forces in 1655 (Duffy 1979, 188–90).

The decision to use the church for defensive purposes was a logical one. Other forms of defence are better known: castles, both royal and private, tower-houses, peles, and fortalices. These were not generally accessible to the common people of the Border whose houses were 'cottages and huts so wretched that they did not care whether they were burnt or not' (Bates 1891, 59), and 'houses such as a man may build within three or four hours' (Tough 1928, 41), 'just like the booths at a fair' (Morris 1984, 173). It was not surprising therefore that the Acts of the Parliaments of Scotland for 1535 required 'that all uther landit men of smaller Rent or Reuenew, big pelis and gret strengthis as thai plese for saifing of thare selfis men tennentes and gudis' (Bates 1891, 59–60); the Act goes on to say that these defences should be 'completit within twa yeres under the pane'. In many cases, compliance with the law may have already been in place where the church had been adapted for use as a communal refuge as there is little evidence that the order was generally observed (MacGibbon and Ross 1887–92, ii, 38). Such adaptation was as much in the people's own interests in terms of safety as from retribution by the Crown. A Scottish decree, issued in 1524, had instructed the head men of the region 'baith spirituale and temporall' to go to their houses and defend them against the English (Murray 1995, 32). As the 'houses' of the clergy, certainly in the case of monastic establishments, may have been considered to include the church, then elements of security and defence were probably renewed in these buildings. Additionally, some higher status dwellings of the common people at least had basic elements of defence, as Sir Robert Bowes, surveying the Border in the mid-sixteenth century, noted in Tynedale that:

> . . . the heddesmen of them have very strong houses whereof for the most parte the utter sydes or walles be made of greatt sware oke trees strongly bounde and Joyned together with great tenons of the same so thycke mortressed that yt wylbe very harde withoute greatt force and laboure to breake or caste downe any

of the said houses . . . roofes be so greatt and covered most parte with turves and earthe that they wyll not easyly burne or be sett on fyre (Frontier I, 232–3).

The Scots and English had clashed many times prior to the early fourteenth century, and the church was the place to which the populace fled. It was not necessarily a safe haven: when in 1129 the townsfolk of Kendal used the church for refuge against a Scottish incursion they were pursued and massacred within the walls (Addison 1982). For this reason, although the term 'fortified' is commonly used, more properly we ought to view the majority of these northern Border churches as 'defensible'. Few, if any, were constructed with offensive motives in mind. That would have required troops and provisions, and whilst one or two were garrisoned for a while during specific campaigns, Tynemouth Priory alone was regarded by the Crown as a fortress against the Scots, and therefore served a truly offensive function. In most cases the church, as the only substantial stone building in a village or town, represented a safe haven. As the local folk were responsible for its upkeep (the chancel apart) it is hardly surprising that they saw the opportunity of providing a local sanctuary for the community in times of trouble (Goodman 1989). On occasion, it was the priest himself, or the appropriate ecclesiastical authority, either monastic or parochial, who adapted the church for defence, as at Newton Arlosh in the English West March where the monks of Holme Cultram Abbey commissioned a fortified church in the fourteenth century. Elsewhere, in addition to, or in place of, the actual fortification of the church, it was sometimes the practice for the wealthier livings to have a vicars' pele tower constructed close by for the personal security of the priest and perhaps other officials. One of the most striking of these is the small tower in the churchyard at Corbridge in the English Middle March, which was built in the second half of the fourteenth century. This was a vulnerable area where, in 1296, the scholars and monks in nearby Hexham had been burnt alive during one of the first Scottish incursions over the border, made in response to Edward I's interference in Scottish politics. However, the practicalities were such that it was the ordinary people who most needed to defend themselves. Money was, on occasion, provided by wealthy landlords, for it was in their own interest to ensure that their tenants were protected from harm. Entries in the account books of the earls of Northumberland during the fifteenth century refer to money spent on repairing church towers for the protection of tenants against the Scots (Addison 1982, 179), and George Clarkson's 1561 survey for the Percy estates emphasised the importance of maintaining both churches and vicarages as places of defence (Keeling 1975, 176).

Churches were not always adapted specially for defence. Many were probably used simply because they were stone buildings which would not burn easily. A few ecclesiastical buildings survive from well before the main period of Border unrest; in all likelihood they were used defensively with little recourse to rebuilding or adaptation (Norman churches characteristically had thick walls, small windows, and, often, stone vaulting). Secular activities commonly took place in churches (Davis 1968) and defence was simply another such function. Churches were also, by the very nature of their purpose, repositories for valuable goods and documents, and the safety of these items was a constant concern for custodians of the buildings. Even during 'safe' hours, the general public were not intended to roam about the building freely, and the internal fittings and layout were in part designed to impede the visitor's progress towards the treasures of the church, usually contained in the eastern portion (Oman 1979). As well as physical defence for the community and priests, churches were therefore also adapted to protect precious objects which would be a prominent target for thieves or looting soldiers.

What then defines a fortified or defensible church? A few examples are obvious: Great Salkeld, Newton Arlosh, and Burgh-by-Sands in Cumbria, Ancroft in Northumberland, Greenlaw and Ladykirk in the Scottish Borders. All had strong towers, some more like castle keeps than campaniles. Nonetheless, deliberate major structural modification of the building in this way, to accommodate military exploitation, is exceptional (Morris 1989, 252). There were, however, other ways of adapting a church to provide defence (Figure 3). Some were self-evident, such as the position and placing of windows well above the ground. Others were more subtle, like the extraordinarily steep stairway in the tower at Brigham, and the numerous stone-vaulted roofs which provided an aegis against enemy fires, as at Kirknewton, Bellingham, and Ladykirk. A specialist device was the deliberate blocking of the tower-arch, or its omission entirely, reducing access into the tower to a narrow doorway; Hartburn, Kirkwhelpington, and Newbiggin, each have good examples. Monasteries mostly had high precinct walls, and churches usually had stout oak doors furnished with good locks, bolts, and perhaps draw-bars (Oman 1979); examples of the last include Morpeth, Edlingham, Bassendean, Kelso, as well as a host of other sites. More rarely an iron yett or yat was used as a doorway defence, and examples survive at Burgh-by-Sands and Great Salkeld. Occasionally these features have been left intact during later restorations, but mostly they have not – leaving, at best, only archaeological indications in the fabric as to the original intention for a particular area of the building, or sometimes an historical narrative attests their former existence. Some features have not survived at all, such as fireproof turf and earth roofs, and we know of them only from contemporary sources (Robson 1989, 149). Of course these churches were intended primarily for the worship of God, and they contained all the usual liturgical features found in any church of the period; indeed, their use as defensible refuges may also have been influenced by the spiritual protection afforded by the house of the Almighty, and a zealous, powerful Church (Kelland 1982).

The architecture of these churches reflected the harsh life and climate of the area. In his discussion of ecclesiastical buildings in Northumberland, Nikolaus Pevsner (1957, 35) remarks on the 'sturdy, masculine, rough character of the county', whilst Addison (1982, 171) notes that Cumbrian churches have an 'all-embracing defensive air and martial character' and that 'the roughness

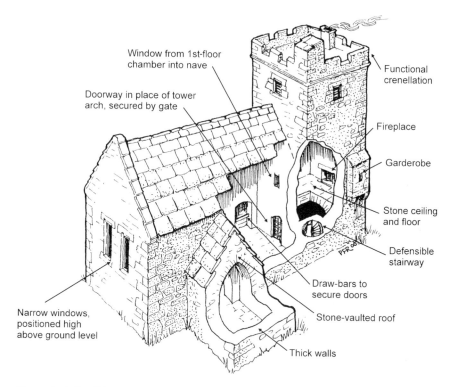

Window from 1st-floor
chamber into nave

Doorway in place of tower
arch, secured by gate

Functional
crenellation

Fireplace

Garderobe

Stone ceiling
and floor

Defensible
stairway

Draw-bars to
secure doors

Stone-vaulted roof

Narrow windows,
positioned high
above ground level

Thick walls

Fig. 3. A defensible Border church. Reconstruction loosely based on Newton Arlosh and Great Salkeld, showing typical features of security.

of construction continued to characterize church building in the north long after more sophisticated styles had been introduced in the rest of England'. This rugged character was to persist for the whole of the medieval period, and is reflected even in comparatively modern buildings such as the parish church of St John the Evangelist at Plumpton in Cumbria, built in 1907 by Sir Robert Lorimer. The church has a tower which, on approach, has the striking appearance of a defensible pele. Over the border in Scotland, many medieval churches were destroyed after the Reformation or left for decay and stone-robbing to take their course (Fawcett 1996). In the buildings which do remain, we can see the same grim, austere character which prevails across the whole of the region.

The decision to strengthen a church appears to have been taken, for the most part, by the community. Unlike Continental analogies, there are very few recorded instances of permission being sought beforehand – in fact the former medieval church at Wigton in Cumbria was the subject of an enquiry in 1374 when it was discovered that it had been fortified without the king's permission (CCR, 48 Edward III: 1374–77. m.27). Subtle adaptations were prob-

ably made over a period of time, and although specific works of defence may
have been put in hand to counter some immediate threat or period of unrest,
the defensible aspect of many churches probably simply came into being over
many years.

Defensible, and a few genuinely fortified, churches existed on the Borders.
Our task is to locate them among the ravages of the rebuilding and remodelling which took place in England largely during the nineteenth century, and
in Scotland from the early seventeenth century onwards. Although a handful
of relatively unaltered examples remain, the vast majority of medieval Border
churches have been subject to severe or complete change since the end of hostilities between the two nations. Despite the numerous changes which have
taken place, enough evidence remains for us to establish a pattern of ecclesiastical Border defence which is surprisingly varied both in style and location, even
though the distribution of surviving examples provides a model which is far
from complete.

In considering what constitutes a defensible or secure characteristic, all fac-
tors of the building's construction, location, and known history are taken into
consideration. The most significant points are: position, design of the tower
(if present) and access into it, general construction, security of windows and
doors, stone-vaulted ceilings, and any other special features indicating 'above
average' strength (Davis 1968; Kelland 1982). A few buildings have the more
obvious attributes of fortification, normally associated with military defence,
such as strong precinct walls, crenellated battlements, machicolation, and iron-
barred gates and doors (Bonde 1994). Buildings which have no evidence of
security or defence are included to present a complete picture.

What follows is an attempt to visualize which Anglo-Scottish Border
churches may have functioned as safe sanctuaries during the period from just
before the commencement of the Wars of Independence in 1296 to the Union
of the Crowns in 1603, a period which, by the sixteenth century, was referred
to as 'troublesome tymes' (Frontier II, 203; Bates 1891) and in this book will
be called the 'Troubles'. The use of churches for military purposes during the
Civil War and Commonwealth between 1642 and 1660 is also briefly explored,
and reference is made to churches which featured in the Covenanter Wars of
1638–1690. The text is divided into six chapters, each examining one of the
original Border Marches. Although Border records reveal fairly well where the
March boundaries lay in the sixteenth century, some sections are far from
clear. Consequently, throughout this book the confines of the six Marches
follow those found by Tough (1928), Rae (1966), and MacDonald Fraser (1989).
Where the extremities of the March divisions are unclear, or very distant (as
in the case of the English West March), a distance of approximately 30 miles
(48 km) either side of the national frontier has been chosen as a boundary.
Inside each March, the text has been further subdivided to reflect distinct geographical regions within these areas with the aim of making the distribution
of churches easier to comprehend.

Each chapter provides a topographical gazetteer of the major churches and chapels. The upstanding fabric and the documentary sources for each building are examined to determine any defensible adaptations. Most sites and ruins have been investigated, but in many instances the exact location of a building has been lost, the remains are too meagre, or the fabric is too altered, to be able to determine any original measures of security. Plans and photographs have been included where these help to clarify the descriptions, but this book is not intended to be a fully analytical investigation of each ecclesiastical site, and detailed measured drawings have therefore been omitted. The spelling of place-names varies greatly in historical sources, and for consistency the spelling of extant locations is taken from that shown on the latest Ordnance Survey maps.

Documentary evidence for this period in Border history, most dating from the sixteenth century, is mainly concerned with the law, land ownership, social and judicial administration, and matters of state, and only infrequently do incidental references occur to the use of churches as refuges from raids and war; indeed, such use may well have been so commonplace that it did not warrant specific written description, or it was not thought befitting of the House of God to record this activity. Castles, fortalices, and other places of strength however were recorded, and one of the most useful sources, on the English side of the border, is the survey made of Northumbrian castles in 1415 for Henry V as part of his defence precautions prior to his invasion of France (Bates 1891); further lists were compiled in 1509 and 1541, the latter, for Henry VIII, was undertaken by Sir Robert Bowes and Sir Ralph Ellerker who also made valuable topographical observations at the same time (Frontier I). Cartularies, registers, and chronicles are of some value in providing details of recompense and exemption from taxation following enemy incursions. In England, licences to crenellate, and to provide men-at-arms for defence are generally recorded in the Patent Rolls, and are most detailed where some element of financial expenditure is being given approval. The Calendar of Border Papers gives fascinating snapshots into daily life during the later sixteenth century and provides important details of raids, means of defence, the administration of justice, and Border geography. The Civil War period is better documented in general histories and military reports. Later sources include, on the Scottish side, the statements of the 'Old Statistical Account' which give many pre-nineteenth-century descriptions, and on the English side the county histories and antiquarian observations contained within individual parish chronicles. Topographic guides and records of the late eighteenth and nineteenth centuries are also useful in that they often contain descriptions, and sometimes illustrations, of churches prior to their restoration. Finally, the ballad sources should not be overlooked as they relate, albeit with some distortion, to significant historical events and characters (Miller 1960), and provide a 'unique record of the life . . . of a remote and precarious frontier community' (Reed 1991, 8).

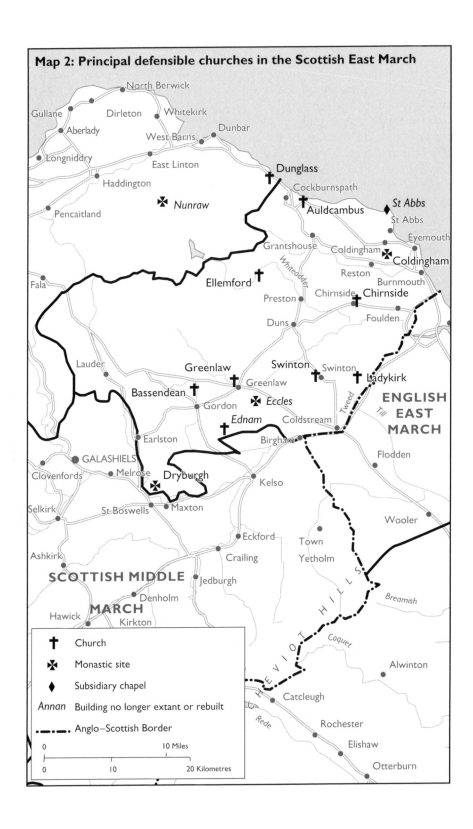

Map 2: Principal defensible churches in the Scottish East March

North Berwick
Gullane
Dirleton
Whitekirk
Aberlady
Dunbar
West Barns
Longniddry
East Linton
Dunglass
Haddington
Cockburnspath
Auldcambus
St Abbs
✠ Nunraw
St Abbs
Pencaitland
Eyemouth
Grantshouse
Coldingham
Coldingham
Reston
Fala
Burnmouth
Ellemford
Preston
Chirnside
Chirnside
Duns
Foulden
Lauder
Greenlaw
Swinton
Swinton
Ladykirk
Bassendean
Greenlaw
ENGLISH
Gordon
✠ Eccles
EAST
Ednam
Coldstream
MARCH
Earlston
Birgham
Flodden
GALASHIELS
Melrose
Dryburgh
Kelso
Clovenfords
Selkirk
St Boswells
Maxton
Wooler
Ashkirk
Eckford
Town
Crailing
Yetholm
SCOTTISH MIDDLE
Jedburgh
MARCH
Denholm
Breamish
Hawick
Kirkton
Alwinton
Catcleugh
Rochester
Elishaw
Otterburn

✝	Church
✠	Monastic site
♦	Subsidiary chapel
Annan	Building no longer extant or rebuilt
·—·—·	Anglo–Scottish Border

0   10 Miles
0   10   20 Kilometres

1

THE SCOTTISH EAST MARCH

The distinctive lowland plain of the Scottish East March largely consisted of the land occupied by the old County of Berwickshire. The town of Berwick-upon-Tweed itself, described in Chapter 2, was a pawn in the war-games of the two nations. Despite being the head burgh, it was for the most part held by the English, as it still is today.

So the border line now starts, not as expected at the Tweed mouth, but three miles to the north on a lonely stretch of coastline between Marshall Meadows Bay and Lamberton Beach. From here the line ran west and south to join the Tweed at the foot of Gainslaw Hill and then followed the river to a point half a mile west of Careham where it turned inland and joined the boundary to the Scottish Middle March.

From Careham, the boundary of the March followed a circuitous route, westward around by Dryburgh before turning north to meet higher ground and finally leaving the edge of the Middle March by Willie's Law, high in the hill country. The northern boundary of the March then followed the line of the Lammermuirs through rugged, inhospitable, and sparsely inhabited territory: over Killpallet Heights to the east, northward again to Spartleton Edge, then twisting eastwards once more over Moneynut Edge before heading towards the coast along the Dunglass Burn, finally to end at the sea by Bilsdean Creek, one mile north of Cockburnspath town.

The Districts of Lauderdale and Lammermuir, although within the Sheriffdom of Berwick, and inside the boundary of the old county of Berwickshire, were a grey area in the outline of the East March for they only sometimes fell within the Warden's jurisdiction (Rae 1966, 23). These two districts have been included in this work, especially given the importance of Lauder town, and the broad definition of the Marches in the 1597 Treaty which specified the entire area as from 'Newcastle to Peareth [Penrith] to Edinburgh and Dumfries exclusively' (Tough 1928, 133).

The coastal boundary of the East March is characterised by rough sea cliffs with few safe harbours saving those at Cockburnspath, Coldingham, and Eyemouth. Although fishing has always been a key industry in this region, the seaboard is savage and dangerous, and in terms of defence during the Anglo-Scottish Wars, its natural eastern boundary served it well.

Despite the high hills to the north and rugged coastline to the east, the Scottish East March was, for the most part, one of the most fertile and productive areas north of the border. Long called 'The Merse', the central and southern parts are a flat plain, intersected by the Blackadder and Whiteadder Waters. To the east the ground rises a little as the March boundary wraps around Roxburghshire, but the valleys of the Tweed and the Leader Water provided fertile land for settlements at Mertoun, Dryburgh, and Earlston. Owing to the richness of this land, combined with the relative ease of passage between England and Scotland, it was one of the most insecure areas of the British Isles.

The natural advantages offered by the fertile lowland plains of the Merse ensured that it was settled and peopled at an early date. There is ample evidence for Iron Age settlement with dwellings at Edin's Hall broch, on Cockburn Law, Preston Cleugh and Earn's Heugh; the stability and strength of the *Votadini* people ensured that the land remained secure until the coming of the Normans. Of the churches which came with the Norman settlement, there is good evidence at Bunkle and Edrom in the east, and at Legerwood and Dryburgh Abbey in the west, with more fragmentary indications at Aldcambus, Chirnside, Coldingham, Eccles, Langton, Mertoun, and Simprim.

Communications through the East March were fairly good during the medieval period. The River Tweed was fordable in several places, notably at Norham and at Coldstream. However there was the ever-present danger of sudden spates which were treacherous and unpredictable. There were three principal roadways: Tweeddale east and west, the Leader Valley, and the coastal margin between the Tweed and the Lammermuirs running north–south. The road along the Leader Valley has an impressive history: Edward I travelled it frequently in his campaigns, the ill-fated Edward II hurried along it to his defeat at Bannockburn, and the equally unfortunate James IV used it to march his army to slaughter on Flodden Field. The coastal route was of less significance than the Leader Valley road, as it had to negotiate the high ground of Coldingham Moor and the steep and perilous defile of the Pease Burn; in the sixteenth century, it was described thus: 'so stepe be these bakes on eyther syde, and depe to the bottom, that who goeth straight doune shal be in daunger of tumbling, & the commer up so sure of puffying and payne, for remedie whereof, the travailers that way have used to pas it not by going directly, but by paths & footways leading slopewise' (Patten 1548).

SOUTH BERWICKSHIRE

North along the modern A1 road from the town of Berwick, the border is now crossed at a place known as Marshall Meadows, at the foot of a steep bank rising up to the west. The first minor road on the Scottish side, running up this bank, leads to the tiny hamlet of **Lamberton** with its ruined church, now no more than a shell, on top of a slight rise. The building itself comprises a single cell which has been sub-divided by a north–south cross wall after its ruination in order to provide for family burial areas. Only the lower portions of the red sandstone walls now survive above ground, except at the east end which rises as high as 2.5 m (8 ft 2 in.); at some stage there appears to have been a render or harling coat for protection against the elements. The walls are fairly thin, nowhere do they exceed 0.81 m (2 ft 8 in.), which is not indicative of a defensible structure.

There was one significant historical event in the history of Lamberton kirk. On 1 August 1503 Princess Margaret of England, the elder daughter of King Henry VII, was received here by the Scottish Commissioners and the Archbishop of Glasgow, to be conducted to Edinburgh on her journey to marry the Scottish King James IV (CDRS, iv, 1680).

A mile and a half south-west of Lamberton, and equally close to the border line, lie the meagre remains of **Mordington** old church. Of the original building nothing now survives above ground as it was destroyed by fire in 1757 (Binnie 1995). However a burial vault of 1662, which stood against its east gable, still exists.

A little to the west of Mordington, the eighteenth-century church at **Foulden** boasts a robust style, with a heavy, crenellated, east gable perhaps echoing the architecture of its past. Foulden was rebuilt in 1786, but probably on the foundations of the original medieval church, and incorporating masonry from it.

Foulden was noted as the place where the Anglo-Scottish Commissioners met (CBP, ii, 1022). In 1587, the kirk was the scene of an important conference between the commissioners of Elizabeth I and James VI, attempting to avoid the renewal of war by discussing the English Queen's action in the execution of Queen Mary. In January 1597 it was set to be the venue of a discussion on Anglo-Scottish Border law, although this was eventually held at Berwick; clearly it was much needed as the Third Lord Eure, writing in December of 1596, commented that 'the Border groweth wylde and disorderlie since the delay of the commissione, our bills increaseth, justice decreaseth, corne fayleth, peoples hartes are gone' (Tough 1928, 264).

Also close to the border, three and half miles to the south of Foulden, lie the remains of **Fishwick** church. The present ruins are all of nineteenth-century date when the building was converted into a private mortuary chapel c. 1835. However, *Fishewie* or *Fyschewike* was one of the Berwickshire manors conveyed to the monks of St Cuthbert, Durham, by King Edgar, between 1098 and 1107, and the manor is mentioned in a charter of David I in 1126, giving it in favour of the same monks; it is clear that there was a church here from around this date. The *New Statistical Account* (1845) describes the kirk as being 'a very plain building, long and narrow, and of small dimensions'.

The present church at nearby **Hutton** dates from 1835, having replaced a structure which was rebuilt in 1765; there is no trace of its medieval predecessor. Although not related to the use of the church as a retreat, the eighteenth-

Fig. 4. Ladykirk, exterior view.

century building was used as a rallying point for the Volunteers of the district on the night of the 'Great Alarm' during the Napoleonic War (*see* page 31).

Two and a half miles upstream from Foulden, standing prominently 30 m (100 ft) up on top of the Tweed's north bank, is the imposing church of **Ladykirk** (Figure 4). The site is almost directly opposite the village of Norham in the English East March, and is well within view of both church and castle there. The old ford across the river at this point was one of the most significant crossing places between the two countries during the Middle Ages. Ladykirk played host in 1559 to a meeting which helped settle the last war between England and Scotland; the commissioners, apparently ignorant of Border affairs, allowed those with local knowledge to meet here to agree 'certain Articles concerning the granting of Safe-conducts to Homicides, Thieves, Rankriders upon the Marches and Fugitives' (Tough 1928, 188).

Both externally and internally, Ladykirk church presents a solid appearance, though in the architectural fashion of the period, moderated only by the top of the tower, rebuilt in the eighteenth century. The building has a nave and chancel, north and south transepts, all surmounted by stone-vaulted roofs (Figure 5), clad with stone tiles and punctuated by a defensible west tower. The whole is constructed from the local, pink Swinton stone, cut in neat ashlar blocks, and heavily buttressed in order to support the massive roofs. The kirk

Fig. 5. Ladykirk, internal stone vaulting of *c.* 1500.

is largely complete from the early sixteenth century, with the exception of
the tower's upper stage, which was rebuilt by William Adam in 1743 (Binnie
1995). Prior to the alteration of the belfry stage, the structure probably had the
appearance of a plain strong tower, able to offer the features of a lookout, and
defensible refuge (Figure 6). Wooden furnishings were only added to the body
of the church in 1861 and prior to this all interior features were made of stone.

The history of the present Ladykirk church appears to commence *c.* 1500,
when, according to local legend, King James IV founded the building in
thanksgiving for being rescued after falling into the River Tweed. He apparently promised that the church should never be destroyed either by fire or
water, hence its solid stone construction (Dobie 1891; Macdougall 1997). There
is certainly evidence to indicate that James IV had some role in the building's
foundation, as recorded in the exchequer accounts of the period, where there
is a reference to the 'ecclesie de Upsedlington' (RSRS, xi, 276). It is also
identified as the 'ecclesia de Steil' in the Royal Accounts of the period, which

Fig. 6. Ladykirk, reconstruction showing the church as it may have appeared on completion *c.* 1500.

show payments for the construction of the church amounting to £483 in 1501 with a further £226 in 1504 (CTRS, ii, 85); further payments were made before completion. The probable identity of the mason was Nicholas Jackson who undertook other work for the king at Linlithgow (Fawcett 1994a).

The site has earlier important connections with the history of the two nations, as it was at Holywell Haugh, a little to the east, that Edward I met the competitors for the Scottish Crown in 1291 (Ferguson 1890).

The measures of security in Ladykirk are clear. The roofs are constructed of stone rib-vaulting and the west tower is without external ingress, save to the ground floor. The upper levels of the tower are reached via a well-worn spiral stairway in a turret which projects from the north-west corner, entered from a small internal doorway in the west wall of the nave, 1.45 m (4 ft 9 in.) high and only 0.73 m (2 ft 5 in.) wide; the head has been renewed, probably in the nineteenth century. Ground, first, and second floors have stone vaulting and there is evidence of checks and bolt holes for heavy doors to each chamber. The first floor has a blocked window in the east wall which formerly gave a view into the main body of the church, whilst the second floor has a disused fireplace in the same position. In the eighteenth and nineteenth centuries there is record of the tower being used as a prison; this would certainly account for the jail-like construction of the ground-floor door, in the west wall, which may lie within an earlier opening. There are substantial mortices for former locks visible in this portal. Holes for bell-ropes have been cut through the stone floors, probably within the last two centuries. There is a blocked opening, of unknown date, in the east wall of the ground floor, which has the appearance of having been a large window formerly opening into the church.

Just outside the isolated hamlet of Whitsome, at **Hilton**, some three miles north-west of Ladykirk, stands a tiny fragment of masonry marking the site of the medieval church. At **Whitsome** itself, all traces of the village church have now disappeared, but it is recorded in the *Old Statistical Account* that the structure was 'a miserable thatched building, which, though now slated, is still very ill seated, narrow, and incommodious' (OSA, iii, 312).

South-west of Whitsome lies the small village of **Swinton** with its little church perched on top of a bank at the east end of the settlement, directly above the main road from the border to Duns. Like the majority of other border kirks it has suffered a considerable amount of restoration and modification; over the south doorway an inscription plaque reads 'Rebuilt 1729'.

Swinton church has a nave and chancel on an east–west axis, with a northern addition of 1782 to create the present north-south orientation. According to Robson (1896, 209), the church was rebuilt in 1593 and again in the eighteenth century, but in the latter restoration the building appeared to be 'uncommonly strong, and might have stood for ages' (OSA, iii, 294). It is clear that the church was not entirely rebuilt in 1729 as a Sacrament House survives in the north wall at the east end, and the main north and south side walls appear to be medieval, constructed of hammered blocks of local red and yellow sandstone, 0.85 m (2 ft 9 in.) thick. Another survival from the medieval period is the bell, dating from the fifteenth century, of Low Country origin and inscribed 'Maria Est Nomen Meum 1499'.

The need for village defence is clearly illustrated by the events of 1558, during a spell of heavy cross-border raiding activity, when Henry Percy, accompanied by Berwick garrison men and border riders – around three thousand men in total – met a Scottish force of roughly the same size at Swinton (MacDonald Fraser 1989). The outcome was a victory for the English, and no doubt during and after the skirmish the majority of the townsfolk needed a safe sanctuary, almost certainly finding this, both spiritual and temporal, in the church. Such a use was apparent in 1482 when a man was reportedly killed whilst defending the church against the English (Binnie 1995, 401).

Just over a mile to the south of Swinton, the fragmentary remains of **Simprim** kirk are now too incomplete to determine its former nature, save that it had a nave and chancel, without a tower, measuring a total of 14 m (45 ft) in length and approximately 4 m (14 ft) in width over walls of 0.75 m (2 ft 6 in.) average thickness. The little church is built of red and yellow sandstone and is positioned at the side of the road.

Along the main road southwards from Swinton and Simprim, and lying one mile north-east of Coldstream town, stand the ruins of **Lennel** church. The remains are situated on top of the north bank of the Tweed, at a very steep point where the land drops away vertically into the river below.

The west gable is almost complete, but the side walls stand only a little above 2 m (6 ft 7 in.) on the south side and lower elsewhere, and are all around 1 m (3 ft 3 in.) in thickness. The whole building has been modified in post-Reformation times for use as a burial area, and much of its original character has been lost.

The little town of **Coldstream** gained its importance through being the first reliable river crossing upstream from Berwick, and in consequence played a major part in the wars and troubles between the two nations; it was a recognised venue for days of truce (Rae 1966, 50). No medieval churches now remain in the town; the present parish church dates from 1716, although there was a Cistercian convent here, founded in 1165.

The convent suffered severely during periods of conflict, and was burnt and despoiled on several occasions throughout the Troubles (Cowan and Easson 1976). Edward I camped at Coldstream during one of his campaigns, with 5,000 horses and 30,000 infantry; on this occasion the priory and its orchard suffered great damage for which compensation was sought and granted (Robson 1896, 67). It was finally destroyed by the Earl of Hertford in 1545, despite the prioress having acted as a spy for the English during his campaigns (Sanderson 1982, 71). The vestige of a vault still remained in 1791 (OSA, iii, 111) and the most likely site is around the present Market Square.

A short distance westward from Coldstream the border line leaves the Tweed and turns south; here, just a little beyond the village of Birgham, Scottish East March meets Scottish Middle March. The only church standing in this corner of the territory is at **Eccles**, five miles north-west of Coldstream, where lie the fragmentary remains of the former convent of St Mary.

Founded *c.* 1160 for Cistercian nuns, the ruins of Eccles Convent lie on the west side of the churchyard, away from the post-Reformation kirk which now stands there; they comprise two barrel-vaulted cells and fragments of walling. The conventual buildings were burnt by the Earl of Hertford in 1545, but it is recorded that the church was spared and remained entire up until 1774 when it was demolished to provide materials for the new kirk (Figure 7). From this, there is a suggestion that the church building itself may not have been strong, hence Hertford's decision to leave it standing. However, this is contrasted by the description in the *Old Statistical Account*, which describes the church as having been a cruciform building of some pretensions, vaulted and covered with large flagstones, with a tower in good preservation; it was apparently so well built that its removal was an operation of extreme difficulty (Ferguson 1890; OSA, iii, 159).

Historical accounts support the view that the church was capable of fortification, and indeed was used as such. In 1523 Lord Dacre wrote that he

Fig. 7. Eccles, church of 1774 on the site of St Mary's Convent.

was 'met at Akles by the convent of nuns, who gave up the keys of the abbey, and promised to cast down before Sunday all walls and ditches of any strength', adding that 'if it is not done, Sir Wm. Bulmer will go and burn the abbey' (L.& P. Henry VIII, iii(ii), 3098). On 27 September, 1544 the English took the church of Eccles 'by assault', and slew eighty people within the abbey and town (Ridpath 1848, 379; Robson 1896, 91). In the following year, the church is listed amongst those places 'brent, rased and cast downe' by the English (Cowan and Easson 1976).

Two miles south-east of the village, close by the river, the village of **Birgham** once had a chapel dependent upon Eccles. There are now no standing remains visible. Similar subordinate chapels also existed at **Leitholm** and **Mersington**.

From Eccles, the boundary of the East March skirts around the town of Kelso, and meets the Tweed near Makerstoun. A little to the west sits the small church at **Mertoun**, apparently newly built in 1658, repaired in 1820, and heavily restored in 1898. Although this church was constructed at a comparatively late date, there was an earlier building nearby, the fragmentary remains of which lie to the east of Mertoun House. The remains are too meagre to determine its original form, but it is recorded that the church was dedicated by Bishop Bernham in 1241 (RCHMS 1915).

Fig. 8. Dryburgh Abbey, gatehouse tower in foreground with high perimeter wall (left) which replaced the west range.

A mile and half due west of Mertoun, lying on a sheltered tongue of land nestling in a horseshoe bend of the Tweed, is situated the ruined abbey of **Dryburgh** (Figure 8). The location was ideal, with fertile land to the north and a river which abounded in trout and salmon.

Dryburgh Abbey was founded in 1140, and was the first Premonstratensian house in Scotland. The layout consisted of an aisled, cruciform church, a cloister 27 m (90 ft) square with eastern and southern ranges of claustral buildings; to the west a high enclosing wall replaced the usual monastic west range. In addition to these principal buildings there was a further wall to the north of the site which sheltered the abbot's lodging, the guest house, infirmary, brewhouse and other utility structures, but there is now no trace of these above ground level (Richardson and Wood 1948). The buildings which survive have evidence from the twelfth to the sixteenth centuries, although the central tower has now disappeared completely and the nave walls are considerably ruined.

Although the abbey cannot be termed defensible, certain security precautions seem to have been taken. The surrounding walls have already been mentioned, and at the southern end of the claustral range is a small gatehouse, dating from the late fifteenth century, which guarded the entrance to the site over a deep ditch, formerly the abbey's water channel. In places the gatehouse walls reach 1.2 m (3 ft 11 in.) in thickness, and access to the upper floor, probably the keeper's accommodation, appears to have been only by ladder, as no trace of a stair is evident. As at Lanercost in the English West March there was appar-

Fig. 9. Dryburgh Abbey, gun-loop in the commendator's lodgings.

ently no attempt to alter the thin lancet windows of the thirteenth century, which, throughout the abbey, have cills well above ground-level. Whether this was a consideration in making the building secure or simply an inertia to new design is not clear.

The one building in the abbey which clearly was adapted for defence is the former commendator's lodging, created in the sixteenth century from an earlier building to the east of the canons' dorter at first-floor level above the chapter house. The evidence for defence is plain: windows bear evidence of heavy barring, and there is a gun-loop located on the south side covering the eastern perimeter of the abbey precinct (Figure 9). The exterior walls of this area of building, along with sections of wall in the north transept, have marks caused by bullets, possibly made when the abbey was attacked by the English. One occupant of this building was probably Andrew Home who was awarded a pension for life in 1535 in return for protecting the abbey (Murray 1995).

Dryburgh appears to have been a relatively easy target for English raids, its location on flat land close to the river being entirely open to attack. There are early recorded raids in 1322, 1323, and 1385 (Liber de Dryburgh, xiv-xv; Mon.Ang., vi(ii), 1152), following which much of the western and parts of the eastern arms of the nave had to be rebuilt. The attack in 1322 was by Edward II's retreating army and may have been made due to frustration at being unable to secure provisions from the abbey (Butler and Given-Wilson 1979). A letter of protection was issued by Robert I in 1328 (though it is possible that this refers to Holyrood Abbey) (RRS, v, 398). Further attacks followed in 1461 and 1523. In 1544, following its elevation to the status of a burgh eighteen years earlier (Pryde 1965), the town was attacked by Sir George Bowes and Sir Brian Laiton, although on this occasion the church was spared (Ridpath 1848). The following year, both town and abbey suffered once more, this time at the hands of the Earl of Hertford.

LAUDERDALE

From Dryburgh the March boundary continues northwards from the River Tweed and follows the Leader Water into **Earlston** village. The present church here is of no great age, the old church being demolished c. 1895, although the bell dating from 1609 still survives. In the exterior east wall is a re-cut inscription stating 'Auld Rymr[s] Race Lyees In This Place', no doubt a reference to the legendary Thomas the Rhymer, otherwise Thomas of Ercildoune, the early Scottish poet who flourished in the late thirteenth century. A small tower-house to the south-west of the town is also reputed to have been associated with Thomas the Rhymer, being known as 'Rhymer's Tower'; however, it is a structure evidently dating from the sixteenth century and there is no credible link with the poet.

Although Earlston church was entirely rebuilt in 1891–2, the site is that of the earlier building, and is in a most commanding position overlooking the town and with excellent views over the valley to the south. Given the important position of Earlston, in the Leader valley and alongside one of the principal north–south roads, the siting of this church on high ground raises the possibility that it may have been utilized as a safe retreat.

Tucked away amongst the low hills to the north of Earlston is the little village of **Legerwood**. The church, in common with many on the Border, lies slightly away from the village, on the side of Kirkhill, its present location hidden away amongst later farm buildings.

Legerwood is important in the Scottish East March as a good survival of twelfth-century work, the chancel being one of the most complete of the period in the area. During the nineteenth century the chancel was used as a private burial vault and the arch between it and the nave was blocked, until the early years of the twentieth century when it was opened up in order to restore the building to its original form. The chancel-arch is composed of three semi-circular orders springing from cushion capitals decorated with geometrical sunk-star ornamentation. Although there has been a considerable amount of rebuilding in the fabric of the chancel, wall paintings in the form of consecration crosses still survive on parts of the original interior walls, which average 0.75 m (2 ft 6 in.) in thickness. There is some evidence for a former vaulted interior. The nave appears to have been largely rebuilt on earlier foundations as can be seen from the splayed base course which is clearly earlier than the present fabric. There is a history of alterations from 1717 (Ferguson 1890; Robson 1896) and the present nave may date from that period.

The main road winds northwards along the valley of the Leader Water to the small town of **Lauder**, important during the medieval period as a royal burgh and the only town in the East March apart from Berwick to have held this status since at least the fourteenth century (Pryde 1965). In 1482, the Scottish nobility, led by the king's half-uncles, held a conference in the church the outcome of which was the seizure of James III as he tried to oppose an English invasion under his brother, Albany. Of the original church at Lauder there is now no trace, it having stood on the north side of the town (OSA, iii, 233), but the present building is of interest as an unusual example of a cruciform building dating from 1673, designed by Sir William Bruce (Hay 1984). The plan is that of a Greek cross with four equal arms extending from a central crossing and tower, and it remains one of the best centrally-planned churches in Scotland (Baldwin 1985; Dunbar 1996).

Just south of the town, and technically within the Middle March, lies the site of **Chieldhelles** chapel, on the left bank of the Milsie Burn. According to the Reverend Adam Milne, writing in 1743 (RCHMS 1956, 291), the chapel was 'fine' and 'built of hewn stone'. It is unclear why a chapel should be built in this position, but lack of historical and structural evidence now precludes conjecture.

North from Lauder the road cuts a path through the hills towards the boundary of the March at Soutra Hill. The one remaining parish in this sparsely inhabited corner of the region, **Channelkirk**, has no visible remains of its medieval church although it was formerly a cruciform kirk, held by the monks of Dryburgh Abbey. A measure of its importance can be gained from the fact that in the thirteenth century, following its consecration in 1241 by David de Bernham, Bishop of St Andrews, Channelkirk was described as the Mother Church of the whole valley. In 1627 the choir was apparently roofless and about to collapse 'to the great scandall off the gospell and prejudice of the parishiners' (Robson 1896, 28). In 1653, 10,000 divots were used in thatching and, despite attempts at restoration in 1702 and 1724, by which time the roof was slated, it was finally demolished entirely and rebuilt in 1817 (Ferguson 1890; Allan 1897). It is possible that the unusual design of Lauder church was modelled on its near neighbour, now destroyed.

Although the evidence for its 'thatched' roof in the seventeenth century implies some weakness in terms of security, the building is nevertheless situated in a very commanding position, well above the main Edinburgh road on a hilltop, and within the confines of a former Roman camp.

Two further medieval chapels, subordinate to Channelkirk, formerly existed at **Glengelt** and **Carfrae**, but of these there are now no standing remains.

The March, whether it be the Scottish East March proper or the District of Lauderdale, ends at Soutra Hill; beyond this point is the Lothian region. However, this place is significant as the site of the medieval hospital and church of **Soutra**, founded by Malcom IV *c.* 1164 for use by travellers (McWilliam 1978). Although all that remains today is a tunnel-vaulted burial aisle of the Pringle family, dated 1686, this was clearly a major ecclesiastical building on a principal route between Edinburgh and the border; in all it covered approximately 128 hectares (320 acres) of the hill top and its buildings were constructed with walls up to 4 m (13 ft) in thickness (Moffat and Fulton 1988). Documentary evidence indicates that both Edward I and Edward II stayed here and it was frequently used as a stopover point by invading and defending armies (Moffat 1988). Such a significant structure, even though it lay beyond the March boundaries, was in all likelihood well defended in serving, as it did, as a lodging place for the military powers of the time.

Two and a half miles to the east of Lauder, standing by the Boondreigh Water, are the remains of old Thirlestane castle, a rectangular tower with projecting stair-wing probably dating from the fourteenth century. This castle was the principal residence of the Maitland family until about the end of the sixteenth century when a new castle was built closer to Lauder town. Half a mile to the north-east of the old castle is the tiny hamlet of **Thirlestane** and hidden away within it are the fragmentary ruins of a simple rectangular chapel. This building was originally the private chapel to the castle, but served for parish worship during the construction of Lauder church (RCHMS 1915). The ruins are too fragmentary to allow an objective analysis of its original form, although the building is shown on Bleau's map of 1654 and was said to have been cruciform in plan (Simpson and Stevenson 1980b, 5).

To the north of Thirlestane, the foothills of the Lammermuirs close in to form rough and rugged upland devoid of further towns and villages, and the main road swings eastwards towards Duns and the coast.

GREENLAW AND THE MERSE

Just north of Corsbie Moor, the road divides three ways, the northern route leading to the tiny village of **Westruther** with its ruined church dating from 1649 but largely rebuilt in 1752 and 1840 (RCHMS 1915). A chapel also existed a little to the north-east at **Wedderley**, close to the late sixteenth-century fortalice there, but the final vestige, a ruined vault, was last recorded in existence in 1834 (Robson 1896).

Fig. 10. Bassendean church.

South of Westruther, lying between the middle and southern roads eastward, is the hamlet of **Bassendean**. The church, now a roofless ruin with its walls reduced to *c.* 3 m (10 ft) in height, is situated on the edge of a gentle plateau away from the present houses and farm buildings (Figure 10). Although the ground is level to the north, it rapidly falls away on the south side to give the building a commanding position.

The only openings through the 1 m (3 ft) thick walls are on the south and comprise a simple square-headed doorway, and two rectangular windows probably of seventeenth-century date, though perhaps originally dating from the fourteenth century (Robson 1896, 217). Whilst the windows are evidently alterations in the medieval fabric, the doorway is probably original and displays chamfered rebates; there is evidence of a substantial draw-bar and lock-mortices to protect a door which must have been of considerable proportions.

The interior of the building is almost completely devoid of features, with the exception of a roughly carved font by the west wall, an aumbry and stoup immediately to the east of the doorway, and niches in the north and south walls at the east end for a piscina and sacrament house. There is no evidence of an east window.

The whole church is constructed of coursed rubble sandstone with sturdy face-alternate quoins, and is surrounded by a shallow bank and ditch. Despite its ruinous condition, Bassendean has all the hallmarks of secure construction and siting.

A little to the south of Bassendean is the village of **Gordon**, whose church was rebuilt entirely in 1763 with modifications made during the nineteenth century; no trace of its predecessor remains today. To the south, the tiny village

Fig. 11. Greenlaw, lower part of tower probably fifteenth century, upper stages *c*. 1700.

of **Nenthorn** once had a medieval chapel of which no standing remains now exist, although its footings were still visible in 1896 (Robson 1896).

Four miles north-east of Gordon, situated at a major road intersection and crossing over the Blackadder Water, the village of **Greenlaw** marks the start of the fertile Merse lands to the east. Away to the north, the moors of Greenlaw and Harelaw gradually yield to the uplands of the Lammermuir Hills, and to the south the rugged outcrop of Hume Crags, on which stands Hume Castle (rebuilt on its medieval foundations in 1789 by the third Earl of Marchmont), indicates the boundary of the Middle March. The former castle was important during the Troubles as a first stage in the warning – by beacons, from the 'watchers' on the Tweed – of an English invasion. It was last used for military purposes during the Napoleonic wars when, on the night of 31 January 1804, a sergeant from the Berwickshire volunteers mistook charcoal burners in the Cheviots for a beacon, and fired the Hume Castle signal; the warning, which caused the lighting of all the beacons to the west, and the turnout of 3,000 volunteers, became known as 'The Great Alarm'.

Granted by the third Earl of Dunbar *c.* 1147 to the monks of Kelso, *in rectoriam*, Greenlaw church proved a useful source of income to the monastery. In about 1316, Kelso was granted permission by William Lamberton, Bishop of St Andrews, to apply revenues to the monastery to pay for the cost of repairs during the Wars of Independence.

As a building however, Greenlaw church is, in all respects, unique. No other church in the six Marches has quite the remarkable intricacy of adaptation and usage to which this site has been put.

The present building is a rectangular kirk, internally fitted with galleries and pews, with a north aisle and vestry extension, and a west tower. The tower is striking: visible on all approaches to the church it rises a sheer 17.5 m (57 ft) to the corbelled parapet without interruption (Figure 11).

The history of the tower at Greenlaw is far from clear. Robson (1896, 126) felt that it had been purpose-built as a jail in 1712 and the Royal Commission in 1915 (RCHMS 1915, 93) agreed, although it was also acknowledged that the pre-Reformation church underwent constructional transformation around 1675. The body of the church was lengthened westwards at some stage during this period – perhaps as late as 1712 (Binnie 1995) – so that tower and nave became joined. Certainly it did serve as a jail and adjunct to the courthouse which formerly lay, attached, on the west side; this layout is shown clearly in a map by Armstrong of 1771 (Figure 12). Gibson (1905) also thought that the tower was built as a dual-purpose jail and campanile: the bells are dated 1702 and 1726. What is certain is that Greenlaw became the county town of Berwickshire in 1696 and new judicial buildings were erected soon afterwards. A prison for 'idle vagrants', previously ordered to have been built at Duns, was, in 1698, ordered to be built at Greenlaw.

A detailed study of the tower however, reveals that it was clearly not built in a single phase, and there are several indications that an earlier structure was modified, probably at the turn of the eighteenth century, to form a prison. This is exactly what took place at Ladykirk, although there the prison was confined to the ground floor and the belfry was completely rebuilt. MacGibbon and Ross (1896–7, iii, 575) thought that the lower vaulted chamber of Greenlaw was of considerable strength, and probably dated from the fifteenth century.

On plan the tower is roughly 3.7 m (12 ft) square within walls which vary between 0.5 m (1 ft 8 in.) and 1.0 m (3 ft 3 in.) in thickness. On the east side, a central projection contains a stone spiral staircase allowing entry to the upper floors, each of which is lit by narrow square-headed windows on the south side. There are no windows whatsoever on the north, and at first-floor level on the west is a blocked doorway now converted into a window; this doorway may have originally communicated with the courthouse, but may earlier have served as an external, upper entrance. There are no belfry windows, and the

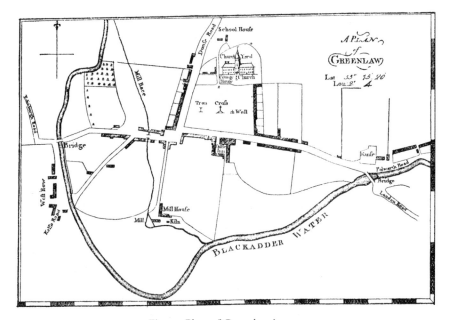

Fig. 12. Plan of Greenlaw in 1771.

top of the tower is crowned by a small octagonal spire at the base of which is a narrow parapet, supported by projecting stone corbels; the sound from the bells escapes from louvres cut into the lower sides of the spire. A staircase leading to the base of the spire and the level of the bells was blocked up in 1856, this date being cut into the blocking.

The interior of the body of the tower has a series of rooms built as, or converted into, prison cells. There are five rooms above the ground floor, each having a heavy door leading onto the stair-turret. However, the first floor may have been used as a guardroom and link through to the courthouse, whilst there was also a fifth-floor cell, now converted into the clock chamber. On the second floor is an account of an alleged miscarriage of justice, carved in the plasterwork by three inmates, and dated 1791, whilst on the third level a small garderobe has been built into the north wall, though there is no evidence of a chute on the exterior.

It is the ground floor however that is the most interesting. Formerly known as the 'Thieves Hole', the roof is tunnel-vaulted in the style of a pele tower (Figure 13) and has an ingress via an iron-studded door in the south wall which is guarded by a yett (Figure 14). This room was apparently used to house the worst offenders and in the wall were staples to which the criminals could be chained. When in use as a jail, there was formerly a small space outside in the form of an iron cage reached through the doorway, which allowed prisoners an occasional breath of air. There was previously no access from the ground to the upper floors until, in 1845 (about 20 years after the jail had become disused),

Fig. 13. Greenlaw, medieval tunnel vault to the ground floor of the tower.

a portion of the vaulting was removed in the south-east angle in order to make a connecting stairway. In the building of this stairway a long-forgotten secret was rediscovered in the form of a human skeleton resting within the vault; no clue to its history was traceable (Gibson 1905).

The archaeological evidence in the fabric indicates that the lower 7 m (24 ft) of the tower are of a different phase of construction from the remainder. The quoins are less well formed and take the manner of roughly cut rubble; above this height the quoins are formed by rectangular blocks of hammered rubble, laid in side-alternate fashion. Although the entire tower is constructed in roughly-coursed rubble on the exterior, the fabric of the lower area has a greater quantity of darker stone which is demonstrably of a different type to that at higher level (Brooke 1996, 674–5). Internally, the ground floor is made up of large rectangular blocks of sandstone cut in a style which indicates a medieval rather than a seventeenth- or eighteenth-century date.

Fig. 14. Greenlaw, iron yett which secured the former entrance to the ground floor of the tower.

With all the available evidence, it appears that the tower may originally have been defensible, with a vaulted ground floor and access to upper levels gained only from an external doorway and ladder, perhaps through the upper doorway in the west wall. At the close of the seventeenth century, the church was altered and new judicial buildings were attached on the west side. At this time, the tower was refitted as a jail, and the upper levels rebuilt entirely.

The main body of the church has been considerably modified since the turn of the eighteenth century and no discernible medieval features now remain. The majority of the alterations and partial rebuilding took place *c.* 1675 when some old portions of the walls were left, 1.2 m (4 ft) in thickness. However, building accounts at the time indicate that the original structure may have been vaulted: 'to take doune the vault and pend and the whole of the south side wall, and so much of the two gables as shall be found fattie . . .

build the south side wall from the ground, and make it two feet higher . . . build therein doors and four large windows in said wall, and repair the north syde' (Gibson 1905). The church at this time may have been detached from the tower, or whatever structure existed at the west end, as the account goes on to detail 'ane door and ane window in the wester gable and ane bell house . . . with dome for ane bell'; apparently the tower was not being used as a campanile at this point. Excavations in 1848 and 1883 found evidence of earlier floor levels, grave-markers, and burials, clearly belonging to the medieval church.

Greenlaw was a significant settlement during the years of Anglo-Scottish fighting. In the Earl of Hertford's raid of September 1545, it was one of the towns which was burnt, and a large booty of cattle, sheep, and horses was carried off. The town was also destroyed by one of Sir Ralph Eure's raids in the same century, but was rebuilt by the following year, indicating that the ordinary houses were of a very simple form of construction (White 1973). In later years, the juxtaposition of church, jail, and court was the subject of a remark made by the traveller and author Robert Chambers:

Here stands the gospel and the law
Wi' Hell's hole atween the twa.

The centre of the Scottish East March is characterized by the fertile lands of the Merse. This stretch of country formerly had its own name, Coldinghamshire. Although never a civil county or shire it was a semi-independent ecclesiastical jurisdiction centred on Coldingham Priory, which in turn belonged to the monks of Durham, given by the gift of King Edgar c. 1098 (Cruden 1986).

The principal ruling authority in this region was the House of Home. So great was the influence of this family that by the sixteenth century they had made Coldinghamshire virtually their own private dominion. Even James IV's successful negotiations with the Pope to get the superiority of Coldingham transferred to Dunfermline Abbey displeased them. It is not surprising to find therefore that the Warden of the March was as often as not a Home; in fact between 1557 and 1600 every recorded Warden was a member of that family and the last, Alexander, 6th Baron Home, was made Lieutenant and Justiciar over all three Scottish Marches at the Union of the Crowns in 1603 (Tough 1928, 282).

Midway between Greenlaw and the county town of Duns nestles the tiny village of **Polwarth**. Its church stands isolated half a mile to the south and had a vital connection with the Home family, acting indirectly in a defensible role as a refuge for Sir Patrick Home in 1684.

The present church, above ground, dates in its entirety from 1703 when it was rebuilt on the site of its medieval predecessor. It has an aisleless nave, chancel, and a west tower; the last has three floors, the first floor being formerly used as an office or vestry, with a fireplace in the south-east corner, and an oval bole-hole window in the east wall giving a view into the body of the church.

Beneath the church however, and visible from the exterior east end of the chancel, is an earlier vault. Formed in a mixture of ashlar and rubble stone with a tunnel-vaulted roof, it is believed to have formed the hiding place for Sir Patrick Home in 1684 after he had been declared a participant in the Rye House Plot, a conspiracy to kidnap King Charles II. Whilst government forces hunted for him, he was kept fed by his young daughter Grizel until eventually he could make his escape to Holland (Lang and Lang 1913; Clark 1956).

Of the medieval church we have little information. There was a building here in 1378 when a restoration is documented, and earlier still, in 1296, the priest, Adam Lamb, is recorded as having paid homage to Edward I (Ferguson 1890, 163). The siting of the kirk may be significant, away from the main road to Duns and elevated on the edge of a very steep bank dropping away to the Kirk Burn at the east end.

A mile and a half to the south-east of Polwarth is the hamlet of Fogo with its little sandstone church positioned at the top of a steep bank on the south side of the Blackadder Water.

Fogo church appears at first to be entirely post-medieval in its present form which is due largely to a major restoration in 1775 (OSA, iii, 180). Various heraldic and memorial panels testify to an earlier church, but most original architectural features were evidently removed during the refurbishment. However, parts of the walls themselves may well be medieval and earlier vaults exist underneath, as shown by the built-up arches in the exterior of the north side. At the east end of the present building is a low stone-vaulted chamber, known as the Harcarse aisle, approximately 6 m (19 ft) in length by 4.5 m (15 ft) in width, standing 3 m (10 ft) high in the centre, with walls averaging 0.85 m (2 ft 9 in.) in thickness. This room may have been the chancel of the pre-restoration church, and although now altered at the east end, with evidence of a later doorway and window, and with its stone vaulting plastered over in 1817 and 1925, it bears some resemblance to the robust and fireproof chancel at Kirknewton in the English East March.

Fogo was a chapel held by the monks of Kelso Abbey, the earliest record being in 1159; the *Liber de Calchou* also records several charters relating to a chapel or small priory dedicated to St Nicholas, granted by Patrick Corbet to Kelso between 1280 and 1297 (Ferguson 1890, 129; Cowan and Easson 1976). During the early years of the Wars of Independence, following Edward I's successful initial campaign against the Scots, the priest, one David 'vicar of Foghow' swore fealty to the English king and thus had his vicarage restored (Robson 1896, 110).

Midway between Fogo and Duns, the spire of **Gavinton** church, dating from 1872, is a prominent feature in the landscape. Of the medieval kirk in the old burial ground, close to the site of Langton House, only part of the chancel now remains, converted in post-Reformation times into a burial aisle. The site now lies in woodland on private land to the north-west of the Greenlaw to Duns road. The building is that of a tunnel-vaulted chamber, standing to a maximum of 4 m (13 ft) above ground level, and constructed of squared limestone; all architectural features appear to be of post-Reformation date.

Duns, the county town of Berwickshire until 1975, held its status only since 1903, the title previously having been held by Greenlaw, Lauder, and originally by Berwick-upon-Tweed itself. The present church is entirely post-Reformation in date, the last vestige of the medieval building having been removed in 1879 following a fire in the same year which also destroyed some rebuilding work of 1790 (Simpson and Stevenson 1981). The early building had a Norman chancel and was cruciform in plan with offset north and south transepts, the north being larger and set further to the west than the south (Ferguson 1890, 119; Lang and Lang 1913, 15).

Berwickshire towns were frequently the target for English military raids, one famous event being recorded by the burgh's motto 'Duns Dings A'!' The story dates to a raid in 1377 by the Earl of Northumberland who, after wreaking much havoc, reached Duns in the evening to camp outside the town overnight. However, during the darkness the townsfolk surprised them, driving away the English horses and causing total confusion amongst Northumberland's men. On this occasion the English were defeated, though many subsequent events probably required the town to make better preparation for defence. In 1544 the English under Bowes, Governor of Berwick, burnt Duns; it was burnt again next year by Hertford and yet again in 1558 by Earl Percy and Bowes.

Two miles north of Duns, a little above the north bank of the Whiteadder Water, lie the ruins of **Preston** church (Figure 15). The village sits at the cross-roads a quarter of a mile further north, leaving the church isolated on the edge of steep slopes to the south and east in a highly defensible position. There has been considerable alteration to provide burial vaults in post-Reformation times, and the walls are in a ruined state, though still standing on all sides. The building is constructed mainly of red and grey sandstone with some rounded boulders, probably from the river below, the whole producing quite a colourful mixture, particularly in the chancel; the thickness of the walls varies between 0.8 m and 1.1 m (2 ft 7 in. – 3 ft 7 in.). The fabric appears to date largely from the thirteenth century as evidenced by the rough-coursed construction of the walls, and the small obtusely-pointed windows in the east and south sides of the chancel, though all the doorways appear to have been altered into a simple square-headed form (possibly to accommodate the post-Reformation use of the church as private burial aisles). The interior of the chancel contains a small piscina under the south window, the only one still *in situ* in the Scottish East March (apart from those in Dryburgh Abbey), and a semi-circular arch links the chancel with the nave.

Bunkle church stands in a secluded valley to the north-east of Preston. The present kirk dates from 1820, when the medieval building, which had been repaired in 1718, was almost completely demolished, and its materials used in the construction of the new church. Of the earlier building, only the eastern apse now remains, but this represents one of the earliest examples of Norman

Fig. 15. Preston, exterior view.

architecture in Berwickshire. On plan, the apse is semi-circular, measuring approximately 3.5 m (11 ft 7 in.) across, within walls 0.75 m (2 ft 6 in.) thick. It was formerly lighted by two small round-headed windows in the north-east and south-east angles some 2.35 m (7 ft 9 in.) above ground-level; there are no other openings from the exterior. The eastern arch is clearly Norman in form, semi-circular and springing from plain imposts, slightly splayed on their lower edges. The whole structure is stone-vaulted with a roof of stone tiles.

There is insufficient evidence in the one small section of the Romanesque building to judge its former character, although if the nave and chancel were built in the same manner as the apse it would in all probability have been a typically robust, Norman structure, capable of being used as a secure refuge. However, as an alternative means of protection, the castle of Bunkle lay only a quarter of a mile to the north-west, in a more easily defended position. The castle, now little more than a pile of rubble, was destroyed in Hertford's raid of 1544, but is still remembered along with two nearby strongholds in the local rhyming prophesy:

Bunkle, Billie, and Blanerne,
Three castles strang as airn,
Built when Davy was a bairn;
They'll a' gang doun
Wi' Scotland's crown,
And ilka ane sall be a cairn
(Lang and Lang 1913, 13)

The place was certainly of some importance in the fourteenth century as on 1 September 1346 there is record of an inspection, by King David II, of a charter of John Graham referring to the lands of Billie in the barony of Bunkle, 'for payment of a rose upon the feast of St James the apostle and to the lord of Bunkle of 8*s*. sterling, with ward and the customary suits of court at Bonkle' (RRS, vi, 107).

South-east from Bunkle towards Chirnside, the ruins of Blanerne Castle are visible just off the minor road north of Edrom.

Edrom, like its neighbour Bunkle, also has an important fragment of twelfth-century ecclesiastical architecture. However, in this instance it is only a doorway from the Norman church which survives, now forming the entrance to a detached burial vault on the west side of the present church. The doorway is remarkably fine in detail, measuring 3.4 m (11 ft) in height and 1.4 m (4 ft 8 in.) between the jambs, with richly decorated capitals and three elaborately carved orders, possibly the work of masons from Durham (Fawcett 1985). The church itself has been considerably restored and rebuilt, mainly in 1732 (OSA, iii, 166), and there are few remains of any medieval work except for two buttresses and possibly core fragments in the south transept, built by Robert Blacadder, Archbishop of Glasgow in 1499, and known as the 'Blackadder Aisle'.

The church was clearly high-ranking during the medieval period being valued at 100 merks in the *Taxatio* of 1176 (Binnie 1995), an unusually high amount for that period. A century and a half later (1331–2) the account rolls of Coldingham Priory record that the chancel was thatched with straw (Ferguson 1890), certainly not a precaution against the kind of attack which must have been expected during that period. However, some element of protection may have been afforded to Edrom, as it was being promoted as a cult centre by the end of the fourteenth century, and in 1393 an indulgence was granted to all those who visited the church (Goodman 1989, 258).

Two and a half miles to the east of Edrom, the large village of **Chirnside** sits at the junction of the Berwick and Eyemouth roads, just a little above the Whiteadder Water. The church is located on rising ground towards the southern end of the settlement, close to the side of the Berwick road.

Chirnside must have been a target for English raiding on many occasions, as it lay within five miles of the border and on a good road through the valley of the Whiteadder. During one such raid in 1565, the Warden of the English East March, Francis Russell, Lord Bedford, took 800 men into Chirnside and Edington and with some slaughter carried off prisoners and booty (MacDonald Fraser 1989, 292). Bedford's raid was typical of the cross-border activity incited at this time by the political activities of both nations.

On approach, the church displays a formidable outward appearance, having a massive west tower 7 m (23 ft) in width by 6.3 m (20 ft 8 in.) in depth, its lower levels windowless, capped by a crowstepped roof within a corbelled parapet and with a taller campanile turret at the north-east angle (Figure 16). Despite its superficial aspect however, the present building belongs largely to

Fig. 16. Chirnside, tower from the south-west; mainly 1750–1876.

the period 1750–1876 and the only obvious feature of the medieval church is a twelfth-century doorway in the south wall, now protected by a Victorian porch. However, it is recorded that the structure was rebuilt in 1572 (Robson 1896, 35) and the south wall appears to belong, at least in part, to the pre-restoration building. There is strong evidence to indicate that the original church was designed for defence, as the tower, pulled down in 1750, was apparently vaulted in stone (RCHMS 1915) and, according to the *Old Statistical Account* (OSA, iii, 78), the remainder of the church was also vaulted. It would appear that the restorers were minded to copy, if not the original design, some elements of the earlier ambience of the building. The tower stands today like a pele tower alongside a simple church, even the rebuilt windows of which are high above the ground.

The tower, or more properly, western annex, has been constructed in two clear phases; the lower, earlier phase, is largely confined to the featureless west side, and angles sharply down on the north and south walls. It is unclear whether any of the tower prior to 1750 survives, although if it does this might explain the unusually robust dimensions of the structure. It is more likely that building material from the old tower was partly re-used in the present arrangement, and that better quality stone was employed during the 1876 restoration to form the upper levels which have ashlar quoins and dressings.

In the *Taxatio* of 1176 the 'Ecclesia de Chirnesyd' is valued at 50 merks, only half that of its near neighbour Edrom, and in the year 1396 it was annexed as a prebend to the Collegiate Church of Dunglass, having been formerly under Coldingham Priory (Binnie 1995).

From Chirnside the coast road to Eyemouth passes first through the village of **Ayton**. Its ruined medieval church, dedicated to St Dionysius, is completely dwarfed by its Victorian successor to the west which was completed in 1865, with a spire 40 m (130 ft) high.

Ayton kirk was formerly of some size and importance. It had a robust nave with north and south transepts, the north with a tower attached, and a chancel, the last standing until about 1840 (Robson 1896, 14). The building is constructed of pink and yellow sandstone in large rounded blocks. A measure of its importance lies in the fact that it was often used as a meeting place for official parleys between Scots and English whilst arranging truces; one of the most important of these was between John of Gaunt and the Scottish Commissioners of Robert II in 1380 (Boardman 1996, 115). In 1555 Archbishop Hamilton found masses being celebrated in the unroofed kirk, or in the open churchyard, as presumably the building had been badly damaged during the Troubles (Keeling 1975). In later years the toll-house, for the payment of road duty, was positioned at the church gate.

Despite the robust construction of the church, with walls averaging 0.9 m (3 ft) in thickness, there is little evidence remaining to determine the extent of any security features, though in a building so often used for important meetings between the two nations some element of security would seem highly probable. There are no complete surviving medieval windows or doors apart from the fine sixteenth-century window in the south transept and the upper doorway in the north transept.

A small tower has been added to the north side of the north transept, which, in its present form, comprises two storeys with a lower south doorway and upper south and blocked north doorways. The exterior of the structure was remodelled in the eighteenth century and is faced with ashlar stone with a blocked upper north opening formed as a segmental arch in Classical style; this may have formed part of the 'several improvements' referred to in the *Old Statistical Account* of 1790 (OSA, iii, 11). The sides and north face however are built in the same rough rubble construction as the rest of the church and appear to be medieval. The original purpose of this tower is not clear, although its later use, after remodelling, is likely to have been for the provision of an external stair-entry to a loft or gallery, perhaps also doubling as a bell-turret.

The present castle, lying north-east of the church, was rebuilt in the early nineteenth century by James Gillespie Graham on the site of its Norman predecessor. In 1498 the Earl of Surrey destroyed the castle just a year after James IV and Surrey had agreed a seven-year truce at Ayton (Mackie 1978, 123). This, like previous parleys and meetings, may well have taken place in the church.

Two and a half miles north-east of Ayton is the coastal town of Eyemouth, important historically as a fishing port, a centre of smuggling, and one of the few safe harbours along the wild and craggy eastern seaboard.

Eyemouth was a dependency of Coldingham Priory and an important centre of trade for the region and country as early as the reign of Alexander II (1214–49). Militarily, the town was the real key to Berwick (Tough 1928) as it defended the coastal road north and south and, during the sixteenth century, housed important forts. In 1547 the English erected a fort on the headland to the north of the town to protect their ships (MacIvor 1981, 148). The French fort on the left bank of the river was destroyed by treaty in 1561.

Of the medieval church at Eyemouth there is now no trace, the original building having been completely obliterated, probably in the early nineteenth century (Ferguson 1890, 128). It was, according to the *Old Statistical Account*, in 'bad repair' in 1791 (OSA, iii, 173). The church stood a little to the north of the present kirk which dates from 1812, probably in the vicinity of the watch-house which still exists in the churchyard.

North from Eyemouth, the coastal road swings slightly inland to the village of **Coldingham**, once dominated by its medieval priory (Figure 17). The village was of considerable strategic importance as it effectively guarded the road between Berwick and Edinburgh. James IV realised its value when, in the late winter of 1496, he ordered gunners to be stationed here, to prevent the passage of the English (Macdougall 1997, 135).

The first monastic house, quite possibly known to Bede as *Urbs Coludi* (Lang 1972), was founded sometime before 673 and was destroyed by the Danes in the ninth century; the monastery was re-founded by King Edgar *c.* 1098, and granted to the monks of Durham. It survived until 1216 when it was burnt by King John of England (Mon.Ang., vi(ii), 1149). Soon after this last destruction, the priory was rebuilt on a larger scale and the earliest standing fabric belongs to this period.

The priory and its buildings were of some significance in the affairs of Anglo-Scottish politics and suffered at the hands of both Scots and English during the Troubles (Ferguson 1890, 107). In 1327 the monastery was taken under the episcopal protection of King Edward III; cited as being an English cell in the priory of Durham it was offered protection with clause *nolumus*, for one year (CPR, 1 Edward III: 1327–30, Pt ii, m.18.). In 1368 similar protection was given by the Scottish King David II (RRS, vi, 398) and ten years later, in 1378, his nephew, Robert II, succeeded for a while in detaching Coldingham from Durham. It was appended to the Benedictine abbey of Dunfermline following a military manoeuvre the previous year, which resulted in the capture

Fig. 17. Coldingham Priory. The present building is part of the original thirteenth-century chancel; to the right are the ruins of the claustral range.

and control of the priory by Scottish forces (Boardman 1996, 113). It was during this period, April 1379, that the prior, Robert Claxton, along with some of his fellow monks, were accused of espionage, as they had been informing English raiding parties when and where to strike (Dobson 1992).

Durham lost control of the priory between 1365 and 1375, and between 1378 and 1398, except for a brief interlude in 1374/5 (Lomas 1996b). In 1485, James III of Scotland tried to connect it to the Chapel Royal of Stirling, but failed, and although it had been returned to Durham, it eventually became permanently annexed to Dunfermline in 1509 (Thomson 1972). The last English monks resident north of the Tweed, at Coldingham, appear to have been ejected by the middle of May 1462, although no record of the circumstances of this expulsion has survived (Dobson 1967).

The church was originally cruciform in plan with an aisleless choir, nave with aisles, north and south transepts, and a great central tower some 28 m (90 ft) in height; to the south lay the conventual buildings (RCHMS, 1915). Only part of the choir now survives, although the foundations of the tower and several other buildings around the cloister may still be seen. Only the north and east walls of the choir are medieval; the remainder was destroyed during the Civil War. After the rebuilding of the south and west walls in 1662 and again in 1850, the building continued to be used as the parish kirk, as it still is today. The restored choir measures 25 m by 7 m (82 ft by 23 ft) within walls which, on the surviving medieval sections, measure 1.2 m (4 ft) in average thickness.

Fig. 18. Coldingham Priory, interior of the thirteenth-century chancel.

The thirteenth-century north and east walls contain an impressive, and finely-detailed, two-tier range of arcading, the lower formed as blind arches, whilst the upper accommodates windows and is arranged as a formal clerestory with a narrow wall passage, reached by a small spiral stair at the north-east angle (Figure 18). The design and ornament point to a date *c.* 1200 (Cruden 1986).

That the building was used defensibly is not in doubt. In 1542 Sir Ralph Eure wrote that 'noe honeste man dothe lye nere the same [the border], but in strong holds . . . and certayne in the churche of Coldingham, in vaults there' (Hamilton Papers, i, 257). In one of the last inroads made by the English, during the raids of 1544, they seized the abbey of Coldingham, fortified the church and steeple, and left a garrison there (Simpson 1939). Eure, writing to the English court on November 17, stated that the abbey had been taken and kept for the king's use (Ridpath 1848, 379). Despite a vigorous Scots attack lasting almost two days, the garrison held out and, with news that English reinforcements were approaching from Berwick, the Scots withdrew. In the following year the buildings were burnt and destroyed by the Earl of Hertford as part of his campaign of despoliation.

During the Civil War the church was once again garrisoned and used as a fortress, this time by Royalist troops (Billings 1845, i). In 1648, parliamentary forces under Cromwell blew-up the building with gunpowder following the capitulation of the soldiers, and destroyed all except the north and east walls of the choir together with the tower and some portions of the transepts (Dent and McDonald 1998, 32). However, in 1650, 'Cothingham Abbey' (i.e. Coldingham) was reported to be one of the 'five strongholds quitted and left' by the Scots following the battle of Dunbar (RCHMS 1915, 42).

Within the same parish, lying alongside the A1 road, is **Houndswood** church, constructed on a new site in 1836 to replace the former chapel-of-ease at **Renton**.

A little to the north-east of Coldingham is the village of **St Abbs**, clustered precariously around its rocky harbour. Above the village the sheer cliffs of St Abbs Head rise dramatically, which provided a sound defence during the Troubles against attack by sea.

Although there are no remains of a medieval church in the village (the present church dates from 1892), higher up, on the hills to the north, are the fragments of two chapels. The first lies on Kirk Hill where only the foundations of a two-celled building of uncertain date remain. The second chapel, known as St Ebba's, is located on a rocky promontory on part of St Abb's Head and is a single-celled structure with evidence of a slight projection at the north-east corner. The promontory is cut by a deep ditch with the slight remains of a mortared wall on top which serve to restrict access to the site.

The location of St Ebba's chapel strongly suggests that it was situated with defence as a primary consideration. However, as it is likely to pre-date the major periods of Anglo-Scottish conflict, the reasons for this must lie in the general social instability of the time. There are many examples of similar chapels throughout the British Isles being sited in dramatic cliff-top positions simply for reasons of isolation and the notion of being 'nearer to God', whose earthwork boundaries, whilst constituting a spiritual and legal border, were hardly physically defensible (Thomas 1971, 29).

LAMMERMUIR AND THE NORTH

Along the coast to the north of St Abbs, situated precariously on a thin promontory of rock, lie the ruins of **Fast castle**, a minor fortress in an impregnable and highly strategic position (MacGibbon and Ross 1887–92, iii, 222–4). Fast played its part in the politics and history of Border affairs and changed hands many times during its eventful life. In 1503, Princess Margaret Tudor, on her way north to marry the Scottish King James IV, slept here for a night whilst her retinue lodged at Coldingham Priory. However, by 1567 the English ambassador to Elizabeth, Sir Nicholas Throckmorton, described the castle as 'fitter to lodge prisoners than folks at lybertye' (Tranter 1987, 64). The remains today are very fragmentary, and it is difficult to interpret the complete form of the original site, although it is highly probable that the castle had its own small chapel

Fig. 19. Cockburnspath church from the south-west.

within its walls which, in terms of defensibility, would have been undoubtedly the most secure of any throughout the Border.

The coast road north from Coldingham bypasses the rugged cliffs and Fast Castle, and leads to the village of **Cockburnspath**, a small settlement clustered around the church and market cross. The parish church, which stands near the side of the former market square, is a complex structure which has been the subject of many alterations and restorations, particularly in 1807 and 1826, but is distinctive for its unusual round tower located at the west end (Figure 19).

Very few features of medieval date remain in the fabric of the building although a two-light window above the exterior of the south-east doorway is indicative of the fourteenth or early fifteenth century. It is also reasonable to suppose that the core walls of the church, averaging 0.9 m (3 ft) in thickness, are largely medieval, and it is to be noted that the building is unusually narrow for its length: 24.5 m long by 5.5 m wide (80 ft by 18 ft). The extent of restoration from the seventeenth century onwards has been such that no indication of the pre-Reformation layout now survives.

The west tower however presents an enigma. Small towers built in a circular form are unusual in ecclesiastical architecture, but there was clearly a definite purpose in its design. The structure is small, measuring only 2.75 m (9 ft) in diameter within walls averaging 0.5 m (1 ft 6 in.) in thickness, and is entirely filled with a stone spiral stair which ascends to a small belfry, approximately 7.5 m (25 ft) above the ground, now housing a single bell dated 1837. The stairway is lighted by narrow rectangular windows whilst the belfry stage has a series of round-headed openings with central cut-outs in the style of the cross-loop-holes seen in castle defences (MacGibbon and Ross 1896-7, iii, 414; RCHMS 1915, 23). The date generally ascribed to this tower is late sixteenth or early seventeenth century, and although restored in the early nineteenth century its principal architectural features remain unaltered. Its original function is unclear, but, given the excellent view attainable from the belfry, its use as a watch-tower is not an unreasonable conjecture (Ferguson 1890). Round towers exist elsewhere, for example in the Scottish West March at Crossmichael, and at Kilmuir Easter on the Cromarty Firth in the Highland region, the latter dating from 1616 (Gifford 1992, 430).

During the Civil War, following the battle of Dunbar in 1650, the church was occupied by Cromwellian troops who clearly found it a useful haven. In the process the building was badly damaged and in 1665 it was recorded that the church was 'not plenished since the English displenished it' (Binnie 1995, 71).

Approximately two miles east of Cockburnspath, on a lofty headland over-looking the sea near Greenheugh Point, stand the ruins of St Helen's church, **Aldcambus**. No village or settlement now exists here and the name Aldcambus survives only in the nearby farmstead of Old Cambus West Mains.

Little now remains of the building with the exception of the west gable, the north wall of the chancel, and portions of the side walls of the nave (Figure 20). The entire church is built of deep-red sandstone, apart from a few yellow blocks in the gable, and despite the construction being of good-quality masonry, the character of the stone, combined with the exposed position, has resulted in severe weathering and largely accounts for the structure's very dilapidated present state. Deterioration has evidently been rapid as there is a description by T.S. Muir in 1845 in which he describes far more of the building than can be seen today, including a narrow east window with pointed exterior head and rounded interior, decorated with a single chevron; Muir's description also relates that the chancel arch was 2.1 m (7 ft) in width (Robson 1896).

The date of the building, from evidence in the fabric, would appear to be of the twelfth to the fifteenth centuries; the earliest records indicate that it belonged to Coldingham Priory. Despite having lost much of its medieval form, there are indications of the remains of springing for stone vaulting over both the nave and the chancel, originally taking the form of simple tunnel-vaults on walls which average 1m (3 ft 3 in.) in thickness. This vaulting may be indicative of an attempt to create a secure, fireproof structure. The position of the building is also significant: to the south a steep descent into a small valley, and to the north a sheer drop over precipitous cliffs into the sea.

Three-quarters of a mile north from Cockburnspath the boundary of the East March is defined by the Dunglass Burn. Although just beyond the confines of the March, the collegiate church of St Mary at **Dunglass** is worthy

Fig. 20. Aldcambus, ruins of the north wall of the chancel, the west gable and parts of the nave side walls.

of serious consideration in the context of defensible ecclesiastical architecture (Figure 21).

The building was begun as a chapel, built by the Home family for their spiritual requirements. During the 1440s Sir Alexander Home formed the priests who ministered there into a college, and rebuilt the church to reflect this change in status. The first building was of a simple design with nave, chancel, and sacristy, but this was soon enlarged with the addition of transepts and a central tower, to take its present form (McWilliam 1978; Fawcett 1985).

Although built in the general manner of other fifteenth-century Scottish churches (e.g., Seton, and the Carmelite friary church at South Queensferry), Dunglass displays all the features of a very sturdy building, capable of withstanding any deliberate attempt at attack. Indeed, the church was used to garrison English troops under Sir Richard Lee in 1547 (Colvin 1963–82, iv(ii), 722) and may earlier have been put to similar use by the Scots during the raid of 1544. Externally the construction is of fine coursed ashlar with roofs covered with stone slabs. Internally the strength of the building is evident from the size of the masonry, with blocks which average 0.6m wide by 0.3m deep (2ft by 1ft) in walls 1.3m (4ft 3in.) thick. Every division except the crossing has a pointed tunnel-vault, and the upper levels of the stocky, central tower could only be reached from a doorway above the north side of the nave crossing arch, probably served only by a ladder.

The nearby church of **Oldhamstocks**, also just north of the March boundary, was largely rebuilt in 1701, apart from the tunnel-vaulted Hepburn aisle

Fig. 21. Dunglass collegiate church.

dating from 1581, and the base of the tower on its west side. Evidence of medieval form has long been effaced by the later alterations, including the upper parts of the modest tower (MacGibbon and Ross 1896–7, iii, 596). On the theme of security, but of a much later date, a watch-house of 1824 still remains at the south end of the churchyard, intended to deter the nefarious nineteenth-century practice of body-snatching.

In 1568, on the day after Queen Mary's escape from Loch Leven Castle, the parson of Oldhamstocks, Thomas Hepburn, along with twenty men, attempted to seize Dunbar, but failed after the arrival of Lord Home's men (Ridpath 1848, 431).

Away from the coast at Cockburnspath, along the narrow route to the south-east, is the small village of **Abbey St Bathans**, nestling between steep hills where the Monynut and Whiteadder Waters meet.

On the south bank of the river, set in this quiet, fertile valley, the restored parish church incorporates the remains of the Cistercian Priory of St Bothan. All that now survives from the earlier nunnery is the east wall and the lower part of the north wall. The east wall, 1.2 m (4 ft) in thickness, contains a fourteenth-century window of two trefoil-headed lights (with restored mullion) surmounted by a quatrefoil, and near the west end of the north wall are the traces of a medieval blocked doorway. Although the conventual buildings were visible at the close of the eighteenth century, the last vestiges disappeared sometime before 1840 (Ferguson 1890), although slight traces of earthworks can be discerned to the east and west of the site.

During the period of the Troubles the nuns seem to have been rather judicious in their choice of loyalties, for on 24 August 1296, the prioress, Ada,
swore fealty to Edward I. However, following the battle of Homildon Hill in
1333, the prioress and nuns submitted to Edward III, clearly having reneged on
their earlier commitment to the English cause. Following their second submis-
sion, Edward granted the abbey protection, but in 1544, during the English
campaign on the Border, the buildings were burnt (Cowan and Easson 1976).

There were two other churches in the vicinity, the standing remains of
which have long since disappeared. The first building, which lay about a quarter of a mile to the south, may have been related to the abbey and could
possibly have been the pre-Reformation parish church (RCHMS 1915, 2); it
was excavated in 1870, revealing a rectangular structure 14 m (46 ft) in overall
length by 6.4 m (21 ft) in width over walls which varied between 1 m and 1.5 m
(3 ft and 5 ft) in thickness (Robson 1896). The second site lay one mile to the
west, at Strafontane (originally *Trois Fontaines* or *Trefontanis*, although there are
many variant spellings), and is thought to be that of a cell of another nunnery
or a hospital. It was recorded in a survey of 1627, and some remains were still
visible in 1794, but had entirely vanished by 1890.

Two and a half miles south-west of Abbey St Bathans is the tiny hamlet of
Ellemford, where the main road north-west from Duns crosses the Whiteadder Water. Ellem church is positioned on top of a steep bank, above the haugh
by the river, to the north of the bridge. It is in a remarkable location with a
near vertical drop to the south and a steep ascent from the west onto a narrow
ridge, which also falls away on two sides, leaving room for no other building
except the church (Figure 22). The plan is rectangular, measuring 17 m (55 ft
9 in.) in length by 5.4 m (17 ft 9 in.) in width, and although part of the centre of
the south wall is all that remains standing, the foundations of the whole building are traceable.

The church was clearly of strategic value as in 1496, whilst leading his army
into England, James IV camped here and met his military commanders in the
church (Binnie 1995), although he spent the night itself in a house, rewarding
the occupants with a gift of £5 (Macdougall 1997). The size of the assembly is
uncertain but was probably at least 30,000 men, potentially the greatest Scottish army of all time (Paterson 1997, 134).

Three miles to the south-west, the village of **Longformacus** straddles the
Dye Water. Its church dates from 1892 and is built on the site of its medieval
predecessor. A church may also have stood on higher ground, above the valley
of the Watch Water near Rawburn farmstead, but only the traces of a graveyard
were discernible at the turn of the century.

Along the main road north-west from Ellemford, the last village in this
corner of the East March is **Cranshaws**. The present church, standing a little
below the road near to the river, was built in 1739 and remodelled in 1899.
The eighteenth-century siting of this building was half a mile east of its pre-
Reformation forebear, the scanty remains of which still survive in the grounds

Fig. 22. Ellemford, the fragmentary remains of Ellem kirk, above the River Whiteadder, on a narrow and restricted site.

of Cranshaws Tower. Although the original church is too ruinous to determine any defensible characteristics, the presence of the fortified tower-house, only a short distance away, indicates that the need for built protection was very real in this remote corner of the March. According to the *Old Statistical Account* this tower was 'used as a place of defence, to which the inhabitants of this part of the country were accustomed to retreat, upon sudden incursions of the English Borderers' (OSA, iii, 127).

The medieval church of Cranshaws played host to one very significant event, the outcome of which fashioned the course of history. It was here in 1513 that King James IV held his council of war, just as he had done 17 years earlier at nearby Ellem church, but this time prior to marching his army to meet with its demise on Flodden field.

From Cranshaws, the road leads over the March boundary below Bothwell Hill. Although in Lothian, and some 20 miles distant from the border, this area was clearly still not immune from raiding and violent incursion. A narrow road leading along the upper reaches of the Whiteadder meanders over the high tops of the Lammermuirs and emerges in the tiny hill village of **Nunraw**. Apart from the few scattered houses and modern Sancta Maria Abbey, the prin-

cipal building here is the castle, now a baronial mansion of 1860 incorporating a sixteenth-century tower-house of the Hepburn family (McWilliam 1978).
The place is of some strategic importance as this narrow pass through the hills
avoided the main thoroughfares on the approach to Edinburgh. It was here in
1548, during an abortive invasion by the English, that William Grey set up a
garrison (Paterson 1997). However, in terms of ecclesiastical defence, Nunraw
is highly significant in that, during the middle of the fifteenth century, James
II gave the nuns then established here, a charter to 'fortify the nunnery' and
to 'have guns aye loaded to shoot at our aulden enemies of England' (Tranter
1962, 44; Lindsay 1986, 383). The exact nature of the buildings is unclear and it
seems unlikely that there was a nunnery at this spot (Cowan and Easson 1976),
though it may have been a grange belonging to Haddington Priory, which lay
a short distance to the north. At a later date, in 1547/8 it is described as a
'fortalice, which the prioress of Haddington undertakes to defend against the
English' (ALC, 572).

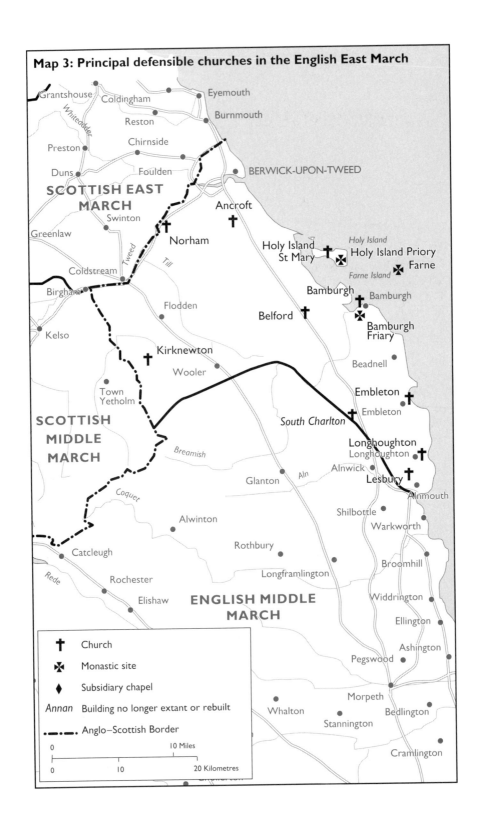

Map 3: Principal defensible churches in the English East March

Grantshouse
Coldingham
Eyemouth
Burnmouth
Reston
Whiteadder
Chirnside
Preston
Duns
Foulden
BERWICK-UPON-TWEED

SCOTTISH EAST MARCH

Swinton
Ancroft ✝

Greenlaw
Norham ✝
Tweed
Till

Holy Island St Mary ✝ ✠
Holy Island
Holy Island Priory ✠ Farne
Farne Island ✠

Coldstream
Birgham
Bamburgh ✝
Bamburgh
Kelso
Flodden
Belford ✝
Bamburgh Friary ✠

Kirknewton ✝
Beadnell

Wooler
Embleton ✝

Town Yetholm
Embleton ✝

SCOTTISH MIDDLE MARCH
South Charlton

Breamish
Longhoughton ✝
Longhoughton

Coquet
Alnwick
Lesbury ✝

Glanton
Aln
Alnmouth

Alwinton
Shilbottle
Warkworth

Rothbury
Broomhill

Catcleugh
Longframlington

Rede
Widdrington
Rochester

Elishaw
ENGLISH MIDDLE MARCH
Ellington

Ashington
Pegswood

Morpeth
Whalton
Bedlington
Stannington

Cramlington

✝	Church
✠	Monastic site
♦	Subsidiary chapel
Annan	Building no longer extant or rebuilt
▬ ▪ ▬ ▪ ▬	Anglo–Scottish Border

0   10 Miles

0   10   20 Kilometres

2

THE ENGLISH EAST MARCH

The East March of England formed the smallest administrative district of the medieval Border. Owing to the fact that it was a sub-division of an earlier, larger March, comprising the whole of Northumberland north of the River Tyne, its southern boundary was especially ill-defined. In the Calendar of Border Papers the area was described as 'that part of Northumberland which is next unto Scotland on the East side of England' (CBP, i, 76), but it is more closely defined as Norhamshire, Islandshire, Glendale, and Bamburghshire, the first two of which formed part of the County Palatine of Durham until 1844. The description of its junction with the border is more explicit: the west corner lay at the 'Hanging-Stone', a feature marked on Christopher Saxton's map of 1579 and which is still to be found on the north-west slope of The Cheviot, alongside a point where the border deviates from its north–south line near Auchope Cairn (at OS grid reference NT 892191). This is close to a crossing road known as 'Gribbheade' which was apparently 'a passage and hye way for the theefe' (CBP, ii, 853). This rocky outcrop has evidently served as a boundary marker since at least the thirteenth century and is documented as marking the boundary between the realms without controversy (Mack 1926). From this point, the East March line struck just north of the Cheviot hill itself and probably followed the Harthope Burn to the Coldgate Water south of Wooler at Middleton. Past Chillingham, which lay within the English Middle March, the boundary line turned south-east until it reached the River Aln, just east of Alnwick; from here it is clear that this river formed the margin up to the sea. That the boundaries were unclear, even in the period of their use, is illustrated by records of those villagers who turned out at East March musters during the sixteenth century: the men of Chillingham, supposedly within the Middle March, appeared at least three times (Tough 1928, 3).

The area is characterized by the extremities of the high Cheviot uplands to the north and west, and the flatter coastal margins in the east. There is only one large town, Berwick-upon-Tweed. The topography of the English East March meant that, apart from the rough hill tracks, many permitting safe crossing of the border only during the summer months, the only direct route north was through Berwick, although there were also important roads from Wooler to Coldstream and from the latter to Berwick via Norham.

BERWICK-UPON-TWEED

Berwick's importance in the history of Border affairs cannot be overestimated. Occupying a position of extreme strategic and commercial importance, it was highly valued in the political and military game of medieval state affairs.

Geographically the town lies at the mouth of the River Tweed, that most significant of Border river valleys which facilitated the export of goods and produce from the northern kingdom to the rest of Europe, without having to travel through England. It has elements of natural defence as it occupies a small peninsula between the river and the sea and is well guarded by offshore rocks and the rugged coastline. Landward however, Berwick is overlooked by hills to the north-west and south-west.

It was the wool trade which enabled the town to rise to prominence during the early Middle Ages and which allowed it, during the thirteenth century, to become Scotland's foremost royal burgh, the most important amongst the 'Four Burghs' of Berwick, Edinburgh, Roxburgh, and Stirling (Gordon 1985). Berwick was, along with Roxburgh, one of the earliest of the Scottish burgh towns, the charter being granted by David I between 1119 and 1124, although by this time the port was already a flourishing centre of trade.

Up until the commencement of the Wars of Independence, Berwick was, in all senses, a completely Scottish town. Indeed, the place was always more important to the northern kingdom than to the southern, and the only real value to England was its strategic location, less than 60 miles from Edinburgh which could be reached easily by both road and sea. It also stood at the gateway to the flat fertile plains of the Scottish East March. It is not surprising therefore that Edward I made Berwick one of his first targets on the outbreak of open war in 1296, taking the town by storm on 30 March and putting many of the inhabitants to the sword. So great was this slaughter that accounts tell of bodies piled high in the streets, and even the sanctuary normally afforded by churches was defiled (Paterson 1996, 9). With this foothold secure, Edward set about rebuilding the castle and constructing stone walls around the burgh to convert it into a garrison post and forward supply base for his military expeditions. Robert Bruce failed to recapture Berwick in 1312 but it fell to him six years later and remained in Scottish hands until after the battle of Halidon Hill, which took place just to the north-west of the town, in 1333. During the reign of Edward III Berwick became the administrative headquarters of English-occupied Scotland, although the Scots gradually won back their lands up to the line of the present border. Winning the town was clearly a great political goal for the Scottish Crown and they succeeded, briefly, in 1355, 1384, 1405, and finally between 1461 and 1482 when the English recaptured Berwick for the last time (Dickinson and Duncan 1977; Tuck 1979).

Owing to King Edward I's fastidious military mind, the ordinary people of Berwick, whether they were Scots or English, enjoyed the relative security and protection of the walled town with its strong castle and garrison. There was therefore, in all likelihood, no need to procure the type of ecclesiastical defensive measures which were to be found in the surrounding districts. Religion flourished within and without the walls, fed by a populous locale and attracted by trade and prosperity.

There were at least five churches around Berwick by the close of the thirteenth century. St Lawrence's and the Church of the Blessed Virgin in Bondington, then a separate village just outside the town walls, and St Nicholas' and the Church of the Holy Trinity within the town itself. Holy Trinity, now rebuilt as the parish church, existed prior to 1156 when it is on record as having passed from the control of Kelso Abbey to Durham (Gordon 1985). The fifth was a chapel, also dedicated to the Holy Trinity, situated on Berwick Bridge and which was destroyed by a flood in 1294. As well as these five churches there were three hospitals, a Franciscan church, founded in 1244, and a house of Cistercian canonesses sited on the southern slopes of Halidon Hill, the last providing a base for Edward I in 1296, prior to his taking the town. The hospital of St Mary Magdalene suffered war damage during the fourteenth century and was restored by Edward II. In the year following the 1333 siege by the English, the church and houses of the Maison Dieu were reported as being utterly cast down by the engines during the siege (Nicholson 1961). There was also a castle chapel, administered by the Carmelite Friars, and a chapel of the Dominican Friars, close to the castle, which, though disused, played host to a meeting in 1291 where the succession to the Scottish throne was debated (Stones and Simpson 1978). However, by the nineteenth century not a trace remained of these ecclesiastical buildings and little of the castle (Tomlinson 1888).

The only major historic church in Berwick today is the parish church of the Holy Trinity which lies within the Elizabethan defences and close to the eighteenth-century barracks. Holy Trinity dates from 1648–1652, designed by a London mason, John Young, in a mixture of Gothic and Classical styles (although in 1855 many Gothic features were converted into Classical form). This church is very unusual in that it was built during the Civil War, and its intended design may have been changed so that it could not be used defensively: the original plan included a west tower which was omitted at the direct request of Cromwell (Pevsner *et al* 1992). To compensate for the lack of a bell housing, the bells of the Town Hall were used to call parishioners to worship (Wilson 1870). The medieval church which stood on or near the site of the present Holy Trinity was described at the time of its demolition in 1648 as being 'very little' and 'meanly built'; it had apparently been necessary to re-dedicate the church in 1242 after blood had been shed within its walls following an argument between two clerics (Lamont-Brown 1988, 38–9). The old parish church was host to one highly significant event in Anglo-Scottish relations, for on 26 March 1603, James Stewart, King of Scotland, was proclaimed at Berwick King of England, France, and Ireland, and after this ceremony

James entered Holy Trinity church to give thanks for his safe entry into his new double kingdom.

Just outside Berwick, at **Tweedmouth**, the church was rebuilt on the site of its Norman predecessor in 1780. The earlier building had been in a poor state of repair, as in 1726 the chancel was ordered to be cleansed 'like a house suspected of leprosy' (Wilson 1870, 34).

THE NORTHERN EDGE

Away from the safe protection of medieval Berwick's walls, the area of the East March which adjoined the Tweed was far from secure and witnessed considerable bloodshed during the years of the Border Troubles.

Four miles south of Berwick, in the flat, open countryside leading up to the coast, the village of **Ancroft** possesses one of the most significant examples of ecclesiastical fortification on the east side of the Marches (Figure 23). The

Fig. 23. Ancroft church, defensible west tower, added to the Norman building.

church of St Anne has an aisleless Norman nave to which has been added, in the late thirteenth or early fourteenth century, a defensible west tower which resembles a typical Border pele in many respects (Kelland 1982). It was evident that this tower was regarded historically as serving this role for in the *Survey Booke of Norhamshire and Islandshire* compiled in 1661, the village is described thus: 'In the same towne of Ancroft is one pile, builded to the end of the church, and dyvers good howses beside' (Bates 1891, 53).

The early church lay in the living of the Priory on Holy Island, witnessed by a dispute in 1145 between Pope Eugenius III and the Prior of Lindisfarne. It may be that, in similar fashion to the prior of Holme Cultram Abbey in the English West March who constructed a defensible church at Newton Arlosh, the monks of Holy Island sought to protect the vicar of Ancroft by erecting a strong west tower which could serve as a home as well as a refuge. The tower is recorded as 'scarcely beinge in good repare' in 1541, though still in use by 1561 (Frontier I, 190; Kelland 1982, 325).

The nave is basically of the twelfth century with an impressive blocked south doorway previously fronted by a stone-vaulted porch. There was considerable restoration in 1836 and 1870 when the chancel and east end were rebuilt and many of the openings renewed, though copied in the Norman style. A Victorian north transept was also added and removed prior to 1870 (Wilson 1870). However, the bulky defensible west tower, partly built over the end of the Norman church, has largely escaped modification, with the exception of the roof and parapet.

Externally the rectangular west tower expresses the stark simplicity expected of a fortified refuge. At the north-west angle is a massive buttress, above which is a vestige of the Norman frieze, seen more completely on the south side. The fabric is extremely complex in the lower part of the west wall, and this attests to some serious alterations which were made probably at the time of the building's conversion to defensible use.

The ground floor is tunnel-vaulted in stone in the typical style of a Border tower-house. The walls, which measure 1.35 m (4 ft 5 in.) in thickness are pierced on the west side by a narrow round-headed light with renewed exterior facing stone, and on the south by a nineteenth-century doorway. Part of this floor, on the north side, has been converted into a family burial vault in the nineteenth century. There was originally no access to the upper levels from the interior basement although at an unknown date the vault has been cut away and a wooden staircase inserted. The original access to the first floor has evidently been through a narrow doorway, 0.5 m (1 ft 8 in.) in width, clearly visible in the west wall at a height of 3 m (9 ft 10 in.) above the ground; no doubt a wooden ladder would have provided admittance during its use.

The first floor of the tower has walls which still retain their plaster, and a stone-flagged floor (Figure 24). In the north and south walls are small windows and in the east a plain fireplace, although the southern lancet opening is a replacement of an earlier, and smaller, rectangular light. From this level

Fig. 24. Ancroft church, first floor of the tower showing position of stair and fireplace.

a spiral staircase leads upwards in the south-east angle and is lit by small stair-lights, formed through the thickness of the wall. One such light, opening east, is now blocked, indicating a heightening of the roof level during the nineteenth-century restorations. Further up, a blocked doorway formerly gave admission to a second floor, now removed, lit by a large Gothic window in the west wall and smaller lights above and in the north and south sides. The stair continues to the parapet level. From the tower head there are fine views in all directions and it is quite possible that this tower may also have served to house a warning beacon.

The scattering of little villages around Ancroft contain no ecclesiastical buildings earlier than the late eighteenth century and many do not possess a church at all. At **Duddo**, a short distance to the south-west, the little church of 1879, partly modelled on St Mary's, Holy Island, sits beneath the fragmentary ruin of a late sixteenth-century tower.

To the north of Duddo, at an important crossing point on the border, the village of **Norham** nestles below its imposing medieval castle. The village itself lies between the castle and the church and found favour for most of the warring period, for although the castle attracted serious military attention from both nations, the protection it offered locally served to deter the casual raiding which so troubled most other villages on the Border.

Fig. 25. Norham castle, the Great Tower.

It is the castle which essentially dominates this small village, and which played a significant part in the political and martial affairs of the region (Figure 25). It was originally constructed in the early twelfth century by Ranulf Flambard, Bishop of Durham, to protect his rights and holdings from thieves and the Scots. The fortification comprises an inner and outer ward with a Great Tower defended by curtain walls, a west gate and barbican, and two moats, all positioned on a naturally defensive bluff high above the river (Dixon and Marshall 1993). Throughout its history, the castle was damaged and modified by repeated attacks and by improvements, so that today the fabric of the building appears as a mixture of periods from the twelfth to the sixteenth centuries (Hunter Blair and Honeyman 1985). Edward I made his headquarters here in 1291 at the start of his campaign to win Scotland by politi- cal means, and the castle remained largely in English custody throughout the remainder of the Troubles. From the 1290s onward, none of the bishops of Durham cared to stay in this part of Northumberland for any length of time, and they relied on their senior episcopal officials, based at Norham Castle, for the day-to-day control of their affairs (Dobson 1992).

At the other end of the village of Norham, the church of St Cuthbert is positioned close to the south bank of the Tweed and near to the present bridge

Fig. 26. Norham church in 1835, prior to restoration.

which may also be the site of an earlier ford, providing access between England and Scotland. The earliest parts of the building belong to the mid-twelfth
century, that is, the chancel, the south nave arcade and wall, and three pillar
bases on the north side of the nave. The eastern bay of the chancel was added
in the fourteenth century. The remainder dates, for the most part, from the
restorations of 1846, 1852, and 1883–84. The present west tower was rebuilt in
1837, its medieval predecessor having been located at least one bay further west;
this portion of the building was evidently destroyed at this time. A painting
made prior to the rebuilding of 1837, shows a narrow tower which appears to
be of seventeenth- or eighteenth-century form and which may have been constructed during an earlier restoration in 1617–19 (Figure 26).

The Norman windows in the chancel are placed unusually high, 4 m (13 ft)
above ground level to the cills, and whilst this may have been to allow for
interior choir stalls to be positioned against the side walls, the pre-restoration
painting indicates that the nave windows, which were later inserted into the
demolished south aisle, were placed almost as high (*see* Figure 26). In the
absence of any other clearly defensive features it is difficult to argue that this
arrangement was for security, especially given that the principal construction
is well prior to the main period of unrest. However, this church is located
uncommonly close to the border and as such may have been considered a
legitimate military target from an early date.

During Robert I's seige of the castle in 1318, the church was utilized as a
stronghold by the Scots who were ensconced within the village (Tomlinson
1888, 551). Norham church had been used a few years earlier, and in marginally

more peaceful circumstances, as an assembly place during the discussions held by Edward I to determine the validity of the competitors for the Crown of Scotland in May and June 1291. The first meeting was held in the church on 10 May and there then followed a period of deliberation. Discussions resumed in early June and nine further sessions were held, some on the green at nearby Upsettlington (in Scotland), two in the King's Chamber within the Castle, and the remainder inside the church (Powicke 1962, 603-4; Stones and Simpson 1978). Later still, in the sixteenth century, the church was utilised, along with its Scottish counterpart at Ladykirk, for March day meetings between the Wardens and commissioners (CBP, ii, 1002), and a peace treaty was concluded in Norham church in June 1551 (Bates 1895).

Norham is immortalised in the opening to Scott's *Marmion*, and was said, according to the original story of the knight William Marmion, to be the most dangerous place in England when he ventured forth from Lincolnshire to seek adventure in 1318.

Upstream along the Tweed, towards the next major river crossing at Coldstream, the old road passes over the fifteenth-century bridge on the River Till at **Twizel**. Of crucial strategic importance (as the lower reaches of the Till are deep and dangerous with few crossing points), it was over this bridge that Howard, Earl of Surrey, led a section of the English army on the way to the Battle of Flodden in 1513. Remarkably, the Scots left this important traverse unguarded.

A mile downstream from the bridge, adjacent to the point where the Till joins the Tweed, lie the isolated ruins of St Cuthbert's Chapel. In its present form, the two-celled chapel dates from the eighteenth century when it was rebuilt by Sir Francis Blake using masonry from its medieval predecessor, the domestic chapel of the early lords of Tillmouth (Tomlinson 1888). Defensive precautions may have been unnecessary due to the presence of the nearby castle, mentioned in 1496 (Bates 1891, 22), and owing to the extreme difficulty of crossing the Till and Tweed at this point.

The road west from Twizel Bridge follows the river up to **Cornhill-on-Tweed**, the next major border crossing after Norham. Although there was a medieval chapel-of-ease to Norham here, the present church dates only from 1840 by Ignatius Bonomi with modifications of 1866, although the nave contains some masonry from its forerunner of 1751-2.

Beyond Cornhill the next Tweedside village is **Wark-on-Tweed** where the remains of one of the most important castles on the Border sit astride a narrow ridge which runs parallel with the river (Figure 27). Originally a motte and bailey castle of the twelfth century, it was converted into a stone structure which consisted of a large east tower with a series of utility buildings in the inner and outer wards below. In 1519 the tower was converted, or rebuilt, as a polygonal gun tower, four storeys high with 'fyve grete murdour holes' so that 'grete bumbardes may be shot out at icheon of them' (Bates 1891; Pevsner *et al* 1992, 610; Cathcart King 1983). The castle changed hands frequently both

Fig. 27. Wark-on-Tweed, site of the castle.

between English and Scots and between private ownership and royal possession, and was attacked with severity on at least thirteen recorded occasions. It
reached the zenith of its importance in the sixteenth century when the Earl of
Northumberland noted that it was 'the stay and key of all this country' (L. & P.
Henry VIII, v(ii), 226). Little remains of the masonry structure today.

There was a chapel here, dedicated to St Giles and belonging to the castle
but probably also serving the village (Vickers 1922). No structure now survives
but the polygonal shape of the churchyard is visible to the west of the castle,
on the far side of the bank between the road and the river.

Two miles west of Wark Castle, the border line crosses the Tweed and runs
south to the Cheviot range beyond. Half a mile east sits the tiny village of
Carham; its church of 1790 and 1870 is positioned close to the river. It betrays
no evidence of its predecessor, a building which was constructed by a small cell
of Augustinian canons from Kirkham Priory in Yorkshire, sometime after 1131
(Knowles and Hadcock 1971). This was a perilous position for any settlement
during the Troubles as the road into Scotland presented no natural obstacles
and the town of Kelso lay only five miles away. Yet the only documented reference to defence is by John Leland who noted in 1538 that 'At this Carham is
a litle towre of defence agayne the Scotts' (Leland, ix, fo.147). Whether this
tower was connected with the monastic buildings, or a separate strong tower,
is not disclosed, though we also know that it was 'wythout barmekyn or iron
gate' and was clearly only intended as 'a place of refuge in a sodenly occur-

rent skyrmyshe'; it was last mentioned in the chain of Border defences in 1584 (Bates 1891, 78–9). Defence was clearly a necessity, as in 1295 the Chronicler of Lanercost recorded that the Scottish army devastated the monastery with slaughter and fire (Chr.Lan., 135). In 1542 the church was presumably in ruins as there is reference to stone being taken from the church to Wark castle, presumably for the latter's repair (L. & P. Henry VIII, xvii, 555).

Between Carham and Wark is the site of a Border skirmish where, in 1370, Scottish troops under Sir John Gordon defeated the English led by Sir John Lillburne, despite having been driven back five times.

South of Carham several roads cross the border until the hills rise too steeply for easy access beyond Yetholm and Shotton. Just to the south of Horse Rigg, some three miles north-east of Yetholm, the tiny hamlet of **Mindrum** possesses the remains of a single celled chapel-of-ease to nearby Kirknewton, later transferred to the priory of Kirkham (though not directly under the control of the cell at Carham); the chapel was extra parochial and enjoyed the rights of sanctuary (Vickers 1922, 15). This place was a dangerous one, and its fortification was urged in 1550 (Bates 1891, 51). Bowes' survey eight years earlier reported that 'there ys nether towre barmekyn nor other fortresse yn it [Mindrum] whereyn the tenents may be releved in tyme of war' (Frontier I, 182–3), but there is no evidence that any defensible structure was ever erected. There were also other minor chapels in the vicinity, at **Howburn** and **Presson**, of which no remains survive.

In Sir Robert Bowes' sixteenth-century Border survey he describes this area in great detail and notes:

> that towne of Mydrom well plenished, lyeth soe in the high streete and waye whereby the Scotts passe and repasse into those merches of England that it would not only be a great reliefe or defence to that frontier, but also having ij litle piles or watch howses, the one upon Teversheughe betweene it and Warke, and the other uppon Heddon Lawe betwene it and Chevyot there could no Scotts men passe into England nor from England, but one of those howses might discover them. And soe by burninge of beacons or shote of a goune to give knowledge and warninge from one to another, whereby they might assemble to resiste repulse or anoye the enemye as occasion might serve them. The uttermost frontyer they fortefyed upon the east marches would cawse that sundrye villages wasted by wares and lying longe tyme uninhabited to be repeopled and plenished which were a great strength to those borders (Frontier II, 203–4).

North-east of Mindrum and a little to the south-east of Cornhill, the village of **Branxton** overlooks Flodden Field where, against all odds, the strong Scottish army, led by James IV, was tactically frustrated by the English forces on 9 September 1513. In the ensuing battle, around 10,000 Scots, including their king and three bishops, were killed. For Scotland the outcome was a catastrophe with her monarch and a large proportion of the nobility dead, but as so often in Anglo-Scottish military history, the victory, little short of a miracle for the English, was not exploited, and the Earl of Surrey quickly disbanded his army (White 1859; Macdougall 1997; Philips 1999).

Branxton church has little of its medieval fabric remaining and now belongs largely to the rebuilding of 1849. However the present building contains some re-used medieval masonry and is evidently set on its earlier foundations, visible on the north side of the nave and at the south-east corner of nave and chancel. The western half of the south chancel wall may also contain medieval work *in situ*. The Norman chancel-arch, modified in the thirteenth century, also survives intact. The early history of the church is colourful, as in the year 1200 it was recorded that, during recent disturbances, certain malefactors had taken possession of the church and had presented it to a clerk named Merlin (Vickers 1922, 96). A visitation in 1369 noted that the roofs of both nave and chancel were in decay and the glazing of the chancel windows needed attention, but there is no mention of a tower at this period; the present small north-west tower dates only from 1849.

Three miles further east the villages of Etal and Ford sit astride the Till and both locations provide safe crossing points, upstream from Twizel, where the river is not so deep or treacherous.

Etal, the northernmost of the two villages, has no remains of its medieval church but does possess the substantial ruins of its castle. This fortification, licensed in 1341, belonged to the Manners family. It was taken by the Scots in 1513, prior to the Battle of Flodden, but by 1541 was decayed (Bates 1891). A quarter of a mile down river the remains of a small medieval chantry chapel, dedicated to St Mary, and founded by Sir Robert de Manners, lie on the wooded slopes of the river.

At **Ford** there is both a medieval church and castle. The castle was licensed in 1338 and was quadrangular in design with four towers, only two of which remain. It was taken by the Scots in 1385, 1513, and 1549 when it was burnt except for the keep which held out. After a final seizure in 1557 the building appears to have been abandoned as a fortress and was rebuilt sometime before 1589 as a mansion house, since when it has undergone several phases of development, particularly in 1761–95 and 1861–5 (Pevsner *et al* 1992, 283).

To the north-west of the church, which lies only a short distance from the castle, are the lowermost courses of a vicar's pele tower, first recorded in 1513 when it was burnt as part of James IV's major raid that year. The stone-vaulted ground floor is still discernible as is a mural stairway on the east side.

The fact that a vicar's pele was necessary, alongside a major castle, underlines the necessity for defence in this location. Ford was open to attack by the Scots from both north and west where the flat terrain allowed easy and unhindered access. The church dates largely from the early thirteenth century, although it was heavily restored by John Dobson in 1853 when the north aisle and east end of the chancel were rebuilt. The west wall typifies the sturdy, northern aspect of church architecture, and at 1.2 m (4 ft) in thickness, with only a bell turret above, it is of robust construction. Below, one original narrow lancet pierces the wall on its north side. This perhaps characterised the building as it existed in the fourteenth century when it may have provided a

Fig. 28. Kirknewton, showing the low chancel and south transept.

third element of sanctuary alongside the castle and pele. It may have been a target for enemy assault as it was damaged by fire in 1341 when Robert Bruce attacked the area, and this was followed by further raids in 1340, 1379, and 1380. The church was reported to be in decay in 1431 and 1598 (Collier and Stewart 1987).

Close to the line of the border, south of Ford, the villages of Westnewton and Kirknewton lie in the shadow of Yeavering Bell and the Newton Tors, and to the south the Cheviot dominates the upland landscape.

The church which serves these two villages, and the remoter settlements at Kilham and Hethpool is at **Kirknewton** (Figure 28). Here, despite the major restoration which took place under John Dobson in 1860 when the nave was rebuilt, and the later addition of the north-west tower, there is considerable evidence for the original defensive adaptation of the building. The chancel and south transept are singular: they are both equipped with stone tunnel-vaults of a very primitive form, that in the chancel springs from only 0.85 m (2 ft 9 in.) above the floor, and thus almost entirely fills the available space, with minimal vertical side walls (Figure 29). In the transept, the springing is even lower – 0.4 m (1 ft 4 in.) and there are no discernible side walls. At its highest point the chancel vault is only 3.79 m (12 ft 5 in.) which is exceptionally low for a major chamber of a church. The walls of the chancel are pierced only by a small window and a low priest's door, cut through the vault on the south side,

Fig. 29. Kirknewton, the tunnel-vaulted chancel.

and by a nineteenth-century triple lancet to the east. The walls of the medieval structure average 1.25 m (4 ft) in thickness. The date of the eastern portion of the building and south transept is unclear – the architecture is practically without parallel, although crude quarter tunnel-vaults are employed at Elsdon, and a similar, but larger, variant exists at Boltongate in the English West March. Although the south door and window appear to be of the sixteenth century, the window is clearly an insertion, having a re-used head, and the main body of construction is likely to be of earlier date, perhaps originating in the fourteenth century, contemporary with the form of the chancel-arch. The chancel also appears to have been the subject of repair or rebuilding as there is a change in the stone coursing of the vault, and an anomalous alteration, on the exterior north side at a distance of approximately 4.5 m (15 ft) from the east wall.

During excavation work in 1857, by F.R. Wilson, the foundations of a Norman building were discovered, probably coeval with the sculpture depicting the Adoration of the Magi now preserved in the nave. The excavations also revealed that the chancel was longer than at present; evidence of this is visible at the north-east corner where the footings of a longer chancel are discernible, projecting beyond the east wall. It may also be the case that the construction of the nineteenth-century north aisle absorbed a corresponding medieval transept to that on the south, and there was certainly a previous north aisle, which dated from the thirteenth century, as shown by the foundations of arcade columns, found during the Victorian restoration (Wilson 1870).

A church at 'Newton in Glendale' is recorded in 1223 (Collier and Stewart 1987), and the nave apparently required rebuilding in 1669. Clearly the construction of this chancel and transept, and possibly of the earlier nave, were a deliberate attempt to make the building secure against attack by fire and, to some extent, direct force. Towards the end of the fourteenth century, the parish was so troubled by Scottish incursions that it was beyond paying its quota and by 1436 the bishop gave licence to the vicar to say Mass and other offices outside the church, in any place in the parish which was safe and suitable, so long as the hostilities continued – provided that the sacraments were celebrated in the church whenever possible (Vickers 1922, 118).

Although the usual East March meeting places for the Wardens on truce days were at Carham and Norham, Foulden-Rig, and the Riding Burn (Tough 1928, 138), it is also recorded that the Warden's deputy went to Yetholm and Kirknewton 'ther to determine of causes' (CBP, ii, 1003), perhaps meeting within the churches there.

The road leading eastwards from Kirknewton follows the contours of the high ground to the south and the lower land of the Glen and Till valleys to the north. Once through the Kirknewton gap, the land of the English East March, and the road to the south, was wide open to invasion or raiding from the west.

The hamlet of **Akeld**, at the junction of the Kirknewton and Coldstream roads, once had a small chapel about which little is known, save that it was in existence by the first half of the thirteenth century and held a chantry to Robert of Akeld. By the fourteenth century it appears to haven fallen into disuse (Vickers 1922). Its site is probably immediately adjacent to the road at the edge of 'Chapel Field' in the heart of the settlement where there was also a 'lytell fortlett or castle house w'thout a barmekyn', recorded in the Border survey of 1541 (Frontier I, 185).

Immediately east of Akeld, the land rises sharply to the south onto the slope of Humbleton Hill where, on 14 September 1403, the battle commonly known as the Battle of Homildon Hill took place between the Scots forces led by Archibald, Earl of Douglas, who had invaded England earlier in the year, and the English led by the Earl of Northumberland and his son Henry (better known as 'Hotspur'). The result was decisive, with the English archers winning the battle virtually alone. Earl Douglas was wounded and captured along with the Earls of Moray and Angus and the son of the Duke of Albany.

The nearby hillside hamlet of **Humbleton**, like Akeld, had a small chapel, the site of which lies just below the high point in the village close to the road. In 1541 the village was described as having 'nether fortress nor barmekyn' (Collier and Stewart 1987) although the remains of an early Norman ringwork castle still exist, and by 1548 there was also a tower or bastle in existence (Cathcart King 1983, 350).

It is likely that the town of **Wooler** provided refuge during periods of disturbance. It is built in a strategic position, high above the valley and road
which mark one of the principal north-south routes. It has the remains of a
castle which was re-garrisoned in the early sixteenth century but which by 1541
was out of use and dilapidated, although noted as being 'a mervelous conveny-
ent place for the defence of the countrye thereaboute' (Frontier I, 185). The
present remains are largely those of a sixteenth-century tower. No doubt this
fortification had served the local population's need for security, and in any
event, Wooler seems to have escaped the worst of the Border afflictions, probably owing to its utilisation of natural defences, despite its description by Lord
Dacre as 'being the outermost town of the realm' and a place of particular
danger (Vickers 1922). In the 1541 Border survey it was remarked that 'nere
thereby ys the common entree & passage of the Scottes for invadynge this
realme or makinge any spoyle in tyme of warre or troubles peace' (Frontier I,
185).

St Mary's church is positioned close by the castle at the east side of the town
and on high ground. The present structure dates mainly from a rebuilding of
1765 with additions of 1834 and 1912-13. Its predecessor was in a ruinous condition by 1501 and was probably seriously damaged in a fire during 1694; by 1762
it was reported that the chancel was in ruins. The scope of the building's use
during the period of the Troubles is unclear, but the fact that both church and
castle were in poor condition during the sixteenth century implies a degree of
enemy damage. This was evidently the case, as on occasion the priest was given
leave to absent himself from his cure due to the 'wasting of the district by war
and burning of churches and houses' (Vickers 1922).

Two and a half miles due north of Wooler, nestling below the crag of Dod
Law, is the village of **Doddington**. The church of St Mary and St Michael is
located at its south-west corner, away from the main road, and comprises a
nave with north aisle and west chamber (now the chancel), and a small vestry.
The evolution of the building is interesting, as the original chancel lay to the
east but was replaced in 1838 by the architect Ignatius Bonomi; in 1893 this
chancel was converted into a baptistery and the west chamber formed into the
present chancel. The purpose of the west chamber is unclear, but it may possibly be the remains of the lower stage of a former tower, a horizonal offset
in the line of construction being evident in the west wall. Such a tower would
have been large; the present area measures 7.3 m (24 ft) east to west and 5 m (16 ft
5 in.) north to south and has a blocked entrance doorway on the north side (the
present floor level is the result of raising in 1893). Restoration has seriously dis-
rupted the fabric, making interpretation difficult, but the west and south-west
windows of the west chamber appear to be original thirteenth-century lancets.
Owing to lack of documentary evidence concerning the possible tower, it may
have been an early victim of destruction during the fourteenth or fifteenth
centuries. In the churchyard is a watch-house of 1826.

Outlying chapels once existed in the vicinity, at **Ewart Newton** and **Fenton**, the fields where the sites lie being called Chapel fields and Church Close respectively.

All the villages around Doddington were hit hard by Wallace's raids of 1297 as the accounts for the manor recorded a nil return for that year, 'on account of the war against the Scots who burnt and destroyed the said manors' (NcNamee 1990, 45).

Four miles due east from Wooler, the village of **Chatton** perches above the River Till. Its church of 1763–70, with additions of 1846 and 1895, possesses a commanding view along the valley to the south. The fabric appears to contain much re-used material from the building's medieval predecessor which was founded in the twelfth century. Adjacent to the church, the old vicarage possibly incorporates part of a defensible tower, recorded in 1415 as the 'Turris de Chatton', the property of the vicar (Hodgson 1820). There was also another tower in the village, on Grieve's Law, both being noted in the survey of 1541 by Bowes and Ellerker (Frontier I, 187). It is reasonable to assume that the people here were in need of a secure refuge as Chatton suffered heavily during the fourteenth-century Scottish incursions, and such attacks, which doubtless persisted until the Union, may account for the necessity to rebuild the church in the mid-eighteenth century.

THE COASTAL PERIPHERY

East of Chatton, the land remains gently undulating but gradually falls away towards the coast. At this point the boundary of the East March was drawn to the south-east, to form a line between Chillingham and Alnmouth.

Belford lies on rising ground, two miles inland from Budle Bay, above and to the west of the modern A1 road and on the line of the old Great North Road. The town was a frequent target for cross-border raids, due to its easy access. The present church lies just above the centre of Belford and dates mainly from the rebuilding of 1827–8 by Dobson, although the chancel-arch is Norman, probably re-set in the reconstruction. There is also evidence of re-used medieval masonry in the south and north walls of the nave, and the south side of the chancel has a fourteenth-century window and a priest's doorway dated 1615.

Higher than the main settlement, and slightly to the north, is the site of a small chapel on the track leading to Chesters Hill. According to Tomlinson (1888, 445) this chapel had been fortified, or enclosed, 'by some high mounds', although it has apparently been built within existing prehistoric earthworks. Certainly the position is defensible and it commands an excellent view of the coast, although its history is obscure. In the survey of 1415, there is named a 'Castrum de Belfurth' belonging to one Dom de Darce, which by 1509 was recommended for garrison by 40 horsemen (Hodgson 1820, 27; Bates 1891).

According to the chronicler, Jordan Fantosme, Belford was attacked in 1174 by a party of Flemish mercenaries, operating for the Scots. He describes the

Fig. 30. Holy Island, the ruins of the priory.

firing of farmsteads, stealing of sheep, and the capture of women, fleeing to
the church for safety, who were snatched away naked, leaving behind their gar-
ments and valuables (Owen 1997, 50). Whilst it is clear that Fantosme's account
is somewhat biased and excessively colourful, the act of people taking flight to
the church for refuge was evidently commonplace, and probably continued in
later years.

To the north of Belford, **Kyloe** has a church of 1792 with alterations of 1868,
replacing a medieval church (Raine 1852). The nearby East Kyloe Tower retains
its tunnel-vaulted lower stage, dating from the fourteenth century. West of
Kyloe, the village of **Lowick** also has a church built just two years after that of
its neighbour, and has lost its tower-house, mentioned in 1338 but in decay by
1584 (Cathcart King 1983, 351). A further chapel also once existed at **Howburn**,
this being a private oratory for Sir Thomas de Forset and his wife Alice (Raine
1852, 95). A violent event is recorded at Lowick when one Sir Alan de Heaton
stole the priest's horse whilst he was saying Mass in the church, and took possession of the churchyard, assaulting the prior's servant and appropriating the
collection (Wilson 1870).

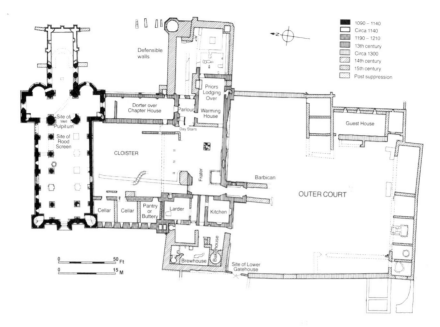

Fig. 31. Plan of Holy Island Priory.

At this point on the coast, the tidal island of **Lindisfarne** or **Holy Island** is accessible along a minor road through the hamlet of Beal. Holy Island is renowned as the site where, following King Oswald's gift of the island in 634 to Aidan, an evangelist bishop from Iona, a monastery was founded which established the Christian mission in Northumbria. It is also notable as the place where, in June 793, the Danes first seriously attacked the English coast, sacking the monastery and murdering most of its inmates. The event is recorded in the Laud Chronicle 'the harrying of the heathen miserably destroyed God's church in Lindisfarne by rapine and slaughter' (ASC, (E), 793).

Today, the ruins of the priory comprise a Norman church dating from about 1090 to 1140, a late twelfth- to early thirteenth-century west range, and the remains of other claustral and secular buildings of the thirteenth to the fifteenth centuries (Figure 30). The whole of the church is of heavy, typically Romanesque, construction which underwent no major alterations after completion, other than the insertion of a number of gothic windows and the defensive adaptations described below. The plan is roughly cruciform with a former central tower (now destroyed) and two smaller western towers flanking the principal external entrance (Figure 31). Above the west doorway is a narrow passage which allowed views both externally and internally. Higher still, over the nave roof vault, the original gable of the Norman building was removed in the fourteenth century when the roof was raised and the elevation heightened.

Fig. 32. Holy Island Priory, parapet and crossbow-loops inserted in the west end, above the Norman nave.

The purpose of this alteration was to provide a parapet and two crossbow-loops set in a modest, defensible westwork, which no doubt also utilised the twelfth-century towers to permit covering-fire upon anyone approaching the building (Figure 32).

Conjecturally, the whole of the upper levels of the church may have been crenellated and the central tower used as a look-out. The grey stone crenellations on the chancel appear to have been added at a date subsequent to the main, red sandstone building of the twelfth century. In common with other monastic buildings of the period and region, side windows are set typically high, those in the south wall of the chancel being around 4 m (13 ft) above ground level to the cills.

Apart from the church, there is strong evidence for the fortification of the claustral buildings. Changes were made during the fourteenth century which included the construction of a barbican, formed by two parallel walls, 1.15 m (3 ft 9 in.) thick, in front of the entrance from the outer court to the frater. The outer, southern part was open and led to a porch, the door of which was protected by a draw-bar (the slot still survives), and possibly also a small portcullis, indicated by parallel grooves (Kelland 1982, 209). The inner east wall of the outer court was strengthened by thickening and by blocking earlier openings and by the formation of defensible walls around the prior's lodging and the warming house. The north wall of this area is 2.1m in thickness and, in common with the east side, has no external openings; entry to the upper levels was gained from a spiral stair in the thickness of the south wall (*see* Figure 31). A description of the rebuilding of this part of the priory appears in the accounts of 1341–2 (Hamilton Thompson 1949) and the outer west gate to the south courtyard is described as the 'yet-howse tower' (i.e. gatehouse) in the inventories, giving some indication of its appearance. The perimeter wall to the courtyard was evidently also defensible and appears to have been battle-mented on the west side (in similar fashion to the chancel); Crossman (1890–1) conjectures that the guns belonging to the priory (see below) may have been located here as this portion overlooks the most likely landing place for boats.

To the west of the barbican and kitchen is a block, added in the fourteenth century, which contained a brewhouse and bakehouse, the walls of which are very thick, no doubt for defensive reasons (Butler and Given-Wilson 1979). This area of the priory was certainly important from a military standpoint as the sixteenth-century survey by Sir Robert Bowes noted that there were store-houses, brewhouses, and bakehouses to conserve and prepare supplies for the English navy who were anchored in the harbour of Holy Island in preparation for war against Scotland (Frontier II, 205).

In 1385, the monks admitted that their church was in some respects a castle, having crenelles and fortifications, and they petitioned King Richard II for licence to destroy the fortified parts of it, claiming that they could not provide the men and armour necessary for their defence. The plea appears to have been rejected as in the inventories for subsequent years, armour is recorded for the 'defence of the monastery', e.g., in 1362, three lances, one helmet with breast plate, and one pair of gloves of iron, and in 1481, two spears, three battle axes, eight cross-bows, eight guns, one longbow, and one sheaf of arrows (Crossman 1890–1). Indeed, not only was the monks' original plea rejected, but an expert in the new subject of artillery was sent to them, along with two guns (Dobson 1992).

The whole site is well protected, the basalt ridge to the south, known as the 'Heugh', formed a natural defence on which there was a medieval fort. A second outcrop, the 'Beblowe', to the south-east of the island, also housed an artillery fort, built in 1542 and still standing, though much altered during the twentieth century.

In the fourteenth century, the island was regularly used by the quartermas-ters of the English army and was therefore a likely target for Scottish attack. However, the defences afforded by the island and its principal buildings appear to have been successful as the priory survived unscathed until the Dissolution in 1537. Only one event of robbery is recorded, in 1325, when one William de Prendergast stole from the bakehouse and brewhouse (Raine 1852), although there was also a skirmish, outside the walls of the priory, during the winter of 1462–3 following the landing of raiding parties on the island (Dobson 1967).

Fig. 33. Holy Island, the parish church of St Mary.

Immediately to the west of the priory is the parish church of **St Mary** (Figure 33). The building has evidence of pre-Conquest construction in the east quoins of the nave, and in a small doorway and the remains of an arch above the thirteenth-century chancel-arch. This raises the possibilities that St Mary's is either a monastic church which survived the Norse raids, or more likely a late tenth- or early eleventh-century building which escaped mention by the Norman chroniclers.

The church has a nave with north and south aisles, aisleless chancel, and west bellcote set on a pair of massive buttresses; the building dates from *c.* 1200 to *c.* 1300 with later modifications. There is some evidence for former vaulting in the west wall of the nave in the form of a slot at wall-plate height, but all traces of actual vaulting have now disappeared in later alterations. The south doorway has once had a substantial draw-bar, and there are further slots within the outer reveal which may perhaps indicate a former gate. Pevsner *et al* (1992) note that 'an impressively fortified appearance' is created by the flat aisle roofs. However despite this visual aspect, there is little tangible evidence of defensive adaptations, aside from the vaulting (the exact form of which is unknown) and strong doorway. It is highly probable that in the event of any Scottish attack the inhabitants of the island would have sought refuge in the adjacent priory which was, as has already been noted, well defended.

The scant remains of a small medieval chapel lie on **St Cuthbert's Island**, a short distance to the south-west of the Priory.

Fig. 34. Bamburgh church, square stair-turret inside the tower.

South of Holy Island is **Bamburgh**, a triangular village dominated by the castle to the east and the church of St Aidan to the west. This place suffered greatly at the hands of the Scots during the period of the Troubles and it was apparently 'absolutely unsafe for anyone to live outside the protecting walls of the castle' (Bateson 1893). By 1332, the situation was so bad that Edward III granted murage rights to the townsfolk 'we have also granted leave to the inhabitants of Bamburgh . . . that they may strengthen, shut in, and crenellate the borough with a wall of stone and lime, as they will, and keep it so crenellated' (Bateson 1893); the charter was confirmed by Richard II in 1382 indicating that there had been little improvement during the century.

Although there is no evidence to suggest that the village was ever enclosed for defensive purposes, nevertheless the people continued to suffer from frequent Scottish raids and therefore it is inconceivable that defensive precautions were not taken. Whilst the castle offered the most obvious, and optimal, refuge, the parish church also seems to have undergone a defensive adaptation.

St Aidan's church is a complex and multi-period structure, the present building being the progeny of a succession of Anglo-Saxon churches, one of which housed the remains of St Aidan following his death here in 651. The church has a chancel of *c.* 1230 with a contemporary crypt beneath, a nave with north and south transepts of the late twelfth to early thirteenth century, and a west tower of similar date, except for the rebuilt upper stage, flanked to north and south by the side aisles.

The tower may have been utilized as a refuge during the later medieval period. Originally, admission to the upper levels was only by ladder, until, in the later fifteenth or early sixteenth century, a stairway was added in a purpose-built turret occupying the interior north-west corner (Figure 34). The stairway and turret are highly unusual in that, unlike most contemporary stairs, these are square in form, set around a square 'newel' or central pier of masonry. The turret measures 1.6 m (5 ft 3 in.) east to west and 2.1 m (7 ft) north to south, with an east-facing doorway only 0.62 m (2 ft) in width. Ostensibly, this square stairway offers easier (and quicker) entry to the high stages of the tower than a ladder, whilst retaining a strong element of defence with short series of steps suddenly interrupted at regular intervals by right-angled turns. There is only one parallel in Northumberland, at Welton pele, a fifteenth-century defensible tower near Horsley-on-the-Hill.

By the end of the principal hostilities, the church was in a poor state of repair. In 1617 an account recorded that

> their steeple is one-half covered with lead, and the other half utterly decayed and open; their church is thatched and indecently kept, and deformed with doves; the windows thereof, as also the quire, not sufficiently glassed, and the steeple is open to the church, whereby the doves especially come (Wilson 1870, 61–2).

As a prominent building the church is eclipsed by the nearby castle, constructed in the twelfth century and enlarged throughout the medieval period, and which was in all probability the primary refuge for the townsfolk in times of need. In 1318 the burgesses of the town petitioned the king to be allowed free access to the castle, to lodge at their own expense and to help with watching duties; the tenants of Shoreston and North Sunderland made a similar request at the same time (Nor.Pet., 156, 157). However, as the 1332 charter demonstrates, this may not have been enough, and certainly it is improbable that in a sudden raid, everyone would have time to reach the safety of the castle. In addition, there was a dispute in the early years of the fourteenth century, when the townsfolk complained to the king that they were being charged for safe accommodation and for entry and exit from the castle (Nor.Pet., 22).

The only other substantial stone buildings (as the permission to construct walls was never executed) were the nearby Dominican Friary and a leper hospital with attached chantry. Part of the hospital may have been defensible, as the survey of places of strength on the Border made in 1415 records: the 'Turris de Bamburgh' belonging to the 'Magri eiusdem' (Master of the Hospital), (Hodgson 1820, 30; Bates 1891).

The fragmentary remains of the Dominican Friary at Bamburgh are located on the western outskirts of the town at Friary Farm. In August 1266 Henry III granted seven acres (2.8 hectares) of land to the friars and the next year gave licence to build suitable houses and habitations (CPR, 50 Henry III: 1258–66, m6., m7., m42.). Further grants of land were made in the following year for the erection of a chapel and other buildings. Although little remains of the friary today, a drawing of the ruined church made *c.* 1780, preserved in the Bodleian library, indicates that the western half, on the north side at least, contained no substantial windows but only five lancet slits at high level, and two doorways, one of which is square-headed and may be a later insertion. The drawing also shows that other windows were placed high above ground level which, although partially to accommodate the interior liturgical layout, may also have been an intentional defensible adaptation to prevent easy ingress. However, some of these features may derive from the conversion, after the Dissolution, into a defensible house of secular nature. A wall replaced the thirteenth-century north arcade, within which still survives a sixteenth- or seventeenth-century doorway with a draw-bar slot.

The castle also had a chapel of its own whose origins lie in the twelfth century. The small building can only ever have served for religious purposes, being well enclosed at the eastern end of the inner ward. There is a link with the parish church in that King Henry I gave the church of St Oswald in the castle, with that of St Aidan in the village, to the Austin canons at Nostell (Caley *et al*, vi, 1830).

The **Farne Islands** lie two miles offshore from Bamburgh. The largest of the group, Inner Farne, is the closest to land and is renowned as the site where, according to Bede, St Cuthbert built a cell in 676. The island continued its ecclesiastical connection throughout the medieval period and today has a restored fourteenth-century chapel and later defensible tower. There was also a second church, and a small Benedictine cell constructed *c.* 1360 of which only a small portion of the guest house now survives.

The church is dedicated to St Cuthbert and was built *c.* 1370 as evidenced by surviving account rolls. It was restored in the 1860s when most of the windows were renewed along with the ogee-headed entrance doorway. This building was originally paired with another church, dedicated to St Mary, which lay to the south, parts of whose walls form sections of the modern buildings now on this site. St Cuthbert's church has indications that defensive traits may have been incorporated into its structure, as the north wall (part of the external perimeter of the buildings of the monastic cell) is totally without openings, and is strengthened by ashlar-built lower courses and a plinth. There is also the obvious security attendant upon its island siting, but clearly by the late fourteenth century the need for built precautions had become necessary, as witnessed

Fig. 35. John Speed's 1611 map of Farne, showing the two churches and tower with a defensible gate and wall.

by the building of Prior Castell's tower. In 1376 the monks had to shelter in Bamburgh after the Scots attacked, and in 1380–1 they are recorded as having to furnish a room in their so-called *castello* (redoubt or fort) for a watchman (Dobson 1992). In 1461 the island was again plundered by a contingent of Scottish sailors, this time from Pittenweem, who forced the two resident monks to move to Holy Island (Dobson 1967). Shortly afterwards Prior Burnby of Durham submitted a bill to the Scottish commissioners for the sum of £58, representing the value of 'divers notable goods' taken by Scottish thieves from the prior's cell on Farne (Neville 1998, 154).

The Prior's tower lies to the west of St Cuthbert's church and, although restored in the nineteenth century, still reveals its medieval, defensible character, having a ground-floor tunnel vault and mural stair. The first floor retains a probable lavabo and a garderobe demonstrating that the room was used for habitation. It was built (or rebuilt) by Thomas Castell, Prior of Durham, around 1500, and, from evidence provided by Speed's map of 1611, originally stood at the rear of a walled enclosure with a fortified gate flanked by the two churches (Figure 35). Following the end of hostilities, the tower served for a long time as a light beacon to aid navigation.

Along the coast south of Bamburgh are three villages whose medieval churches have completely disappeared in later campaigns of rebuilding. St Hilda's, **Lucker**, is built on a small hill above the rest of the village and in its present form dates from the late eighteenth century, with much reworking in 1874. The graveyard continues slightly higher than the present church and it is quite possible that its medieval predecessor was located in this position. In December 1362, David de Lucker and others from the district were accused of causing the death of John de Coupland, a March Warden. Lucker turned outlaw and fled north to Scotland after joining with Scottish reivers in attacking one Thomas Muschance in 1366. The estate, including the village, was confiscated and given to the barony of Alnwick.

Ellingham, a short distance south of Lucker, has a church which dates from 1862, probably on the site of the earlier building of which only a piscina and one lancet window head were salvaged for re-use. A Norman church here was founded by Radulph de Guagy in the twelfth century. Although no evidence survives for its medieval form, its position is noteworthy as it stands isolated from the main part of the village on a promontory with steep drops on the north, east, and south sides. In 1567 the church was documented in the Duke of Northumberland's records as being in good repair, but by the Archdeacon's Visitation of 1604, the roof appears to have been removed and the whole building was in decay. There was also a small chapel in the vicinity, dedicated to St Mary, which is recorded as having a new thatched roof in 1333 (Bateson 1895); the site has long since vanished.

Ellingham parish is singular in the Bursar's Account Rolls of Durham Priory for the years 1318–19 as being the only parish in the priory's Northumberland possessions to provide an income – ten pounds, all other parishes having been wasted by the Scots (McNamee 1997).

The coastal village of **Beadnell** has a church of 1740 with additions of 1792 and 1860. Of the earlier church here there is scant record before the sixteenth-century Archdeacons' Visitations which, in 1578, recorded that there was neither a curate nor churchwardens. The remains of an earlier chapel at Beadnell are located at Ebb's Nook to the north-east of the harbour, although the foundations are so fragmentary that any construction date is conjectural. From excavations undertaken in 1853, it appears that the building had a nave and chancel with a west annexe of a different date; the whole may be thirteenth-century and earlier (Pevsner *et al* 1992).

At nearby **North Sunderland**, the church was newly built in 1790 (though subsequently rebuilt in 1834). It is located on the site of a defensible tower.

Two miles south-west of Beadnell, the deserted medieval village of **Tughall** (or Tuggal) was located around the present Tuggal Hall, and the foundations of its church are situated close to a sharp bend in the road. The building was still

standing in 1852 and drawings by S.H. Grimm made *c.* 1786 show it to be ruined
at that time, but with the gables and walls largely intact. The whole construction was clearly Norman in style and date, having had a simple rectangular
nave with north and south doorways and an apsidal chancel with a Norman
arch between. There were no windows whatsoever on the north side, a trait
seen elsewhere in Border church construction at all periods and which may
have implications for security (although the exclusion of the fierce northern
weather may have been a key factor). The building evidently suffered the same
vicissitudes and fortunes as its neighbours, as in 1340 it was recorded as not
being taxed and in 1534 there was no incumbent. Towards the end of the period
of the Troubles some colourful records appear in the Archdeacon's Visitations,
illustrating the nature of the people and place: in 1599 Thomas Forster was presented for 'strickynge the minister of Tughill upon the heade with his dagger',
and Thomas Hopper was presented for that 'he shott a pistall when all the congregation were cominge out of the church at Tuggill in the middest of them'; in
1601 John Forster was admonished for 'rideinge into the church on horsebacke
in service time' (Bateson 1893, 347). It would seem that the church was no
defence against this anti-social behaviour, typical of the period.

Close to the coastline, south from Tughall, the village of **Embleton** shelters
from the sea under the ridge of a low hill. The church is located close to the
road, on the south side of the village, and comprises a tall west tower, its lower
stage Norman and upper two stages fourteenth-century, a nave with south
porch, north and south aisles and a chancel. The nave and aisles were heavily
restored by John Dobson in 1850 and again in 1867 by Frederick Wilson who
also rebuilt the chancel, and discovered some re-used lengths of parapet from
Dunstanburgh Castle (Wilson 1870). The tower however survived these restorations largely intact, and is strikingly unusual for the north of England in that
it has a decorative pierced parapet with open, trefoil-headed panels capped
by pinnacles. That the tower may have been adapted for defensive use is evident from the ground-floor stone barrel vaulting, set on three north-south ribs
and inserted into a pre-existing Norman tower, shown by the blocked twelfth-
century windows cut by these ribs (Figure 36). Formerly, the only access to
the upper floors was by ladder, now replaced by a modern steel spiral stair in
the south-west corner. The upper floors have small window openings in the
west and south walls. Both floors were conjecturally designed for temporary
residence (Bateson 1895); the second stage was formerly more spacious than at
present, demonstrated by projecting corbels in the lower chamber which originally supported the second floor.

In the vicars' and bursars' rolls it is recorded that the Scots did great damage
to the parish in 1384, and in 1395–6 a sum of £1 13s. 4d. was paid to persons
guarding the church of Embleton, in the time of vacancy (Bateson 1895, 67).
This may refer simply to a secular care of the building whilst there was no
priest, but may also imply a physical defence.

That there was a need for defence against the Scots is plain. In 1395 a sum

Fig. 36. Embleton church, stone rib-vaulting in the ground-floor ceiling of the tower.

of £13 6s. 8d. was paid to the vicar '*pro suo novo edificio*' (Bateson 1895, 67). This was the vicar's pele tower or defensible house, which still exists to the south of the church. Despite the implications that this was a new building, the tower may be earlier than this date and may have been modified for defence at this time, following the severe raid by the Scots (Pevsner *et al* 1992, 271). It has two vaulted chambers on the ground floor and the original entrance was probably at first-floor level, however later alterations have made interpretation of the present building difficult. In the fifteenth century the tower was recorded as the 'Turris de Emyldon, vicarij eiusdem' (Hodgson 1820, 30).

The remains of **Dunstanburgh** castle are located on the coast a short distance from Embleton. Dramatically positioned on a narrow promontory, this fortress occupies the largest area of any castle in Northumberland, although it guards no routes of communication and serves no obvious strategic function other than to house a garrison, or as McNamee (1997, 141) and Bowes (four hundred years earlier) suggest, to accommodate refugees: 'then surely it would be a great refuge to the inhabitants of those partes, yff enemies came to annoye them, either arriving by sea or coming by lande out of Scoteland' (Frontier II, 206). Construction started in 1314 by Thomas Earl of Lancaster following the English defeat at Bannockburn that year, and was largely complete

by 1322, with major alterations being made in 1380-4 (Pevsner *et al* 1992). The
principal buildings are arranged around a gatehouse in the south-west corner
and along the southern perimeter wall, with the Lilburn Tower positioned
along the west wall. There was presumably a chapel located somewhere in the
vicinity of these buildings, as the receiver's accounts for 1439 record that the
ornaments of the King's Chapel in the castle were conveyed from London to
Dunstanburgh by land, the cost of their transport being 2s. 8d. The site of this
chapel has now been lost, although according to the antiquarian John Wallis
it lay close to the main entrance (Wallis 1769).

Inland from Embleton and Dunstanburgh, the village of **Rock** has a small
towerless church, dating from the twelfth century, restored by Anthony Salvin
in 1855, with a north aisle by Frederick Wilson of 1866. The Norman work is
well attested by the west doorway and the chancel-arch, but there is no evidence of any adaptation for security either at this or any subsequent date.

Close to the church, the present Rock Hall encapsulates the remains of an
early medieval building which in 1549 was chosen as the headquarters of Spanish mercenary troops led by Sir Julian Romero. An oratory is recorded here in
1359 (Bateson 1895), and there is a building immediately to the north of the hall
still called the Chapel, although there is no evidence of an ecclesiastical use in
the present structure, which is probably of a later date.

Two and a half miles west of Rock is **South Charlton**. The present church
dates from 1862 and replaces a medieval chapel-of-ease (within the parish of
Ellingham) which lay on the opposite side of the road in the field known as
Kirk Croft. This earlier building was of some considerable interest in ecclesiastical Border defence, as it is recorded in the Earl of Northumberland's account
books that in 1450, the incursions of the Scots had become so serious that
the earl's steward contributed a sum of £3 6s. 8d. towards the building of a
tower at one end of the chapel, specifically designed for the protection of the
villagers in time of war: '*Ad edificationem unius nove turris defensabilis ad finem
capelle ibedem, pro salva custodia dicte ville tempore guerre*' (Bateson 1895, 310). Evidently it was much needed, as worship had been suspended sometime during
the middle of the fourteenth century and the inhabitants of both North and
South Charlton were required to contribute to the parish church at Embleton,
presumably due to the depredations of war and raiding. Of the tower, and
the medieval church to which it belonged, there is now no trace, the building
having become ruined towards the end of the eighteenth century.

South of the village of Rock, the church at **Rennington** is also a nineteenth-
century replacement of an earlier chapel. It dated from the Norman period,
denoted by sketches made prior to its demolition in 1831, and by notes made by
the Rev. John Hodgson. The medieval building was a simple two-celled structure with a west bellcote but no tower; the south side had a twelfth-century
doorway and a series of Gothic style lancets, whilst the north side contained
three blocked arches of a former aisle. There are no records or evidence of this
church ever having had a defensive role.

Fig. 37. Longhoughton, a pre-fourteenth-century church later utilized as a defensible refuge.

At **Howick** the old church lay close to the hall, away from the present village although within the former medieval settlement, now deserted. The present structure dates from 1746, remodelled in 1849; it replaced a medieval church of which no trace remains.

The southern edge of the English East March, east of Alnwick, is defined by the line of the River Aln where it envelops the three coastal villages of Longhoughton, Lesbury, and Alnmouth. **Longhoughton** church stands towards the southern end of the village and has pre-Conquest origins, attested by the style of the chancel-arch which appears to be Saxo-Norman and earlier in form than the tall Norman tower-arch (Taylor and Taylor 1965, 324–5). The likely period of the nave is also Saxo-Norman, with a south aisle added *c.* 1200. The tower was originally much taller, with a gabled top (Pevsner *et al* 1992) but this was replaced *c.* 1840 with the present roof, following a fire (Figure 37).

The tower is strongly built, and has a robust outward appearance. The lower walls are 1.1 m (3 ft 7 in.) in thickness, and access to the upper levels is by ladder. The three windows in the lower stage are all small and placed above 2 m (6 ft 7 in.) from the floor to their cills.

That the church was used as a defensive refuge is affirmed by a survey of the manor, made about the year 1567, where it is stated that: 'The chirche and steple of this towne is the great strenth that the poore tenants have to draw to in the tyme of warre' (Bateson 1895, 372). The higher portion of the tower, destroyed in the nineteenth-century fire, may have been connected with this purpose, providing secure, temporary accommodation. Incredibly though, in the visitation of 1601 it is recorded that the church door had no lock.

A short distance south of Longhoughton, the mother church of the medieval parish is at **Lesbury**. This building has a heavily restored nave with north aisle, chancel, and west tower. The principal restoration took place in 1846–9 when the south side was largely rebuilt and the tower was given its present pyramidal roof. Excavations in 1999 revealed evidence of an earlier south nave wall (Ryder 1999). However, considerable portions of medieval work remain above ground, and the tower is largely intact from late twelfth through to the thirteenth centuries, although the south-west corner has been rebuilt at some period.

Like its near neighbour at Longhoughton, Lesbury has a tower with walls 1.1 m (3 ft 7 in.) in thickness and has upper levels reached only by ladder. It also has a reconstructed roof; a sketch in 1773 indicates that the roof was half-round in form and may, unusually, have been stone-vaulted (Figure 38). On a visit to

Fig. 38. Lesbury in 1773 showing the unusual form of the tower roof (Beilby, 1773).

Fig. 39. Alnmouth church in 1771 (after Bateson 1895).

the parish in 1604, the bishop criticised the churchwardens noting that 'their steple is like to fall' (Hickes n.d., 38), clearly indicating a lack of maintenance, and possibly also a problem with the heavy structure, as in 1847 some strengthening of the tower was undertaken. Wilson (1870) noted that a sketch of 1823 showed the tower with a corbelled-out parapet, and that the small windows of the fabric as a whole conduced to the general strength and security of the building. The present west window in the lower stage of the tower is a Victorian addition, and apart from this there are no other openings below the top stage where only two narrow lancets on the south and west sides provide minimal apertures, although the 1773 sketch also shows a similar opening in the east wall.

The termination of the East March lay at **Alnmouth** where the River Aln joined the sea. Here, until the early nineteenth century, stood an impressive church dedicated to St Waleric, located on Church Hill, a prominent knoll lying to the south of the town. The church was in ruins by the late eighteenth century when it was profusely sketched, and was finally destroyed during a severe storm in 1806 when the Aln broke through the narrow spit of land connecting the hill and church with the town.

From the sketches and descriptions made prior to its destruction, it is known that the church was a large cruciform building without aisles but with a clerestory and impressive gables, and having no central or west tower. The architecture was a mix of twelfth- and thirteenth-century forms with a few post-Reformation additions. Most windows were placed high, at an estimated 2 m (6 ft 7 in.) above ground level, and there was an unusual narrow projection on the west wall (Figure 39). The building conceivably had a pre-Conquest predecessor.

There are no records of the church being used defensively. A survey in 1567 recorded that it was covered with lead, and also noted that a large number of foreigners, for the most part Scots, were living in the town. The position of the church is significant and has defensive imports, although its location probably owes as much to prominence in the twelfth century, and to its probable pre-Conquest origins, as it does to matters of security.

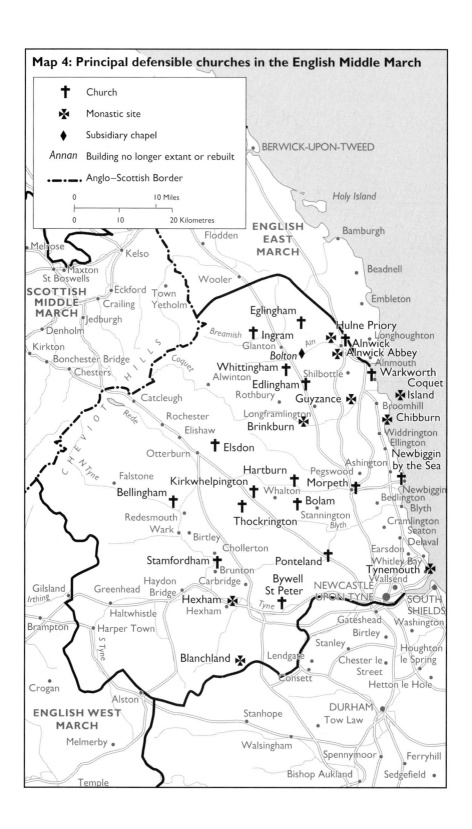

Map 4: Principal defensible churches in the English Middle March

† Church

✠ Monastic site

◆ Subsidiary chapel

Annan Building no longer extant or rebuilt

•—·—•· Anglo–Scottish Border

0   10 Miles

0   10   20 Kilometres

BERWICK-UPON-TWEED

Holy Island

Flodden

ENGLISH EAST MARCH

Bamburgh

•Melrose

Kelso

•Maxton
St Boswells

SCOTTISH MIDDLE MARCH

•Eckford
Crailing
Jedburgh

•Denholm

Kirkton

•Bonchester Bridge

Chesters

Wooler

Town Yetholm

Breamish

Beadnell

Embleton

Eglingham

† Ingram
Glanton

Bolton ◆

Whittingham †
Alwinton

Edlingham †
Rothbury

Guyzance ✠

Hulne Priory
Longhoughton

✠ †Alnwick
✠ ✠Alnwick Abbey

Alnmouth

† Warkworth

Ain

Shilbottle

Coquet
✠ Island

†
Broomhill

Longframlington

Brinkburn
✠

✠ Chibburn

Catcleugh

Rede

Rochester
Elishaw

C H E V I O T
N Tyne

ENGLISH WEST MARCH

† Elsdon

Otterburn

Falstone

Kirkwhelpington †

Bellingham †

Redesmouth
Wark

Birtley

Hartburn
†

† Bolam

Pegswood

Morpeth †

Whalton

Thockrington †

Stannington
Blyth

Widdrington
Ellington

Newbiggin
by the Sea

Ashington

Newbiggin ✠

Bedlington

• Blyth

Cramlington
Seaton
Delaval

Earsdon

Whitley Bay

Tynemouth ✠

Wallsend

SOUTH
SHIELDS

Chollerton

Stamfordham †
Brunton

Ponteland †

Gilsland
Irthing

Greenhead

Haydon
Bridge
Carbridge

Bywell
St Peter

NEWCASTLE
UPON TYNE

Hexham ✠
Hexham

Tyne

†

Gateshead
Washington

Brampton

Haltwhistle

Harper Town

S Tyne

Blanchland ✠

Birtley

Stanley

Lendgate

Houghton
le Spring

Crogan

Alston

ENGLISH WEST MARCH

Melmerby •

Temple

Stanhope

Walsingham

Consett

Chester le
Street

DURHAM
Tow Law

Hetton le Hole

Spennymoor

Bishop Aukland

Ferryhill

Sedgefield •

3

THE ENGLISH MIDDLE MARCH

The English Middle March consisted of the majority of modern Northumberland, with the exception of the north-east quarter which belonged to the East March, and the extreme south of the county beyond the Tyne. The population was varied, for in the north and north-west of the district the land was high and unproductive and supported only a scattering of villages and farmsteads, whilst in the centre and south, settlements were more commonplace and people more numerous.

The frontier line was defined simply along the Cheviot hills which formed a powerful physical barrier to the wholesale movement of troops and artillery but which still allowed passage for smaller bodies of men and horse, and for the exploits of the reivers. The major medieval routes of communication lay along the line of the modern A1 and A68 roads. The former passed from Newcastle northwards through into the English East March, whilst the latter formed a direct route from Corbridge through into the Scottish Border heartland, crossing the frontier at Carter Bar. An important thoroughfare also lay through Wooler, leading to Morpeth and the south. To the west there was a good road alongside the line of Hadrian's Wall which led to Brampton, in the English West March, and then to Carlisle.

The major watercourses which provided the valleys and fertile land for settlement were the Rede, Coquet, and Tyne, with the lesser rivers of Font, Wansbeck, and Blyth which fed the central region of the March.

The March was administered, in the main, from Alnwick, and the abbey there was the usual residence of the Warden (Tough 1928), who, when not actually one of the Earls of Northumberland, worked with them to attempt a form of justice and rule of law. There was good reason, apart from political considerations, for the Wardens to operate out of Alnwick, for this town was close enough to the frontier to permit good intelligence, and to intercept minor incursions, whilst maintaining good communication links with the south.

In 1583–4, Christopher Dacre and other Royal Commissioners reported on the condition of fortified places in Northumberland with a view to their repair or regarrisoning. It is clear from the reports they made that the area of the upper Coquet valley, encompassing Rothbury, Harbottle, and the Vale of Whittingham, was of great strategic importance (Watts and Watts 1975) and

91

from this region southward towards the North Tyne delineated what Dacre termed the 'plenished ring of the border'.

The survey of 1541, reporting to Henry VIII, noted that the leaders of local society in the upland regions lived for the most part in strong wooden houses with turf roofs (Frontier I, 232–3). It is known that in the years following this report, many bastle-houses were built in the north and north-west of the March (Ryder 1996a).

The ecclesiastical situation in Northumberland on the eve of the Wars of Independence was surprising: only 63 parishes, some covering ten or more separate townships (Lomas 1996a). This was clearly a reflection of the structure of the ministry founded in the previous centuries, although the scattered, upland population undoubtedly assisted in the formation of this pattern. During the twelfth and thirteenth centuries a further 100 or so subordinate chapels had arisen, to serve the settlements which had no church building.

Monasteries were situated mainly in the east of the March and there were important Norman foundations at Tynemouth, Hexham, Brinkburn, New-minster, Blanchland, and Alnwick. Benedictine nunneries were established at Holystone, Newcastle, and Lambley, and there were a number of friaries, one of the most significant being that of Hulne near Alnwick.

ALNWICK AND THE NORTH

The village of **Chillingham** lies in the shadow of its castle, rebuilt by Sir Thomas de Heton in 1344 which replaced an earlier tower sacked by the Scots in 1296. Mentioned in the musters of the East Marches in 1580 (CBP, i, 47), Chillingham is more usually regarded as belonging to the Middle March, although the boundary was unclear.

The location is close enough to the border to provide the motivation for de Heton to build his strong castle. Once built, this castle naturally attracted trouble, and it was attacked and taken by James IV on the eve of the battle of Flodden.

The church lies to the north of the castle and is built into sloping ground, its chancel rising higher than the nave. The earliest portions are of the twelfth century; the south doorway and parts of the south chapel belong to this period, and possibly the crypt beneath the chancel. The remainder is a mixture of thirteenth- to sixteenth-century dates and there is a fine monument to Sir Ralph Grey of *c.* 1450. There is no evidence that there has ever been a tower.

The residents of Chillingham do not appear to have adapted their church for defence. The nave walls, although 1.10 m (3 ft 7 in.) in thickness, are largely Norman in date and therefore not unusual; in fact all later walls are much thinner, not exceeding 0.65 m (2 ft 2 in.). The adjacent castle probably offered, in this instance, the safest option for the local populace seeking refuge. This is

Fig. 40. Ilderton, exterior view.

confirmed by the precautions which the patron afforded to the priest, for in 1348 Sir Thomas de Heton gave to whoever should be vicar at Chillingham a chamber above the gate of his castle with one stable for two horses at the west hall (Bates 1891).

Three miles west of Chillingham, close to the road leading south from Wooler, stand the remains of West **Lilburn** Tower, a fifteenth-century defensible tower which belonged to the Ogle family. Close by was another minor castle, recorded in 1541 as belonging to Cuthbert Proctor but which has now disappeared (Rowland 1994). Also close by are the fragmentary ruins of a small Norman chapel with a thirteenth-century addition to the south.

Just south of Lilburn, the tiny village of **Ilderton** sits atop one of the low Cheviot foothills. The church, dedicated to St Michael, was largely rebuilt in the late eighteenth century with the exception of the medieval west tower (Figure 40).

The tower is constructed of large sandstone blocks; its upper stage was evidently restored at the same time as the body of the church. The west wall has late thirteenth-century angle buttresses and a single lancet in the ground floor. Inside, a well-worn spiral stair of crude construction leads to the first floor, and above this a former second stage would only have been accessible by ladder. There are few openings, a narrow light in the south wall may be a restored original, and the square hatch in the west wall appears to be comparatively modern.

Little remains to determine the original character of the building, although the tower appears to have been used frequently judging by the worn stairs. The church was burnt during a Scottish raid *c.* 1300 and the village was a frequent target for such forays in later years; hence it would be surprising if the church, and especially the tower, was not used as a refuge.

In 1464 a battle took place at Hedgeley Moor to the south of Ilderton, close by the side of the Morpeth road. Unusually for the Border region, the subject of the fight was not exclusively concerned with Anglo-Scottish relations, but was part of a series of battles and skirmishes which made up the Wars of the Roses, the struggle for political power in England between the Houses of Lancaster and York. The battle came about as a result of an attempt by the Lancastrians to disrupt negotiations between Edward IV and James III which threatened to interfere with their use of Scotland as a military base. At this spot near Wooperton, the Lancastrian forces led by Sir Ralph Percy ambushed the Yorkist ambassadors heading for Norham under Lord Montague, but were defeated by the stronger force and their leader killed.

A little further south from the battle site is the River Breamish, where a minor road heads westwards into the hills. The first village along this road is **Brandon**. There was once a medieval chapel here, of which only the foundations remain, in a field just to the east of the present settlement. The likely date for this building is the thirteenth century, although it may be founded on a pre-Conquest site (Pevsner *et al* 1992). There is no evidence of a tower.

A mile and a half further, the road crosses the Breamish at **Ingram**. Here, isolated from the village and above the river, stands the church of St Michael (Figure 41). This was almost certainly utilised as a defensible refuge (Bates 1891), but unfortunately the building has been reconstructed to such a great extent that much of the evidence for this purpose has now been effaced.

The church has a nave and aisles, transepts, chancel, and west tower. The original south aisle, demolished in the eighteenth century, was apparently vaulted (Pevsner *et al* 1992), although whether this was Norman vaulting or later medieval work is not known. In 1803 the north aisle was also levelled and both aisle arcades were blocked. During the 1870s the church was heavily restored and the tower was underpinned and largely rebuilt; new side aisles were added in 1879. However, large areas of original fabric have remained from the medieval building including the early Norman tower-arch, the fourteenth-century chancel-arch, and the piers and arcades of the side aisles.

Prior to the restoration in the nineteenth century, contemporary accounts and plans reveal that the tower-arch was blocked with a thick wall and the entrance to the ground floor was reduced to a small doorway (Wilson 1870; Tomlinson 1888, 364) (Figure 42). The tower was lighted only by windows and

Fig. 41. Ingram, the reconstructed tower.

openings of the smallest dimensions. Even following the rebuilding of the tower, the openings are minimal, clearly accordant with the idea of defence, whilst access to the upper levels has evidently always been by ladder. The filling of the tower-arch probably followed the same pattern seen at Kirkwhelpington, Bolam, Hartburn, and Newbiggin, where the restriction of access into the tower would have undoubtedly assisted in its use as a secure refuge.

Ingram lay well inside the main danger zone for Scottish raids. It was attacked on 23 June 1587, and again in July that year when four webs of lead were torn from the church roof by the Teviotdale men (CBP, i, 535). By the end of the Troubles the church was described as ruinous and destitute.

There was formerly a defensible parsonage tower at Ingram, first recorded in 1509 but in serious decay by 1541 (Cathcart King 1983, 350). Bowes' sixteenth-century survey noted that 'At Ingrame ys a lytle toure which ys the mansion

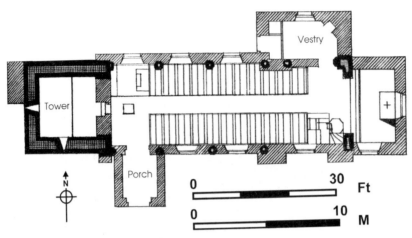

Fig. 42. Plan of Ingram showing blocked tower-arch prior to 1870 (after Wilson 1870).

house of the parsonage there . . .' (Frontier I, 210). No trace survives above ground.

To the north-east of Brandon and Ingram, below Cateran Hill and the two Iron Age forts at the edge of Bewick Moor, the small Norman church of **Old Bewick** lies almost hidden at the end of a narrow track leading along the Kirk Burn.

The church has no tower or aisles, and comprises a nave and chancel with a small eastern apse, a porch, and a vestry. The entire fabric is indicative of a twelfth-century date, having typical Norman masonry and some original openings. Alterations in the fourteenth century included the squaring of the east end externally, and the insertion of new windows. The church lay in ruins for some considerable time following a storm in the early years of the eighteenth century; it was restored in 1866–7.

No obvious adaptations have been made for security, and the building may well have sufficed for this purpose in its original form, with large sturdily built walls, 0.85 m (2 ft 9 in.) in thickness and narrow openings.

Tynemouth Priory held the living here from c. 1100, and the Prior of Tynemouth is recorded as the owner of the now destroyed Bewick Tower in 1509 which Bowes described as standing in a 'fytte place for the defence of the countrye thereaboutes' (Frontier I, 209).

A short distance along the Alnwick road from Old Bewick is the village of **Eglingham** with its multi-period church dedicated to St Maurice (Figure 43). The church is a complex blend of medieval and later builds, with much post-medieval reconstruction in the nave and rebuilding in the chancel, probably from the seventeenth century through to the nineteenth century, but leaving

Fig. 43. Eglingham church, exterior view.

the original thirteenth-century west tower largely intact apart from its remodelled arch.

The tower has, like many others on the Border, minimal openings and no permanent access to the upper levels, entry now being provided by a vertical ladder. It is evident that there has been a chamber below the present first floor as there is a blocked window in the east wall 6 m (20 ft) above the ground, and at the same height an arched aumbry in the north wall. The window provided a view into the church, above the tower-arch, and so it is likely that this chamber was used for accommodation, either by a sexton or priest, or as Tomlinson (1888, 400) speculated, as a retreat for the villagers during Border frays. The narrow double lancets of the belfry stage have close parallels with those at Ingram church and the barbican of Alnwick castle. The tower is strongly built, with 1 m (3 ft 3 in.) thick walls and has obviously been repaired on one or more occasions.

The amount of rebuilding and repair manifest in the fabric from the seventeenth century onwards may probably be explained as a result of the sacking of the church by the Scots in 1596, and again during the Civil War, when it was apparently a deliberate target, strengthening the argument for its former use as a refuge.

Further towards Alnwick, the remains of **Heiferlaw Tower** stand on a hill-top a mile to the north of Hulne Park. This three-storey tower was constructed as a lookout point for Alnwick Abbey (*see* below). The two sets of Percy arms built into the heavy 1.2 m (4 ft) thick sandstone walls date it to between 1470 and 1489 (Bates 1891; Pevsner *et al* 1992). Although now much ruined, the remains of all but the uppermost stages of the tower are largely intact, and a fireplace is still visible on the west side of the first floor. Although the surviving openings all have restricted apertures, the floors were suspended on timber beams with the stairway or ladder also likely to have been of timber, and there are no major defensible traits associated with this tower. The building's size, 8.7 m by 7.4 m (28 ft 7 in. by 24 ft 3 in.), and position indicate that it was unlikely to have been used for permanent residence, but it played an important role in the defence of the abbey and town of Alnwick, by providing early warning of an approaching enemy.

Alnwick sits in a strategic position astride the Great North Road, and only a short distance upriver from the coast. The origins of the present town, which takes its name from the River Aln, are largely due to its position in the defence of the north following the Norman Conquest. The site was a magnet for administrative power (with all the attendant troubles of such office) from an early date. In the winter of 1093, King Malcom III of Scotland pillaged the northern parts of Northumberland in retaliation for the disrespectful treatment he had received at the court of the English King William II. Just to the north of the town, on 13 November, Malcom clashed with the governor of Bamburgh Castle, Robert de Mowbray, and was killed and his son Edward mortally wounded in the ensuing battle. He was one of two Scottish kings to die in battle on Northumbrian soil, the second being James IV, killed at Flodden in 1513.

At the place where Malcom III was killed, a hospital, dedicated to **St Leonard**, was founded by Eustace de Vesci *c.* 1163. It came under the patronage of Alnwick Abbey after 1376 (Prescott 1992, 146). The buildings, which comprised a hall with a narrow chapel to the east, were in ruins by the Reformation, and little now remains above ground.

The earliest castle was constructed by the de Vesci family, the first Norman barons to occupy the town, sometime before 1136 when it was captured by David I and the Scots. At this time Alnwick was the largest barony in Northumberland and its catchment included over 60 townships (Lomas 1996a). Nearly a century after the death of Malcom III, his great-grandson, William the Lion, was taken prisoner after destroying Warkworth and its church in 1174, thwarting his attempt to dislodge William de Vesci at Alnwick (Owen 1997).

Although much troubled between the eleventh and thirteenth centuries, it was during the Scottish Wars of Independence when Alnwick assumed its pivotal role in Border politics, and it was the dynasty as much as the place which made it so. Like their Scottish counterparts the Douglases, the Percy family rose to power in the north following the purchase of Alnwick in 1310, and again like the Douglas clan, the House of Percy originated outside the principal arena of conflict, their main estates being in Yorkshire (Lomas 1999). By the year 1400, they dominated the county, the Crown generously rewarding their Border services (Brown 1998).

Although the castle was rebuilt and strengthened between 1318–52, and became symbolic of English power in the region, it was controlled by the Percys and remained a local family stronghold. The town which grew up around it was the strongest in the English Middle March (except for Newcastle) but was still vulnerable to Scottish attack and occasional raiding. As late as 1596 the Scots raided Alnwick, making off with horses and oxen (CBP, ii, 351). It is perhaps surprising therefore that the town was not walled until 1434 when a licence to crenellate was issued by the Crown (Hodgson Hinde 1858). Even then the building took 50 years to complete (Lomas 1996a), which may be the result of the town's inability to pay for the work during a period of escalating political tension on the Border.

Although the castle undoubtedly had a private chapel for use by the Percy family, the present chapel was designed by Anthony Salvin and dates only from the 1850s. However, the fourteenth-century Abbot's Tower survives, at the north-west corner of the outer ward, which was for the use of the abbot of Alnwick Abbey when the need arose.

During the sixteenth century, Alnwick was a focus for administration and the dispensation of justice. The abbey was the usual residence of the Warden (Tough 1928) and courts were frequently held in the town. There is some evidence to suggest that Bailiffgate was a settlement separate from the main town, closely related to the military functions of the castle at one end, and possibly the parish church at the other (Conzen 1969). This area may have provided lodgings for militia in times of war or unrest as rents were paid direct to the castle reeve rather than the town.

Alnwick Abbey is located to the north-west of the town, close to the parish church but on lower ground by the River Aln. Its foundation was the result of local patronage, in common with many other twelfth-century religious houses. It was Eustace Fitz-John who first introduced a body of Premonstratensian canons here in 1147 from the English mother house of the order at Newhouse in Lincolnshire.

The sole surviving building from the abbey is the gatehouse, which stands intact, close to the Eglingham road (Figure 44). It consists of a central block, flanked by four square turrets, surmounted by battlements and machicolation, with a tunnel-vaulted passage at ground level. The whole is distinctly defensible in nature and designed to protect the former church and claustral buildings which lay beyond. As the residence of the March Warden, it is not surprising that such precautions should have been taken.

Of the abbey church and related claustral buildings there are now no remains; however, excavations in the late nineteenth century showed that the site was complex, having a church 61m (220ft) in length, of cruciform plan

Fig. 44. Alnwick Abbey gatehouse, showing battlements and machicolation.

with a small central tower; the chapter house was unusual in having a near circular east end. There was a large precinct wall, no doubt aiding the defensive aspect of the gatehouse which protruded from it (St John Hope 1887).

The parish church of **St Michael** is located a short distance towards the town from the site of the abbey and is built on a spur of high ground at the west end of Bailiffgate. It is an impressive building both internally and externally, presenting a richness of form and ornament little seen in the northern counties during the Middle Ages (Figure 45). Externally, the church is entirely of the fourteenth and fifteenth centuries, and has a strong west tower with tall stepped buttresses, a contemporary south porch, imposing perpendicular windows in the side walls, and a curious turret and caphouse at the south-east angle of the chancel. Inside there is evidence of earlier work in the *ex situ* Norman carvings above the chancel-arch and the re-used grave-markers in the lintels of some clerestory windows. The capitals of the chancel arcades are richly decorated with stylized foliage, probably a result of the patronage afforded by the Earls of Northumberland.

The tower is positioned at the south-west corner of the building and has walls 1.4 m (4 ft 7 in.) in thickness. The ground floor has quadripartite stone vaulting, and access to the upper floors is gained through a small rectangular

Fig. 45. Alnwick, the parish church of St Michael.

doorway positioned just above the floor in the west wall, which leads to a spiral stair offset from this doorway in the south-west angle. The present first-floor chamber is plain, with deeply splayed windows in all but the north wall, and there are indications that a floor once existed 4 m (13 ft) above this, supported on large beams. The spiral stair is truncated between the first and second floors, although it appears formerly to have continued upward, and the present belfry is reached via a straight stairway set at right-angles to it. Evidence for a defensible use of the west tower is generally lacking, although it was certainly capable of fulfilling this role with its narrow off-floor entrance, stone vaulting, and spacious upper floors with minimal openings.

At the opposite end of the building is a structure which is far more enigmatic in its use than the west tower. Rising through a narrow turret at the south-east corner of the chancel, a spiral stair (largely renewed) yields to a narrow straight section with an awkward offset, possibly a deliberate attempt to hinder ascent. This is a similar device to that found elsewhere for this purpose, e.g., Craigmillar Castle, Lothian (Simpson 1954), and curiously also found here at Alnwick in the west tower (*see* above), although this may be due to alterations made at the renewal of the upper stage.

The stair now leads onto the present roof, although from evidence in the

Fig. 46. Alnwick St Michael, caphouse and stair above the south-east corner of the chancel.

fabric it once led into a room running north from the existing structure and which has now disappeared. What remains is a small, narrow caphouse with a single room east of the stair, reached through a low doorway from the roof (Figure 46). This room measures only 1.5 m (5 ft) in width (north to south) by 2.2 m (7 ft 3 in.) in length, and has a steep stone-vaulted and stone flagged roof, a single rectangular window in the south-east angle, and a deep recess in the west wall, the purpose of which is unknown. The mouldings around the exterior of the structure date from the sixteenth century, although these may represent a phase of repair or refacing as they do not sit comfortably with the north wall of the caphouse.

The purpose of this building above the chancel is unclear. It has restricted access, only one small window, and is constructed entirely of stone. It has once been slightly larger and, speculatively, served as an emergency retreat for clergy worshipping in the chancel during periods of unrest. The theory that it was a lookout point (Wilson 1870; Tomlinson 1888; Graham 1994) appears fundamentally flawed as there is only one window in the surviving portion and better vantage could certainly be gained from the west tower which is higher. The remaining possibility, that it was a residence for a chantry priest, cannot

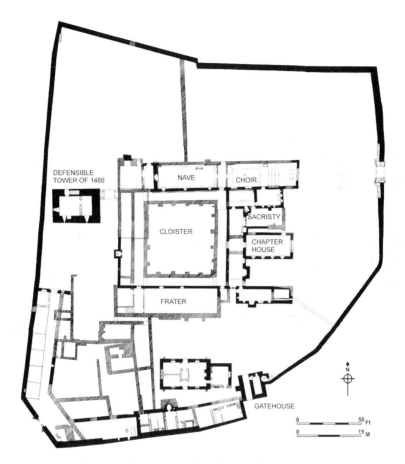

Fig. 47. Hulne Priory, plan (after St John Hope 1890).

be verified as the structure is now incomplete and any evidence of a fireplace
or other domestic features has been lost. One final feature of note however,
which tends to support the idea of a retreat, is the presence of holes in the
lower stonework of the turret, caused by musket shot, though possibly dating
from the Civil War.

About two miles north-west of Alnwick, the ruins of **Hulne Priory** overlook
the River Aln from a high prominence. The site is one of the best preserved
medieval friaries in England and is a superb example of ecclesiastical defensive
construction.

Hulne was probably founded by William de Vesci in 1242 and belonged
to the Carmelite order. The thirteenth-century buildings may largely have
been constructed of timber, as a contemporary charter of confirmation by de
Vesci's son John confirms the right to take timber for building purposes (St
John Hope 1890). The site selected is one of natural defence with the only

Fig. 48. Hulne Priory, defensible precinct wall.

level approach being from the north. By the fifteenth century the site had developed into a complex of ecclesiastical, domestic, and defensible buildings, no doubt necessitated by the friary's isolated position within easy striking distance of the frontier.

The middle of the site is occupied by the usual layout of church, central cloister, and surrounding claustral buildings including a sacristy, chapter house, warming house, and frater (Figure 47). The buildings to the west of the cloister were partially destroyed by the construction of a summerhouse in 1778–9. This formed part of a landscaping programme, designed by Robert Adam and 'Capability' Brown, who also added Gothic features to other parts of the medieval ruins. To the south there are remains of the kitchen, a brewhouse, stables, and an infirmary with attached chapel which has now been made into a house. The sacristy has an upper chamber with a fireplace and a window looking into the church. There is no evidence of a stone stairway and access must therefore have been by a wooden stair or ladder, perhaps partially for security reasons, as the chamber was most likely occupied by a sacristan who watched the church at night to prevent the theft of valuable ecclesiastical treasures (Patrick 1903; Oman 1979; Tracy 1992).

The site is surrounded by an irregularly shaped curtain wall, 3.6 m (12 ft) in height, constructed in the fifteenth century and probably originally designed with battlements or parapets (Figure 48). A contemporary gatehouse tower

Fig. 49. Hulne Priory, fortified tower built in 1486, and ruins of the church to the left.

punctuates the south wall and contains a narrow tunnel-vaulted passage and an external stair to the upper floor and wall head. There appears to have been two smaller exits on the north and west sides of the curtain which are now blocked and there have been small turrets on several of the angles, the latter evidently having been in better condition at the beginning of the twentieth century (Patrick 1903). Gothic gateways on the east and south-west sides were fashioned during the eighteenth-century landscaping. Beyond the curtain lay an outer precinct wall, 2.7 m (9 ft) in height, of which a large section to the north is intact. To the east and north-east the land drops away sharply, making extra defences unnecessary on these sides.

Inside the friary walls, as an extra defensive precaution, the fourth Earl of Northumberland, Sir Henry Percy, had a strong tower constructed in 1486 (Figure 49). A contemporary plaque, now repositioned on the interior first-floor wall, states this. Although the whole structure was heavily modified during the eighteenth century, the original intention of the tower as a refuge is clear. Placed close to the prior's lodgings on the west side of the cloister, it has a Gothic stone bridge at first-floor level, perhaps replacing a medieval one which would have allowed easy access during times of trouble. The tower originally had two upper storeys, now formed into one, and a tunnel-vaulted ground floor. There is a straight mural stair, within the 1.7 m (5 ft 7 in.) thick walls, which communicates between the first and ground floors, and a spiral stair leads up to the battlements.

There is no evidence to indicate that Hulne was ever disturbed by the Border Troubles, probably due to the extensive precautions taken both in location and construction. At the dissolution of the house the annual income was recorded as being £194 7s. The site's natural defences may have continued to be exploited by the dukes of Northumberland in the later sixteenth century, as in 1578 the estate accounts record expenses in Hulne Park on 'keys to the gaol door 8d.' and 'mending a bolt for the door 2d.' (Nor.Est.Acc., 57).

Four miles upriver from Hulne Priory lies the tiny village of **Bolton**. Its chapel, which lay within the parish of Edlingham, has been severely restored and largely rebuilt, though the west end appears to sit above a chamfered, medieval plinth. It stands on top of a natural mound and consists of a Victorian nave, a large vestry of *c.* 1868, and a much restored twelfth-century chancel. From the character of the Norman chancel-arch, it may be inferred that this represents the *'capella de Boulton'* which was annexed to the vicarage of Edlingham in 1291 (Hodgson 1904). There is nothing to indicate any adaptation for defence.

In 1225, the Lord of Wark, Robert de Ros, founded a leper hospital here, dedicated to St Thomas the Martyr, which had its own chapel, located in a field known as The Guards. No evidence now remains above ground of either of these buildings. However, unusually for a hospital, defensible precautions appear to have been taken, for in June 1336, the Keeper, Thomas de Baumburgh, was granted a licence 'to crenellate the dwelling place of the hospital' (CPR, 10 Edward III: 1334–38, Pt i ,m.1).

Three noteworthy historical events occurred at Bolton. The first, in 1209, was an abortive conciliatory meeting between the Scottish King William the Lion and the English King John which ended at Norham after reaching no agreement (Owen 1997, 101). In 1295, Edward I's army camped here under Sir Hugh de Cressingham, and the latter was still here two years later when he was recalled by the king. He was subsequently killed at the battle of Stirling Bridge (Traquair 1998; Watson 1998). The third event took place on 5 September 1513, on the eve of the battle of Flodden, when the Earl of Surrey camped here and met with the leaders of the English army. Tradition has it that this conference took place in the church (Wilson 1870; Tomlinson 1888). Surrey's adversary, King James IV, also met his leaders in a church prior to the campaign (*see* page 51).

Three miles to the south, nestling in a valley below the Alnwick road, lies the mother church of the parish at **Edlingham**. Church and castle sit juxtaposed at the end of the hamlet and form an impressively austere group, each outwardly portraying their defensible nature.

The church of St John the Baptist has a nave with south porch and north aisle, chancel, and a strong west tower (Figure 50). The nave dates from the eleventh century, and the original exterior west doorway and tympanum are

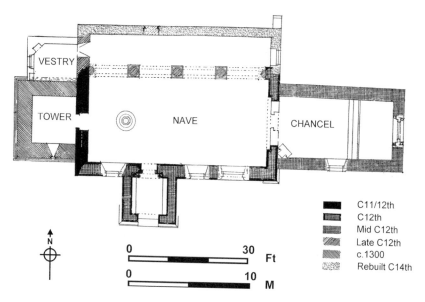

Fig. 50. Plan of Edlingham church (after W.H.Knowles 1901).

visible from within the later tower. Additions of the twelfth century included the south doorway and the north aisle (Knowles 1896). The stone barrel-vaulted south porch may also be of this date, but some seventeenth-century work is evident (there is a keystone in the arch) and a rebuilding has been suggested (Pevsner *et al* 1992). The doorway has been modified at a date subsequent to the Norman period when it was made square-headed on the interior, and a hefty draw-bar slot, 1.45 m (4 ft 9 in.) deep on the east side, bears witness to defence against would-be intruders. The re-used medieval grave-marker which now forms the cill may be a later insertion.

Most of the fenestration was restored in 1864 and 1902, but it is interesting to observe that there are no windows whatsoever on the north side of the building, and the only opening is a former doorway. The north wall appears to have been rebuilt sometime in the medieval period.

It is the tower however which provides the clearest indications of defence. Of uncertain date, due to its extreme architectural severity, it is entered only from the nave through the former early Norman west doorway rather than an arch (Figure 51). It may have retained a heavy door in this position, judging from the surviving hinges which, however, must be later than the deep draw-bar slot probably used in securing the Norman entrance. The interior of the structure is dark with the lowest chamber lit only by a single lancet 2.4 m (8 ft) above the floor. Access to the upper levels is by ladder, and even on the first floor the windows are no more than narrow slits through the 1 m (3 ft 3 in.)

Fig. 51. Edlingham, west doorway of the nave with draw-bar slot in the south jamb.

thick walls. Between the ground and first floor is a small early Norman window in the east wall, and higher in the same wall, in the upper chamber, a small bole-hole would formerly have given a view down into the church. This small window is now blocked but may be seen externally in the tower wall, clearly positioned inside the medieval roof line. Although difficult to date precisely, the most likely period of construction for this tower is *c*. 1300 (Figure 52).

There is no doubt that Edlingham was a legitimate target for Scottish raiding, and being located so near to Alnwick must have suffered many times. In the ecclesiastical accounts for 1401–2, the amount received for corn tithes is recorded as only 73s. 4d. 'and no more', as the remainder was destroyed by the Scots, probably during Earl Douglas' revenge raid of August 1402 (Hodgson 1904; Paterson 1997).

The castle lies only a short distance to the east of the church and was originally constructed as a moated enclosure by John de Edlingham around 1250.

Fig. 52. Edlingham, showing the austere west tower with a minimum of openings.

The first stone buildings were constructed by Sir William Fenton *c.* 1295–1300 and comprise a hall-house block approximately 24 m by 9 m (80 ft by 30 ft) with a first-floor defensible hall, reached by an external stair on the north side. As Border tensions and hostilities grew, a three-storey tower was added to the south of the hall in the early fourteenth century, and a gatehouse and stone curtain wall were built. These additional defensive precautions were probably constructed at about the same time as the west tower was being added to the church.

To the north-west of Edlingham is **Whittingham**. The village is divided by the River Aln, and the church stands on the north bank, overlooking the valley. The architecture of Whittingham church is unmistakably Anglo-Saxon in the lower portions of the west tower and parts of the side walls of the nave (Taylor and Taylor 1965, 657–60). The building has a nave with north and south aisles and south porch, transepts, chancel with north vestry, and west tower (Figure 53). A major restoration and partial rebuilding in 1840 has unfortunately destroyed much early evidence, including the Anglo-Saxon belfry. This was recorded by Thomas Rickman in 1834 (Hodges 1893) which showed that the battlements and uppermost parts had been altered in medieval times. As well as the destruction of the upper portion of the tower, the

Fig. 53. Exterior view of Whittingham church.

aisles were practically rebuilt and much of the original twelfth-century work was replaced in a pseudo-Gothic form by the architect John Green. In 1871, Frederick Wilson recast the chancel in Gothic form, but this was merely a restoration of an early eighteenth-century rebuilding. The remainder of the church is medieval. The south porch appears to be of the fourteenth century and is stone-vaulted with two supporting transverse ribs. The south arcade and transept are thirteenth-century as are the responds of the restored chancel-arch.

   Owing to the considerable alterations, it is extremely difficult to gauge any measures of security which may have been implemented. The entrance porch is stone-vaulted as has already been observed. The tower, which was constructed well before the principal Troubles, lends itself naturally to a secure refuge. It measures only 3.4 m (11 ft) square internally and originally rose to an estimated 18 m (60 ft). There is no stair and access to the upper floors was by ladder. According to nineteenth-century accounts, the tower-arch was formerly built-up in the medieval period restricting access between nave and tower to a small doorway 0.8 m (2 ft 8 in.) in width with a stout door which, on removal in 1840, was found to contain a bullet hole (Dixon 1895). Similar deliberate blocking of the tower-arch is seen as a defensive measure elsewhere (e.g., Bolam, Hartburn, Ingram, Kirkwhelpington, and Newbiggin).

The necessity for a safe place of refuge in Whittingham is certain. There were formerly two strong towers in addition to the church. One, belonging to the rector, was probably close by and was destroyed during the nineteenth-century rebuilding of the vicarage. This 'vicar's pele' is recorded in the 1541 survey of Border strongholds: 'At Whyttyngane bene two towers whereof the one ys the mansion of the vycaredge & thother of the Inheritance of Rb't Collyngewood esquier & bothe be in measurable good repac'ons' (Frontier I, 210). The second tower, which still survives, lies to the south of the village and was first recorded in 1318 (Cathcart King 1983, 344).

In the wooded uplands south of Whittingham is hidden the castle of Callaly, a fifteenth-century tower now incorporated into a multi-period mansion house. Further south, on the hillside above Rothbury, sits **Cartington Castle**, a fortified manor-house licensed in 1442, though containing fabric from earlier periods. The building appears to have had its own private chapel and several medieval religious artefacts have been discovered during excavations here (Dixon 1903, 359). Half a mile south-east of the castle, on the northern edge of Chirnells Moor, is the reputed site of another chapel, but there is no physical or documentary support for this tradition.

Rothbury lies within the Coquet valley and served as an important bridging point on the river. The town had the status of a borough, and by the early fourteenth century formed part of the barony of Warkworth which reverted to the Crown in 1332 on the death of Sir John Clavering, then baron. The parish church of All Saints has early origins, indicated by the magnificent cross shaft of c. 800, part of which now serves as a base for the font (two more pieces, including part of the head, are now in the Museum of Antiquities in Newcastle). Like its neighbour at Whittingham, the building was considerably reconstructed during the nineteenth century, but unlike Whittingham, which preserved much of its pre-Conquest fabric, Rothbury was practically rebuilt and its possible Anglo-Saxon tower entirely demolished (Pevsner *et al* 1992). In fact all but the chancel and the east walls of the transepts was rebuilt in 1850, leaving little evidence of the medieval arrangement.

Dixon (1903, 391) described the church prior to restoration as having an 'ancient porch' and a 'sturdy Edwardian tower of four stages, having square-headed window openings'; he also published several engravings of the building which show that the tower had an unusual upper portion, with three diminishing stages and a high parapet (Figure 54). None of the illustrated windows were large; indeed they are all depicted as narrow slits even in the belfry, and there are no openings apparent at lower levels. The use of narrow window slits and lack of lower openings is a widely recognized defensive trait and this may have

Fig. 54. Rothbury church in 1840 prior to the demolition of the nave and tower (after Dixon 1903).

been an adaptation made at Rothbury, especially given the vulnerability of the town's location in the valley. As an alternative refuge there was also a castle, about 45 m (150 ft) south-west of the church, which had developed (on the site of a Norman motte and bailey) into a prison and hall; it was entirely destroyed in 1869 (Dixon 1903).

In the middle of the sixteenth century, Bernard Gilpin, a priest from County Durham, visited this area in order to try and instil some religion into an otherwise recalcitrant local populace. He was at first shocked on learning that some parishioners failed to attend church because of feuds, and was later alarmed when they did come but congregated in two armed groups, one in the chancel and one in the nave (Goodman 1989).

Rothbury and its church had a reputation for being in the thick of the Troubles, colourfully portrayed by a sixteenth-century ballad about the rector of Rothbury:

> Hue an' cry, hoond an' home, ca' to the fray,
> For the Scots hae been Rothbarrie waie i' the mirke,
> An' left na a galloway, sheepe, hogge, or stirke,
> Fired a' the haudins, an' harried the kirk,

An' faur waur then a'
Oh! wae ti'll us wae
The Meenister missin', they've lifted him tae'.
(Ward Davis 1991)

Adaptation of the church tower for defence may have originally been undertaken at the instigation of the prelacy (Rothbury was annexed to the Priory of St Mary at Carlisle) who, in later years, utilised the strong tower at **Whitton** high on the hillside above the town to the south (Figure 55). Whitton Tower dates from the fourteenth century, and may have been built by the Umfravilles, but is first mentioned in 1415 when it was in possession of the rector of Rothbury (Hodgson 1820, 29; Bates 1891). In the 1540s it was described as a 'toure and a lytle barmekin being the manc'on of the p'sonage of Rothbery' (Frontier I, 214). The building is unusual in that, being built into the hillside, it has vaults on two of its four storeys to maintain a defensible aspect for the

Fig. 55. Whitton Pele Tower. Fourteenth-century with later alterations. This was the residence of the later medieval vicars of Rothbury.

upper floors. In 1871, a semi-octagonal piscina within an ogee niche was discovered in a window recess on the first floor, indicating that this area was used as a private chapel or oratory for the use of the occupier (Dixon 1903, 447). Close to Whitton Tower, a watch is recorded as being kept in 1553, 'Whettone to watch at the Quarle-Yate with two Men in the Watch' (Nicholson 1705).

A short distance to the east of Rothbury, the village of **Longframlington** sits astride the Morpeth-Wooler road and has a small towerless church located close to the centre of the settlement, lying within the medieval parish of Felton. The date of the fabric is essentially late twelfth-century, contemporary with nearby Brinkburn Priory, with alterations of 1740, 1882, and 1896. The early, small windows have generally been retained and all openings are placed high above ground level, between 2.5 m (8 ft) and 4 m (13 ft) to the cills, possibly to impede easy ingress. This high level was kept even at the restorations in 1882 (when the east and much of the south walls of the chancel were rebuilt) and 1896. The soffit of the outer arch of the fourteenth-century porch has a deeply-cut recess which has clearly once contained a heavy gate or grill to protect the entrance.

In a loop in the Coquet, a little over four miles downriver from Rothbury, **Brinkburn Priory** lies hidden in a sheltered hollow. It was founded between 1130 and 1135 by William Bertram I of Mitford for Augustinian canons who came from the priory of Pentney in Norfolk, to which house it remained subordinate until its independence in the late twelfth century.

The church consists of a nave with north aisle, chancel, transepts, and a low central tower. Construction started at the east end in the late twelfth century and moved westward, reaching completion in the early thirteenth century. The whole building is a fine illustration of the transition from Romanesque to early Gothic architecture (Figure 56). To the south-west of the church, the remains of the south range are now incorporated within a later manor-house and include a cellar, with an inserted tunnel vault, possibly of the late sixteenth century.

Until its restoration under the guidance of Thomas Austin in 1858–9, the priory lay in ruins. During the restoration the south-west angle of the nave was rebuilt, new roofs and floors provided, and some features were removed in order to attempt a 'purist' reconstruction. Of the features destroyed, two were of particular importance: a chamber above the choir, and an upper floor over the nave aisle. These upper chambers appear to have been additions of the fourteenth century when the nave aisle wall and the side walls of the choir were raised, apparently specifically to accommodate these areas. A similar room above the chancel existed at Tynemouth Priory. No documentary evidence is available to explain the use of these additions, but it seems highly probable, especially given their period of construction, that they were designed as secure areas, most likely serving both for the storage of valuable items and as an emergency refuge at a safe, high level to which access was limited.

The architecture of the church itself never evolved beyond the late twelfth-

Fig. 56. Brinkburn Priory church.

to early thirteenth-century form, despite thriving as a successful priory until the Reformation. It is possible that, like Lanercost Priory in the English West March (also first colonized from Pentney), the narrow windows, placed high above ground level, served as a useful barrier to unwanted ingress and were never changed to more fashionable styles for this reason. This may also account for the unusual insertion of mullions and transoms into the large lower lancets of the chancel which would have acted like grills, narrowing the openings. These were also removed in the restoration of 1858.

Brinkburn certainly needed to adopt defensive precautions, and there are accounts surviving of the predations suffered at the hands of the Scots. Between the years 1331 and 1334 the prior and convent petitioned the king for relief on account of the losses they had sustained, and various adjustments were allowed in rents due. In August of 1333 they even received 20 quarters of wheat on account of their 'much depressed state' (Page 1893; Hodgson 1904). In 1391 the canons again complained of poverty on account of Scots, and in 1419 the priory was raided and robbed of charters, muniments, books, chalices, vestments, ornaments, and other goods (Storey 1956).

The road above the priory led north-west to Rothbury. Beyond, a network of small byways percolated into the valleys of the Coquet and the Aln, to serve a diffuse cluster of small farming settlements which lay scattered below the Cheviot foothills to the north.

The first villages west of Rothbury are Snitter, Thropton and Hepple. All suffered heavily at the hands of the Scots during the Troubles, and there is a defensible tower in Hepple which dates from the fourteenth century. The extent to which the inhabitants of the locality had to guard their possessions is revealed in various sixteenth-century accounts where frequent watches were kept nightly on the roads and tracks leading from the border (Nicholson 1705).

None of these villages retain any medieval ecclesiastical buildings. However, the site of the original church at **Hepple** is located on top of a hill to the west of the village in an obvious position of defence, well above both road and valley. The building was destroyed around 1760, although excavation has shown that an earlier destruction took place when the chapel was burnt, probably in the fourteenth century, perhaps during the most damaging Scottish raid of that period in 1346 (Miket 1974). Both the original twelfth-century chapel and the later medieval building were of no great size; each had a simple arrangement of a nave and small chancel.

At **Thropton**, there was a medieval hospital, probably in the vicinity of the present Wreighburn House, and another lay on the opposite side of the river at **Allerdene**. No remains survive.

To the north of Hepple, the church of St Mary's at **Holystone** represents a mere fragment of the former nunnery, established in 1124. The house was originally founded by the Benedictine order but in the thirteenth century it became Augustinian.

The present nave has been created from the chancel of the nunnery, although the only medieval parts are the south and lower north walls, along with the east respond of the former south arcade, the last being visible at the exterior south-west corner. In 1848–9 considerable restoration and rebuilding was carried out, leaving no clear evidence of the medieval form of the church. The building was destroyed after the Reformation and fragments of carved and worked medieval stonework appear throughout the village.

The incumbents of the nunnery were never numerous, generally within single figures, and the building and lands suffered considerably during the Troubles. In 1311 the bishop assigned the vicarage of Harbottle and the churches of Holystone and Corsenside to the nunnery on account of the deprivation caused by Scottish raiding, not least in that same year when Robert Bruce devastated much of the area on his way to Tynedale. Nine years later, the prioress and convent petitioned the king for relief due to yet more destruction caused by the Scots (Nor.Pet., 162).

West of Holystone, the land rises into wild moorland, devoid of villages, until it descends again into the lonely valley of the Rede. To the north lies **Harbottle**, a tiny village which once boasted a powerful castle, founded by the Umfraville family to control the route into Scotland along the River Coquet. The site of the fortress lies to the west of the settlement and extensive earthworks of the twelfth century and later remain. A thirteenth-century shell keep was appended to an earlier motte and projecting towers were added. In 1541 the castle was in a very poor state of repair although it was recognised as being 'a stronge place & metely for the defence of all that countrye aswell againste the Invasion & Incourses of Scottes in tyme of warre as for the defence of the theftes & spoyles of the Ryddesdayle men' (Frontier I, 212). In keeping with many key Border castles, the structure was converted to allow the use of artillery (Cathcart King 1983, 334); however by 1584 it was once again in a bad condition.

The castle was attacked on several occasions, being taken by Robert Bruce in 1318 when it was dismantled. In 1515 it was the residence of the Warden of the Middle March, Lord Dacre, along with a garrison of around eighty men.

Although no parish church is now extant in Harbottle, one evidently did exist, as there is a record of a member of the Umfraville family having been baptized in the 'church of the vill' (Dixon 1903). In addition there is likely to have been a private chapel within the castle's defences.

A short distance past Harbottle, the last village before the Cheviot hills lies at **Alwinton**. Snugly positioned in the valley, between the rivers Coquet and Alwin, the settlement is located at the foot of Clennell Street, and the road north-west to Windyhaugh and Browhart Law. This road fed the small tracks and passes or 'swires' leading over the border into Scotland which provided easy ingress for Reivers (Figure 57). This location was highly vulnerable

Fig. 57. Looking northwards along Clennell Street near Alwinton. This road constituted one of the 'swires' or hill paths which crossed the border and which provided access for raiders.

as Alwinton was effectively the 'gate' into Coquetdale, and by the sixteenth century regular nightly watches were kept.

The church was of course susceptible to any raiding party coming from the north, although its slightly elevated position to the south of the village is more likely to be due to the constant danger of flooding than any defensive considerations. Built into the slope of the hillside, the chancel is 1.6 m (5 ft 3 in.) above the nave, necessitating a rise of ten steps, the space beneath which has been excavated to make a burial vault. Of the medieval church, only the chancel, and parts of the north aisle and west wall remain, the rest having been rebuilt in 1851 in the thirteenth-century style.

As early as 1293 there is a reference to the church being used by a sanctuary seeker, one Thomas de Holm, who, having escaped from Harbottle Castle, fled to the church to seek refuge. His bid however proved unsuccessful for he was taken and beheaded at Simonside, his head being hung on the gallows at Harbottle (Tomlinson 1888, 349).

By the sixteenth century, a secure refuge was essential for the parson of Alwinton, and in Bowes' sixteenth-century account it was recorded that 'At Allaynton [Alwinton] ys a lytle Castell house of stone the mansion of the vycaredge scaresly in good repac'ons' (Frontier I, 211).

At nearby **Biddlestone** the remains of a pele tower, formerly attached to the now-demolished eighteenth-century hall, still retain a basement tunnel vault. A Roman Catholic chapel was constructed at first-floor level in the nineteenth century.

The tower was held by the Selby family, who were, in the early years of the Troubles, variously on the sides of both the Scottish and English causes. Addressing a raid by the Kerrs in 1549, the poet James Hogg wrote:

Turn, Captain of Biddleston, turn and flee!
Thy arm was never a match for mine,
I'll hold at bay thy men and thee,
Till I'm across the Border line.

In a narrow valley to the north-east of Biddlestone the church of St Michael's at **Alnham** lies juxtaposed with a strong vicar's pele tower, both located close to the vanished medieval village and site of Alnham castle.

The church has no tower and consists of a nave with a tunnel-vaulted south porch, transepts, chancel, and a former north aisle. The construction of the nave indicates that the earliest portions may be pre-Conquest, attested by the heavy side-alternate quoins at the east, whilst elsewhere the construction is of a robust form, with very heavy buttressing at the west end. The present roof is of local stone tiles throughout, and if this reflects the original intention then it makes for a very compact, fire-proof building. The majority of the windows have been renewed; indeed the building was in a ruinous state until restored in 1870 by Frederick Wilson (Dixon 1895). The only outward indication of security, other than the generally sturdy character, is the tunnel vaulting of the south porch which probably dates from the late sixteenth century.

Alnham is positioned right at the foot of the Cheviot hills, and lies only five miles from the Scottish border. This was a very dangerous location during the Troubles, and raiding parties could descend easily down the valley of the River Breamish, along the 'Salters Road' from the north-west. Twice in the space of a month, in the autumn of 1532, the Earl of Northumberland had cause to write to King Henry VIII complaining that the Scotts of Teviotdale, and then the Kers, had come over the border and run forays on several villages, burning Alnham in the process. For this reason, when eighty additional men were allocated to the Border for military service in 1596, a quarter of them were sent to this location (CBP, ii, 234).

The strategic position of the village was recognised from an early date during the Border wars, and a castle is first mentioned here in 1405 when it was surrendered to the king (Cathcart King 1983). In 1566 the Earl of Northumberland's agent reported that there was a strong tower, vaulted, and with gates and doors of 'great strong Iron Barres' (Rowland 1994, 34), but the building was by then ruinous, having, in all probability, been partially destroyed during the raids of 1532. Today there are no upstanding remains of the castle, although its position and foundations can be traced a short distance to the south-east of the churchyard.

The danger which was posed by the vulnerable location also led to the construction of a defensible tower for the vicars of Alnham. In the mid-sixteenth century the 'two lytle toures' on 'the mansion of the Vycaredge' were 'scarcely in good reparac'ons' (Frontier I, 211), and by the mid-seventeenth century both had been abandoned. The vicarage tower was restored during the nineteenth century when the upper areas were rebuilt, although it retains a tunnel-vaulted ground floor with walls 2.75 m (9 ft) in thickness (Figure 58).

To the north of Alwinton, Clennell Street winds its way towards Yarnspath Law and the Usway Burn by way of the Kidland Forest. This rugged upland area, now planted with dense conifers, was once owned by the monks of Newminster Abbey who used the hillsides and steep, narrow valleys for their summer grazing (Newminster Chart., 37a; 37b). Deep inside the modern forest, at the foot of the Rigg, where the Sting and Yoke burns meet, are located the fragmentary remains of an unremarkable building known as Memmerkirk or **Memmer Kirk**.

The foundations of the building lie on a level platform where the land slopes upwards on all sides except the west, providing one of the most sheltered locations in the area. The walls stand to a maximum of only 0.6 m (2 ft), and there is insufficient detail to be able to determine its former purpose.

The origin of the name Memmer Kirk is obscure, but it first appears on record in 1650 when it is described as 'Member Kirke' by the commonwealth commissioners who were seeking to unite it and Kidland with Alwinton and Holystone (Hodgson 1835, lxxvi). Edward Chandler, Bishop of Durham, wrote

Fig. 58. Alnham, the restored vicar's pele tower.

some historical notes *c.* 1736 when he described the building as having been an old chapel (Dixon 1903).

Excavations were carried out in 1887 and again, more thoroughly, in 1962, which revealed a rectangular building 14.6 m (48 ft) long by 4.6 m (15 ft) wide. Two internal walls divided the area into three rooms, the centre and western of which had external doorways and were paved with irregular flat stones. Finds included three fourteenth-century pottery fragments in the core of one of the external walls, and a group of seventeenth-century pieces; a hearth was found in the western room (Harbottle and Cowper 1963).

The building bears no resemblance to a medieval chapel in its plan, and no ecclesiastical finds were made during the excavations. The most likely explanation is that the building was a seventeenth-century farmstead owned or tenanted by local men (Harbottle and Newman 1977). It was abandoned after a short period of use. However, during its brief existence, groups of Scottish Covenanters, escaping from persecution north of the border (Paterson 1998), may have utilised its remote and somewhat secret location for their conventicles, thus giving rise to the 'kirk' place-name. This explanation would fit both the archaeological and historical evidence, and the site may therefore be an exceptional example of late ecclesiastical security in the form of a secret, secular refuge.

The main road from Alwinton continues far into the Border hills to the north-west, passing small farming settlements at Linshiels, Shillmoor, and Blindburn until, after eight miles, it intersects the important cross-border medieval road of Gamel's Path, at the site of the Roman Camp on Chew Green. Here, just below the ridge of Brownhart Law, was a small early medieval village which also seems to have taken the name 'Gamelspath' or 'Kemylspethe', within which have been excavated the foundations of a small Norman chapel. This was one of the appointed places for truce meetings between the Middle March Wardens and the men of Redesdale, Coquetdale, and Teviotdale (Bates 1895; Robson 1989).

To the west of Gamelspath the land is wild and rugged as the border line passes over Hungry Law and on to Carter Bar at the head of the River Rede. To the south, the old Roman road of Dere Street passes through the Otterburn military range (where access is now restricted). Also in this area, a track leads to the hamlet at **Byrness** where a small church, rebuilt at the end of the eighteenth century and remodelled in 1884, stands on the site of its medieval predecessor.

A little to the south of Byrness is **Rochester**, the site of the Roman fort of *Bremenium*. Between here and Horsley, a mile to the south-east, is the Victorian church of 1844, a church first having been proposed for this location in 1650 (Hodgson 1835, lxxvi). Further south-east still, the site of a small medieval chapel is located at **Elishaw**, where the roads divide either side of the Rede. Around the year 1240 there is mention of the 'master of the hospital of Rede' in the exchequer accounts, perhaps referring to a small hospital foundation of which this chapel formed a part (Hodgson 1827, 146). No structural remains are now visible.

Along the upper road from Elishaw is the site of the Battle of Otterburn where, on the night of 5 August 1388, James Douglas successfully held his Scottish troops against an attack by the English, commanded by Henry 'Hotspur' Percy, the eldest son of the Duke of Northumberland. Percy attacked soon after his arrival, making two fatal mistakes: his men were tired and hungry after their long march from Newcastle, and the lack of daylight prevented the use of his archers. By using good military strategy and guided by a strong leader, the Scots counter-attacked the English flank from higher ground and in the fight which ensued Douglas was killed. The undisputed victory however was to the Scots, who routed the tired English forces, causing over 1,000 of their number to be killed and taking Percy prisoner.

The village of **Otterburn** has a small church which dates from 1857 by the local architect John Dobson and which stands close to the site of Otterburn Tower, formerly held by Sir Robert Umfraville. In 1300 the place lay within the large parish of Elsdon, and when John Leland visited in the early sixteenth century the situation was the same, indicating that there has never been a major church in Otterburn (Charlton 1986; Lomas 1996a).

A short distance to the east of Otterburn lies the village of **Elsdon**, dominated by its wide green, its church, and defensible tower (Figure 59).

Fig. 59. Elsdon church, located centrally in the village with a pele tower on higher ground to the north-west.

St Cuthbert's is a cruciform church with a nave, chancel, north and south transepts, south porch, and narrow aisles to the nave and west sides of the transepts. A modern vestry occupies the space to the north of the chancel. The west end is capped by a small bellcote, constructed around 1720, which may have replaced an earlier tower. The evidence for this is apparent internally in the blocked tower-arch of uncertain date, but probably Norman reset in the fourteenth century, and now pierced by a nineteenth-century window. It may also have been the case that a tower was planned but never executed.

The archaeology of the building is complex. In addition to the evidence for the possible former west tower, there are indications that the present south wall has been cut back from an earlier, wider aisle, which probably belonged to a twelfth-century building, attested by the west responds of the arcades. The lower north external wall of the nave also demonstrates significant changes as there is a break in the low plinth two-thirds of the way along its length, and the remaining wall along with part of the north transept has evidently been burnt as shown by the oxidisation, or reddening, of the stonework. Internally, the nave aisles have been extended into the once aisleless transepts.

It appears that the building was largely reconstructed during the fourteenth century; this is the date of the present octagonal nave arcades and the chancel. Later, possibly during the sixteenth century, the narrow side aisles were added, almost certainly for reasons of defence. These aisles are only 1.12 m (3 ft 8 in.)

Fig. 60. Elsdon, quadrant vaulting in the nave aisles.

in width, and have stone quadrant-vaults, a most unusual feature, but a sound protection against ingress and fire (Figure 60). They sit against exterior walls which are thicker than the width of the aisles at 1.2 m (4 ft), and which had no openings (the present windows date from the nineteenth century). Although the present south entrance has no evidence of a strong door or draw-bars, there has been much Victorian alteration, at which date two medieval grave-markers may have been inserted to form the head of the doorway.

Elsdon was clearly of great importance in Redesdale. Only three churches of significance existed when John Leland visited in the late 1530s or early 1540s, Holystone, Corsenside, and Elsdon. He wrote that 'to thes parochis resorte the witriding [outriding] men othar wyse theues [thieves] of that Englishe marche' (Leland, ix, fo.143). The area certainly lay in the thick of reiving country, a fact which did not go unnoticed by the Bishop of Durham, who in 1498 noted that most of the inhabitants were reivers and cattle-lifters and that the clergy were no better than their parishioners. Three-quarters of a century later little had changed, and Bishop Pilkington commented that many clergy were reluctant to accept the Elsdon living because they were afraid for their personal safety, writing that: 'priests go with sword, dagger, and such apparel as they can get' (Charlton 1986, 39). In 1583, a Scottish raid took place resulting in three deaths and the loss of 100 kye and oxen, and in the following year the Elliots and Armstrongs burnt the town, killed 14 men, took 200 prisoners and drove away much valuable livestock, money, and insight gear (Taylor n.d.).

It is highly probable that Elsdon parish church served as a secure refuge for the people of the village during raids or periods of unrest. Its rebuilding, following the massive Scottish incursions of the early to mid-fourteenth century, may have resulted from destruction wrought in that period. The adaptation of the vaulted aisles for defence may have followed the Scots raids of the 1580s.

Excavations in the churchyard during 1810 and 1877 revealed large numbers of skeletons in a single grave pit (Hodgson 1827, 90). These may have been victims of the Battle of Otterburn who were taken to the parish church for burial.

The vicar of Elsdon had his own retreat in the form of a pele tower, positioned on higher ground to the north-west of the church. This tower appears in the survey of 1415 as the 'Turris de Ellysden' in possession of the rector (Hodgson 1820, 30; Bates 1891). The present tower appears to have been modified in the sixteenth century and although it was heavily remodelled in the 1700s (Ryder 1996b), it still retains its fourteenth-century core, a tunnel-vaulted basement, and machicolation defences.

At the north side of the village are located the remains of the Norman earthwork castle of the Umfravilles, constructed in the early twelfth century. The fortifications were probably dismantled sometime after 1157 when Henry II regained Northumberland.

Four miles south-west of Elsdon the little Norman church at **Corsenside** overlooks the valley of the Rede from its lonely, windswept position on the hillside by the edge of Dere Street (the modern A68 road). Along with Elsdon and Holystone, Corsenside was considered to be one of the major parish churches in Redesdale during the sixteenth century. However, owing to the local topography, the parish was always sparsely populated and the church appears today, as it always has, isolated, and above the valley and main settlements at West and East Woodburn. In 1311 the living was given to the nunnery at Holystone in order to help offset the losses incurred by Scots raiding.

The church is built simply, with a nave and lower chancel, probably all of twelfth-century date with modifications of the seventeenth, eighteenth, and nineteenth centuries. There are no aisles, no tower, and no north windows, and apart from its hillside position the building has no indications of defence or security.

NORTH TYNEDALE AND THE GREAT PARISH OF SIMONBURN

The land to the west of Dere Street and to the north of Hadrian's Wall is mainly upland fell and forest, largely devoid of villages and with few roads. The northern half of this area contains the high hills of Oh Me Edge and the Earl's Seat, below which the sykes, linns, and flows of upland drainage made habitation challenging. The region has long fostered the fabric of legends and romantic Border tales.

Along with Redesdale, North Tynedale was an ecclesiastical 'Liberty', granted in the twelfth century, which originally enabled the enjoyment of the right of extended sanctuary (Robson 1989; Barrow 1992), thus benefiting the more unruly members of society who proliferated in later years. Indeed, this area had a reputation for lawlessness unequalled elsewhere in the English Middle March, despite having its own Lord's deputy, styled 'Keeper'. This extended even to the point where the Warden was driven out, as happened in 1525 when Sir Ralph Fenwick was expelled from Tarset Castle. In the mid-sixteenth century, Sir Robert Bowes, making his survey of the Borders, commented that 'North Tyndall is plenished with wild and misdemeaned people' (Frontier II, 228).

At a point between Saughtree in the Scottish Middle March and Kielder in the English Middle March, where the only sound road in the area crosses the Border, lies the site of the **Bells Burn** chapel. The actual position is in a sheltered spot near the Bells Linn waterfall, to the west of the road and close to where the Bells Burn meets the River North Tyne. The first mention of the chapel is in 1590 when the Wardens of the Marches met here at the 'Belles Kyrke' (CBP, i, 668), the little structure perhaps affording both physical shelter as well as the neutrality of hallowed ground. Whilst the site appears on later maps, the last mention is just fourteen years later, in 1604, when it was annexed to Castleton, along with Ettleton and Wheel; all except Bells lay within Scotland (Watson 1921). This area of North Tynedale was, by special arrangement, ceded to William the Lion by Henry II (Owen 1997), and may have remained a part of Scotland until Balliol's forfeiture by Edward I in 1295. During the reign of Robert I the district was occupied by the Scots and there is evidence to suggest that North Tynedale had once again become a part of Scotland (McNamee 1997; Traquair 1998).

Some remains of the Bells Burn chapel were visible in the early years of the twentieth century (Mack 1926, 190), but the building has now largely disappeared. It was probably a small Norman foundation, like its neighbours at Ettleton and Wheel, and was never intended to be defensible, despite its immediate proximity to the Border line.

To the east of Kielder, and the late twentieth-century reservoir, lie a number of small scattered settlements. Those at **Falstone**, **Thorneyburn**, and **Greystead** each have churches designed by, or modelled on, H.H. Seaward's scheme of 1818 for the Commissioners of Greenwich Hospital (Pevsner *et al* 1992). At Falstone there was a chapel in existence in 1318 (Barrow 1974) which in 1541 was 'used for pryvate masses at sometymes' (Frontier I, 231). In the surrounding area are the remains of many defensible secular buildings, in the form of early seventeenth-century bastle-houses; the best preserved group is in the vicinity of Gatehouse.

From the uplands of the Kielder Forest, the road leads south-east to the village of **Bellingham**. The church of St Cuthbert stands on a high point, above and to the west of the village centre, and has an aisleless nave, south transept, and chancel. The earliest fabric dates from the thirteenth century, although this is now confined to the north and east walls of the chancel, and parts of the east wall of the south transept and the west wall of the nave. Four contemporary responds, embedded in the angles of the nave side walls, show that aisles once existed. The remainder of the structure was rebuilt in the early seventeenth century, post-1609.

The most remarkable feature about Bellingham is that, despite the date of reconstruction falling after the Union, it retains important defensive features. The nave and transept roofs are constructed with stone vaulting, carried on rounded, transverse arches, each of which is chamfered in a decidedly medieval fashion (Figure 61). On the exterior, the roof is made up of alternate strips of single and double thickness stone slabs in almost identical form to those at Ladykirk in the Scottish East March. The rebuilt side walls of the nave also average 1.3 m (4 ft 3 in.) in thickness, 0.45 m (1 ft 6 in.) thicker than the surviving thirteenth-century walls. To underline the protective nature of the rebuilding, the windows in the nave are formed as narrow lancets, possibly partially re-using earlier material, but clearly unlike windows coeval with the period, having, like the south doorway, a double arch construction; they were evidently designed to restrict ingress. The reveal of the south doorway is now obscured by plaster and dado panelling but is partially cut-away on the east side, adjacent to an infilled hole at high level in the wall, which may be indicative that a strong doorway or gate has once hung here.

Bellingham was clearly in a highly vulnerable position and must have taken the brunt of Scottish raids on many occasions. One such event happened in 1597 when the Earl of Buccleugh raided and spoiled the town and church on Fair Day, the church being used as a centre of defence by the townsfolk who suffered eleven casualties after artillery was deployed by the attackers (MacDonald Fraser 1989; Allen n.d.). However, the church was as much at the mercy of the Tynedale men as from the Scots, as at Easter in 1524, one Hector Charlton took the Sacrament out of Bellingham church and carried it with a firkin of wine and 800 breads to Tarset Hall where a Scottish friar (probably an itinerant priest) gave the thieves communion (Bates 1895, 210–11; Robson 1989, 129). Parts of the exterior stonework on the south side are unusually reddened, probably caused by fire.

To the south of Bellingham, the village of **Wark-on-Tyne**, once the capital

Fig. 61. Bellingham, the interior, showing stone vaulting of the nave.

of the regality of Tynedale, has a motte and bailey castle, later developed by the addition of a stone tower, but long abandoned by 1538 (Cathcart King 1983, 343). The place was never an independent parish but had a medieval chapel. This was supplanted by another church built to the designs of Seward in 1818, which lies a third of a mile to the north of the village.

On the opposite side of the River North Tyne, to the east of Wark, the hill-side village of **Birtley** has a small church which lies outside, and slightly above, the main settlement. The Norman structure was built by the Umfraville family and given to Hexham Priory at some time before 1180. The village formed part of Chollerton parish until 1765 when it became separate.

The building is largely constructed of grey and yellow sandstone and on plan has an aisleless nave with chancel, and a Victorian west tower and porch. The core fabric is twelfth-century and the chancel-arch is of this date. There is a sixteenth-century blocked doorway in the north of the nave and indica-tions of other alterations both in this wall and in the corresponding wall to the chancel, but apart from an unclear square anomaly towards the east end, there is no evidence that there have ever been any other openings on this side. In 1610 the church was described as ruinous, and in 1723 Sir Cuthbert Heron commissioned repairs and some alterations which included the fenestration. There was a major restoration in 1884 when the eighteenth-century windows were renewed and the tower and porch built. There is no evidence of any security measures in the building other than its elevated position and windowless aspect to the north. A small tower of uncertain date stands nearby to the southwest, which may have been utilised as a defensible parsonage house.

South from Birtley, and close above the bank of the North Tyne, is **Chipchase Castle**, first mentioned in 1415 as a tower; by 1541 a house had been attached to it. The tower was a major stronghold and had a portcullis, barrel-vaulted ground floor, internal well, and apartments at upper level. At the northeast corner of the third storey is a small oratory with the remains of a stone altar and piscina (Bates 1891; Toy 1939, 180). A chapel was also constructed outside the tower, and, although the present building is post-1735, the north wall appears to contain medieval masonry. This may be the remains of the chapel mentioned in a fourteenth-century licence from Bernard, prior of Hexham, authorizing a chantry *'in capella de Chipches'* (Hexham Charters, XVIII).

At nearby **Gunnerton**, the present church of 1899 has replaced an earlier chapel. Further east, at **Great Swinburn**, the now-vanished castle of Roger de Widdrington, licensed in 1346, may once have included a private oratory, in addition to the chapel which formerly existed here and which was part of the parish of Chollerton (Lomas 1996a).

It is at **Simonburn**, two and a half miles south of Wark-on-Tyne, that the mother church of the medieval 'Great Parish' is found. Around the year 1300, the parish bounded some 52,600 hectares (130,000 acres) and extended as far north as Carter Bar, although the population of this area was small and, apart from Bellingham, contained no settlements of any appreciable size.

Simonburn lay close to one of the principal roads leading north, and was an obvious target for raiding. The church was infamous as early as 1294 when, although rated at 70 marks, had 'pleated withies, smeared with fresh cow dung, in place of the panel over the high altar' (Chr.Lan., 110). In 1490, Bishop Fox of Durham ordered that the Rector should have an 'honest and sufficient chamber' near to the castle for his personal safety (Ward Davis 1991), and in the survey of 1541 the rectory was described as 'a nother lylte towre the manc'on of the p'sonage there in measurable good repac'ons' (Frontier I, 216); today there are no remains of this building, the site lying a short distance to the west of the church. Despite the protection afforded by the rectory tower, it was clearly difficult to persuade priests to stay here. In 1595 Sir Ralph Eure, March Warden, asked permission to present his own candidate, one Mr Crakenthorp, who then promptly refused the living stating that he was 'unable to live in so troublesome a place' and that his nature was 'not well brooking the perverse nature of so crooked a people' (Rowland 1991, 37).

St Mungo's church at Simonburn is a large thirteenth-century building, with a nave, north and south aisles, and a long chancel, all heavily restored by Anthony Salvin in 1863-4. A south transept was removed in 1763, and there were further alterations made in the late 1870s. Fragments of pre-Conquest sculpture attest to an early foundation, but the fabric has been so altered that the previous form of the building cannot easily be determined. The length of the church, a total of 34.5 m (113 ft) is unusual, and probably reflects the status of this site as a major parochial centre. Although there is no evidence of a tower, the west wall of the nave, which has survived the restorations and is original medieval work, is 1.07 m (3 ft 6 in.) in thickness and has an exterior, battered plinth, and two buttresses.

There was a castle to the west of the village, of which little now remains, though a vaulted basement is largely intact. It was first mentioned in the survey of 1415, was in fair repair in 1541, and in 1766 was partially rebuilt as a pictur-esque ruin (Wallis 1769). The castle was probably originally the private resi-dence of the Heron family, and it was recommended to King Henry VIII as a suitable lodging for the Keeper of Tynedale, who was to have 50 horsemen to ride against the Scots (Hugill 1939). It is most unlikely that the inhabitants of Simonburn would have been able to use this castle for protection during times of danger, and in all probability would have resorted to the church which lay in the heart of the village (although Bishop Fox intended the priest to use the castle should danger threaten).

Further down the North Tyne valley, the villages of **Humshaugh** and **Chol-lerford** have no medieval ecclesiastical remains. The present church at Hum-shaugh dates from 1818 and is another example of H.H. Seward's work.

Situated above a bend on the east bank of the river, where the Erring Burn once divided the Regality of Hexham from the Liberty of North Tynedale, lies the village of **Chollerton**, formerly a manor in the barony of Prudhoe. The impressive medieval church has a nave with north and south aisles, a chan-cel, and a west tower. The earliest portions date from the twelfth century and include most of the south aisle which, remarkably, has four Roman columns, probably salvaged from nearby *Cilurnum* (Chesters). The north aisle is of the fourteenth century, and the chancel was rebuilt c. 1769 except for the north wall which appears to be medieval and has no windows. The puzzle lies with the west tower, ostensibly of the eighteenth century, except for its lower east wall. An upper floor and wooden spire were added in 1873. However the fabric of the lower walls appears to be earlier and the lower portion of the structure may therefore be medieval. Entry to the tower (other than by the modern external stairway to the first floor) is through a post-Reformation doorway, 1 m (3 ft 3 in.) in width, in the west wall of the nave (Figure 62). Although altered from its medieval form, and largely rebuilt, this may reflect an earlier intention to restrict entry into the tower and may have been constructed as a defensive feature of the type seen elsewhere on the Border.

To the south-east of Chollerton is the ruined tower-house of the Errington

Fig. 62. Chollerton, interior, looking west, showing a post-Reformation doorway in place of a tower-arch.

family at **Cocklaw**. At first-floor level an east doorway communicated via a wooden bridge to an adjacent building, possibly a chapel (Hugill 1939, 67).

A mile and a half south of Chollerton, in a field just to the north of the modern B6318 road is the church at **St Oswald's**, commonly known as Heavenfield, after the battle which took place here in the year 635 (Bede, iii.2). The present building is two-celled with a small western annexe, and dates from 1737, although it contains some re-used medieval fabric and apparently occupies the site of its predecessor. The position is striking, high above the valley with fine views to the north and south. There is no historical evidence for its use as a refuge.

THE CENTRAL REGION

The area which lies between the Coquet and South Tyne valleys is bounded on the north side by the Simonside Hills and Harwood Forest, and to the west and east respectively by the principal highways of the modern A68 and Great North Road. Through this undulating region run the rivers Blyth and Wansbeck and one principal route, leading from Newcastle north-west to Otterburn, and thence to the border at Carter Bar.

Of the cluster of small village churches just to the east of the modern A68, **Bingfield** and **Kirkheaton** have sparse medieval remains and have been extensively rebuilt; **Matfen** has a new church started in 1841 and completed in 1854, and **Colwell** and **Ingoe** have fragments of their medieval chapels-of-ease. In 1293 William Perles, who had killed Thomas Scherwynd, took sanctuary in the chapel at Ingoe (Hope Dodds 1926).

The church of All Saints at **Ryal** was also a chapel-of-ease, originally served by the vicar of Stamfordham, and has a greater survival of medieval fabric than its neighbours. The building has a nave and chancel dating from the twelfth and thirteenth centuries, although extensive restoration in 1870–9 has resulted in the rebuilding of the south wall and the renewal of all window openings. The west wall of the nave is complex; there are, for example, at least three building phases visible on the interior, along with many inserted thirteenth- and fourteenth-century cross-slabs. The exterior west wall has two uneven buttresses; that on the north is larger, and rises higher than its southern counterpart. However, these buttresses have been formed from the scar stubs of the side walls belonging to a former west tower which had an original wall thickness of approximately 1.2 m (4 ft).

To the south-east of Ryal and Matfen, the larger village and parochial centre at **Stamfordham** sits astride the Corbridge to Belsay road. The settlement today is largely the product of the eighteenth century, with its rows of houses centred around the long green. The church of St Mary, however, is much earlier, and is set just to the west of the village at a point where the lands drops away markedly (Figure 63).

Stamfordham was a vicarage, normally held by a canon of Hexham, and made an annual payment of 50 marks to the Priory. In 1340 there was evidently a serious problem with Scottish incursions and other troubles, 'propter frequentes Scotorum incursus, [et] varia exactionum onera' and the payment was reduced by ten marks on the orders of Bishop de Bury (Hexham Charters, XLIII). The 'other troubles' continued, for in 1374 thieves broke into Walter the vicar's close and with their dogs chased and killed swine worth ten marks, 'urging on the dogs to bite them so that the swine died by the chasing and the bites of the dogs' (CPR, 48 Edward III: 1374–77, Pt ii, m.25d).

The building is chiefly of the thirteenth century, although there is some evidence in the south-west nave quoins for a Norman or late pre-Conquest date. A major restoration in 1848, under the architect Benjamin Ferrey, resulted in the aisle walls largely being rebuilt, but the majority of the remaining fabric is medieval. The plain west tower has walls 1.2 m (4 ft) in thickness, and is built of grey and yellow sandstone blocks in a robust fashion, with a pronounced batter to the base. Against the exterior west wall, a massive buttress rises in four stages to the level of the first floor. The ground floor is entered through a very low thirteenth-century arch, more like a doorway, perhaps a deliberate

Fig. 63. Exterior view of Stamfordham.

feature to restrict access similar to that at Bywell St Peter's. The chamber is lit by a deeply-splayed lancet window in the south wall, and a blocking in the west wall may be the arch of an earlier window. Access to the upper levels is by ladder, which leads to the dimly lit first stage and thence up to the belfry which is scarcely better illuminated. Structurally the tower would be well suited to serve as a defensible refuge and perhaps also a look-out point, offering fine views to the north and west.

Amidst wild and lonely countryside between the Hexham to Rothbury road and the Roman Dere Street, north of Colwell, lies the hamlet of **Thockring-ton**, now scarcely more than a farm and a church (Figure 64).

The church is positioned dramatically atop a sharp hillock, a position that, were this building a tower- or bastle-house, would unquestionably be regarded as defensible. Scattered around are the earthworks of the medieval village. The structure itself is simple, having its origins in the twelfth century as evidenced

Fig. 64. Thockrington, the small Norman church positioned on a knoll.

by the chancel-arch and by two tiny Norman windows on each side of the chancel. The east wall was rebuilt in the thirteenth century and two massive buttresses were erected at the corners, perhaps concealing evidence of a previous Norman apse. Much of the nave belongs to later rebuildings of c. 1769 and 1864, including the robust bellcote and heavy buttress on the west.

The interior has a tunnel-vaulted chancel with the upper portions of the Norman windows let in. Above this heavy stone vault is a low chamber, reached only through a small doorway high above the west side of the chancel-arch (Figure 65). Below the doorway is an offset cut into the wall which appears to have supported a floor or gallery projecting above the nave. As the western part of the building has largely been reconstructed it is now not possible to determine the original arrangements, but it is plausible that this upper chamber was designed as an emergency refuge, fireproof and difficult to reach, and may have a parallel in the similar, but larger, chamber at Warkworth.

An indenture of 1505 required that Sir Thomas Cartington and others of the parish should 'fynd an able prest on ther proper costes and expenses . . . to celebrate divine service in the church of Thokeryngton . . . and buyld a sufficient stone hous . . . for defence of the preste and ye fermer and ther guddes there for the tyme being aganest the Scottes and other adversaries . . . and uphold the same'. This was supposed to be built specifically outside the churchyard,

Fig. 65. Thockrington, interior looking east showing entrance to chamber above the vaulting of the chancel.

'... the said house sufficiently to be belded upon acres which is the prebendaris owne grounde without the church yard' (Hodgson 1897, 392). There is no evidence that this house was ever constructed.

The population of Thockrington was never large; just eighteen were eligible to pay tax in 1296, and the income from the parish was just £10, a mere 4 per cent of the annual sum that derived from Bamburgh or Holy Island (Lomas 1996a). This income was claimed by the Archbishops of York following the surrender of the parish, in the early thirteenth century, by Richard de Umfraville as a penalty for his misdemeanours against Hexham Priory and the archbishop. In consequence the building never grew in size. Refuge for the small number of inhabitants was probably provided by its rugged Norman design with a defensible upper chamber which met such exigencies as from time to time arose.

Fig. 66. Kirkwhelpington, exterior view of the tower.

Four miles north-east of Thockrington, **Kirkwhelpington** sits by the New-castle to Jedburgh road, its church centrally positioned within the village (Figure 66).

St Bartholomew's church is a long, thin building with a chancel, nave, south porch, and a sturdy west tower. Excavations have revealed that the building once had aisles and later medieval transepts (Salter 1997a), but these have long since been swept away by a series of restorations culminating in 1896. The side walls of the nave, porch, and the east end of the chancel have been renewed in part, although evidently using earlier masonry. Sections of the interior north wall are especially puzzling, having a complexity of archaeological evidence for alterations. The thirteenth-century south doorway survived the restora-tions and has slots to either side indicating the former presence of a heavy draw-bar. A deep check appears, cut into the earlier fabric, which may be a fourteenth-century strengthening of this entrance.

Fig. 67. Kirkwhelpington, showing the infilled tower-arch and restricted access (the doorway is a nineteenth-century replacement).

It is in the tower however that the soundest evidence for defence is to be found. Built of large blocks of yellow and grey stone, and surrounded by a series of remarkably massive buttresses, it gives a strong visual impression of robustness. The arch leading from the nave is ostensibly of the twelfth century, but its steeply pointed form suggests that it has been reconstructed at some subsequent date. This arch has been infilled with masonry, and although some of the material used consists of carved fragments, placed here in 1896, the main blocking is of medieval origin and has been done intentionally to restrict entry from the body of the church (Figure 67). A simple nineteenth-century doorway has been inserted through the wall, which probably replaced a similar sized, earlier opening. The ground floor is now lit by a Victorian two-light window in the south wall, and there is an earlier west doorway which, in the early nineteenth century, was 'half-buried in the earth . . . its upper part used as a window' (Hodgson 1827, 203). Between the ground and first floors a massive stone tunnel vault, of fourteenth- or fifteenth-century date, pitched east-west, cuts across the earlier opening of the tower-arch. A quarter-round stair-turret has been constructed in the south-east angle which is also an addition to the earlier tower, and is probably contemporary with the vault. The spiral stair leads to a spacious first floor approximately 4 m (13 ft) square, which has a rough stone floor and walls of 1.1 m (3 ft 7 in.) in thickness. The narrow opening from the stair-turret has evidence of a door which could be locked from the interior, and there are further steps, of irregular construction, from here to the first floor proper. The chamber is poorly lit with just two narrow splayed windows in the north and west walls. The stair continues upwards to the roof, but at a height of 2.5 m (8 ft) above the first floor there is a blocked doorway which obviously once led to another chamber with a wooden floor, the support slots for which still remain in the tower walls at this height. From this second-floor room a small opening once gave a view down into the nave through its west wall.

Kirkwhelpington has the classic form of a secure west tower with bulky, heavily-buttressed, exterior walls, restricted ingress from the nave, a defensible stairway, fireproof ground and first floors, and an upper chamber giving a view down into the body of the church.

A little way beyond the church is the vicarage. Although largely of the eighteenth century it contains the vestiges of an earlier tower-house, no doubt the same 'little toure, the mansyon of the vycaredge' recorded c. 1541 (Frontier I, 214).

Two miles to the north-east, the church at **Cambo** was rebuilt in 1842, with a tower and vestry added in 1883–4. It is positioned high above the road on the edge of a steep bank, but the building which it replaced lay to the east of the village, and was down to its foundations in 1795 when the last vestiges were removed in order to construct a barn (Hodgson 1827). This building was formerly a chapel-of-ease in the parish of Hartburn. Defensive precautions were as much a necessity here as anywhere in the district, as witnessed by the nearby three-storey bastle-house later converted to the village post office. A little to the north, the remains of a chapel were still visible in the early nineteenth century at Hartington Hall, on Kirkhill.

The church of St Wilfred at **Kirkharle** lies close to the road, south of Kirkwhelpington. It is a simple building of nave and chancel with a west porch and vestry, and has seen two major restorations, the first in 1771–8 and the second in 1884. The medieval fabric is largely of the fourteenth century, dated by the surviving unrestored windows in the north wall of the chancel, and two low-side windows in the side walls. However, the west wall has been rebuilt, probably closer to the east, and the church appears to have lost the west part of the nave and possibly a tower.

Further to the south, **East Shaftoe** and **Belsay** once had dependent chapels of which there are now no remains. At Belsay there is a defensible tower,

Fig. 68. Ponteland, the south porch from above.

part of a larger fortified house, that belonged to the de Middleton family, and which has survived in an unusually good state of preservation; it is deemed to be one of the finest Border towers. The first record of this castle is in the survey of 1415, but on the exterior is an armorial stone which is recorded as having carried the arms of Middleton impaling Strivelyn and which dates from *c.* 1371 (Cathcart King 1983, 327). The building had rooms on three principal storeys above which are battlements and machicolations. At first-floor level, a small chamber in the south-west angle, reached from the main stairway, is generally thought to have been a chapel (Johnson 1984).

Ponteland is the last major settlement along the road before Newcastle-upon-Tyne and was of some strategic importance as a crossing point on the River Pont, the surrounding land being largely undrained marsh until the early nineteenth century. In 1244 a treaty of peace was negotiated between the Scottish King Alexander II, who brought his army here, and Henry III who was residing in nearby Newcastle (Bates 1895).

Much of the ground around Ponteland is low-lying but the old village core is built on Pont Island, an area of slightly higher ground. The church is large and of several periods, beginning with Norman work in the sturdy west

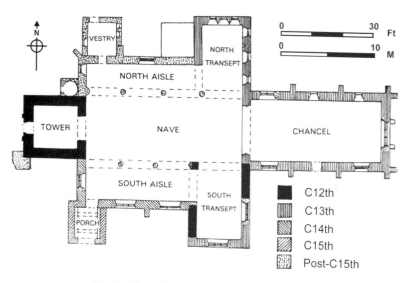

Fig. 69. Plan of Ponteland (after Salter 1997a).

tower, sections of the south transept, and parts of the side walls of a contemporary aisleless nave. The chancel and north transept are almost entirely of the thirteenth century, the *ex-situ* south porch is late thirteenth or early fourteenth century, and the south aisle and uppermost stage of the tower belong to the mid- to late fourteenth century. Restorations of 1810, 1861, and 1880 have resulted in many interior alterations and the remodelling of the north aisle.

The south porch has a pointed stone tunnel vault, supported by three heavy transverse ribs, and was probably rebuilt when the south aisle was re-cast during the later fourteenth or early fifteenth century. It is positioned oddly at the south-west angle, resulting in the doorway being offset relative to the side walls and putting the entrance hard against the west wall of the aisle (Figure 68). Whilst the purpose of this arrangement was most probably to allow two windows to fit in the south aisle wall, it would also have provided a more secure entrance, as an angle-opening of this type is more easily defended from within (Figure 69).

The west tower is substantial, measuring approximately 4.6 by 4.9m (15 by 16ft) internally. Access to the spacious upper levels was by ladder. At the second stage, a large rectangular window formerly opened eastwards into the upper part of the nave.

Immediately to the west of the church, the Blackbird Inn incorporates the remains of a fourteenth-century fortified house, with a tunnel-vaulted ground floor, substantial draw-bar socket, and a murder hole above the lobby. It therefore seems unlikely that the church, built even more substantially, would not be used for the same defensible purpose as need dictated. In August 1388 the

Scottish army led by James, Earl of Douglas, attacked and captured the castle at Ponteland, burning it along with the rest of the town (Froissart, iii). This same army went on to camp at Otterburn where the English army led by Percy attacked and was defeated (*see* page 121). In 1552, defence of the area was still a very serious business: 'the watch to be kept at the Water of Pont with 2 men nightly of the inhabitors of Hecallerton and Blakecallertone: Setters and searchers of these 2 watches William Foster and Rauff Collingwood' (Nicholson 1705, 194).

That the church was capable of being used defensibly is borne out by an account of the church preserved in the Merton College archives, written sometime between 1292 and 1302. The letter details how, in 1286, on the death of Master Robert of Driffield, Rector of Ponteland, 'David Deverel . . . entered by force the said church, prebends, and the rector's house, and held the church with an armed band like a castle' (Hope Dodds 1926, 412). Although the purpose of this act was essentially a political dispute over patronage, it demonstrates the effective use of the church as a secure refuge.

A short distance to the south-west of the church are the old rectory, and the vicarage of 1860. In the grounds of the latter stand the ruins of a defensible tower, most probably a vicar's pele. The structure is of three storeys and dates from the late thirteenth or early fourteenth century when it formed part of a cross-wing. This was later heightened into a tower, probably in the sixteenth century, evidenced by the fabric. In the 1415 survey there is listed a '*Turris de Ponteland*', belonging to the '*vicar eiusdem*' (Hodgson 1820, 30; Bates 1891).

To the north-west of Ponteland, the church of 1869 at **Milbourne** has replaced the chapel-of-ease which was in existence by 1202.

North of Ponteland, the former medieval village of **Ogle** is now visible only as earthworks in the fields to the west of the castle, and the church has long since disappeared. The castle, which has been considerably restored, was licensed in 1341, and still has parts of its original double moat.

A short distance from Ogle is the village of **Whalton**, with its church located below the village, on the south side. The building consists of a nave with north and south aisles, and south porch, a chancel with north chapel, and a west tower. The body of the church dates almost entirely from the thirteenth century, representing an extensive phase of rebuilding, but which left some earlier work: the twelfth-century west respond of the north aisle, and the late pre-Conquest west tower.

The southern entrance to the nave has been protected by a heavy draw-bar, the deep slot for which still remains in the wall. Entry to the tower appears to have been unrestricted through the tall eleventh-century arch, but the upper levels could be approached only by ladder. The first floor, 5 m (16 ft) above the ground, was unlit by any external opening whilst the second and belfry levels are only dimly lit by narrow windows. The uppermost parts of the tower were restored in 1783 and the body of the church was largely refenestrated at the same time (Hodgson 1827).

Fig. 70. Exterior view of Bolam.

On the east side of the lane running down to the church is the old rectory which incorporates the remains of a defensible tower, probably a vicar's pele. In the west wing are two stone-vaulted chambers with a mural stair, dating from the fourteenth or fifteenth centuries, which became part of a larger house during the following hundred years (Pevsner *et al* 1992).

Two and a half miles north-west of Whalton is the scattered settlement of **Bolam.** The church of St Andrew is located to the north-east of the nineteenth-century hall and parkland (Figure 70). The tall west tower, with the exception of the later parapet, is clearly of Anglo-Saxon workmanship, with twin bell openings at two-thirds of its height, and single lancets in the uppermost stage, three having triangular heads. There is further evidence of the pre-Conquest church in the west quoins of the nave and parts of the south side wall, now cut by later arcades (Taylor and Taylor 1965, 78–9; Briggs 1982). The tower-arch is late Norman in style, and this period is also represented in the construction of the north wall of the nave and the west part of the chancel. The remainder of the building belongs mainly to the thirteenth century, with the exception of the Victorian vestry added onto the north-west corner.

The tower, in common with other pre-Conquest church towers in Northumberland, has no stair, the upper levels being reached by ladder. In all likelihood this was as much a constructional expediency as it was a design for security. However, at some period the arch between the nave and the tower appears to have been blocked: an entry in the Bolam Vestry Book for 24 September 1792 records that it was resolved that the arch in the belfry should be opened out, that it be lofted above, the floor flagged, and two windows introduced. Although there are no further details to explain the nature of the work to the (partially) blocked arch, it may well have involved the removal of a feature similar to that found at nearby Kirkwhelpington, the purpose of which was to prevent easy access into the tower which could thus be used as a refuge. Alternatively, it is entirely possible that this blocking was of more recent origin, and was undertaken simply to create a separate space for a room such as a vestry or office. It is also worth observing that the top of the tower is the highest point for some considerable distance around, and although no specific mention is made in documentary sources, this would have been an excellent vantage for the watch or for a beacon.

The village of Bolam was once larger and more prosperous than it appears today. Edward I gave a grant of a market and fair, and in 1305 the town had a church, a castle, and two rows of about 200 houses separated by a green (Tomlinson 1888, 268). In the early fourteenth century half the barony came into the possession of the Reymes family who held the nearby fortified tower at Shortflatt.

The church of St John at **Meldon**, positioned on a knoll at the highest point in the parish, is a single-celled building with nave and chancel under one roof. The date is a uniform early thirteenth century, except for a small vestry which was added onto the north side in 1849.

In 1310 a dispute arose between the priors of Durham and Lanercost, the latter claiming Meldon to be a dependent chapelry of nearby Mitford. The patronage of Durham was proved and the church declared to be an independent parish (Lan.Cart., A8, A9; Donnelly 1988).

There are no features in the present building, nor indications in documentary sources that this building was ever used or intended as a refuge. Close by the church, in a field to the south-east, is the site of a small tower-house belonging to Nicholas Heron, mentioned in the 1415 survey (Rowland 1994). The tower also included a barmkin and other buildings which, no doubt, served to protect the villagers in times of danger.

To the north-west of Meldon, lying on the main thoroughfare between Morpeth and Cambo, is the village of **Hartburn**. Its church, dedicated to St Andrew, sits on the top of a steep bank which falls away to the Hart Burn below (Figure 71). The building is large and consists of a nave with north and south aisles and contemporary south porch, an aisleless chancel, and a robust west tower. The earliest portions are the east quoins of the nave which are characteristically pre-Conquest, but the majority of the fabric dates from the thirteenth century. The lower portion of the tower is late Norman, the upper levels are thirteenth century and include a massive plain parapet and project-

Fig. 71. Exterior view of the west tower at Hartburn.

ing corbel table. The setback buttresses are an addition of the fifteenth century. Internally, there are indications that the south doorway was protected by a draw-bar, the slot for which is now filled. The interior stonework has been variously repaired and the north wall of the chancel was rebuilt in the early nineteenth century. There is no sign that there has ever been a north doorway, and some of the masonry in the north aisle wall is of considerable proportions; several blocks measure up to 0.62 m by 0.37 m (2 ft by 1 ft 3 in.) in size.

The defensible characteristics of this church are found principally in the tower. Like its neighbours at Kirkwhelpington and Bolam, Hartburn also has a tower-arch which has been deliberately blocked, doubtless for the purpose of restricting entry into the tower itself (Figure 72). The archaeology of this feature is far from straightforward, for the arch of c. 1200 is clearly an insertion into an earlier wall as it cuts a round-headed, high-level doorway. Into the blocking has been inserted a window, possibly at a much later period, in order

Fig. 72. Hartburn, showing infilled tower-arch with inserted window and restored door-way.

to provide extra light into the room which has become the present vestry. This may be the window referred to in the Vestry Book of 1755 when the 'Vestry window' was repaired and enlarged (Donnelly 1988, 22).

The ground floor of the tower is entered through a narrow doorway whose head and jambs are of Victorian date, matching the characteristics of the rebuilt north wall to the chancel, and therefore probably dating from the restoration of c. 1832. Major work was also carried out in 1889–92 when the plaster was removed. The infilling wall is 1.32 m (4 ft 4 in.) in thickness and is composed of large blocks of stone, similar to the surrounding walls. The entrance passage is heavily plastered, which obscures evidence of any earlier features, and leads into a chamber with a stone-vaulted ceiling, pitched north to south. In the west wall, a window has been inserted during the fifteenth century, evidently to provide extra light into this dark area; its cill is 2 m (6 ft 7 in.) above the present exterior ground level. In the south-west corner is a disused fireplace which has a stone flue cut through the vaulting into the higher levels.

The upper floors of the tower are reached by a spiral stair, set into the thickness of the north-west angle. Entry to this stair is through a narrow doorway in the north wall, unusually set slightly to the east so that the base of the

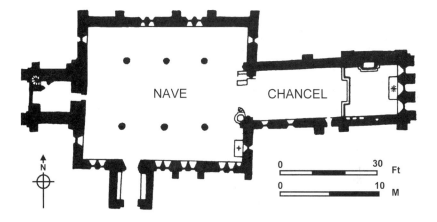

Fig. 73. Plan of Hartburn showing the restricted access to the tower and the offset entrance to the stair.

stair proper is reached through a small passage, 1 m (3 ft) in length and 0.45 m (1 ft 6 in.) in width, and which is offset from the doorway at a sharp angle (Figure 73). The underside of the stair has been deliberately blocked in order to form this passage. Against the wall, above the third and fourth steps, are the remains of a masonry construction and a blocked vertical section of stone-work, both of which align with a cut-out in the central newel, indicating that there has been another doorway or contrivance to impede access at this point (Figure 74).

There have been two upper levels in the tower. The first floor was formed on top of the stone vault, above which is a doorway leading to a second-floor chamber, now destroyed. Both doorways leading off the spiral stair have heavy checks and evidence of hinges and locks. However they appear to have been locked from the exterior and this may be a post-medieval feature. There are four large belfry windows at first-floor level, although all have been blocked with masonry except the south, and replaced by lancet openings at higher level. In the east wall, a small window has been created in the blocking of the door-way, visible from the nave. In common with other defensible church towers, this gave occupants of the upper levels of the tower a view directly into the body of the church below. The stair continues upwards to the parapet.

The old rectory is another example of a secure vicars' pele. Although the present house appears to be eighteenth century in form, the style of construc-tion suggests a sixteenth-century date for the core fabric, and the lower north wing incorporates stone tunnel vaulting of an earlier building.

Amongst the tree-lined banks of the River Font, three miles north, the tiny church of **Netherwitton** was formerly a dependent chapelry in the parish of Hartburn. The building was extensively remodelled in the eighteenth century, and again in 1881 and 1886–7, leaving little of its medieval form intact. The

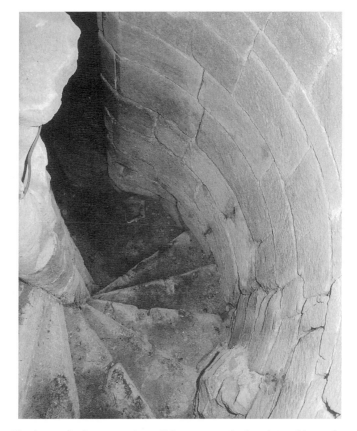

Fig. 74. Hartburn, the lower portion of the tower stair showing evidence for a feature to restrict access.

chancel however retains some of its fabric from the fifteenth century, and has a contemporary east window with a cill 3 m (9 ft 10 in.) above ground level.

Downstream towards Morpeth, the village of **Mitford** stands where the River Font meets the River Wansbeck. Here, overlooked by the Norman castle, and surrounded by trees, the church nestles in a loop of the river where it was established by the Bertram lords when they cleared the earlier settlement to make way for their new fortress (McCord and Thompson 1998). In 1307, Edward I granted the church to Lanercost Priory in Cumbria, on account of the serious hardships the monks there had suffered at the hands of the Scots (Lan.Cart., 248).

The church of St Mary Magdalene has a complex and chequered history. There are remnants of the twelfth-century building in the south aisle arcade, the entrance to the north transept, and in the priest's door in the south wall of the chancel. The core of the nave and chancel belongs to the thirteenth century and the transepts to the fourteenth. The west end of the nave, the porch, and the whole of the tower were built in 1870 when the building was extended westwards. Prior to this time there was a plain west front, itself a truncation of a previously longer nave, containing a single lancet window, above which rose a gabled, double bellcote (Hodgson 1832). The lancet windows of the chancel are all positioned well above the ground, approximately 3 m (9 ft 10 in.) to the cills, and the north wall of the nave has three similar windows.

Being juxtaposed with the castle, the church shared many of its misfortunes. In 1216, King John took the castle from Roger Bertram, who had opposed him in the Northern Revolt. Local legend has it that the villagers took refuge in the church which was then burnt by John's troops. An army composed mainly of foreign mercenaries would certainly have been capable of such an act, many atrocities being recorded during this campaign (Poole 1954). A year later, Alexander II made a retaliatory raid into Northumberland and unsuccessfully besieged the castle, undoubtedly wreaking damage on the church at the same time. During the fourteenth century the castle was again attacked, and this time it was reportedly wholly burnt (Rowland 1994). Such burning may well have extended to the church, as reddening of the stonework on the north side of the chancel shows where this area was set alight. The castle was finally put out of use between 1318 and 1323 when it was occupied by the Scots.

Within the bailey of the castle, on the edge of a later quarry, is a fragment of a late twelfth-century chapel. This represents the private chapel of the Bertrams, positioned within the defensible enclosure of the castle walls, thus providing a safer place of worship than the parish church. Mitford also had a medieval hospital, the site of which is on a hill to the north of the bridge over the Font.

North of Mitford there is a large area devoid of churches, and the only one between here and Brinkburn is at **Longhorsley**. The present church started life as the village school in the mid-nineteenth century but was converted to its current use when its forerunner fell into disrepair. The old church lies isolated in a field by the Paxtondean Burn, to the south-east of the village. It is now in a ruinous condition and dates entirely from 1783 and 1798, having replaced its medieval predecessor on the same site. A Norman arch and piers were noted as having been in the original building (Hodgson 1832).

Horsley Tower, nearby, is a strong, early sixteenth-century tower-house with a vaulted ground floor and stone spiral stair. During the late eighteenth and early nineteenth centuries the third floor was used as a Roman Catholic chapel.

MORPETH AND THE COAST

The coastal plain of the Middle March stretches down from Alnmouth to Whitley Bay where it becomes absorbed into the spreading conurbation of Newcastle

Fig. 75. Warkworth town and castle looking south from the church tower.

and Tynemouth. The area has a strong industrial history, and in the nineteenth and twentieth centuries coal mining dominated the southern part, resulting in the rapid expansion of towns and villages. Morpeth is the principal settlement but Ashington, Bedlington, Blyth, Longbenton, and Woodhorn also feature prominently in the landscape. In the north, Warkworth and its major castle oversee the locality, and the influence of medieval architecture is still strong.

Two and a half miles south of Alnwick is the village of **Shilbottle**. Its cruciform church, rebuilt in 1884 by William Hicks, replaces an earlier Norman building, traces of which may be seen in two blocked north nave windows, a re-used doorway, and the repositioned chancel-arch. The old church is shown in engravings of 1824 and 1870 (Wilson 1870) and had a nave and chancel with a tall western bell turret, and a south porch. Windows in the medieval building appear to have all been positioned high, the three in the south wall of the chancel being mere slits. Those in the nave had been redesigned in the Gothic style although a high central window on the south side may have been unrestored. The chancel had a priest's door (Hodgson 1899).

To the south-west of the church is a small defensible tower, once probably a vicar's pele, though not described as such in the 1415 survey when it was listed as belonging to the king's son, the Duke of Bedford (Hodgson 1820, 29; Bates 1891). The ground floor is tunnel-vaulted and some narrow splayed windows remain at basement level, but otherwise the building was comprehensively remodelled and extended in 1863.

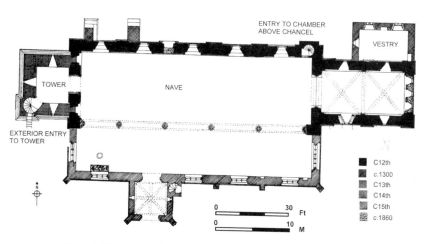

Fig. 76. Plan of Warkworth church (after W.H.Knowles, 1898).

South-east of Shilbottle, towards the coast, is the town of **Warkworth**, its major medieval castle dominating the surrounding area. The town is largely juxtaposed between the hilltop fortress and the parish church of St Laurence; the latter is positioned prominently in the lower part of the settlement (Figure 75). The River Coquet neatly surrounds Warkworth on all sides, and provided, in the time of the Troubles, a vital defensive barrier, allowing only two means of access: past the castle to the south, or over the fortified bridge, of *c.* 1380, to the north.

St Laurence's is a substantial building, and is the most complete Norman church in the English Middle March. The twelfth-century building had a long nave and a chancel, to which was added a west tower of *c.* 1200 with a four-teenth-century belfry and spire. Also added were a thirteenth-century north vestry, and a sixteenth-century south aisle (Figure 76). The only significant pieces of Victorian restoration were undertaken in 1860 when Ewan Christian rebuilt the east wall and blocked the priest's doorway. John Dobson also renewed the aisle window tracery and destroyed a fifteenth-century clerestory.

As a building capable of being defended against aggressive attack, Wark-worth has several virtues. In its twelfth-century form the nave had high win-dows, *c.* 4 m (13 ft) to the cills on the exterior (Figure 77), and there is evidence to suggest that these may have been shuttered inside. On the interior, the chan-cel is entirely rib-vaulted in stone, in a design clearly adapted from Durham Cathedral. Such vaulting is comparatively rare, and may have been introduced here for both aesthetic reasons and for security. The real security however comes, not under the vaulting, but above it. On the northern exterior of

Fig. 77. Warkworth, exterior of the twelfth-century north nave wall.

the junction between the nave and the chancel, a massive projecting buttress houses a tiny doorway, 0.55 m (1 ft 10 in.) in width, 1.17 m (3 ft 10 in.) high, and 1 m (3 ft) above ground level, which leads to a small spiral stair. A doorway has been created below this stair, opening directly into the east end of the nave. This was subsequently blocked with ashlar stone at an unknown period, but may have been the original entrance (it has a partially cut-away Norman head). It was closed up, possibly for reasons of added safety. The stair rises to an extremely narrow, stepped passage in the thickness of the wall above the chancel-arch which leads to a square hatch opening into a space above the chancel (Figure 78). Although long-disused, this space was evidently once a functional area, having a ledge at the level of the wall plate, probably to support a wooden floor above the uneven stone vaulting. By 1860 the roof of the chancel had become low-pitched, and a contemporary photograph shows that a doorway led into the former upper chamber where the present square hatch now exists.

At the opposite end of the church, the tower may also have been adapted with elements of defence in mind. Although the approach to the upper levels is conventional, by a spiral stair in the south-west angle, there are two doorways, one inside the ground floor of the tower, and the second positioned in

Fig. 78. Warkworth, stair-passage in the thickness of the nave east wall leading to a chamber above the chancel.

the exterior south wall of the stair-turret, 1.6 m (5 ft 3 in.) above ground level (Figure 79). The exterior doorway has been roughly cut through the masonry and is of diminutive proportions, 1.2 m (4 ft) high and 0.63 m (2 ft) wide. Below this second entrance, there is evidence that the stair has been reconstructed as the newel posts are of shorter sections than the main stairway above. Conjecturally therefore, the smaller, elevated, outside doorway may have been constructed to restrict access into the tower whilst the lower stairs were removed or in some way disabled. At some subsequent date the normal thoroughfare has been restored, and the stairs are now reached through the interior doorway from the ground level. The upper parts of the tower have had two thirteenth-century chambers, the uppermost now removed, leaving only traces in the walls where it once existed. The stair above is truncated where, in the fourteenth century, the present belfry and spire were added. At the level of the first floor the walls of the tower are 1.25 m (4 ft) in thickness, which confirms the robust appearance of this structure.

Fig. 79. Warkworth, external raised doorway giving access to the tower stair.

Warkworth has two further upper chambers. Above the south porch, entered from an exterior doorway and projecting stair on the east side, is a small room with an east window, and blocked west window. A south light was added in the nineteenth century. The porch below has a stone, rib-vaulted roof, and this upper chamber sits above the vaulting with a stone flagged floor. The present entrance cuts through the vault and has clearly been added at a subsequent period. The vestry to the north of the chancel has also had an upper floor, demonstrated by the small high-level windows. Although such two-storey vestries are not unknown, they are uncommon, and the construction here may have carried defensive overtones, or may have provided secure accommodation for a priest or anchorite, perhaps similar to that at Morpeth St Mary.

On 13 July 1173, the lives of the townsfolk were devastated by a violent Scottish attack, led by Duncan, Earl of Fife, acting for King William the Lion. It was an event which tested the church as a safe refuge, and the inhabitants took shelter within the walls. On this occasion the use of the building proved flawed, the priests were assaulted and all others were put to death, some 300 in total, although it is unclear whether all were sheltering within the church at the time (Fantosme, 1700). In the following year the castle was again sacked, but nothing is said of the church. Better precautions may have been put in place, and there is no further mention of the church being used for such a communal retreat, despite the fact that the town and castle came under attack by the Scots several times during the next three centuries (McNamee 1997; Brown 1998). These precautions most likely benefited the clergy who had suffered in the original assault of 1173. In 1567 the building housed the manorial court hearings, although it was apparently unfit for such a purpose (Hodgson 1899). The Troubles were far from over however, as Scottish and English reivers appear to have been in the area during the autumn of 1597, 'to the very sea syde at and about Warkworth' (CBP, ii, 380).

The castle probably afforded the ordinary townsfolk their best chance of refuge during times of danger. Originally constructed as a Norman motte and bailey, it was strengthened in the twelfth century by the addition of a curtain wall, and buildings were added throughout the medieval period. Within the outer ward, just west of the gate tower, was the chapel. In its present form it is a simple rectangular block, rebuilt in the early fourteenth century and later divided into two storeys at the west end. The castle is most unusual in having, as well as the normal chapel, a separate church within its walls. It seems to have been the aim of the first Earl Percy to found a college of secular canons within the castle, and for this purpose a new church was planned, extending right across the northern part of the outer ward. The foundations for this building were put in place during the early fifteenth century, and it was intended to build a nave with side aisles of four bays, a central tower, transepts, and a chancel of either two or three bays. Below were cellars, perhaps intended to form a treasury or other secure area (Honeyman and Hunter Blair 1990). However, the church was probably never completed, and no evidence for its upper parts now remains.

In the vicinity were four other ecclesiastical establishments. Close by the church, on the east side, once stood a small Benedictine chapel, probably belonging to the prior and convent of Durham, which by 1616 was in ruins (Hodgson 1899). Just outside the town, to the south, was the chapel of St Mary Magdalen, also pertaining to Durham, which was founded in the early part of the thirteenth century. There was also a hospital, extant in the thirteenth century, ownership of which passed to Hulne Priory (Knowles and Hadcock 1971), and whose walls probably stood until the end of the eighteenth century. Whilst there are now no remains of these buildings, the fourth has survived virtually intact, and takes the form of a small hermitage on the north bank of the Coquet.

Warkworth hermitage was created in the fourteenth century and originally consisted of three chambers, cut out of a protruding section of cliff above the river. The only practicable means of access was by boat from the opposite bank. Living accommodation was added later, adjacent to the chapel and sacristy, which included a kitchen with an oven, a hall with a fireplace, and a solar above the hall. The chapel was dedicated to the Holy Trinity and first appears on record in 1487 when Thomas Barker, who had been appointed chaplain by the fourth Earl of Northumberland, at an annual stipend of 66s. 8d., made a payment for grazing privileges. It was apparently out of use by 1567. The doorways bear evidence of locks, and at the base of the cliff are signs that a rough wall once enclosed the frontage to the complex, perhaps for the purpose of keeping livestock. By 1531, the duties were restricted to a single requiem mass each week, and were combined with the chaplaincy to the Earl of Northumberland. It seems highly unlikely therefore that this chaplain, one George Lancastre, would have been resident in the hermitage at this time (Hodgson 1899).

Owing to its relative inaccessibility, the hermitage was probably reasonably safe from raids and military activity, and can properly be regarded as a safe sanctuary, although it was clearly never designed to protect more than its single occupant.

At the mouth of the River Coquet is the fishing village of **Amble**, which increased in prosperity when a harbour was constructed in the early 1840s to serve the flourishing coal trade. The present church was built in 1870 to cater for the increased population. Although there was no previous church here, a

Fig. 80. Coquet Island, the lighthouse of 1841 built above a defensible tower.

fragment of a wall containing a fifteenth-century window exists on the north side of High Street, which represents the remains of the manor-house belonging to the Priory of Tynemouth. This building may also have housed a small monastic cell (Hodgson 1899; Pevsner *et al* 1992), and a chapel probably existed as late as 1765 (Wilson 1870).

A mile out to sea, east of Amble, lies **Coquet Island**, a roughly flat, wind-swept rock. On its west side is the prominent tower of the lighthouse, completed in 1841, and built on top of an earlier defensible tower which formed part of an ecclesiastical establishment dependent on Tynemouth Priory (Figure 80). The religious buildings appear to have been a chapel, a two-storey domestic range, and a strong tower to the south of this range, which may have been linked to it by a bridge. The chapel has now largely disappeared, having been replaced by a lighthouse-keeper's cottage, although this building incorporates parts of the medieval structure. Sufficient evidence remains to show that the chapel had a west gallery and a first-floor sacristy or safe-room, which was reached via a turret at the north-west angle, and whose upper door was secured by a heavy draw-bar. The tower and domestic buildings were incorporated with the lighthouse and its ancillary structures in 1840–1. The domestic range has a tunnel-vaulted undercroft, over walls 1m (3ft 3in.) in thickness, and a blocked spiral stair. The small three-storey tower also has a stone-vaulted ground floor, no doubt for reasons of security.

There are indications that the island contained a monastic cell in the pre-Conquest period (Morris 1989). In 1415 the tower of 'Coketeland' is recorded as being a place of strength, and belonging to the Prior of Tynemouth (Hodgson 1820, 30). After the Reformation the island was given to the Earl of Warwick, and became a haven for law-breakers; an examination of 1569 recorded that coin forgers had been at work here (Hodgson 1899). During the Civil War, the Royalists had a garrison of 200 on the island with seven guns; it was captured by the Scots in 1645.

Inland from the coast and upstream along the River Coquet, are the ruins of the chapelry of **Brainshaugh** or **Guyzance** which lie on flat land alongside a meander in the river. The church has been 18.6m (61ft) in length by 4.8m (15ft 9in.) in width. Although the north and west walls survive to some height, there is little evidence to assist with dating the structure. The style of the masonry indicates a late eleventh- or early twelfth-century date. The north wall is entirely devoid of window openings, but a fragment of a twelfth- or early thirteenth-century west light remains. A circular pier of a former two-bay arcade exists on the south side, along with the base of the east respond. Beyond lie the fragmentary ruins of the chancel, which appears to have been rebuilt in the fourteenth century. A priest's doorway in the south wall remains intact, and has low draw-bar slots and locks; on its east side is the base of a fourteenth-century window. To the north is a blocked doorway with a roughly pointed head of uncertain date. There are indications of the foundations of other buildings within the churchyard.

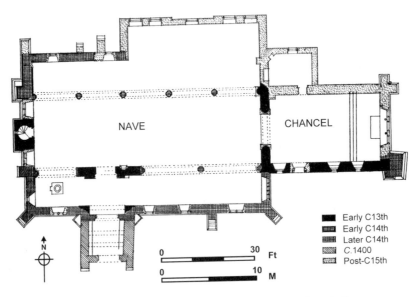

Fig. 81. Plan of Felton church (after W.H.Knowles, 1898).

The establishment had monastic origins, as the chapel of nuns of 'Gysyns' was founded by Richard, son of Gisbert Tison, the first lord of Alnwick, and subsequently given to the canons of Alnwick around 1147 (Hodgson 1899). The last record of a prioress was in 1313, and it is probable that the foundation became depopulated at the Black Death, being occupied afterwards by two canons of Alnwick (Knowles and Hadcock 1971). The chapel was dependent on the parish of Shilbottle, although it was generally regarded as extra-parochial. Despite the removal, at or shortly before the Reformation, of the endowments which supported a Master and Fellow, the building continued in use for occasional services until the end of the eighteenth century.

There is no record of the building coming under attack, or suffering from Scottish raids. However, the heavy, blank north wall and secure south doorway indicate precautionary traits which are typical of Border churches, and the siting of the foundation, within a tight loop of the river, may also be a measure of security.

In 1595, the nearby village was able to provide five men for the general defence of the area, of which three had weapons, including a petronel (CBP, ii, 169). Previous musters in the century had provided similar numbers.

Two and a half miles south-west of Guyzance is the village of **Felton**, with its once strategically important bridge across the Coquet. The church of St Michael is situated above and to the west of the settlement, on the north side of the river. The building has a heavy appearance, with its bulky west wall and low-pitched nave roof, and consists of a nave with narrow north and south

Fig. 82. Felton, the stone-vaulted porch of *c.* 1400.

aisles, south porch, a chancel and vestries, and a heavy central buttress supporting a bell turret.

The construction is multiphase and complex. The second arch in the south
arcade from the west is the site of a late twelfth-century south doorway leading
into a porch, the latter being encapsulated within the later aisle in such a way
that the present south doorway contains part of the original porch entrance.
The south, west, and north walls of the nave were built in the fourteenth
century, and the porch was rebuilt *c.* 1400. However, the centre of the west
wall, including the turret and the greater part of the chancel, belong to the
thirteenth century, as does the chapel in the south-west corner of the south
aisle which existed either as a chapel or the base of an unfinished tower, prior
to the construction of the aisle. Alterations were made in the middle of the
nineteenth century when the north aisle was extended. A vestry was built in
1870, and further restoration took place in 1884 (Figure 81).

The walls are not of great thickness and vary between 0.6 (2 ft) and 0.9 m
(3 ft), but are nevertheless constructed in a robust fashion, with numerous buttresses. The approach on the south side is protected by a heavy, low porch,
which has a stone flagged roof and rib-vaulted interior (Figure 82); there is
evidence in the fabric to show that the outer entrance formerly carried doors

or a gate. A former north doorway into the nave has been partially blocked
by a buttress. The western central buttress contains a narrow spiral stair which
leads onto the roof of the nave, and is capped by a sixteenth- or seventeenth-
century bellcote. However, the stairs have clearly once continued higher and
this structure may be part of a former tower, now lost. The thirteenth-century
portions of the building have narrow external openings or, as in the north wall
of the chancel, no windows at all (although a disturbed area of the external
fabric at high level may represent the blocking of a former window). The south
door to the chancel has been blocked at an unknown date prior to the mid-
nineteenth century.

As early as *c.* 1199 the church and its possessions were given by William Bertram II to Brinkburn Priory (Hodgson 1904), though little now remains in the
fabric of the building from this time. In 1302, the barons, knights, good men,
and whole commonality of Northumberland met at Felton, most probably
in the church, in the presence of Walter, Bishop of Coventry and Lichfield.
They entered into an agreement to meet at Wark on the Thursday after Christmas, to make an expedition into Scotland to prevent the Scots from doing
harm, and to recover such castles as were under seige (CPR, 31 Edward I: 1301–7,
m.44).

A small dependent chapel formerly existed in **Cawsey Park** ('de Calceto'
in historical records), on the road south towards Morpeth, all traces of which
have now disappeared (Hodgson 1904).

Westward from Felton, the road leads to the wide inlet of Druridge Bay at
High Chibburn. At nearby **West Chevington**, the site of a medieval chapel,
previously marked only by a large mound and a pile of dressed stones, has
recently been excavated.

A little to the north of the road, and now accessible only by footpath, are
the remains of a preceptory of St John of Jerusalem at **Low Chibburn**. The
earliest mention of the Knights Hospitallers here is in 1313, and the next record,
25 years later, reports that their number was 11 (Pevsner *et al* 1992).

The building visible today represents the remains of the chapel to this preceptory, and dates mainly from the fourteenth century, although during restoration work in the 1990s, some loose architectural fragments were identified
as dating from the twelfth century (Rushton 1996). The east and south walls
stand to some height, although the structure has been converted into two storeys and a domestic, cross-passage west range added, probably in the mid-sixteenth century, when Sir John Widdrington acquired the site (Figure 83). The
windows of the upper floor were projected on corbels, perhaps as a defensive
aid. Other buildings, now vanished, may have included a hospice and accommodation for the Order. A defensible courtyard, with a barmkin, was added,
probably during the seventeenth century, and in the Second World War, a pill-
box was inserted into the chapel. Surrounding the whole is a medieval defensive moat, partially destroyed by opencast mining activities in the twentieth
century.

Fig. 83. Low Chibburn, the converted chapel from the exterior.

This structure is untypical of the usual parish church, as it was served, not by an appointed parish priest, but by a dedicated religious body of knights. In the fourteenth century, and founded by a military order, it is not surprising that the site was made defensible, nor, given its vulnerable location, close to the sea, that these precautions were maintained and even strengthened when the building fell into domestic use in later years. The Knights Hospitallers evidently took security seriously at their establishments, as gatehouses and walls are known at Temple Bruer and Aslackby in Lincolnshire, and at Quenington Court in Gloucestershire.

Chibburn is located in the parish of **Widdrington**. The church of the Holy Trinity stands a little to the south of the village, on a slight rise above the road. The building has no tower, and comprises a short nave with side aisles, and a chancel with flanking north and south chapels. The south and east walls, the porch, and the northern return wall of the chancel date from the fourteenth century (although the south nave doorway is thirteenth-century, *ex situ*). The west wall of the nave is earlier, and, excluding the window, it is of the twelfth century, contemporary with the two bay north arcade. The remainder of the church on the north side belongs to a rebuilding of the late nineteenth century.

There are no indications that Widdrington church was used defensibly, but close by was a very strong tower, the *Castrum de Wodryngton* built by Gerald de Widdrington who received a licence to crenellate in 1341 (Bates 1891; Cathcart King 1983, 355). The tower was demolished in 1777 (Bates 1895, 173).

The two villages to the south of Widdrington, **Ulgham** midway along the Morpeth road, and **Creswell** on the coast, both have Victorian churches. That at Ulgham has replaced an earlier building which had Norman origins, whilst Creswell's church was newly built in the early nineteenth century. Both villages had strong secular buildings: the manor-house at Ulgham is positioned immediately to the south of the church, and at Creswell a medieval tower-house with a tunnel-vaulted ground floor lies on the east side of the village.

Further down the coast is the large village of **Newbiggin-by-the-Sea**, which had achieved the status of a borough by the beginning of the fourteenth century (Lomas 1996), and had a thriving port supporting considerable foreign trade (Fraser 1968). During the early part of the Anglo-Scottish wars, the port was used for the storage of supplies, and was asked to provide ships for the king's navy (Hodgson 1835; McNamee 1997). The church, originally a chapel-of-ease to Woodhorn, stands on the rocky headland known as Newbiggin Point, above the bay and to the east of the settlement, where it forms an imposing landmark, conspicuous for several miles (Figure 84).

Although its position may be due in part to a pre-Conquest origin, the present fabric dates mainly from the thirteenth and early fourteenth centuries. The medieval work includes most of the chancel, the aisle arcades, and the small unbuttressed west tower. The remainder was heavily restored in 1845 and 1898 after years of neglect, and in the early years of the twentieth century the north aisle was rebuilt.

The body of the church has no evidence of defensive precautions, and in any case it has been too heavily altered for any such features to have survived. However, the west tower, despite its diminutive size, appears to have served as a secure refuge, possibly for the parish priest alone. The evidence points to a fourteenth-century alteration of the earlier tower as the pointed tower-arch was subsequently blocked up when a stone tunnel vault was inserted behind. A very low, chamfered doorway was created within the blocking, measuring 1.4 m (4 ft 7 in.) in height by 0.7 m (2 ft 4 in.) in width and which was secured by a strong door, the deep draw-bar slot for which still remains on the interior (west) side, 1 m (3 ft 3 in.) in depth.

The ground floor of the tower is lower than the nave, making the east side of the blocking doorway taller than the west. At the original period of construction this room was provided with a west doorway, but this too was closed up, probably at the same time as the vault was inserted, in order to create a defensible space.

The inserted vault established a secure upper-floor area to which entry was gained from a rough stone stair, which penetrates the vault at the south-east corner, cuts across the former tower-arch, and ends at first-floor level with its

Fig. 84. Newbiggin-by-the-Sea, exterior of the tower.

own stone-vaulted ceiling. This stair has a strange feature in that it terminates abruptly, without leaving any space for a proper door fitting, but leaves a vertical slot over the stairway between the vaulted roof and the original tower side wall (Figure 85). It has been conjectured that this slot, which could be reached from above the level of the stair, may have served as a form of machicolation for defence (Briggs 1998).

The first-floor chamber is formed directly on top of the stone vault and has a rough, uneven finish, although when in use it may have been levelled by sand, earth, or plaster. There are two deep recesses in the north and south walls, which represent the blocking of the side windows, each measuring 1.15 m (3 ft 9 in.) in height, which may have been created for storage in addition to added security. The interior dimensions of the room are minuscule, measuring only 2.7 m (8 ft 10 in.) east to west, by 2.5 m (8 ft 2 in.) north to south.

Fig. 85. Newbiggin-by-the-Sea, top of the stair in the first-floor tower chamber, formed above the inserted vault.

Access to the second level was by ladder, this probably having been the original first floor when the tower was constructed in the thirteenth century. This chamber probably also functioned as occupational space when the tower was in use as a retreat, and the windows to the north and south have been blocked to form recesses, leaving only a square opening on the west side to provide light. In the east wall a blocked doorway once opened out over the tower-arch into the space above the nave. The bells are positioned at high level, just below the springing of the spire.

Newbiggin did not escape the attentions of marauders. Piracy was rife along the coast (Tough 1928), and as late as 1597 there is a record of the Scots raiding East and West Newbiggin, carrying away fifteen head of cattle and five nags and mares (CBP, ii, 803).

The settlements in this area were largely subsumed in the nineteenth and twentieth centuries into an industrial landscape, where mining dominated and produced large communities such as those at Ashington, Ellington, and Lynemouth. However, a short distance from Newbiggin the much smaller village of **Woodhorn**, lying in the midst of this landscape, has preserved a little of its pre-industrial character.

The pre-Conquest church at Woodhorn is preserved in the side walls of the nave where two single-splayed windows may be seen to have been cut away by the westernmost arch of each Norman arcade. The most likely date for the windows, and hence these walls, is the early eleventh century (Taylor and Taylor 1965, 682). Much of the remainder of the building is of the twelfth century including two bays of the arcades and the base of the tower. In the thirteenth century the aisles were extended eastwards, transepts added, and a new chancel constructed. However, much of the medieval church has now been radically restored or destroyed: the chancel was rebuilt entirely in 1842–3, as were the upper portions of the tower, and the exterior was heavily refaced. Prior to the rebuilding of the chancel, the east wall contained three narrow lancets, and the south wall a further two smaller windows, one perpendicular style opening, and a round-headed doorway towards the west. All these windows were placed high above the ground, and a further two tiny openings in the east wall of the south nave aisle were at even greater height (Hodgson 1832).

Although there is no direct evidence for defence dating from the period of the Troubles, the construction of the surviving lower parts of the Norman tower hint at an earlier attempt to make some provision for security. The stairway is placed in the thickness of the wall, with a very narrow entrance from the nave, to the south of the tower-arch, measuring only 0.55 m (1 ft 10 in.) in width by 1.7 m (5 ft 7 in.) in height. There are no ground-floor windows in the north or south walls, and probably only a minimal light in the west wall prior to the restoration. The narrow stair terminates at first-floor level without a doorway, but with a large block of masonry abutting the stairhead, a feature which in part reflects that at nearby Newbiggin, and which may originally have served a similar purpose. The large chamber is now windowless, there being only one narrow deeply-splayed light in the north wall, long-since blocked. The east wall retains much of its original Norman masonry, including a closed-up doorway at the level of the second floor, again echoing that seen at Newbiggin.

A sketch made in 1842 shows a lofty tower of robust appearance, apparently windowless apart from narrow belfry openings, and with a high-pitched roof. An earlier drawing published by Hodgson (1832, 184) also shows this roof and hints at a plain, but deep parapet (Figure 86). However, there is a reference in 1764 to 'repairs to the battlements', implying that the head of the tower may once have been crenellated (McGuinness 1986, 8).

Woodhorn village, like its neighbours, was severely damaged by Scottish raiding, and it appears to have been abandoned for a while at the end of the thirteenth century as the income from the manorial court in 1298–99 is recorded as nil (McNamee 1990, 47).

Fig. 86. Woodhorn, exterior from the south-east before restoration (after Hodgson 1832).

Bothal lies midway between Woodhorn and Morpeth. The church is located at the higher end of the village and below a steep hill. Nearby, on a prominence overlooking the River Wansbeck, is the fourteenth-century castle founded by the Bertram family.

St Andrew's church belongs mainly to the thirteenth and fourteenth centuries, and has a nave with flanking aisles, a chancel, and a Victorian south porch. Despite a restoration in 1887 when the east end of the chancel was rebuilt, the building has survived largely intact from the medieval period, but the west bellcote may be post-Reformation. Although many of the windows are between 2 m and 4 m (6 ft 6 in. and 13 ft) above ground level, there are no obvious signs of defence or security, and the walls are unusually thin, around 0.7 m (2 ft 4 in.). The immediate proximity of the castle is likely to have offered the villagers a more attractive, and certainly more secure, refuge than the parish church.

A little way to the north of Morpeth is the village of **Hebron**. Its small two-celled church is positioned slightly to the north of the village, and was heavily restored in 1793 when much of its medieval character was lost. The walls of the twelfth-century chancel and a fifteenth-century chancel-arch have survived, but too little is left to determine the overall medieval character.

Morpeth is situated in a wide loop of the River Wansbeck. It was a vital bridging point, its town defended by a strong medieval castle and its road controlled by a tollbooth, the fifteenth-century tower of which still remains in the centre of Oldgate. Despite its strong position and defences, the settlement was vulnerable to attack, and nightly watches against incursions by the Scots were established in September 1552 (Hodgson 1832, 511).

There were two medieval churches: the parish church of St Mary, which

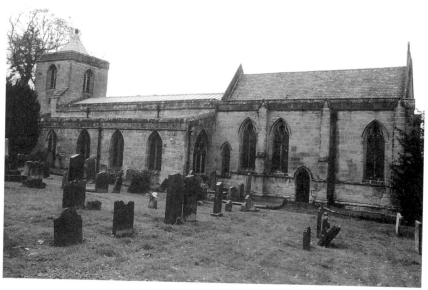

Fig. 87. Morpeth St Mary's, exterior view.

stands in an elevated position, well away from the centre, south of the river and the castle, and the chantry chapel of All Saints at the east end of Bridge Street.

St Mary's belongs, in its present form, almost entirely to the fourteenth century (Figure 87). There are a few thirteenth-century remains, including the side walls of the originally aisleless nave, but the greater part of the church was rebuilt between 1300 and 1350. In addition to the nave, aisles, and chancel, there is a medieval south porch, a low west tower, and a two-storeyed vestry, or sacristy, to the north of the chancel.

Defensive measures abound in this building, and that is perhaps not surprising given its location, as it was an obvious target for the more ambitious Scottish raids, and a certain target in war. The major recasting of the building occurred at precisely the time of greatest danger to the English Borders, during the first Scottish War of Independence, and it is likely that security was an integral part of the design.

The south entrance into the nave is defended by a contemporary robust oak door which was secured by a substantial draw-bar, the slot for which is still in use. The present porch is most probably of the sixteenth century.

The vestry to the north of the chancel, although of contemporary date, may at one time have been free standing. The evidence for this is mainly within the west wall, which has an originally external window now looking along the north aisle which may have been extended to meet this building. There is a butt-joint at the point where the aisle meets the vestry which helps to reinforce this argument. It is possible that this two-storeyed structure was intended to provide living accommodation and a defensible refuge for the priests serving the church.

It is the tower, however, which gives the best indication of defence. The ground floor is stone-vaulted, octopartite, split with diagonal and transverse ribs. Within the north wall is a spiral stair, protected by a stout, original, planked door which has formerly had a sizeable lock. The stair leads to the first-floor chamber where it terminates. This room has once had a substantial door, rebated on the interior and this too had a significant lock. The floor is covered by stone flags, each approximately 0.3 m (1 ft) square, and is of high quality. A comparison may be made with the first-floor chamber of the tower at Newton Arlosh in the English West March. It is evident that this room was intended to be occupied, although the lack of a fireplace indicates that such occupation was probably of short duration. In the east wall a deeply splayed window opens out at high level above the tower-arch, giving a comprehensive view from the chamber into the body of the church (Figure 88).

Raiding certainly took place this far south in the March, and there are accounts of forays reaching Morpeth as late as 1558 when the townsfolk were

Fig. 88. Morpeth St Mary's, interior of the tower first-floor chamber showing stone floor and splayed window looking into the body of the church.

duped into believing that a Scottish army was approaching (Watson 1974). However, the security precautions built into St Mary's probably originated after Bannockburn. Two tax collectors in Morpeth recorded that when the king was retreating from Stirling with his army, his followers were terrified and sought refuge in towns, castles, and forts (McNamee 1997). Edward Bruce and Thomas Randolph led the Scottish army down to Newburn via Morpeth shortly afterwards, wreaking destruction, stealing cattle, and carrying off prisoners *en route*.

Morpeth's other medieval chapel is the bridge chantry of **All Saints**. Now converted into a museum and gallery, the building is thought to have been founded by Richard of Morpeth prior to 1300 (Hodgson 1832). A substantial restoration in 1738 altered the medieval interior and has also changed the south and east sides of the building. In its present form it is impossible to determine if it was used as a secure refuge, but given its highly vulnerable location, on the north side of the river by the bridge, some defensive precautions would be highly likely.

The site of the Cistercian abbey of **Newminster** is located half a mile to the west of the town. Founded in the late 1130s, it was practically demolished at the time of the Reformation, and even as early as John Leland's visit it was spoken of in the past tense: 'A qwartar of a mile owt of the towne on the hithere syde of Wanspeke was Newe Minster abbay of White Monks, plesaunt with watar and very fayre wood about it' (Leland, ix, fo.144). The hasty demolition (and, no doubt, pillaging for building stone) was probably the result of the last abbot's resistance against Henry VIII, an action which led to his being made a 'terrible example to others' (Hexham Memorials, cl). However, unlike the contemporary resistance made at Hexham Priory, there is no evidence that the buildings of Newminster were defended or garrisoned by armed men.

Almost nothing now remains of the abbey, apart from the overgrown lower walls of the abbot's house and infirmary buildings, some architectural fragments, and the reconstructed doorway to the chapter house. The plan is known from excavation and appears to have taken the usual form for a Cistercian monastery. Little is revealed concerning the buildings in documentary sources, although it is recorded that there was a gatehouse (Newminster Chart., 55a). The abbey, in common with the castle and the parish church, was sited to the south of the river, this undoubtedly helping to provide a defensible barrier against unwelcome visitors from the north. Such visitors certainly came, as in 1330 the abbot and convent reckoned their losses at the hands of the Scots to be £20,000 since the time of Edward I, and they petitioned the king for a pardon on money which they owed (Nor.Pet., 172). Three years later, a further petition, this time for alms, indicates that Edward II had previously maintained the abbot and certain of his monks in the safety of a castle for several years on account of the war (Nor.Pet., 180).

Five miles south-east of Morpeth is the large village of **Bedlington**, standing just above the wooded valley of the River Blyth. Like the majority of churches

Fig. 89. Bedlington, exterior of church *c.* 1832 (after Hodgson 1832).

in this heavily industrialized area to the north of Newcastle, St Cuthbert's Bedlington has been radically altered from its medieval form during the last three centuries. The nave and tunnel-vaulted south chapel are essentially medieval, dating from the twelfth and fourteenth centuries respectively, though with seventeenth-century alterations. The main entrance to the church is through the south side of this chapel. The chancel was rebuilt, apart from the original Norman arch, in the eighteenth century, and again in 1868 when the Norman tower was also demolished and replaced by the present structure. Finally, a wide north aisle was added in 1911–12, replacing its medieval predecessor. In its present, heavily modified form, there is no evidence that this building was used defensively, unless the tunnel vaulting in the south chapel was constructed in an attempt to create a more secure entry point into the building. However, a drawing published by Hodgson (1832, 352) shows the west tower with business-like merlons in its crenellation, untypical of a decorated form (Figure 89).

To the south-west of Bedlington, lying on the former Great North Road, is **Stannington**. Here once stood an important medieval parish church, which was rebuilt in 1871 after it had fallen into dereliction. The only remains of the earlier building are in the re-used north arcade which dates from the thirteenth century, though this has been heavily restored. Prior to its demolition, the tower appears to have been tall and plain, with massive quoins and simple single-light belfry openings with large cills (Hodgson 1832, 279) all of which suggest that it may have been pre-Conquest in date. West of Stannington, at **Herford Bridge**, no traces now remain of the church and hospital, which were in ruins in the late eighteenth century, nor of the former chapels at **Shotton** and **Plessey**.

The Victorian church at **Horton** stands alone in an elevated position, on the site of its medieval predecessor, and still retains some twelfth-century decorative work in the reset tympanum over the south doorway. The original building was a towerless chapel with a north aisle, and was a chapel within the parish of Woodhorn, although it was transferred to Tynemouth Priory by Bishop Kirkham in the early 1250s (Craster 1909). The Scottish invasion of 1340 resulted in considerable damage to the area and tax relief was allowed on account of the losses incurred (CPR, 18 Edward III: 1343–5, Pt ii, m.22d).

Between Horton and Whitley Bay is Seaton Delaval. The parish church at **Seaton** lies a little way to the east of the village, adjacent to the hall, and was originally a private manorial chapel to the Delaval family. The original build-ing was Norman, consisting of a nave, chancel, and probably an apsidal sanctu-ary, similar to the plan found at Old Bewick. The walls are 0.65 m (2 ft 2 in.) thick and, in the exterior north wall, two blocked windows appear to be of Saxo-Norman design. In the second quarter of the fourteenth century a longer, square-ended sanctuary was constructed and a new window inserted; this later window was renewed in the nineteenth century and the old tracery inserted over the door in the porch. This porch was added in 1895 to the west end of the building, covering the twelfth-century doorway which has a weathered, carved tympanum. Internally, both the chancel and the sanctuary have simple north-south tunnel vaults, clearly contemporary with the Norman arches, whilst the nave has an eighteenth-century plaster ceiling.

The earliest mention of the church is in a charter dated 1174, in which Bishop Pudsey confirmed the list of churches and chapels in the gift of Tyne-mouth priory, and includes Seaton Delaval. In the early years of the seven-teenth century Sir Ralph Delaval had 'repayred the chappell, built new the west end of it, slated it, put up the steeple new, glased it, plaistered it all over without and within, new hewed the pillars and arches, and new stalled and seated it all, and hung up two bells in it' (Craster 1909, 189). There is no evi-dence that this church ever had any features pertaining to defence, although the stone vaulting may be a standard twelfth-century precaution against fire in this vulnerable, coastal position.

Although distant from the Border, the parish did suffer from Scottish attack, as the value of land holdings, recorded in the *Inquisitions Post Mortem*, reduced considerably in the years between 1258 and 1483. In the early sixteenth century, Sir John Delaval actively supported the king with £100 annually and the provi-sion of fifty horsemen, and also served with the Warden (Hodgson 1897).

Adjacent to the church is the hall. The present building of 1718–29 was designed by Sir John Vanbrugh. However, in 1415 there is reference to a defen-sible tower in this location (Bates 1891), and in 1549 the beacon on Seaton tower-head formed part of the early warning system in the event of an invasion (Craster 1909).

On the coast to the south-east of Seaton is a tidal rock now known as **St Mary's Isle**. There was once a small chapel here, dedicated to St Helen, and which was still in use for burials in 1680, as recorded in the Earsdon parish reg-isters. It was entirely destroyed when the lighthouse was constructed in 1898.

Further south is the village of **Earsdon**, now on the outermost tip of the conurbation that forms Whitley Bay and Tynemouth. There was a chapel here before 1250 when the vicar of the mother church was called upon to provide a chaplain and clerk for Earsdon. From sketches made prior to 1837, and from records of the Archdeacons' Visitations, the building is shown to have been a simple structure comprising nave and chancel without tower or aisles, and with west and south porches. A post-Reformation belfry was added to the west end, and the windows were altered, probably in the seventeenth century. This chapel was pulled down in 1837 and a new church built in the same year, designed by John and Benjamin Green.

Longbenton was a major parish during the medieval period but its church was rebuilt in 1790, and considerably modified during the nineteenth century. Some re-used medieval masonry appears to survive in the chancel which was rebuilt in 1855, completing the demise of the early building.

At the termination of the River Tyne, eight miles east of Newcastle city centre, is **Tynemouth**. Built on a commanding limestone promontory, with three of its four sides guarded by the sea, this is an unusually strong location and is naturally defensible. The priory is positioned to take the full advantage of the site. On the north and east sides cliffs fall almost vertically to the sea, and the slope to the south is very steep, making the buildings on the plateau almost impregnable, and approachable only from the west. The present structures are the successors to earlier settlement here. The headland was occupied by an early Christian monastery, sacked by the Danes in 800, and finally destroyed in 875. The priory offers a rare glimpse in Britain of what is commonplace in parts of continental Europe, a prime example of an *ecclesia incastellata* on a grand scale, and is unique in English chancery enrolments, being treated by the Crown as a fortress for defence against the Scots (Coulson 1982; Bonde 1994).

From the outset, the priory appears to have been intentionally fortified, as much a castle as it was a monastery; indeed it was often referred to as Tynemouth Castle. Robert de Mowbray, Earl of Northumberland, refounded the monastery in 1085 as a dependency of St Alban's Abbey, and building had commenced by 1090. The Laud Chronicle records that only five years later King William II besieged and took the castle at Tynemouth (ASC (E), 1095); this is the first occasion on which the place is recorded as being a fortified position. In 1296 Edward I granted the prior and convent a formal licence to crenellate, to surround their monastery with a wall of stone and lime, and to hold it without let or hindrance on the part of the king or his officers (CPR, 24 Edward I: 1292–1301, m.8). So useful was this place to the king, that he exempted the prior from rendering military service, except for the maintenance of his own defences (Knowles 1910).

Surrounding the whole site was a continuous wall with towers, but much has now been lost; on the south side to quarrying and erosion, and on the north to later rebuilding. At the north-west angle of the defences are the remains of

Fig. 90. Tynemouth Priory and castle in the eighteenth century.

the Whitley Tower, originally more than three storeys high. Other towers and defences along the curtain wall have now disappeared, such as the 'tower in the madder garth' mentioned in a survey of 1577 and which was probably the tower depicted in an eighteenth-century illustration (Figure 90). It was located at the south-west angle of the south court, and had heavily corbelled machicolations (Craster 1907).

The plan of the priory commences with the gatehouse at the west end of the peninsula (Figures 91 and 92). The foremost structure is a barbican which has a tunnel-vaulted entrance flanked by guardroom. Beyond this was a high-walled, open area and a drawbridge crossing the now filled-in ditch. A portcullis controlled entry into the first zone. Another tunnel-vaulted arch led into the gatehouse proper, then through another open area, defended by projecting machicolation slots, before meeting a final gateway (Figure 93). A hall and solar lay above the gatehouse, and a kitchen wing extended to the south. The broad arrangement of barbican and gatehouse can be identified in the early fourteenth-century work at Alnwick castle.

Beyond the gatehouse, an outer court led directly to the priory church which had an aisled nave, central tower, transepts, and a short chancel with

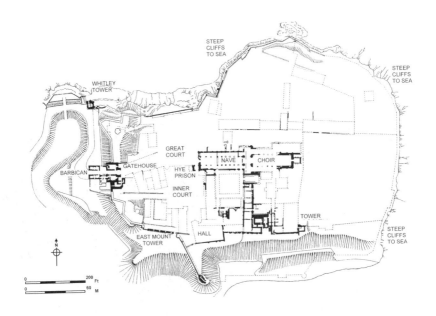

Fig. 91. Plan of Tynemouth Priory.

Fig. 92. Tynemouth Priory, the gatehouse from the south-west.

Fig. 93. Tynemouth Priory, machicolation slots on the east side of the gatehouse.

radiating chapels, on the far side of which was a presbytery. To the north of the presbytery lay the Lady Chapel, and to the east, still intact, is the fifteenth-century Percy Chantry, restored in 1852. The body of the church belongs mainly to the twelfth century but the presbytery was constructed around 1200, and the west end was added in the mid-thirteenth century.

The church itself, the nave of which served for parochial purposes, probably needed no separate defensive measures, as the gatehouse and walls of the castle provided sufficient protection. However, in the fourteenth century, a tower with massive foundations was constructed just west of the church, on the south side, and probably linked to it at high level (Figure 94). The purpose of this structure is unclear, but in the sixteenth century it was referred to as the 'Hye Prison' (Saunders 1993). About the same time as the west tower was built, a chamber was added above the vault of the presbytery and choir, akin to that found at Brinkburn Priory. This upper room was probably made for storing valuables (Oman 1979) as ingress was very restricted along the inter-mural passages, but it may additionally have served as an emergency retreat in case the outer defences of the castle were breached. There was also a room above the south choir aisle, which contained a fireplace, and which was prob-

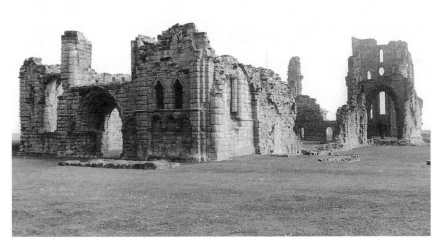

Fig. 94. Tynemouth Priory church from the south-west, showing the foundations of the 'Hye Prison'.

ably constructed in the fifteenth century (Hadcock 1936). This room may have served as an extension to the cloisters, for the purpose of private study.

To the south of the church lay the claustral buildings, little of which now remain. The plan indicates a conventional arrangement of chapter house, refectory, dormitory, warming house, and west storage range around a central cloister. Further to the south were the prior's lodgings, private chapel, and the 'New Hall'; the last most likely provided accommodation for guests (*see* Figure 91).

The defences of the priory were put to the test during William Wallace's campaign of 1297, just one year after permission had been given to build fortifications. On learning of the Scottish invasion, the prior ordered that all houses built against the defensible wall should be burnt down in preparation for the assault (McNamee 1990, 54). In the event no attack took place. Wallace perhaps considered that the strength of the place was too great, especially given that he had no siege equipment with him (Paterson 1996, 20).

According to the terms of the licence granted by Edward I, the prior and convent were to hold and defend their monastery under their own terms of office. However, in the reign of Edward II, consent was obtained from the prior to put John de Haustede in charge, on behalf of the Crown, and a writ of aid was granted 'for repelling the Scots' (CPR, 11 Edward II: 1317–21, Pt ii, m.17). In Prior de Tewing's office, between 1315 and 1340, a garrison of eighty armed men was maintained, despite an attempt in 1322 by the Warden to arrest forty-one of these, the action being disallowed by the king (Craster 1907). Such a garrison was clearly needed, as in 1315 the Scottish army had advanced to the walls of the castle, and a couple of years later, Gilbert de Middleton, an English rebel, besieged the monks. Both incidents failed to breach the defences.

In 1346, Ralph de Neville tried to use the priory as a royal fortress but was thwarted by Prior Thomas de la Mare who restored the original terms of fortification, and obtained from the king letters of protection and injunctions against the March Wardens from staying in the priory or stealing from it. Edward III considered Tynemouth to be one of the strongest fortresses in the Marches and dissuaded Rome from unduly appropriating revenues which were otherwise needed to maintain the garrison.

Despite the efforts made by earlier monarchs and priors, by 1390 the defences were in a poor state, with the gatehouse in ruins and the best part of the seaward-facing walls destroyed. Richard II gave £500 towards the repairs, which included the building of the present gatehouse. Even apart from monetary gifts such as this, the priory could, for the most part, well afford to undertake repairs and new building, as it was one of the wealthier establishments in the region, having much land, tithes, and the proceeds of local coal deposits.

In January 1539, Prior Blakeney and his monks surrendered the monastery to the king. In 1544 the Earl of Hertford, whilst preparing for his infamous invasion of Scotland, realised the importance of Tynemouth, and in the following year converted the former priory into a royal fortress. The parish church was reported as being in use for a powder store in 1558. In 1583/4 there were ten pieces of ordnance in the castle, but little shot or powder, and the walls were beginning to fall into ruin, and ten years later this had reduced to two sakers, one dismounted; three falcons, dismounted; a cast iron culverin, and a demi-culverin (CBP, i, 957). In January 1596, Richard Musgrove wrote to Lord Burghley, the queen's principal advisor, stating 'it is most needful that the ordnance at Tynemouth Castle should be mounted and placed, for the defence of the castle and haven' (CBP, ii, 467); clearly the place had become significant in the defence of the Tyne estuary but little was being done to put this into effect. By the end of the century the situation had grown worse, and in 1599, the Bishop of Durham wrote 'Tynemouth castle, a promontory in the mouth of the haven seven miles off [Newcastle], utterly disfurnished; no blockhouse or other piece or platform for defence on the river between that and Newcastle' (CBP, ii, 1041). The castle was again garrisoned in 1640, this time by the Scots during the Civil War, and ownership kept changing until it was finally taken by parliamentary troops under Sir Arthur Heselrig. Military occupation of this strategic site continued until 1960 (Saunders 1993).

THE SOUTH TYNE VALLEY

At the extreme western edge of Northumberland is the small village of **Gilsland**, sitting astride the Poltross Burn which divides it between the English West March and the English Middle March. Close by, the remains of the

Roman Wall further divide the settlement. Although technically the village is in Northumberland, the present church, which dates from 1852, lies just inside Cumbria.

The 'Gilsland Gap', a pass about four miles in length, allowed easy passage between the two administrative zones, and provided the main communication route between Newcastle in the east and Carlisle in the west; although by the 1370s there is evidence to suggest that the road had become so dangerous that dealings between the two towns had seriously diminished (Summerson 1992). Because of the strategic nature of the place, its inhabitants suffered very heavily during the Troubles, and it is not surprising therefore that no trace of the medieval church now remains.

As early as 1256 the monks of Lanercost Priory were granted leave to carry bows and arrows on the roads and paths through the barony of Gilsland, presumably for personal defence as they were not permitted to injure the wild beasts of the forest (Lan.Cart., 201). The village of Gilsland itself, and the surrounding area, were hit hard by Scottish raiding, and there are numerous accounts relating to such forays (Chr.Lan., 212, 228, 277, 325; Barrow 1988; MacDonald Fraser 1989); every tenant in the barony was required to keep a hound for protection (Watson 1974, 138). The authorities did little to help the inhabitants and by the late sixteenth century both Gilsland and Bewcastle were described as 'places . . . ill governed by their officers' (CBP, ii, 613).

Along the Newcastle road to the east lies **Haltwhistle**, a larger village than Gilsland but which suffered no less from the frequent raiding which took place in this dangerous area, and especially so during times of war. In 1311, Robert Bruce's first major raid into England used the 'Gap' and resulted in the burning of the town and the kidnapping of the vicar, Robert de Pykwell (Barrett and Watson, n.d.; Paterson 1996). Despite its precarious position, medieval Haltwhistle flourished, and in 1307 a regular market was founded, this being combined with three-day fairs every May and December (Robson 1989). However, as late as 1601 the village was still being attacked and buildings set alight (CBP, ii, 1378).

The parish church is positioned on a slope at the west end of the village and slightly below it, and comprises a nave with north and south aisles, chancel, and a nineteenth-century vestry. The period of construction is almost entirely of the thirteenth century, but with a major restoration of 1870 when the windows in the aisles, which had already been changed in the eighteenth century, were removed and replaced by the present lancets. In the chancel where the original medieval windows survive, they are positioned 2m (6ft 7in.) to the cills above ground and, conjecturally, like Lanercost Priory, may have been deliberately retained to prevent easy ingress. Surprisingly, for such a vulnerable church, there is no other evidence of defence in the building.

Despite the lack of evidence for the use of the church as a defensible structure, there were plenty of other buildings capable of such use. On Castle Hill was an early fortification, and there were other towers and bastles in the village

(Cathcart King 1983). One of these may have been the old vicarage, now heavily restored, which stands at the south-east corner of the churchyard.

Upstream, and south of Haltwhistle once stood a small nunnery at **Lambley**. All that now remains are a few architectural fragments in and around Lambley Farm. The religious establishment was, in common with all others in the Border region, a legitimate target for Scottish raiding. In the major campaign of 1296 it was reported as being destroyed (Chr.Lan., 174), and in 1321, Archbishop Melton granted an indulgence to the '*monasterii Sancti Patricii de Lambeley*' on account of '*hostilis Scotorum incusrus consumpsit*' (Hexham Memorials, XLIV). The church, situated to the south of the village, dates from 1885, but replaces an earlier single-celled structure, which, curiously, had a Scottish curate between 1577 and 1583 (Hodgson 1840).

On the south bank of the Tyne, opposite the village of Bardon Mill, is the small late medieval church of **Beltingham**, formerly a chapel-of-ease to Haltwhistle. The plan is very simple: a single rectangular chamber of nave and chancel, with a Victorian vestry added to the north side, which has a stone tiled roof. The earliest architectural style appears to indicate a date of *c.* 1500, but by 1650 the building was reportedly ruinous, and between this date and the end of the seventeenth century much of the western part of the church was rebuilt (Salter 1997a). In 1884 a further major restoration took place and the vestry, built at this time, appears to have replaced an earlier chapel or sacristy, as a medieval squint into this area from the body of the church still exists.

There are no surviving indications of defensive adaptation of this church, although its position, on an elevated spur above the Beltingham Burn, and with the South Tyne to the north, gives a marked territorial advantage. Adjoining the churchyard is a bastle-house, altered in the eighteenth century, and a mile to the west at Willimoteswick is the medieval fortified manor of the Ridley family, now incorporated into a farmhouse. Edward III may have spent the night at Beltingham in 1327, whilst hunting for the Scottish army (Hodgson 1902).

Between Bardon Mill and Hexham lies **Haydon Bridge**, the major river crossing for the Newcastle road. Its church, dating from 1796 with later additions, is on the north bank, on land given by the Governors of Greenwich Hospital. The settlement here dates mainly from the eighteenth century and its medieval predecessor was located half a mile to the north, where part of **Haydon Old Church** still stands. The building today is a mere fragment of its antecedent and comprises the original twelfth-century chancel and a fourteenth-century south chapel, restored in 1882. The remainder was demolished and used as building material for the eighteenth-century church in the present village, but had additionally consisted of a west tower and nave with a south aisle. The roof is constructed of stone tiles in diminishing courses and this, combined with the rough, coursed blocks of stone and lack of openings on the north side (apart from a plain blocked doorway towards the east end), give the building a robust appearance. The position is dramatic: the church sits on a

small knoll, atop a hill overlooking the valley of the Tyne, and lying well above
it. No doubt this position was favoured by the original medieval villagers who
utilised it, in part, for purposes of security. It is interesting to note that the
church occupies the highest point within the former village area.

Like most of the South Tyne valley, Haydon Bridge was extremely vulnerable to raiding and consequent destruction of property. In 1587, 400 Scottish
horse came and 'tooke upp the towne and burnt dyvers howsys' (CBP, i, 556).
The population at this time, in terms of eligible fighting men resident in the
town, was put at 200 (CBP, i, 563).

The main road from here follows the southern edge of the river towards
Hexham, whilst on the north bank another road leads north-east towards
Chollerford. This second road passes through **Newbrough** where the present
church of 1866 replaced its predecessor of 1797, itself on the site of a medieval
foundation. In the mid-nineteenth century the church is depicted as a tall
building with a plain, almost windowless west tower, not unlike that of its
neighbour at Warden (Hodgson 1840). Edward I was forced to make a halt here
when he was taken ill in July 1306 (Bates 1895).

Sitting in the elbow formed between the rivers North and South Tyne, two
miles north-west of Hexham, is the hamlet of **Warden**. The church, dedicated
to St Michael, has obvious Anglo-Saxon origins, and is reputed to be the site of
an earlier oratory (Bede, v.2). The building has a tall unbuttressed west tower,
a wider aisleless nave with south porch, north and south transepts and a long
chancel.

The nave, except for the transepts, was rebuilt in 1765, at which time the
present belfry of the tower was also reconstructed. The transept arches are
nineteenth century, though on earlier jambs, and the transepts themselves
appear to date from the thirteenth century, and have typical lancet windows.
The chancel was rebuilt in 1889.

It is the tower which contains the most complete, and least restored, aspect
of the medieval building. Dating from the late pre-Conquest period, probably the second half of the eleventh century (Taylor and Taylor 1965, 632–4),
it is unusually plain, having no string courses and very few openings. The
approach from the nave is through a small contemporary arch, only 1.7 m
(5 ft 7 in.) in width and 2.1 m (7 ft) in height, and apparently utilising Roman
masonry. There is no evidence for the historic screening or blocking of this
arch to restrict ingress, a feature seen occasionally elsewhere, as in the pre-
Conquest towers at Bolam and Whittingham. The upper floors, of which the
original three below the belfry have been replaced by two, have always been
reached by ladder. The positions of the earlier floors may be seen in the internal fabric. Like other pre-Conquest and Norman towers in the Border region,
it is difficult to conjecture that it was built with defence in mind, although it
is hard not to conclude that this was intended, at least in part, given the basic
features of its design.

A short distance to the west of the church are the remains of a partial earthwork castle which utilises the edge of a low promontory, the natural slope, and a ditch, for defence.

On the west bank of the River North Tyne are the villages of Acomb and St John Lee. The latter has a church of 1818, rebuilt on the site of a medieval chapel, by John Dobson. The chancel was added in 1886. As early as 1310 the building was in a poor state of repair, the archbishop requiring faults to be put right (Hexham Charters, xxxiii, iii). It was here that the men of Hexhamshire and Tynedale met together in 1536 to resist the royal commissioners who had been sent to assess the value of Hexham Priory, 'being assemblyd at a place callyd Sanct John Ley, reght unto Hexham' (Hinds 1896, 51).

On the opposite bank of the river is the town of **Hexham**, a short distance downstream from the confluence of the North and South Tyne; the position of the large watercourse gave an obvious strategic advantage. There were two principal medieval churches in the town, the parish church of **St Mary** and the **Priory**. The former is now represented largely by the remains of the north nave arcade, embedded in later houses off Market Place. It is known that the thirteenth-century church was a large seven-bay rectangle, which replaced an earlier church having a tower surrounded by a porticus (Pevsner *et al* 1992). In 1878 one of the aisle arches was exposed and found to have been blocked since the medieval period; Hinds (1896, 204) conjectured that this was probably done for defensive purposes, though more likely the aisle was destroyed during a Scottish raid. Of a third church, founded before the Norman conquest, and dedicated to St Peter, nothing is known.

The first priory church in Hexham was built by Wilfrid *c.* 675, and was described as being built with deep foundations, having crypts of beautifully dressed stone, and with walls of remarkable height and length (Wilfrid, 22). Of the church built at this time, only the crypt now remains, though virtually intact. In 876 the Danes sacked the town and in all likelihood the ecclesiastical buildings above ground were destroyed. During the late eleventh century, Malcom III of Scotland attacked Northumberland but spared the monastery at Hexham (Hinds 1896). In 1113 the priory was refounded by Augustinian canons who rebuilt the church, created a nave with north aisle, and a chancel with an apsidal east end. The tower and transepts followed, completed in the thirteenth century, from which period most of the remaining claustral buildings date (Figure 95).

The plan is thus cruciform, with the core of the early building being contained largely under the nave, including the Anglo-Saxon crypt which sits just west of the crossing. Large transepts spring from beneath the low tower, each having a separate eastern aisle. The south transept contains the night stair which led from the former monastic dorter, and its southern bay is partitioned as a slype, with a rib-vaulted roof. Access from the west range, and probably the prior's lodgings, was possible along a mural passage in the west wall of the nave, now blocked. The upper chambers of the central tower are reached from a spiral stair in the south-west angle of the south transept, at the head of the

Fig. 95. Hexham Priory, exterior view of the tower and south transept.

former night stair, and then along the clerestory passage to a second spiral stair. An alternative route to the upper levels leads from another mural stair in the north transept. This arrangement, whilst somewhat convoluted, is not unusual in greater and monastic churches.

In the fourteenth century, two additions were made to the priory: a sacristy or chapel was built on the south side, and a range of five eastern chapels were constructed. These additions were probably made after 1336, as the buildings had suffered considerably during Scottish raids earlier in the century, and repairs to these would certainly have taken priority over new works (Cambridge and Williams 1995). The eastern chapels were demolished in July 1858.

The present building reflects the amount of damage which war and raiding inflicted on the priory in the centuries following its completion, through the necessity for periodic rebuilding (although neglect, following the Reformation, also played its part). The south and west walls of the nave are of the fifteenth century, though the west wall has been heavily restored. The entire east end of the chancel was rebuilt in 1858 by John Dobson using Whitby Abbey as a model, and the north aisle of the nave was reconstructed in 1907–8 by Temple Moore. The claustral buildings have fared worst of all; parts of the cloister, chapter house, warming house, lavatorium, and refectory are still visible but in a fragmentary and ruined form, or otherwise heavily restored. The west range survives better, but the upper parts were all rebuilt in the late eighteenth century, and again following a fire in 1819 which also destroyed the prior's house. A gateway of *c.* 1160 still exists to the north of the site, but with its former upper floor, once set on stone vaulting, removed. There was also a precinct wall which defined the boundary to the priory and which may have assisted with its protection.

The priory had huge land holdings, with scarcely a parish in the English Middle March where the prior and canons did not have an interest; in all, it amounted to over 8,100 hectares (20,000 acres)(BBH). This was a rich prize for the invading Scots, and the priory had the richest pickings of all.

In the eleventh century Malcom III had respected the monastic buildings and had allowed people to take refuge there. David I also permitted the right of sanctuary in the church when he invaded in 1137 (Hinds 1896). However, with the onset of the Wars of Independence attitudes changed dramatically.

The first serious attack on the priory occurred right at the start of the principal Troubles, in 1296, when some 200 boys were burnt alive in the grammar school (which was associated with the priory); the Scots apparently blocked the exits to prevent escape (Chr.Lan.,136; Hexham Annals, lxxxi). The church was severely damaged, and was gutted by fire from end to end, treasures were stolen, and relics were destroyed. The canons managed to escape on this occasion by running away. The following autumn, after three canons had returned to set up an oratory in the ruins, the Scots army led by Wallace returned and destroyed the priory again, although most accounts relate that Wallace himself wished no harm on the priory (Wright 1823; NcNamee 1990).

The next series of attacks took place in 1311, 1313, and 1315, when Robert Bruce invaded England and troops occupied the town. In the last incident the monastery was valiantly defended (Chr.Lan., 230–2), but the monks fled the area and sought refuge in Yorkshire and Nottinghamshire.

Such was the impact which these raids had on the priory (and other religious establishments in the region) that in 1342 Edward III authorised the arming of the 'sanctuary men at Hexham' (Hexham Annals, xcvi). This did little to help the monastery when, four years later, David II looted it and despoiled the town, using it for a supply dump in his campaign (Chr.Lan., 332; Paterson 1996). However, in the spring of 1351, a commission for peace between the two nations was held there. By the early years of the fifteenth century, the monks were complaining that their lands and goods were worth almost nothing owing to the destruction caused by the Scots, and in desperation they sought to arrange a private truce, only to result in condemnation and accusations of treason by the Archbishop of York (Neville 1998, 104–5).

The most significant incident involving the priory's use in a defensive role happened in September 1536, following the royal commissioners' valuation of the monastic holdings earlier in the year. In April, Archbishop Lee had written that 'there is never a house between Scotland and the Lordshippe of Hexham; and menn feare, if the monasterie goo downe, that in processe all shall be wast moche within the land. And what counfort that monasterie is daylie to the contre ther, and speciallie in tyme of warr' (L. & P. Henry VIII, x, 716), implying that the priory served either as a spiritual or physical refuge during periods of fighting, or perhaps as both. With the Reformation in full flow, and the monks' living about to be removed, anger and bitterness at the perceived injustice of this act following the usual heavy losses at the hands of the Scots, spilled over into direct action. On 28 September the commissioners heard that Hexham Priory had been garrisoned, and on riding to the town discovered that it was filled with armed men and that the gates and doors of the priory had been secured. They observed that the leads of the roofs and the tower were manned by twenty men 'in harness' (i.e. wearing armour), including the Master of Ovingham who carried a longbow (Hexham Annals, cxiii-cxxv). The rebellion was part of the 'Pilgrimage of Grace', a general reaction to the Reformation in the north of England, which was suppressed the following year by the Duke of Norfolk (Knowles 1959; Lomas 1992). The king wrote to Norfolk saying:

> as all thise troubles have ensued by the sollicitation and traitorous conspiracyes of the monkes and chanons of those parties; we desire and pray you, at your repaire to Salleye, Hexam, Newminster, Leonerdcoste, Saincte Agathe, and all suche other places as have made any maner of resistence, or in any wise conspired, or kept their houses with any force, sithens th'appointement at Dancastre, you shall without pitie or circumstance, nowe that our baner is displayed, cause all the monkes and chanons, that be in anywise faultie, to be tyed uppe, without further delaye or ceremony, to the terrible example of others; wherin we thinke you shall doo unto us highe service (Hexham Memorials, cl).

Of the twenty who made a stand on the roofs of the priory, only fourteen remained in Hexham afterwards, though most may have been spared execution (Lomas 1992).

That the priory building was considered to be of some strength is confirmed in Henry, Earl of Northumberland's letter to the king in September 1536. Following the armed takeover and consequent exclusion of the commissioners, the earl wrote complaining of this and reminding the king that the monastery had been promised to Richard Carnaby, 'thought it desirable for him to have a house of strength for the safeguard of the King's money' (L. & P. Henry VIII, xi, 449).

There is nothing in the present fabric to indicate that the priory church was in any way contrived or used for defence. The building itself, through its size and general construction, could have been utilised for this purpose, as indeed it was, briefly, during the sixteenth century, but no special adaptations appear to have been made. In all likelihood, a reliance on the security of a religious establishment, so badly undermined in the early fourteenth century, and its location within a large town, served to deter the majority of minor raiding and subsequent damage. However, Hexham was an important target during periods of war, and the damage inflicted on the buildings over the medieval period reflects this. Security was most likely obtained by routine strengthening of the claustral buildings, although too little remains now for confirmation. One final reminder of the priory's use for defence against the Scots survived until the mid-eighteenth century, as there was a 'Fray Bell' until 1742 when, along with the other bells, it was broken up (Wright 1823; Watson 1974).

To the south of the river, between Hexham and Corbridge, the castle and chapel at **Dilston** sit juxtaposed by the side of the Devil's Water. Dilston chapel is a complete example of an early seventeenth-century building with a rectangular nave and chancel under one roof, and a small tower on the southern half of the west wall, carrying a stair to a former gallery. A rib-vaulted undercroft lies beneath the eastern part. The chapel was built as a private manorial establishment for the Earls of Derwentwater who occupied the adjacent castle and hall.

The earliest reference to the chapel is in 1379 when one John Adamson was presented as chaplain (CPR, 2 Richard II: 1377–81, Pt ii, m.40), but of this building nothing further is known. The present structure has a marked secure appearance, having no windows close to ground level, with those on the south side all above 2m (6ft 7in.) to the cills and most of diminutive proportions (Figure 96); the robust west turret is virtually windowless. It is unlikely that defence was planned here, as the adjacent castle would be a safer retreat. However the design appears to reflect a secure architectural form in what were still relatively unstable times.

Corbridge, unlike its larger neighbour Hexham, is mostly situated on the north bank of the Tyne, due mainly to the small Roman settlement which once existed half a mile to the east. There is also the higher risk of flooding on the south side. In order to compensate for this positional disadvantage, the town was protected on the north by a ditch.

The church of St Andrew is located in the centre of the town, by the side of the market place, a short distance above the river. On plan the building clearly demonstrates its development from a pre-Conquest rectangular nave, a chancel, and a west tower, to the present form which has a large thirteenth-century chancel, a contemporary north nave aisle, later thirteenth-century north and south transepts and south aisle, and a north aisle in the chancel. In addition, there is a west bay to the north nave aisle, in the form of a northern extension to the ground floor of the tower. This appears to have served as a residence for the priest, or possibly as an anchorite's cell (Craster 1914). The Norman south doorway is *ex situ*, placed in a thirteenth-century wall and protected by

Fig. 96. Dilston chapel, exterior view.

a twentieth-century porch. Of the pre-Conquest building, the whole of the tower and parts of the nave walls survive, much of the masonry employing re-used Roman material. The tower is of two Anglo-Saxon periods, and started its life as a west porch of one or two storeys, probably in the eighth century. It was later raised to provide the present tower, most likely in the eleventh century (Taylor and Taylor 1965, 172–6). The belfry openings were altered in 1729 and the crenellated parapet replaces an earlier gabled cap (Pevsner *et al* 1992).

There is little direct evidence for the use of St Andrew's Corbridge as a defensible refuge. There are no heavy draw-bar slots or signs of locks or other means to prevent easy ingress, although the thirteenth-century lancet win-dows have generally been retained, the chancel being similar to Rothbury and Ovingham. The tower, like others in its class and period, is tall and thin, with its upper levels reached only by ladder, but this form has been retained from the eleventh century to the present day and no special safeguards are evident; there was also an earlier west entrance, now blocked (Parsons 1962). The only possible hint at extra security lies in a blocked upper doorway within the north wall of the tower base, which formerly led through to the residen-tial chamber previously mentioned, and which might have been designed to hinder easy access into this area, assuming that there was no entrance from the north nave aisle.

Fig. 97. Corbridge, the vicar's pele tower.

Corbridge, however, had certain need for security measures. In 1296, along with Hexham, Lambley, and Lanercost Priory in the English West March, it was attacked and burnt by the Scots (Ridpath 1848). The town was attacked again in 1311 and 1313 (Hexham Annals, xc). Probably as a direct result of these repeated incursions, a vicar's pele tower was constructed to the south, and in the grounds of, the parish church (Figure 97). The tower remains in a remarkably intact state. It has an east doorway of oak set onto an iron grille, which opens into a stone tunnel-vaulted ground floor, set within 1.4 m (4 ft 7 in.) thick walls. Above this vault, a mural stair leads to two upper storeys, designed for accommodation, the lower having a latrine and a fireplace. The parapet was reached by a ladder, and has the remains of corbels which formerly supported machicolated bartizans at the corners. This pele is described as the '*Turris de Corbrigge*' belonging to the vicar in the 1415 survey (Hodgson 1820, 29; Bates

1891), and was probably constructed in the latter half of the fourteenth century (a worn cross-slab of *c.* 1300 has been re-used as a lintel).

In addition to the parish church, there were three other ecclesiastical establishments in the medieval town. **Trinity church** which lay to the north-west, outside the boundary of the defensive ditch, and the chapel of **St Helen**, which was located a short distance to the north-east of the centre. The third, dedicated to **St Mary**, formerly stood on the bridge (Craster 1914).

To the north of Corbridge, the fortified manor of the de Reymes family at **Aydon** occupies a spur above the Cor Burn. Probably containing a private chapel (but not identified as such in the existing ruins), this is a fine example of a defensible Border house with a licence to crenellate dating from the early fourteenth century.

A mile north of Aydon is the small village of **Halton**. Typically for the area, the church lies adjacent to a castle – here the fourteenth-century stronghold of the de Halton family. The church is built partially of Roman stone, has a Norman chancel-arch and side walls, and possibly earlier work in the north-west quoins of the nave. There were major restoration schemes in the seventeenth century and again in 1706, which have resulted in the present battlemented parapet and low roof. There is no evidence of the building being used for defence.

The hamlet of **Bywell**, four miles south-east of Corbridge, has two churches, both with evidence of pre-Conquest origins. That the two churches should be positioned so close together is not altogether surprising, as they stand at the edges of two Norman baronies, the boundaries of which may reflect previous Anglo-Saxon land divisions. The circular shape of St Andrew's churchyard indicates early origins, although the fabric of the tower appears to be of the eleventh century. Though this is generally thought to be the place where Egbert was consecrated bishop in 803, it may alternatively have been in St Peter's which has still earlier fabric.

St Andrew's church has a two phase pre-Conquest tower, the lower parts of which are built partially from re-used Roman stones, and which may be of the tenth century. The upper stage is about a century later (Barrett *et al* 1990), and may be an extension to an earlier west porch. The tower is plain and unbuttressed with a minimum of openings, and, apart from the belfry, has only two original windows, one in the west elevation at first-floor level, and one in the south lighting the ground floor. There is also an upper doorway in the south wall just below the bell opening. Internally the tower-arch has been altered but may retain the original pre-Conquest jambs (Taylor and Taylor 1965, 122). Approach to the upper floors is by ladder and from the first floor a blocked doorway once led out into the nave at high level.

The remainder of the church dates principally from the thirteenth century, although major restorations and alterations of 1830, 1850, and 1871 have changed its character and have removed much medieval work. The aisleless nave, south porch, transepts, and chancel bear no evidence of use for defence, although

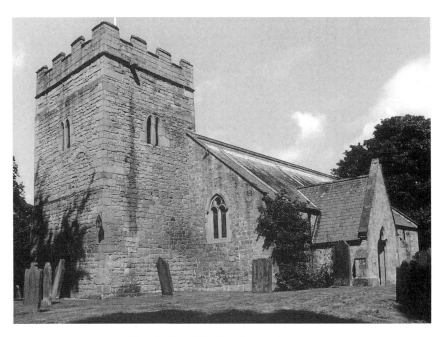

Fig. 98. Bywell St Peter's, exterior view.

the south doorway may have been secured by two draw-bars, the slots for which are now plastered over.

A short distance to the south-east is the church of **St Peter**. The building has a strong west tower, nave with south aisle and north chapel, and a chancel with a Victorian vestry (Figure 98). The south porch and outer walls of the eastern extension to the south aisle belong to Benjamin Ferrey's restoration of 1849. The earliest portions are the north wall of the nave and west parts of the chancel side walls, which are pre-Conquest. The remainder of the body of the church dates from the thirteenth century, although the tower and north chapel are additions of the fourteenth century. A drawing of the church by William Bellers made c. 1754 and published in the *History of Northumberland* (Hodgson 1902, 96) shows the north aisle wall with virtually no windows, and a windowless chancel.

The design of the west tower of St Peter's church bears the typical hallmarks of a defensible refuge. It is of the first half of the fourteenth century and is constructed against the earlier west wall of the nave, the evidence for which includes a buttress on the north side, which extends through to the first floor. The entrance from the nave is through a simple doorway, 1.2 m (4 ft) in width and 2.1 m (7 ft) high, cut through the wall. There is no tower-arch, and this arrangement has parallels in other Border churches where the intention was to restrict entry. The ground floor has no windows and the walls are 1.1 m (3 ft

Fig. 99. Bywell St Peter's, the elaborate set of draw-bar slots in the west entrance.

7 in.) thick on average. There is a west doorway which has been secured by an elaborate series of three draw-bars, the slots for which are set vertically into the opening on the inner face with a further four notches (perhaps for locks) also positioned vertically, closer to the door itself; these slots reach 0.9 m (3 ft) in depth on the south side (Figure 99). There is a modern wooden stair which now leads to the top chambers; however, in the south side of the west face of the tower, what appears to be a blocked doorway is apparent at first-floor level, and the original approach to the upper levels of the tower may have been confined to this highly defensible arrangement. This is commonly found in tower-houses and bastles, but is seen externally only in one other Border church, at Ancroft in the English East March (though external upper access may also have once existed at Greenlaw in the Scottish East March). However this blocked opening has no jambs, and although it apparently serves no con-structional purpose, its original function is far from clear. The first-floor cham-

ber has no external windows, but the belfry openings are set unusually low so that they assist in lighting this area. There is a single narrow lancet, now blocked, in the east wall, which would formerly have provided a view down into the nave. Above this chamber, another upper doorway at one time gave entry through the east wall of the tower into the nave at high level.

Bywell also has a castle, constructed by the Neville family in the fifteenth century. It takes the form of large rectangular gatehouse tower, probably intended to be part of a larger fortified enclosure which was never completed; it was out of use by 1608 (Salter 1997b).

The village was accidentally burnt and both churches damaged in 1285 (Chr.Lan., 46), and was attacked as early as Wallace's invasion of 1297 when roughly half the land in the demesne was laid waste (McNamee 1990, 47). In 1570 both the castle and the church tower were used for defence by the towns-folk, Bywell having been a target for raiders from Tynedale. Cattle and sheep were regularly herded each evening into the main village street with a sentry posted at each end (Hugill 1939; Dodds 1999).

East of Bywell, the village of **Prudhoe**, the centre of a former Norman barony, was granted by Henry I to Robert de Umfraville, who first started construction of the castle. The fortress is situated at the end of a sharp ridge, almost 50 m (164 ft) above the Tyne, and comprises an irregular walled enclo-sure with a gatehouse, keep, and many ancillary buildings. Parts of the outer walls, the gatehouse, and the keep belong to the twelfth century, and other structures were added subsequently. Above the gatehouse, a chamber was formed into a chapel sometime during the thirteenth century. The chapel is reached by an open stair on the west side, and has two chambers, nave and chancel, divided by a massive pointed arch. The chancel has a stone roof, but that of the nave was altered in the fourteenth century when the gatehouse was heightened and divided internally into two floors. An earlier chapel, dedicated to 'Our Lady of the Pele-yard', lay between the castle moats, but no visible trace now remains above ground (Hope Dodds 1926).

Opposite Prudhoe, to the north of the river, **Ovingham** church is another in the South Tyne group of pre-Conquest churches. The west tower is, like its neighbour at Bywell St Andrew, tall and unbuttressed, though larger, and has similar bell openings and a high level south doorway placed just below the upper stage. The lower stage of the tower is without any openings in the north face, and has only two windows, one in the west elevation lighting the first floor, and one in the south side to light the ground floor. At high level a doorway leads through the east wall into the upper area of the nave. The pre-Conquest tower-arch has been cut away and in 1880 a new organ was placed into the opening; only a few fragments of the original arch now remain (Taylor and Taylor 1965, 479). The rest of the building has a nave with south porch, north and south aisles, transepts, and a chancel. Most of the fabric, which has architectural similarities with Corbridge, dates from the thirteenth century, with the exception of the outer walls of the north aisle which were rebuilt in

1857. A vestry has been placed to the south of the tower. The south doorway is Norman, but evidence of any original fastenings is obscured by later plasterwork. As in other pre-Conquest towers, the approach to the upper floors was by ladder, but there are no other specific indications for defence, either in the tower or the body of the church.

Ovingham was in a vulnerable position, easily reached along the corridor of the Tyne valley, and suffered from major Scottish raids between 1311 and 1316. In 1340 the Scots stole cattle and destroyed crops, with such severity that in 1357 the people of the town were still receiving tax relief (CCR, 31 Edward III: 1354–60. m.14d). In 1378 the advowson was granted to Hexham Priory by Gilbert de Umfraville III and Henry Percy, Earl of Northumberland, and the church was served by three Augustinian canons of that priory (Hope Dodds 1926). A house to the south of the churchyard was constructed in the fourteenth century as a residence for these canons. Although now much altered to form a later vicarage, parts of the medieval building still survive, described in 1586 as 'well buylded with stone' (Hope Dodds 1926, 55). It was the Master of Ovingham who led the rebellion at Hexham in 1536 and who suffered the ultimate penalty for his defiant gesture.

Wylam, just to the east of Ovingham, was a possession of Tynemouth Priory, and there was a monks' house here in the fourteenth century which was destroyed by the Scots and rebuilt in the early fifteenth century (Craster 1907, 101). Wylam Hall contains a medieval core with a tunnel-vaulted ground floor, and may represent the site of the monastic grange (Salter 1997b).

East of Wylam is **Heddon-on-the-Wall**, its pre-Conquest church sitting in an elevated position in the centre of the village. The building has a nave, with north and south aisles, a south porch, and a chancel with later vestry to the north. At the south-east corner of the nave is evidence of the earliest work in the form of massive Anglo-Saxon quoins. This was superseded by the Norman building, now represented by the chancel with its rib-vaulted ceiling, chancel-arch, narrow south doorway, and tiny round-headed north window. The aisles are thirteenth-century and the south porch, built with a steep tunnel vault, was added, probably in the late fourteenth century. A major restoration took place in 1839–40 when the west end of the church was added and the north walls were renewed.

As the building has been re-fenestrated, apart from the small twelfth-century window previously mentioned, it is difficult to gauge the medieval appearance of the exterior. The placing of the tunnel-vaulted porch however, partially cutting across the earlier doorway, is perhaps an indication of a defensive precaution.

Newburn is situated on the north bank of the Tyne, and now forms part of the City of Newcastle, but was formerly an independent parish. Here was the lowest safe fording point on the river, and the head of the tideway, and as such it was of strategic significance, in the medieval period, to the city which lay just beyond its administrative boundary.

Fig. 100. Newburn, exterior view.

The church is positioned on a small hill above the village. It has an early Norman west tower, a probable pre-Conquest nave with twelfth-century north aisle and thirteenth-century south aisle – both extended westwards to embrace the tower in the nineteenth century – later medieval transepts, and a Norman chancel (Figure 100). Restorations and alterations of 1827, 1885, and 1896 have resulted in the addition of a vestry and south porch, and the remodelling of much fabric including the clerestory and the aisle walls, and the side arches into the base of the tower.

There is no evidence whatsoever in the body of the church of its adaptation for defence. The tower is typically Norman, and like others of its period (e.g., Ponteland and Woodhorn) may have been designed with the possibility of such use, but has no specific defensible traits, although its original west entrance has been blocked. A modern ringing gallery now interposes between the ground floor and the upper storeys, and original access was by ladder. The first-floor chamber has a small blocked doorway leading through the east wall to emerge formerly at high level in the nave. This doorway has evidence to show that it could be locked from the interior of the tower using a draw-bar, an unusual contrivance for a door in this position, and possibly indicative of a former first-floor entrance (cf. Scaleby, English West March). The room has two twelfth-century splayed windows to the south and west, above which are the contemporary belfry openings. The second floor has been removed to make way for the modern bell frame.

Newburn is a considerable distance from the border and sits in the lee of Newcastle, with its major medieval perimeter defences, and therefore suffered less from the effects of casual raiding parties and open-day forays which so troubled the villages and towns further north. However, its useful position did not escape the eye of military leaders during periods of war. In 1314, following Edward II's defeat at Bannockburn, Edward Bruce led an invading force down to Newburn, where it stayed camped for three days (McNamee 1997, 72). David II most likely used the Tyne crossing point here in 1346 on his way to the battle at Neville's Cross.

One incident in which the church played a significant, if brief, military role, occurred in August 1640, during the Civil War. The Scottish army, commanded by Sir Alexander Leslie, had, like Bruce many years previously, marched south to encamp at Newburn (Terry 1899). They were met by a small royalist force led by Lord Conway, whose objective was to hold the Scots until reinforcements arrived from York. As the English threw up temporary earth-work defences, Leslie mounted his ordnance on the sloping banks and on the tower of Newburn church, and on 28 August quickly defeated the vastly out-numbered royalists (Charleton 1885; Bates 1895). The view from the tower para-pet offers a commanding panorama of the surrounding area.

Beyond Newburn is the city of **Newcastle**. Its medieval population and their churches were contained within the municipal defences, and it is unlikely therefore that ecclesiastical buildings were specially adapted for defence. Of the medieval churches, three have survived until the present day in varying degrees of completeness.

In 1291 the inhabitants of Newcastle petitioned King Edward for money to construct a defensible wall around the town (CPR, 18 Edward I., 1281–92, m.3). The wall was completed during the later fourteenth century and was originally between 3.6m (12ft) and 9.1m (30ft) in height and 2.1m (8ft) to 3m (10ft) in thickness; it had a broad fosse in front and contained a total of seventeen towers, six gates, and two posterns with other minor turrets and gates (Pevsner et al 1992; Dodds 1999).

The present cathedral, **St Nicholas**, is a substantial cruciform building with an imposing west tower and spire, and reveals building phases dating from the late twelfth century onwards, but the majority is of the fourteenth and fifteenth centuries. The tower is striking: it rises 59m (193ft 6in.), and was probably completed in the fifteenth century. Until 1892 there was a medieval bell (probably by William Dowe of London and therefore not later than 1418) known as the 'thief and reiver' bell (Charlton 1885, 109).

St Andrew's, close to the city wall, has the lower stages of a twelfth-century tower with early fourteenth-century upper parts. Also of the early four-teenth century are the chancel, south porch, and north transept, and shortly after 1380 the north chancel chapel was added. The tower is robust and has a stair-turret, separately buttressed at the north-west angle. Like Newburn, St Andrew's was also briefly utilised for military operations during the Civil War when a gun was mounted on the parapet of the tower. The response from the Scottish guns, located at Castle Leazes, probably caused some damage to the building. The damage was not confined to St Andrew's, and indeed, the other churches within the walls of Newcastle may also have been used to defend the townsfolk during the siege of 1644. Scots prisoners were even taken into the lantern of St Nicholas' to prevent the spire from being deliberately fired upon by Sir Alexander Leslie (Charleton 1885, 48).

The only other medieval parish church to survive in the city is that of **St John the Baptist**. The tower is fifteenth-century, as is the clerestory and south transept; the nave arcades and north transept are of the previous century. The chancel was largely rebuilt in 1848, although a Norman window survives in the north wall, indicating that part of that wall may be twelfth-century. Other churches and chapels have been rebuilt on or near the sites of their medieval predecessors, St Anne's of 1764; St Thomas, Barras Bridge, of 1827, which replaced the medieval chapel at the end of the Tyne bridge; and All Saints, Pilgrim Street, rebuilt in the late eighteenth century and now converted to secular use. A nunnery, dedicated to St Bartholomew, once also flourished, founded in the early twelfth century. A hospital, dedicated to St Mary, lay within the walls, and in 1290 the bretheren were permitted to make a postern gate through the town wall, then in the course of construction (CPR, 18 Edward I. 1281–92, m.6).

The Dominican Friars set up a foundation in Newcastle during the thirteenth century, and appear to have been established by 1239. They constructed a friary church, now known as **Blackfriars**, with a claustral range to the south, with the usual arrangement of central cloister, chapter house, kitchen, refectory, dormitory, and guest house. Only parts of this range survive today, the church having been demolished in the sixteenth century, and the remaining buildings have been used for a variety of secular purposes. There is no evidence of defensive precautions, but there have been radical alterations and severe restoration of the fabric since the Reformation, which has destroyed much of its medieval form.

In 1280 the friars were permitted to make a narrow gate through the newly constructed town wall (the line of which had cut through their gardens), on condition that the sheriff or constable could close it as they pleased (CPR, 8 Edward I. 1272–81, m.5). In June 1312 they obtained a licence to construct a wooden bridge to span the ditch which had been added to the town's fortifications (CPR, 5 Edward II.,1307–13, Pt ii, m.5). Although this was granted, it was on the condition that if danger threatened, the bridge and paling around the garden were to be removed with all speed. The friary must have been recognised as both a safe and comfortable place, as in 1322 Edward II and Queen Isabella stayed here for two weeks, and in 1334 Edward Balliol did homage here for the Kingdom of Scotland, in the presence of Edward III and the Archbishop of York (Willis-Fear 1965). One incident which hints at the need for security, even within the protection of the city defences, occurred in 1341, when the friars petitioned the king for the right to reinstate their gates which had been broken down during a fight between the townspeople and other Northumberland men (Heslop 1986).

The castle, which gives its name to the city, was first started in the eleventh century to guard the lowest bridging point on the river. The present keep dates from the re-fortification of 1168–78 under Henry II. The ground floor of the keep contains the castle chapel which has a two bay nave, and a single-bay chancel to the north.

The remains of two other medieval chapels exist further east of the city centre, in areas which were once separate villages. In **Jesmond** there are the ruins of the Chapel of St Mary which comprise the fragments of the east end of a Norman nave, a chancel and fourteenth-century north chapel. Further east, at **Wallsend**, the remains of the church of the Holy Cross consist of a twelfth-century nave and chancel, and a seventeenth-century south porch.

BEYOND THE TYNE

The area of Northumberland to the south of the River Tyne technically lies beyond the English Middle March. Across the river from Newcastle is County Durham, and below Hexham lie the open moorlands of Hexhamshire Common and Blanchland Moor. It is on the edge of the latter, in the remote upland area of the Derwent valley, that a Premonstratensian abbey was founded at **Blanchland** in 1165 (Knowles and Hadcock 1971).

The medieval layout was that of a large church with nave, chancel, transepts, and tower beyond the north transept. The claustral buildings lay to the south of the church and formed the usual arrangement about a central cloister. Beyond, to the south-west, was an L-shaped outer courtyard, defended by a gatehouse on its north side, around which were ranged the monastic dormitory, mills, stores, and a lead or silver refinery.

The present church is largely an adaptation of the eighteenth century when the Crewe Trustees recreated a parish church out of the medieval monastic ruins. The early thirteenth-century chancel, crossing, and later thirteenth-century north transept and tower (with fourteenth-century upper stage) were repaired and utilised as a complete church (Figure 101). A small post-Reformation chapel, which had been constructed against the west side of the tower, was removed. Parts of the transept were rebuilt in 1854 and 1881. Whilst no clear indications survive of defensive modifications to the surviving portions of the body of the church, the massive tower has a very high, stone rib-vaulted ceiling

Fig. 101. Blanchland Abbey, exterior view showing the thirteenth-century tower with fourteenth-century upper stage.

with west and south lancet windows placed well above ground level, and the external doorway was secured by a heavy draw-bar, the slot for which survives in the south jamb. The spiral stair leading to the belfry has been protected by a hefty door, evidenced by the deep rebate with a mortice for a lock, and has also had a draw-bar. The stairs, which are extremely worn, lead directly to the upper fourteenth-century stage without interruption or evidence of intermediate floors. At the termination of the stair, the re-entrant angle leading to the belfry is constructed through a narrow passage, 1.1 m (3 ft 7 in.) in length and 0.5 m (1 ft 8 in.) in width which is clearly designed to restrict access into the chamber (Figure 102). The outer face of the passage, on the side of the stairs, is rebated and hinged to take a door, though no door is now extant.

Further obvious signs of security are contained in the defensible gatehouse to the outer courtyard, and in the tower in the former west range which probably formed the abbot's lodgings (Figure 103). The gatehouse is fifteenth-century and probably had a linked perimeter wall to secure the outer court-yard. The tower in the west range, which now forms part of the Lord Crewe

Fig. 102. Blanchland, the wall-passage at the top of the church tower stair.

Arms Hotel, is also probably fifteenth-century and has a tunnel-vaulted lower stage, clearly designed to be defensible. The battlements on both buildings are, however, fanciful additions, probably of the eighteenth century.

At this distance from the Border, small raiding parties and reiving bands did not much trouble the abbey. However, during periods of war, just like the South Tyne valley churches, Blanchland became highly vulnerable. In 1327, following a major incursion by the Earls of Moray and Douglas (Paterson 1996), the abbot and convent petitioned the king, who had stayed in the abbey (Hodgson 1902), stating that they had often been despoiled by the Scots and had lost 40 acres (16.2 ha) of wheat and rye, 100 acres (40.5 ha) of meadow, and 500 sheep; Edward III granted victuals worth 20 marks for relief of the canons (Nor.Pet., 169). Four years later, the king was again petitioned, this time the complaint being that the English army, whilst at Stanhope, had beggared the

Fig. 103. Blanchland, abbey gatehouse (right) and prior's tower (left).

monks, leaving houses burnt and fields untilled (Nor.Pet., 173). Throughout the later medieval period Blanchland was frequently in debt, and the condition of the abbey buildings was poor (Addleshaw 1951). After the Reformation the nave was destroyed and many of the perimeter buildings disappeared.

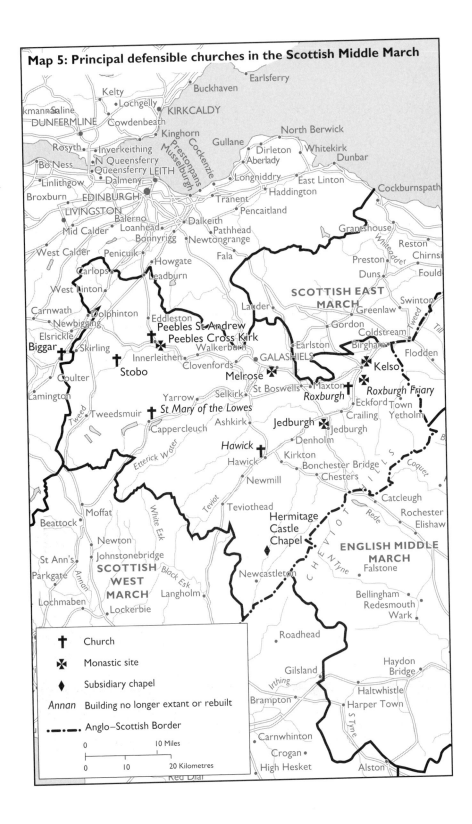

Map 5: Principal defensible churches in the Scottish Middle March

Earlsferry

Kelty · · Buckhaven
· Lochgelly
kmannaline KIRKCALDY
DUNFERMLINE Cowdenbeath
Kinghorn North Berwick
Rosyth· ·Inverkeithing Gullane Dirleton· ·Whitekirk
Bo'Ness· ·N Queensferry ·Aberlady Dunbar
·Queensferry LEITH
Linlithgow· ·Dalmeny ·Longniddry East Linton
Broxburn EDINBURGH ·Haddington Cockburnspath
LIVINGSTON ·Tranent
Balerno ·Pencaitland
Mid Calder· ·Loanhead· ·Dalkeith Granshouse·
Bonnyrigg ·Newtongrange Reston
West Calder Penicuik· ·Pathhead Preston· Chirnsi
·Howgate Fala Duns· ·Fould
West Linton· ·Leadburn
SCOTTISH EAST
Carnwath· ·Dolphinton Lauder· MARCH Swinton
·Newbigging ·Eddleston Greenlaw·
Elsrickle· Peebles St Andrew Gordon· Coldstream
Biggar· ·Skirling Peebles Cross Kirk Earlston· Birgham· Flodden
·Walkerburn ·
Coulter Stobo ·Innerleithen ·Clovenfords GALASHIELS Kelso·
Lamington Melrose Roxburgh Friary
·Yarrow ·Selkirk St Boswells· Maxton· Town
St Mary of the Lowes Roxburgh· Eckford· Yetholm
·Tweedsmuir ·Ashkirk Crailing
·Cappercleuch Jedburgh· Jedburgh
Hawick Denholm
·Hawick ·Kirkton
·Newmill ·Bonchester Bridge· Chesters·
Moffat· ·Teviothead Catcleugh·
Beattock· Hermitage Rochester
Castle Elishaw·
·Newton Chapel ENGLISH MIDDLE
St Ann's· ·Johnstonebridge MARCH Falstone·
Parkgate· SCOTTISH ·Newcastleton
WEST Bellingham·
Lochmaben· MARCH ·Langholm Redesmouth·
·Lockerbie Wark·

·Roadhead

Gilsland· Haydon Bridge·
Brampton· ·Harper Town Haltwhistle·

·Carnwhinton
Crogan· Alston·
High Hesket·

4

THE SCOTTISH MIDDLE MARCH

The Middle March of Scotland stood at the heart of the former medieval Border conflict. Its character was made up of wild, high hills intersected by imposing lowland valleys containing a scattering of small towns, villages, and hamlets. The terrain was akin to a horseshoe, surrounded on all sides, except the east, by hills and fells, never much lower than 440 m (1450 ft). Within lay a plateau divided by the deep-cut glens and valleys of many rivers: Jed, Gala, Teviot, Ettrick, Yarrow, and the Tweed. It was an exacting territory with the dispersed settlements linked together by dales routes, and with the outside world by narrow hill crossings except where the land fell away into the Merse plain of the Scottish East March (Figure 104).

The area covered by the March was vast, over 2,000 square km (800 square miles), and comprised the former counties of Roxburghshire, Selkirkshire, and

Fig. 104. The Cheviot Hills from Linton churchyard.

199

Peeblesshire (Rae 1966, 23). Roxburgh lay at the core and was the largest of the old shires in extent. Selkirk was the smallest, and for the most part encompassed sparsely populated hill country which formed a buffer zone between the south and north of the region. The third and most distant quarter, was centred on the former county town of Peebles.

The frontier line between England and Scotland is well served by its natural defences. The boundary starts at Carham, where the Scottish East and Middle Marches, and the English East March all met. Here the land is relatively flat, allowing easy passage from all directions, and this situation pertains for five miles to the south, over Horse Rigg and the aptly named Wideopen Moor, until the border reaches the hills north of the Bowmont Water near the village of Kirk Yetholm. Beyond, the character of the frontier changes dramatically; sweeping southwards across the high hills of White Law and The Schil, the line swings south-west just below The Cheviot, along the lofty bounds of Windy Gyle and Beefstand Hill, to Brownhart Law, where the former Roman outpost of Chew Green lies astride Dere Street. At this point, good communication between the two nations was viable: the medieval roads of Gamel's Path (following the old Roman road), Hexpathgate, and Clennell Street, negotiated the rangy and dangerous terrain through to the Kale and Bowmont valleys on the north, and Upper Redesdale and Upper Coquetdale on the south.

From Chew Green, the border line is drawn westwards over Hungry Law, to the place near where the River Rede has its source at Carter Bar. Here lies the only principal road to traverse the central Cheviots, and it is still a major communication route between the two countries. Not surprisingly therefore, Carter Bar was one of the key meeting points on truce days to discuss legal business, and was also the infamous setting for the last major pitched Border battle between English and Scots.

On 7 July 1575, the March Wardens, Sir John Forster for England and Sir John Carmichael, Keeper of Liddesdale, for Scotland, met at Reidswire just below Carter Bar on the Scottish side of the frontier. What actually triggered the fighting is unclear, as is the question of who started first, but the outcome was several Englishmen killed and captured and an amount of spoil taken. Were it not for the fact that one of those captured was the English Warden, Forster, this event would have been run-of-the-mill, and might not have assumed the significance it seems to have taken with historians and ballad writers:

> The seventh of July, the suith to say
> At the Reidswire the tryst was set;
> Our wardens they affixed the day,
> And, as they promised, so they met.
> Alas! that day I'll ne'er forgett!
> Was sure sae feard, and then sae faine –
> They came theare justice for to gett,
> Will never green to come again . . .
>
> (Marsden 1990, 50)

From Carter Fell the Border line continues south-westward, intersected by the Wheel Causeway, another important medieval crossing road, over the lonely Larriston Fells to a further truce day meeting spot at Kershopefoot which adjoined the English West March. From here, at the Liddle Water, the March line struck away to the north and the boundary dividing Scottish Middle March from Scottish West March traversed some of the bleakest upland fell country on the Border. Some of the names of the points encountered along this line speak for themselves: Windy Edge, Black Knowe, Foulbog, Mirk Side, North Black Dod, and Gathersnow Hill. Other names hint at the time when these remote hills were used for other, more sinister, purposes: Watch Hill, Bloodhope Head, Stock Hill, and the Devil's Beef Tub.

To the north, the perimeter of the Middle March lay just to the east of Biggar town and continued upwards into the Pentland range before turning east into the Moorfoot hills, finally meeting the Scottish East March near Soutra Hill. From this important crossing point, the line of the boundary ran south through Lauderdale before following a convoluted route just north of the Tweed, around the village of Nenthorn and on to Sweethope Hill, finally sweeping below the castle of Hume and back to Carham.

The lack of easy access from the heart of the Scottish kingdom made the task of the feudal overlords of medieval Scotland very difficult. In order both to administer and defend this vital Border region, it was essential to ensure that good communication routes existed from Edinburgh (the Scottish capital from about 1503). One of these routes came down via the Fala Moor gap between the Moorfoot and Lammermuir Hills and split two ways, one over to the valley of the Gala Water and the other by Soutra Hill and on to Lauder; the latter thoroughfare was known in the Middle Ages as 'Malcholmisrode' (Rae 1966, 3). Other roads led east and west into the two adjoining Marches. However, the situation had not improved even by the early eighteenth century, for Sir Robert Sibbald, writing about the communications in the Border region in his *Description of East-Lothian* sometime prior to 1722, remarked that 'all thir three passages very uneasy' (Graham 1949, 206).

Within this 'uneasy' district, religion flourished from an early date. The abbey at Dryburgh on the edge of the March has been described in Chapter 1, but close by lie three further important monastic establishments: the abbeys of Jedburgh, Melrose, and Kelso, all within a radius of 12 miles. Each of these buildings reveals archaeological evidence dating back to the twelfth century and each in turn was a result of the influence of the powerful Scottish King David I (Scott-Moncrieff 1964; Cruden 1986). In addition to the monastic sites, there is also evidence of twelfth-century fabric in the parish churches of the region, for example at Linton, Smailholm, Ettleton, and Stobo, albeit often in fragmentary form.

Clearly, in a troubled frontier region which mainly consisted of upland and hills, the principal economy was concerned with the rearing of sheep, horses, and cattle, although arable farming did extend well into the higher land. The livestock were an obvious, and principal, target of the reivers – the bands from both sides of the border who lived above the law and survived by stealth, daring, and sheer effrontery.

THE CHEVIOT FRONTIER

A little beyond the gateway from Redesdale into the March at Carter Bar, the road forks, northwards to Jedburgh, and westwards into higher country at Bonchester, eventually leading to Hawick.

The first hamlet along the western route, nestling in the valley of the Jed Water and surrounded on all sides by hills, is **Southdean**. The scanty remains of the church lie below the road on the flatter haugh beside the upper reaches of the Jed. The building has had a nave with narrower chancel and a small west tower (Figure 105). All but the few lowest courses of the building have now disappeared, the roof having collapsed in 1688 (RCHMS 1956, 419).

The building was excavated in 1910 by the Hawick Archaeological Society and restored to its present appearance. Prior to this, only the east wall of the tower stood to any height, around 1.8 m (6 ft), the remainder having been built up afterwards to form a shelter for excavated carved fragments.

Known variously as 'Southdean', 'Zedon', and 'Souden', the church appears to have been of some significance, surprising perhaps for such an isolated location, dangerously close to the Border. This is supported, according to the chronicler Froissart, by its use as the mustering point for James, Earl of Douglas' troops prior to his raid into England which culminated in the battle of Otterburn in 1388 (Froissart, ii, 362). For the same reason that, 125 years later, James IV needed a secure building in which to meet on his way south to invade England (*see* page 51), the Earl probably chose Souden kirk as it was a sound stone building. It was close to the border, and large enough to accommodate his leaders and tacticians, whilst providing enough security in the event of a surprise attack, and shelter in the event of bad weather. The church also provided a focal point for such a muster, being comparatively easy to find amongst the Border hills.

The building appears to date from the thirteenth century, although it is clear that the chancel was rebuilt about the middle of the fifteenth century. There were formerly two doorways into the nave, one each on the north and south sides, though these underwent later modification as their cills were found to be made up of early medieval grave markers. A third doorway opens westwards into the tower which is tiny in comparison to most Border churches, measuring only 4.6 m (15 ft) by 3.4 m (11 ft) over walls 0.9 m (3 ft) in thickness. Ostensibly, this tower could never have served as a refuge for more than one or two individuals, although the body of the church itself, the nave being some 18.3 m (60 ft) in length, could have accommodated many more people.

In view of the hazardous position of Southdean in relation to the Border

Fig. 105. Southdean, the foundations of the church.

and to the Wheel Causeway coming north from England, it seems likely that the inhabitants would have taken defensive precautions as an essential part of everyday life. Indeed, there are a proliferation of small pele towers in this area which bear witness to the necessity of self-preservation; one of these, Dykeraw Tower, was burnt in 1513 by Sir John Ratclif, and lies only a few metres away from the church, on the north bank of the Jed. However, the nature of the terrain allowed comparatively easy escape into the forests, hills, and hidden valleys which abound here, a tactic well known of the lowland Scots who would hide with their cattle during English raids (Summerson 1992). It is therefore questionable if the church was ever a fundamental part of the local defensive network.

The area was evidently more important in a commercial sense than it appears today, for three miles closer to the border, between the Jedburgh and Hawick roads, lies the hamlet of **Lethem** where two important yearly fairs were held, and a subsidiary chapel of Southdean was located. Of the latter, there is now no trace (Lang and Lang 1913, 165).

A mile further along the Hawick road, in the tiny village of **Chesters**, are the remains of the church which replaced Southdean in 1690 as the new parish church. There are no defensible implications as the structure was built some eighty-eight years after the Union, and has itself now been superseded by a kirk of 1874. The south-west entrance into the nave appears to have been reassembled and may have been brought from the earlier building at Southdean, though in date it seems no earlier than the fifteenth century.

Chesters village lies on a crossroads. The main route leads to Bonchester Bridge whilst two narrower roads lead respectively east and north. The northern way tracks around the far side of Bonchester Hill (on which sits a major Iron Age hillfort, 200 m (650 ft) above the surrounding land), and passes a little way from the isolated ruins of **Abbotrule** House and church. The church lies to the east of the ruined house and sits alone on a slight rise above a small burn. The remains are fragmentary; all that survives are the two end gables and the grass-covered foundations of the side walls. In plan the building is rectangular with walls which vary from 0.7 m to 0.9 m (2 ft 4 in. to 3 ft) in thickness and there is only one discernible doorway, on the north-east side. None of the surviving openings, nor the bellcote on the east gable, are easily dateable but they are probably post-Reformation. It is more difficult however to assign a date to the fabric of the church itself, although its core is possibly medieval.

Abbotrule was formerly called 'Rule Hervey' and was a separate parish until 1777; the demise of the present structure may well date from this period. However, it is plain that the earlier building was of some significance in its own right, as the canons of Jedburgh Abbey are recorded as having acquired the barony in 1153 and, in consequence, the church (RCHMS 1956, 421). There are no obvious defensible features in Abbotrule church.

On the south side of Bonchester Hill, nestling in the narrow valley of the Rule Water, the hamlet of **Hobkirk** has a nineteenth-century kirk built in a manner which displays all the potency of a secure medieval church, with its immense west tower and severe Gothic style, and the effect is spoilt only by the excessively large size of the windows. Although rebuilt in its entirety between 1862–69, there was a church recorded on this site as early as 1220, recorded in the *Registrum Episcopatus Glasguensis*, and in 1296 the priest, one Allan vicar of Hobkirk, swore fealty to Edward I. The building had yet earlier origins as evidenced by fragments of Norman work which still survive inside the present kirk; this early church is supposed to have stood just to the north-east of the present building, on a small eminence called Cowdie's Knowe. There was at least one rebuilding between the medieval church and the present, although the intervening structure was partly composed of earlier masonry (Robson 1893, 8). If the style chosen by the Victorian builders reflected the intention of the medieval designers then we have here a good example of the lingering and emotive response to a secure style of construction in this precarious corner of the Middle March.

Four and a half miles due north of Hobkirk the tiny village of **Bedrule** perches on the east side of a steep valley. The present church dates from the rebuilding of 1877, with alterations of 1914. It is located on the site of its medieval predecessor which, according to the *Old Statistical Account* was 'partly below ground, and the windows, or rather slits, are not made to open and shut . . .' (OSA, iii, 348); it was in ruins at the time of writing (1793). Some attempt at restoration was made in 1803–4 but by 1876 it needed a more thorough overhaul; the tower was added in 1914. It was in the medieval building that William Turnbull was baptised, later to become Bishop Turnbull, founder of Glasgow University.

Bedrule church is strategically positioned, on the edge of a spur jutting out high above the glen of the Rule Water. At a distance of 180 m (591 ft) to the north-west lie the fragmentary remains of Bedrule castle, which formerly stood on a promontory jutting west from the rising ground on the right bank of the river. The plan of the castle was an oval enceinte with a gatehouse and at least three circular towers, which suggests a date late in the thirteenth century (RCHMS 1956, 62). It was undoubtedly of some importance as it was visited by Edward I in 1298 when it belonged to the Comyn family (though it later passed to Sir James Douglas and then to the Turnbulls); it was finally destroyed by the English in 1545 (TSA, xxviii, 35).

Over Black Law, to the north-east of Bedrule, the deep valley of the Jed Water marks the principal route leading from Jedburgh to the border crossing at Reidswire. **Jedburgh** was of considerable importance during the Middle Ages as the town was, geographically, the first settlement of any appreciable size in the Scottish Middle March and was, in effect, the gateway into the central lowland region. First created a royal burgh by David I sometime between 1124 and 1153 the town later had its status renewed by Robert I who granted it to Sir James Douglas in 1320 (Pryde 1965). Jedburgh served as a key centre for trade, justice, religion, and political administration. It has been described as 'almost a miniature Edinburgh' (White 1973, 150), in having a basic pattern of a castle (demolished in 1409 and replaced by a jail in 1823) high on the hill, dominating a long high street which has a market place roughly in the middle. In Border affairs it served as both a meeting place for days of truce and as a location for judicial court hearings: Queen Mary came here in October 1566 to deal with a particularly unpleasant outbreak of 'crewell murthere' which had apparently 'becum commoun' (MacDonald Fraser 1989, 293), though in the event she did little to stem the problem.

In the southern part of the town, just above the broad sweep of the river on its high left bank, stand the ruins of **Jedburgh Abbey**, one of the four principal Border abbeys on Scottish soil (Figure 106). Although there has been a church on this site from at least the ninth century, the present fabric dates from the foundation of the Augustinian house by David I sometime around the year 1138 (Tabraham 1986a). There is a marked lack of documentary evidence relating to the early history of the abbey, the one notable (and fateful) event being the marriage in the church of Alexander III to Yolande de Dreux in 1285. There is an incidental reference in 1318 to the expulsion of Ralph de Chollerton and all the Englishmen from the monastery (Let.Nor.Reg., No.

Fig. 106. Jedburgh Abbey, view from the south.

CLXVIII); no violence is recorded, but this was clearly the pattern of things
to come.
   The position of Jedburgh town, only eight miles inside Scotland, ensured
that there was no lack of disturbance during the Troubles. The abbey was ransacked in 1297 by the English under Sir Richard Hastings, and by 1300 was
reported to be uninhabitable, the monks having fled to Thornton-on-Humber
in 1313–14 (RCHMS 1956, 196). In the following century the abbey was again
attacked, during the years 1410, 1416, and 1464, as a result of which both transepts and the south presbytery chapel had to be rebuilt. The damage may
well have been greater than was at first thought, for between 1478 and 1484
Abbot John Hall rebuilt the south crossing pier following the disclosure that
the tower had become unstable. The work was continued by Thomas Cranston,
Hall's successor, who undertook a major restoration of the central supports,
but by 1504–6 repairs were once again needed. It was not only the English who
caused problems for the monks, as in May 1409, Pope Benedict XIII issued a
mandate to pardon some canons of Jedburgh who had mortally wounded one
of a band of robbers who had been terrorising the monastery and stealing its
goods (Pap.L.Scot. Ben.XIII, 204).
   The major incursions by the English under Surrey, Eure, and finally Hertford, in the sixteenth century, spelt disaster for the abbey. It was burnt in the

raids of 1523, 1544, and 1545, but evidently the chief damage was confined to the choir as the church was reportedly still in use in 1552, and by 1671 the five western bays of the nave had been converted into the parish kirk. Even as late as 1875 part of the church was still in use as a place of worship (OSA, iii, 495; Tabraham 1986a, 7). In Surrey's raid of 1523 the people of the town may well have fled to the abbey for safety after they had removed the thatch from their houses and set light to it in the streets so that 'the smoke was very noisome', after which the burgh was 'so burnt that it must be rebuilt before new garrisons are lodged there' (L. & P. Henry VIII, iii, pt ii. 3360, 3364).

Although the damage from war is evidenced both in documentary sources and by archaeological study of the surviving fabric, the use of the buildings during these episodes is not so clearly revealed. As the principal, and largest, stone building accessible to the common folk, the abbey undoubtedly served as a refuge during times of trouble, and such use is unlikely to have warranted detailed description. However, it is interesting to note that the abbey was the target of such vehement attacks by the English during the campaigns of the sixteenth century. Dryburgh abbey escaped comparatively lightly during the 1544 incursion and earlier raids that century, and only suffered major damage during the general devastation of Hertford's 1545 operation. The explanation may lie partly in the fact that Jedburgh was said not to be fortified when the Earl of Surrey attacked in 1523, and in 1549 it was reported that the English then intended to fortify the town, though French troops intervened to prevent them (Ridpath 1848). The abbey would have been a natural point of defence, next only to the castle which was on higher ground. It is known that Hertford had considered using Jedburgh Abbey as a fort but chose instead to fortify Hume and Roxburgh castles, but he was well aware of the local practice of using both Jedburgh and Kelso abbeys for defence, and it is recorded that in 1523 Kerr of Ferniehirst used the abbey for just this purpose (Jeffrey 1864, 293). The attacks on the abbey were probably not confined to the church and claustral buildings as the burgh and abbey defences appear to have run together congruously. Although there is no record of the precinct walls, it is known that there were defensible towers at several points along the monastic boundary, three of which protected gates into the precinct; in 1551, St Ninian's Tower, which lay between Canongate and Abbey Place, was described as the residence of the chaplain of the altar of St Ninian's (Lewis and Ewart 1995, 10).

One piece of physical evidence survived until the early twentieth century to hint at the use of the church as a secure refuge. Prior to 1913, the north and east crossing-arches contained screen-walls which were subsequently removed as they were considered to be post-Reformation alterations. However, both these walls previously supported two or more upper floors which suggests a domestic use at a time when the presbytery had been abandoned, and it may be that the monks of the abbey took to dwelling in chambers within this area following the destruction of 1523 (RCHMS 1956, 201).

A 'rampart' associated with the abbey was described in 1857 as being about

12 yards (11 m) broad and 8 ft (2.4 m) high (Jeffrey 1864, 109). This accords well
with the typical design of mid-sixteenth-century defensible earthworks, built
on the principles of 'Trace Italienne' the ultimate development of which may
be seen at Berwick-upon-Tweed (Hughes 1991), and which may have formed a
defensible barrier to protect the east end of the abbey. Further evidence for the
use of the abbey for military purposes was discovered during the excavations
in 1984 when two paved areas in the south range were uncovered which could
have represented gun platforms, set on a terrace within an earlier monastic
building; an eroded bank may have been the remains of an associated earthwork (Lewis and Ewart 1995, 150–2). Such an arrangement would have provided
a south-west corner bastion in a circuit which was centred on the abbey church
tower and which included the Market Place tower to the north.

   As well as the abbey, there were other possible ecclesiastical places of refuge
for the inhabitants of Jedburgh. Blackfriars church, standing just back from
High Street at its north-west end, was built in 1746 and reconstructed in 1818.
However the site is close to that of an **Observant Franciscan friary**, founded
in the early sixteenth century (Fawcett 1994b), which was also a building of
stone, the foundations of which are still visible. The friary did not enjoy a
long life as it was caught up in the English assaults of 1523, 1544, and 1545 and
may never have been reoccupied after the last attack (Yeoman 1995). There is
scant reference to a nearby *Maison Dieu* where the Master apparently swore
allegiance to Edward I in 1296 (Robson 1893, 110). Just outside the town to the
south-east, at **Scraesburgh**, and further upriver at **Old Jeddart**, were also subsidiary chapels, no remains of which now survive.

   Two miles to the south of Jedburgh, high above the Jed Water on its eastern bank, stands the castle of **Ferniehirst**, home to the Kerr family who were
rivals with their cousins, the Kerrs of Cessford, for the Wardenship of the Scottish Middle March. The present building dates largely from 1598 though it is
built on the site of an earlier Kerr stronghold, demolished by the Earl of Sussex
in 1571, rebuilt, and demolished again by Lord Ruthven in 1593 on the orders
of James VI (MacGibbon and Ross 1887–92, ii, 156; Evans 1987). The present
castle chapel, a separate building to the east of the site, dates from the seventeenth century.

   Due east of Ferniehirst, lying at the foot of the Cheviots, the village of
Oxnam sits peacefully in a quiet, hidden valley. The scene was not so peaceful on 20 October 1544 when the English attacked and burnt the town along
with corn to the value of 100 merks (Armstrong 1883), nor yet again on the
night of 18 April 1570 when Sir John Forster, Warden of the English Middle
March, 'burnt along Oxnam Water on each side of the stream' (Tough 1928,
214). The present church is of 1738 with additions of 1880, though clearly the
site is that of an earlier building, possibly the one mentioned in 1153 (Robson
1893, 77), as evidenced by many grave markers which pre-date the existing kirk.
The siting is of note as it lies 45 m (150 ft) above the floor of the valley, and
although not at the top of the hill, it sits favourably in a secure position. It is

said that, during the Troubles, one of the bells was carried away by the English to Durham Cathedral.

A chapel once existed further into the hills at **Plenderleith**, on the north-west side of the medieval border crossing road, Gamel's Path, but no traces of it now survive.

North of Oxnam, the road and river run into the valley of the Teviot, first crossing the old Roman road of Dere Street. Close to the mouth of the Oxnam Water, astride the modern A698, lies the village of **Crailing**. Its present parish church dates from 1754 and lies on flat land between the road and the river. The old church however is in a much more secure position, sited high above the village on the edge of a steep bank behind Crailing House, where it may be approached with ease only from the south or east.

The church has been a simple building, rectangular on plan and single-celled, measuring about 23 m (75 ft) in length by 8 m (25 ft) in width over sandstone walls which, in places, reach 0.9 m (3 ft) in thickness. Little of the walls remain standing, except at the north-west corner where a monument has been set into the exterior wall. However, sufficient remains of the foundations to indicate that an outbuilding has adjoined the west gable, though its function is unknown.

Crailing kirk existed in the twelfth century when it was recorded that lands were given to the abbot of Jedburgh for the sustainment of the chaplain of Crailing. The village however was in a vulnerable position as it lay on a principal road along the flat valley of the Teviot, and, during the English raids of 1544, it was burnt by Giles Heron with the Tynedale and Redesdale men, along with the neighbouring hamlets of Cragsheil and Crailinghall; twelve prisoners were captured and 130 cattle and horses were taken (BM.Harl.MS. 1757). In 1570 Hunsdon and Forster chose Crailing as their meeting point on their joint march of destruction towards Jedburgh when they left 'neyther castell, towne nor tower unburnt' (MacDonald Fraser 1989, 307). It is not surprising therefore that the church is sited in a position where defence was a real possibility, and where an assailant would find it more difficult to effect a worthwhile attack, or, during periods prior to the sixteenth century, when the area was less well known by hostile forces, missed altogether, hidden in the trees. The villagers may have used the church for purposes of refuge along with the caves cut into the sandstone cliff on the opposite bank of the Oxnam Water (OSA, iii, 323; RCHMS 1956, 127).

In the year 1612, the parish of Crailing was united with that of **Nisbet**, a tiny village on the north bank of the Teviot about one mile distant. The church of Nisbet was granted to Jedburgh Abbey in 1126 following a meeting there to settle a dispute between the Archbishop of Glasgow and the Abbot of Jedburgh. The building was demolished around 1757, following the completion of the new kirk at Crailing and nothing of the fabric now remains above ground.

Eckford church is located just to the north of the main Jedburgh to Kelso road, approximately two miles north-east of Crailing. The building is isolated

on rising ground in a bend of the river Teviot near its junction with the Kale
Water, more than half a mile away from the village which it serves. Eckford
first comes on record in the year 1220 when it was in the possession of Jedburgh
Abbey, but accounts for the latter part of the medieval church's history are
remarkably sparse (TSA, xxviii, 97). The current building dates from between
1662 and 1668 with modifications of 1722 and 1775 (Robson 1893, 63; RCHMS
1956, 127). There is a local tradition that during the wars the bell was carried off
to Carham church, just over the Border in the English East March, though the
present bell there, by Samuel Smith of York, dates only from 1724. Although
not associated with the period of the Troubles, defences against a different
kind of enemy, the body-snatchers, had to be taken during the nineteenth century, and at Eckford there is a fine example of a watch-house in the form of a
small crenellated tower built of red sandstone.

At the scattered settlement of **Caverton**, two miles to the east of Eckford
village was once another chapel but all traces, except the churchyard, have now
vanished.

South-east towards Morebattle, a narrow road leads along the Cessford
Burn to the ruins of **Cessford** Castle. This castle was once reckoned to be
the third strongest in Scotland after Fast and Dunbar (L. & P. Henry VIII,
iii(ii), 3039) and played an influential part in the history of the Anglo-Scottish
conflict (Figure 107). The building, which dates largely from the mid-fifteenth
century, stands in an elevated position overlooking the Kale valley and has a
massive L-shaped tower with walls 4.25 m (14 ft) in thickness, and an outer barbican with a strong earthen fore-wall or 'vawmure'. An idea of its strength may
be gained from the English commander's report at its siege in 1523 where he
commented that, if the defence had been continued (it was in fact surrendered
by the March Warden, Sir Andrew Kerr), he did not see how the castle could
possibly have been taken (Stell 1981, 39). The besiegers had used eleven canon,
scaling ladders, gunpowder, and all the usual methods of assault to little effect
against the massive walls and determined efforts of the defenders.

Cessford belonged to the Kerr family who held the Wardenship of the Scottish Middle March throughout most of the sixteenth century. Whether the
building ever contained a private chapel for the use of the Kerrs is not clear,
and given the ruinous nature of the upper levels it may now prove impossible
to determine this.

The kirk of **Hownam** lies in the steep valley of the Kale water to the south-
east of Cessford and is surrounded on all sides by the high slopes of the Cheviot range. The small village lay at the end of the important border crossing
points into Upper Coquetdale along 'The Street' and related tracks, past the
aptly named landmarks of Murder Cleuch and Beefstand Hill. The main trackway may have been in existence as early as the twelfth century where it is
referred to as 'Herdstrete' (L.de Melros, i, 126).

The earliest dateable feature in the fabric of Hownam church is a late
fifteenth- or early sixteenth-century doorway in the south wall. However the

Fig. 107. Cessford castle, exterior view.

remainder of the building has been so severely altered in 1752, 1844, and following a fire in 1907, that it is now virtually impossible to determine its original form.

The village of **Morebattle** occupies an elevated position above the river, where the sheer-sided valley of the Kale gives way to the flatter haugh below Grubbit Law. It was a significant place in the medieval period as the seat of the Archdeacon of Teviotdale, one of the two Archdeacons of Glasgow. The present church dates from 1757–9 with additions of 1899 and 1903, but occupies the site of its medieval predecessor as proven by excavation (Fawcett 1994a, 216). At the end of the nineteenth century the foundations were traceable, and traditions of a large aisled church, with stained glass windows, lingered in the village (Robson 1893, 25). Without doubt the earlier building was important and in the northern boundary wall to the churchyard were discovered the foundations of a building which is conjectured to have been the residence of the Archdeacon. It seems probable that security precautions would have been taken where high office was concerned, although whether such measures were confined to the residence, or whether they extended to the church, is impossible to determine.

Fig. 108. Linton, showing the church positioned on a pronounced knoll.

The effect of fighting between Scotland and England clearly had a significant impact here, for in 1395 it is recorded that the revenue of the parish church was 'much diminished by wars' (Pap.L.Scot. Ben.XIII, 43).

Of two subsidiary chapels to Morebattle, at **Whitton** and **Clifton**, no structural remains now survive above ground.

Visible from Morebattle, and lying less than one mile distant to the north, the parish church of **Linton** sits squarely on top of a pronounced hummock of glacial sand (Figure 108). The village itself is a dispersed series of farms and houses along the lower ground, the medieval settlement having all but disappeared by 1791 (OSA, iii, 550).

The church has references back to 1127 when Blahan was the presbyter, and 1160 when Edward was the parson (Mackie and Robson n.d., 6; Robson 1893, 81). The present fabric is a complex mix of medieval and later work and although a little of the structure, mostly the lowest courses of the nave north wall and east gable, probably derive from the twelfth century, the remainder is considerably later. Some of the fabric dates from *c.* 1426, following the 'perpetual excursions and burnings of the English', and a great deal dates from the restoration work which took place in 1911–12 when the chancel was completely rebuilt by James Leishman, minister at the time. Apart from the font, another piece of Norman work survives in the form of a carved tympanum above the south doorway, which depicts a bearded knight on horseback thrusting a lance into the jaws of one of two animals; it is unique in Scotland though similar examples are found elsewhere in Britain. A measure of the strength of the original building may be gained from the account of the renovations undertaken in 1813, when the south wall was largely rebuilt and it was found that the old masonry was so compact that gunpowder had to be used to demolish it (RCHMS 1956, 258).

Although there is nothing secure in the form of the church as it appears today, its prominent siting, on a knoll above the surrounding countryside, coupled with its proximity to the former Linton Tower, which previously lay immediately to the south of the kirk, lends some weight to support its potential use as a defensible refuge. The Somerville and Ker families, who respectively held the parish, had powerful enemies and were likely to have attracted trouble from either side of the Border at almost any time. However, it may also be noted that churches formerly dedicated to St Michael were often positioned in elevated situations in recognition of the Saint's heavenly activities (Morris 1989 52–56).

Parallel to the valley of the Kale, the confined glen formed by the Bowmont Water extends far back into the hills. Four miles down the narrow road from Primsidemill the little settlement of **Belford**, crouching beneath the rugged hills and upland, has one of the Border's least known churches. This place must have been significant during the Middle Ages because, like Oxnam and Hownam, it lay on key crossing routes: over Cock Law and into Northumberland down Clennell Street, and along to the frontier on Windy Gyle. Somewhere on this point of the bleak and windswept Border was 'Mayden Cross', mentioned as an important 'ingate' between the two nations during the sixteenth century (L. & P. Henry VIII, xviii(ii), 538; CBP, ii, 853) and marked on maps long after the Union.

Belford was formerly known as Mow or Molle and was, until the middle of the seventeenth century, an independent parish (it is now united with Morebattle). A church is on record here during the twelfth century when it was granted to the monks of Kelso Abbey, the grant being confirmed first by Malcom IV and later by William the Lion. However, there is no mention of the actual church fabric in the brief documentary accounts of this parish.

The church is situated in the most unlikely position, high on the east bank of the Bowmont Water, 18 m (60 ft) above the valley floor, and is perched precariously on the edge of a bluff overlooking the village below; few churches are ever sited quite so markedly high above their associated settlement. Although only the foundations of the church now remain, along with a few meagre gravestones, the plan and size of the building can be traced easily. It has been a two-celled structure of nave and chancel, the overall length being approximately 14.5 m (48 ft) by 7.3 m (24 ft) in width, over walls 1 m (3 ft 3 in.) in thickness. Despite the lack of documentary support and upstanding fabric, it seems possible that this church, like that at Crailing, was positioned high, at least in part to be defensible. It is also likely that its elevated position was chosen to avoid the prospect of flooding by the Bowmont.

At the northern entrance to the valley, the main road follows the river into **Yetholm**, the largest village in the area, which is divided into Town Yetholm and Kirk Yetholm by the Bowmont Water. Although there was a twelfth-century church here, this is represented now only by a few fragments of carved stone in the garden of the manse. The present building is entirely early Victorian, its predecessor having been reconstructed in the seventeenth century, and which was still covered by heather thatch at its demolition in 1836. In October 1401, Kirk Yetholm played host to a well-attended meeting to discuss peace between the nations, but these talks collapsed, resulting in a renewal of fighting and cross-border raids (Neville 1998).

More enigmatic in nature is the site of a subsidiary chapel, located high above Yetholm village close to the Halter Burn on **Humbleton Sike**. It is virtually on the Border line, and was mentioned as such in 1604 (RCHMS 1956, 453). No structural remains have survived, but the position is of some interest, being well away from the main thoroughfare of the valley below; it evidently served as a chapel-of-ease for the hill farming community. The chapel was dedicated to St Ethelreda and was in use up to the end of the eighteenth century.

Between Yetholm and the edge of the March boundary, north-east of Kelso, the land becomes undulating as the Cheviots spill outwards onto the flat haughs of the Tweed basin. At **Hoselaw**, in the northern part of Linton parish, a memorial chapel of 1906 now occupies the approximate site of a medieval church which became disused after 1560 (Mackie and Robson n.d.), and which lay only a mile and a half from the border.

The hamlet of **Lempitlaw** once also had a medieval church, the site of which is now marked by a graveyard. Unlike many of the neighbouring villages, this settlement is located close to the top of a hill and its church site commands excellent views over the valley to the south, and towards the English border on the east. Of the history of this parish there is little trace, but the church is known to have existed in the thirteenth century when it was granted, with all its lands, to the house of the Holy Trinity of Soltre (Soutra) (RCHMS 1956, 433–4). The ruins of the building existed in 1791, although no detailed description is extant (OSA, iii, 650). As observed elsewhere, the elevated position of both village and church may indicate endeavours to achieve a level of security from hostile incursions.

On the southern bank of the River Tweed, just outside Kelso, the village of **Sprouston** lies astride the main road leading to Wark and Cornhill in England. The little church was built in 1781 with alterations of 1822 and 1911. Not surprisingly, in the twelfth century the patronage was in Kelso Abbey, granted by David I between 1128 and 1147, but of the later medieval church there is little record. In more recent history, on the night of the 'Great Alarm' in 1804 (*see* page 31) the minister of Sprouston, Dr Andrew Thomson, headed a large body of volunteers from this parish into Kelso.

KELSO AND THE BURGH OF ROXBURGH

Kelso is situated at the place where the two great rivers Teviot and Tweed meet, in the broad valley which marks the conclusion of the Cheviot range. The town has a cluster of fine Georgian and Victorian houses huddled around its market place and medieval abbey.

The origins of the town owe much to its close neighbour, the burgh of Roxburgh, which already had a thriving market when David I, acting on the advice of the Bishop of Glasgow, moved the monks of Selkirk Abbey to Kelso c. 1128, founding a new abbey in the process. The place was of some considerable significance to the king as he already had a powerful castle to defend the adjacent burgh and the important river crossings, upon which hinged the prosperity of the site.

The new foundation probably replaced an earlier church and quickly achieved a position amongst the most important monastic houses in Scotland, eventually becoming the second wealthiest. At the outbreak of the Wars of Independence, the judicious Richard, Abbot of Kelso, at first sided with Edward I in his disagreement with Balliol and the Scots – it is recorded in 1296 that the lands of the abbot were restored by the English king. However, three years later, Richard was being described as a 'rebel and an enemy' and had clearly changed to the Scottish cause (Moffat 1985, 72).

Throughout the main periods of war, Kelso suffered a great deal through its adjacency to the much fought-over Roxburgh. At this stage, the town was divided into two parts: Westerkelso, which had received burgh status probably around 1237 (Pryde 1965), and Easter Kelso, which was completely under the control of the abbot and which is first mentioned in records in the early fourteenth century (Simpson and Stevenson 1980a). In 1332, Edward Balliol, whilst trying to usurp David II as king, sheltered in the abbey during his attempted abduction by Sir Andrew Moray, which ended in Moray's capture (Chr.Lan., 273).

The abbey was laid open to attack on numerous occasions, as recorded in Papal letters of the fifteenth century, and during the period of Henry VIII's 'rough wooing' it was mercilessly harried by the English. In 1473, the abbey appointed Walter Ker of Cessford as bailie for the defence of the monastery and its goods; the appointment was reaffirmed in 1478 (Murray 1995). In 1522 the lords Ross and Dacre attacked and burnt Westerkelso but seem to have left the abbey alone. However Dacre returned the following year and destroyed the gatehouse, the abbot's house and adjacent buildings and part of the claustral range, along with the Chapel of the Blessed Virgin (Simpson and Stevenson 1980a; Moffat 1985, 81). Dacre had apparently rated the importance of the gatehouse tower alongside other castles and towers of strength in Teviotdale and its razing was needed 'for the utter destruction of Tevidale and the Merse' (L. & P. Henry VIII, iii(ii), 3098). The abbey's revenue suffered greatly as a result of these English attacks, and in 1533 there is a record of the monastery and its goods being put directly under the king's protection owing to the immediate danger (RMS, iii, 1330). In 1542 the Duke of Norfolk burnt the town and abbey, though it is not clear how much damage was caused to the fabric of the church on this occasion. It is, however, in 1545, during the Earl of Hertford's infamous Border foray, that the abbey played a truly defensible role, and was virtually the only building during the incursion which offered any real resistance.

The summer of 1544 had seen extensive raiding by Sir Ralph Eure for the English, and it had been proposed that the Abbey of Kelso should be garrisoned for the king's use; in the event these plans were not effected and the abbey must have remained largely intact. Early in the following year Eure was killed at the battle of Ancrum Moor (*see* page 227) and the Earl of Hertford took the lead in the autumn with his savage advance through the Scottish East and Middle Marches. When he reached Kelso however, around 10 September, he found that the abbey was garrisoned and defended by 300 men (Ridpath 1848, 382). The Spanish mercenaries who were in the English party attacked, but failed to make any serious headway before nightfall and were ordered to retire; during the night several Scotsmen escaped under the cover of darkness. The following day the assault on 'the steeple' was renewed and the church was taken; Hertford was determined to 'rase and deface this house of Kelso so as the enemye shal have lytell commoditie of the same' (State Pap. Henry VIII, v(iv), 515). Despite Hertford's attempts to neutralise the abbey's military worth, it was reported in 1546 that the English soldiers had again taken 'the church of Kelso, wherein was 31 footmen' (Moffat 1985, 83). After this last attempt at using the buildings for military purposes, the abbey went into decline following the successful English capture and partial dismantling. In 1649 part of the abbey was converted into a parish kirk, and a wall was erected to close off the east end of the west crossing. This arrangement was in existence until a new church was built close by in 1773.

Little of the original abbey is now left, with the exception of the west end of the church (Figure 109). Indeed, surprisingly little is known of the original layout, including the claustral buildings and the gatehouse, and even excavation has been unable to advance our knowledge greatly (Tabraham 1972). Fortunately, in 1517, a deposition was made before a papal representative by one John Duncan, a cleric in Glasgow, who reported that 'the church, in size and shape . . . has two high chapels on each side, like wings, which give the church the likeness of a double cross . . . it has two towers, one at the first entrance to the church, the other in the inner part of the choir; both are square in plan and are crowned by pyramidal roofs' (RCHMS 1956, 241; Fawcett 1994b, 31). Duncan made it clear that the ravages of war had taken their toll on the buildings as part was apparently 'unroofed through the fury and impiety of enemies' and he noted that there were places where 'merchants and the neighbours store their corn, wares and goods and keep them safe from enemies'. The use of the

Fig. 109. Kelso Abbey, view from the south.

abbey for direct defence is also alluded to in Duncan's statement 'the inhabitants are husbandmen and cultivators of the fields . . . they receive payment
from the Abbot, that they might be able to withstand and repel from the monastery the continual attacks of enemies' (RCHMS 1956, 241).

The plan and structural form of the church buildings have exceptional
merit, and are unique in Scotland. Kelso is the prototype for the unfinished
twin towers, planned at Stirling (Fawcett 1996, 92). The surviving fabric is
almost wholly of the twelfth century and displays the sturdy simplicity and
prodigious strength which are characteristic of the greater Norman churches.
There are features within the remaining buildings which are of some interest in
giving consideration to the building's defensible role. Over the slightly projecting porch in the north transept gable is a 'watching-chamber', with five lancet
windows which provided a view outward to the doorway below and which was

Fig. 110. Kelso, interior of the 'watching-chamber' above the north entrance.

reached along a mural passage in the interior of the transept (Figure 110). This
chamber probably served for the observation of sanctuary-seekers (Cruden
1986, 52) but equally would have provided a safe view of would-be adversaries
approaching the entrance (Tracy 1992). The north doorway itself was secure,
demonstrated by the massive hinges and supports, and by the mortice and slot
for a heavy draw-bar. Above the corner buttresses of the transepts there are
small round turrets, each containing a series of plain rectangular slits at the
head of the stairways. The purpose of these turrets is not clear, but, although a
certain amount of restoration has taken place, their original form is apparent,
and they may indicate a protective measure, being akin to watch-towers on the
angles of the building.

Perhaps most interestingly, Kelso is constructed with a westwork, a structure
forward of the west transepts, which, although very ruinous, displays some of
the features of defence associated with other westworks, for example Lincoln

Cathedral (Gem 1986), including observation points and a multiplicity of inter-mural passages connecting with the tower and transepts, all of which have a close association with castle architecture. Unfortunately, the west wall is now so ruinous that any evidence for a similar chamber to that above the north door has long since been effaced. However a deep slot has survived on the north side at ground-floor level, indicating that the main doorway was secured by a substantial draw-bar.

In common with some other Border churches (e.g., Ladykirk and Greenlaw), part of the church was converted into a prison during the eighteenth century; in this case it was the clerestory which was used for this purpose (Tranter 1987, 93).

A short distance to the north and north-east of Kelso, on the outer edge of the Middle March boundary, are two small villages, both doubtless dependent upon Kelso for the majority of the pre-Reformation period. **Stichill**, some three miles to the north, now has only an isolated pier of masonry in the churchyard and traces of earlier foundations in the east wall, surviving from its medieval church. Little of its history is recorded, although in the twelfth century it is listed as belonging to Coldingham priory. **Ednam**, two miles north-east of Kelso, is better chronicled and evidently provided an important service to the new monastery by virtue of its corn mill (Moffat 1985, 15); the church, dedicated to St Cuthbert, then belonged to Durham. The present kirk was built in 1800 and modified in 1902 although there are signs within the fabric of re-used medieval masonry, and the possibility of some surviving core fabric. To the north-east is a roofless burial aisle which also appears to be constructed of medieval or early post-medieval masonry, and it has been conjectured that this may be the remains of the earlier church (Robson 1893, 107). The medieval building here may have been of some strength, and was regarded as such by Dacre in June 1523 when he planned a raid into Scotland: 'The garrison and inhabitants of the country to meet at Howtell Sweyre at 4 p.m. on Wednesday 10 June, to ride into Scotland, and cast down the tower and great steeple of Ednam, which is double vaulted' (L. & P. Henry VIII, iii(ii), 3097).

Immediately to the south of Kelso, on the opposite side of the Tweed, lay the important **Burgh of Roxburgh**, not a trace of which now remains except for the earthworks and a little masonry of the castle (Figure 111). The burgh is first recorded in the foundation charter of Selkirk Abbey, which was granted about 1120 by Earl David (later King David I). The rights of the burgh were confirmed by the English King Edward III in 1368, but by 1460 there was only the castle and the church of St James left.

The site occupies a highly defensible place, Kay Brea, at the elevated western end of the haugh adjacent to the River Teviot, which was immediately east of the royal castle. From documentary evidence the town was obviously of some size, had a wall and gates, and contained many houses and churches. In total, three churches were in existence within the burgh and a further one inside the castle defences. St James' is the earliest recorded of these buildings,

Fig. III. Roxburgh Castle, view of the earthworks.

dedicated in 1134. The Church of the Holy Sepulchre may have been contemporary, but only appears in historical sources in 1329, where it is described as standing on the south side of the main street (RCHMS 1956, 253). The third ecclesiastical property inside the burgh was a house of Minorite Friars, their second foundation in Scotland following their arrival in 1231, which included a church dedicated to St Peter. Part of one building of this complex survived through into the nineteenth century thus accurately identifying the site and the approximate position of the south wall of the burgh.

Roxburgh, despite its readily defensible position and strong castle, was attacked and burnt on numerous occasions; indeed its prosperity and importance seem to have attracted a plethora of repeated incursions, the burgh being sacked in 1311, 1313, 1377, 1398, during the siege of the castle in 1460, and no doubt at other times as well. The offensives were by both English and Scots, depending upon who held the burgh at the time (Barrow 1992; Paterson 1997). As the houses of the people were mainly built of wood, it must be assumed that the stone-built churches, and more particularly the castle, were used as places of refuge during these assaults. That the churches were built of stone is likely, but as yet unproven with the exception of the friary. In 1547, following its destruction two years earlier by Hertford, the English built a guard-house at the gate of the friary and roofed over part of the church for stabling, the purpose being to create a defensible position to guard the ford over the Teviot (Cowan and Easson 1976; Moffat 1985, 38). A contemporary account reveals that the buildings were used for stabling and that the gates were guarded; Sir Ralph Bulmer wrote that 'I have brought timbers from Kelso "whitche hayth maid a ruffe at the Freraige, wherby thre fayr vautes ar saved, whitch will serve for XX horses", and I have caused them to set up a warding house at the gates' (CSP, i, 98). This is the only positive evidence of ecclesiastical fortification in the burgh apart from the inferred case of St John's church which lay within the walls of the castle.

Roxburgh castle, also known as Marchmount, was once one of the most potent of the Border strongholds. It is first mentioned in 1125 when the Church of St John the Evangelist is recorded. This church was undoubtedly for use by the king when in residence, and for the sheriff and garrison. It seems to have played an important role during its early years, a church council having been held there in 1125 headed by the Papal Legate, John of Crema, to discuss the Archbishop of York's claim over Scottish ecclesiastical affairs. Two years later, another meeting took place in the church of St John to witness the formal declaration that Coldingham Priory should remain in the possession of Durham. Surprisingly, in the winter of 1282, the marriage of Lord Alexander, son of Alexander III, to Margaret de Dampiere took place here, rather than in the larger and more prestigious abbey at nearby Kelso.

As the castle was so heavily re-cast during its four and a half centuries of occupation by both Scottish and English forces, it is not surprising that there is no trace remaining today of the church, nor of most of the other important buildings such as the great 'Douglas tower', mentioned with prominence in the site's turbulent history. Of the famous assault by James Douglas in 1313, the poet John Barbour wrote (of the attack on the tower):

> The wardane that was in the tour
> That wes a man off gret valour
> Gilmin the Fynys, quhen he saw
> The castell tynt be clene and law
> He set his mycht for to defend
> The tour, bot thai without him send
> Arowys in sa gret quantite
> That anoyit tharoff wes he . . .

(Duncan 1997, 385)

The castle was the scene, in 1460, of the death of James II, killed when one of his own cannons exploded. On hearing of his death, his wife and son, the young James III, rode to the siege, probably in time to witness the Scottish victory, the new king afterwards being crowned in Kelso Abbey (McGladdery 1990, 112). Roxburgh castle was finally destroyed in 1550.

THE VALLEY OF THE TWEED

Two miles upstream along the Teviot from Kelso, **Roxburgh** (the village has the same name as the former burgh) has a kirk constructed in 1752. It stands close to the site of an earlier church, the only survivor of which is a much restored stone-vaulted structure, dated 1612, used as the burial aisle of the Scott-Kerrs of Chato and Sunlaws. Although all traces of the medieval church have now been effaced, the *Old Statistical Account* describes this building before its demise:

> ... the kirk of Roxburgh was almost wholly under ground, roofed with a strong arch, and totally overgrown with grass. The people entered to the place of public worship through an aisle of the same construction, and descended by six or seven steps into the body of the church (perhaps the particular construction of that edifice had been intended as a kind of security to the worshippers in times of persecution and danger) (OSA, iii, 621).

The reference to security may have been based upon the partially subterranean aspect of the building (TSA, xxviii, 311), a feature also observed at Bedrule. However the 'strong arch' and aisle of similar construction seem to imply stone vaulting, which may have been a defensible adaptation.

Smailholm lies on the road leading west from Kelso towards the Leader valley. Its towerless church is positioned immediately by the side of the road, and comprises a nave and chancel, with a post-Reformation apsidal projection to the north. The pre-seventeenth-century building is largely of cubical ashlar, ascending from a chamfered base course, and it seems likely that the date of this work is twelfth-century. The only surviving medieval opening is a tiny blocked window, of splayed form, at the east end of the north wall. Despite much of the primary fabric being of early medieval date, the alterations of the seventeenth and subsequent centuries have all but effaced the building's original form and it is now impossible to conjecture its potential value in terms of defence. However, judging from the devastating effects of the English raids, late in 1543, on Smailholm town and surrounding villages, the need for refuge was unquestionable; this area was extremely vulnerable. Nearby is an unusually complete example of a Border tower-house, Smailholm Tower, which dates, most probably, from the latter half of the fifteenth century when it served as a residence for the Pringle family. The tower rises above an outcrop of bedrock which provided a strongly fortified position. Its entire upper storey was rebuilt in the late sixteenth century, possibly to comply with the 1587 Act of Council requiring lairds on the Border to 'keip watch nyght and day' (Tabraham 1985, 8), though this was only a reiteration of earlier laws 'For bigging of strenthis on ye Bordouris' (Tough 1928, 167; Rae 1966, 208).

South of Smailholm, on the gentle hillside above the River Tweed, the tiny nineteenth-century kirk of **Makerstoun** lies alone, to the north of the hamlet which it serves. Although a church is on record here during the twelfth century, when it was given to the monks of Kelso Abbey, there are no remains of this building today. The present construction dates from 1807–8.

Beyond Makerstoun, the road passes through the Scottish East March parish of Mertoun before crossing the river onto one of the major north-south thoroughfares, as important in the Middle Ages as it is today. Beyond lie the Eildon Hills, rising above the junction between the Leader Water and the Tweed, and forming a narrow entrance to the broad valley within which sit the towns of Melrose and Galashiels.

The site of **Old Melrose** is situated on a promontory jutting out into the Tweed, some two and a half miles east of the present town, and a little way north of Dryburgh Abbey. Although no structural remains survive, this is the site of a pre-Conquest monastic establishment (Thomas 1971, 35), and is also the location of a later chapel dedicated to St Cuthbert. Around the year 1321, this chapel was burnt by the English, but was rebuilt and was in existence as late as 1437 (RCHMS 1956, 303). The strategic position of the site is obvious, surrounded as it is by the Tweed on all but its west side where the pre-Conquest vallum forms a partial closure of the promontory. The disposition of the medieval chapel is not so clear, although evidently it was a target for enemy action.

The town of **Melrose** lies on the south bank of the Tweed, on the flat haugh below the Eildon Hills. Its abbey, one of the four major monastic establishments in this area, was first founded by David I in 1136 and dedicated to the Virgin Mary ten years later. It is the earliest Cistercian settlement in Scotland (Figure 112).

From humble beginnings, as a simple cross-kirk and cloister, the abbey prospered and grew in size. During the thirteenth century, a new chapter house was built and the claustral range was considerably extended. However, despite promises of immunity by Edward I at the outbreak of the Wars of Independence, the abbey's properties in Northumberland were seized, and by 1307 Melrose itself had been attacked and was in need of repair. In 1322, the abbey was again despoiled by English troops, this time under the leadership of Edward II. On this occasion a fight seems to have ensued, after the English advance party, who were resting inside the abbey precinct, were attacked by a guerilla band of Scots. The confrontation ended in the death of Prior William de Peebles and three other monks, as well as at least four Englishmen (Billings 1852, iv). Although there is no direct record of the abbey being used defensibly, this is clearly what took place on this occasion, but gauging from the extent of the damage caused it was not particularly successful. Shortly afterwards, the abbey fell into English hands, and in 1340 the Chronicler of Lanercost recorded that the English king kept Christmas at the abbey where 'he was exposed to much danger by cunning assaults of the Scots, losing several of his men' (Chr.Lan., 324). However, after this, great care was taken by the Scots to ensure that the monastery did not suffer unduly, and David II commanded that, although the abbey was in the hands of the English, it should not, for that reason, lose control of its Scottish possessions (RRS, vi, 151, 164). In 1361, three years after this

Fig. 112. Melrose Abbey, exterior from the south-west.

proclamation, David gave the monks further rights to treat with the English as they should find necessary (RRS, vi, 254). The English found the abbey a very useful base from which to conduct military operations. There was ample room for safe storage in cool, fireproof undercrofts, and secure lodging for troops, and in 1341 and 1356 Edward III launched major campaigns from the abbey precincts (Brown 1998).

In August 1385 came the monastery's most severe blow when it was burnt and all but completely destroyed by an English army under Richard II. However, four years later, Richard granted a reduction in wool taxes to the monks in restitution for the destruction caused, and by 1398 the abbey was in the process of reconstruction, the quality of the new work being outstandingly high (Fawcett 1994a). Nevertheless, in 1402 the abbot and convent complained that their monastery was ravaged by war and that they had insufficient money to effect repairs (Pap.L.Scot. Ben.XIII, 100). The monks never fully recovered from the financial losses caused by the war, and as late as 1505 the building work had failed to reach completion. Despite this, Melrose represents one of the most architecturally accomplished churches ever erected in Scotland. One of the master masons involved with the building works, a Parisian called John Morow, was also responsible for work at Lincluden in the Scottish West March.

The abbots of Melrose, in common with other monastic establishments in the later Middle Ages, called upon the services of the laity to assist in the defence of the Abbey. Thus in 1527, there is a record of one William Hamilton of McNariston who bound himself to the abbot to 'ride and gang with thame and mak thame service' in return for grants of certain lands in feu-ferme (Murray 1995, 33).

The Troubles of the sixteenth century brought about further misfortune when, in 1544, Sir Ralph Eure burnt the abbey. In the following year a repeat attack was carried out by the Earl of Hertford. Following these attacks, and despite attempts at raising money for rebuilding, the abbey gradually fell into ruin and was used as a source of building stone. In 1618, the parish kirk was, in common with Kelso and Jedburgh, formed out of the ruined nave, and the present vaulting was added for reasons of structural stability. It remained in use until 1810 when a new church was built in the town (Richardson and Wood 1949, 6).

The only hint at security within the fabric of the church is the heavy draw-bar arrangement which is evident at the entrance to the dormitories, at the head of the night-stair; this was clearly a sensible precaution against attack by night. Signs of strong locks also appear on the doorway to the south transept. One structure on the site however had an undisputedly defensible role, though not of an ecclesiastical nature. The Commendator's House, lying to the north of the claustral buildings, was converted in 1590 by James Douglas, the commendator of the time, from a two-storey building which originated as the private residence of the abbot, and was described in 1609 as the *'palatium de Melros'*. It is not now evident if this earlier, wholly monastic, building had been in any way designed for security, but by 1618, after alteration for secular use, it was called a fortalice and manor place. The archaeological evidence for this is clear: there are gun-loops in the walls of the added south-east wing, and a watch-chamber at the head of the stair (Figure 113).

Tradition has it that the heart of Robert I ('Bruce') is interred at Melrose after first being taken overseas by Sir James Douglas on a military campaign. Evidence of this relic came to light during excavations at the abbey in 1996 when a probable heart casket of lead was re-excavated (Turner 1996, 89). Although it is now impossible to determine the originator of the burial, there is much symbolic value in this find, and it is fitting therefore, after so many turbulent years, that the (possible) heart of this major figure in Anglo-Scottish politics should now lie peacefully where:

> . . . No sound of dangling sword or spear
> Nor foray wakes the warrior's ear;
> No breasted fight, nor parlied truce,
> Beats to the throbless heart of Bruce . . .

South of Melrose the road passes along the base of the Eildon Hills to the village of Bowden, first passing **Holydean**, once the site of a medieval chapel

Fig. 113. Melrose, the Commendator's House to the north of the church.

perched high above a deep glen, whose recorded history is unusually deficient (Robson 1893, 93). It may have been associated with the former castle here, whose fragmentary walls were incorporated into an eighteenth-century farmhouse.

The parish church of **Bowden** is on record as belonging to Kelso Abbey before 1180, though most of the present fabric dates from the major restorations of 1794 and 1909. Prior to its first major overhaul, the building was described as 'old, long, narrow, and needs reparation' (OSA, iii, 375). It is evident from a study of the fabric that the church was not entirely rebuilt during the late eighteenth century, and probably retains the basic form of its predecessor with new openings and internal fittings. The archway into the north chapel is of fifteenth-century form and the surrounding wall is probably, at least in part, contemporary, being some 0.5 m (1 ft 8 in.) thicker than any other wall in the building. During restoration work, evidence transpired that the nave had once been tunnel-vaulted, a feature which suggests a possible measure of security. The vaulting was reconstructed in wood in 1909. The elevated chancel of Bowden kirk has been formed from a 'retiring room', formerly behind the laird's loft (now moved into the body of the church), below which is a burial vault.

The village of St Boswells has a modern church dating from 1959; its earlier building lies on a knoll above the steep south bank of the river, about a mile to the east, at a place now known as Benrig cemetery.

St Boswells old church at Benrig stood intact until 1952, when it was unroofed and its interior gutted. Decline and further demolition followed, and what remains today are merely the foundations of a building which dated from 1652, but was practically rebuilt in the late eighteenth century (RCHMS 1956, 413). The surviving remnants stand only just above the ground, but the plan is clearly visible and comprises a single cell nave and chancel with a small east porch, a slightly larger west entrance porch, and a large north transept with a structure to the west. The transept and west annexe appear to have been sub-divided by internal walls, probably of late date as part of a conversion of the building into a series of private burial aisles.

Less than a mile east from St Boswells' old church, is the kirk of **Maxton**, similarly perched on a high and steep bank above the Tweed, a little way from the village. The place was clearly of some significance by the sixteenth century as it was created a burgh of barony, and granted to Kerr of Littledean in 1587/8 (Pryde 1965).

The familiar pattern of early origin, neglect, and rebuilding seen so often in Scottish Border churches, is typified here at Maxton. The kirk is rectangular in plan with a chapel on the north side, clearly replacing an earlier aisle or chapel in the same position, as its west wall partially covers a blocked arch in the body of the church. Although the lower parts of the walls may be sub-stantially medieval in date, the only recognisable feature of the period is the south doorway on the west side, which is probably of the fifteenth century. A tiny blocked window above the opposite south doorway is of seventeenth-century date judging from its rough quoins. The building underwent a thor-ough restoration in 1812, although work had been carried out in 1790, prior to which it was thatched with broom. As a result of the various repairs and altera-tions the form of the medieval kirk has largely been lost and, apart from its position, its early character is indeterminate. Downstream, at **Rutherford**, a further church may have existed (OSA, iii, 558; Robson 1893, 88), though the site has now been lost.

Two miles due south of Maxton, the stretch of land above Lilliardsedge Park marks the site of the battle of Ancrum Moor, where in February 1545, angered by the repeated incursions of the English under Sir Ralph Eure, the Scots, led by Archibald Douglas, 6th Earl of Angus, took their revenge. The ploy was simple and effective: Eure, with a much larger English and renegade Scottish force, was caught in a cleverly laid ambush on ground which strongly favoured the smaller company headed by Douglas. As he faced his enemy directly into the setting sun, Eure realised his mistake; events grew worse as his fickle Scottish riders, seeing the way the battle was going, changed sides. From this point the outcome was certain, and Eure, along with hundreds of his men, was killed, and at least a thousand were taken prisoner.

A short distance south of the scene of the battle, **Ancrum** village extends along the ridge above the Ale Water, its present church dating from 1889–90. The old church lies hidden alongside the river, below the village to the north-west. Much of the fabric is now very ruinous (although the west gable still stands entire), and dates from the eighteenth century, probably between 1750–62 (Robson 1893, 112; TSA xxviii, 17). The siting and construction of the church are in no way indicative of defence. In Hertford's invasion of 1545, one of the three 'spitelles and hosbitalles' destroyed is given as 'Angeram Spittel' which may indicate that there was a hospital in the vicinity. There was also a palace belonging to the bishops of Glasgow which, in 1297, an enraged William Wallace raided, following the capitulation of his friend Bishop Robert Wishart to the English (Barrow 1988).

A church once existed at **Longnewton**, which was formerly a dependency of Lessudden or St Boswells, and the parish was annexed to Ancrum in 1684. Judging from the size of the site the building has not been large, and only the burial ground remains today.

Lilliesleaf is five miles west of Longnewton, upstream along the Ale Water; its kirk stands in an elevated position, slightly away from the village. The original building was situated on a knoll to the south of the present structure which dates from 1771 with alterations of 1883 and 1910. The medieval church is first recorded in the middle of the twelfth century, although the building may have been reconstructed around 1430. By 1771 it had become 'off the plumb with rents in several places', and to allow for enlargement the new church was built further to the north (RCHMS 1956). The Norman font is the only surviving feature remaining from the original building. However, the burial aisles of the Riddels and the Stewarts of Hermiston, which now occupy the knoll to the south, may in part stand on, or be built from, the foundations of the medieval kirk. The location of this church, with slopes on two sides and flooded wetland below, would have been useful if the building was ever used for purposes of refuge, although it is clearly questionable if this was a primary consideration in its siting.

Five miles to the south-east, along the winding road by Greenhouse and Standhill, the tiny settlement of **Minto** nestles beneath two crags. The village church is a cruciform building of 1831, one of the few ecclesiastical neo-Gothic works of the Edinburgh architect William Playfair (1790–1857). The original church lies a short distance away to the east, in the grounds of Minto House, and now within the bounds of a golf course. However, the remains comprise only a later burial enclosure, one wall of which may have formed part of the medieval building, being 1.2 m (4 ft) in thickness, with fragments of Romanesque work inserted (Wood 1987). The church was demolished in 1831 (Strang 1994).

It is impossible to conjecture the original form of Minto church from the fragmentary remains which now exist, but its proximity to the large mansion house implies a manorial foundation. The house, originally a sixteenth-century tower, was later encased by a William Adam house (1738–43), and further developed by Archibald Elliot and William Playfair during the nineteenth century. The rectory of Minto is recorded in Baiamond's Roll of 1275, and the church is first mentioned towards the close of the thirteenth century, in the Ragman Roll of 1296. Evidently this building enjoyed a long and successful history, as in 1796 it was described as standing in the middle of a grove of trees, 'neat, clean, and well seated' (OSA, iii, 578).

In times of trouble, the villagers of Minto had a number of choices in seeking refuge. Probably more attractive than a retreat into the church would be escape into the Minto Hills to the west, or onto the crag to the east, where in later years stood Fatlips Castle, a typical Border tower-house, reputed to have belonged to the freebooter, Turnbull of Barnhill. Fatlips still stands, partially restored, and commands an excellent view over the surrounding countryside, a feature which must have been exploited by the watchers of the medieval settlement at Minto.

A little way south, by the side of the River Teviot, formerly stood the chapel of **Hassendean**, but by 1796 the church and most of the churchyard had been swept away by the frequently flooding waters nearby. The Reverend William Burn, writing at this time, stated that the people had continued to bury here, even though the church had vanished, having been all but swept away one winter. He also noted that after every flood 'the haughs were covered with human bones' (OSA, iii, 579).

UPPER TEVIOTDALE AND LIDDESDALE

Along the lower reaches of the Teviot, the main road passes through **Denholm**, a former stocking-weaving village, with the typical planned layout of the eighteenth and nineteenth centuries found elsewhere in the Border region. There is no medieval church or chapel, and the present kirk is Victorian. A tiny chapel once existed at **Spittal-on-Rule**, a quarter of a mile north-west of Rule Bridge, but no visible remains now survive.

The topography is dominated by the sturdy bulk of Rubers Law to the south and the Minto Hills to the north, and where the land falls away towards Hawick, the irregular uplands are home to the villages of Kirkton and Cavers.

At **Kirkton**, the church stands perched upon a mound which surrounds the building and is itself on a platform. The whole village is in an elevated position above the valley floor, tucked into the side of the hill. The kirk is a simple rectangular building made up of nave and chancel, with a vestry annexe on the north side, and a small west porch. It dates from the turn of the eighteenth and nineteenth centuries, and replaced the 'old, incommodious, pitiful edifice' which was 'not sufficient to contain a third of the inhabitants' in 1793 (OSA, iii, 529). There is no evidence in the present fabric of anything earlier than this date.

A short distance away to the north, the scattered houses and farms which make up the settlement at **Cavers** overlook the valley of the Teviot and the town of Hawick. The present kirk lies on the northern slope of the hillside, beside the present roadway, and dates from 1822. The earlier church however remains intact, at the top of the hill, close to the now ruined Cavers House, a building with a similar history to that of Minto.

The church is rectangular on plan and measures 29 m (96 ft) from east to west, and 7.3 m (24 ft) in width, with a north transept which was added during a major reconstruction in 1662. A former south transept was demolished in the mid-eighteenth century. Although standing entire, its interior fittings and fixtures have long since been removed, the building having been used for secular purposes since its redundancy. Despite the reconstruction of much of the building in the mid-seventeenth century, there is evidence of twelfth-century work *in situ* at the east end, where the masonry is of cubical ashlar, and where a tiny Romanesque window survives in the north wall. This portion of the building was partitioned off, at about the time of the reconstruction, in order to provide a burial-place for the Douglases of Cavers, and thus escaped destruction; the remainder of the church is constructed of rubble stonework. The lost portions of the church, destroyed at the time of its reconstruction, were those which stood at the time when the advowson was granted to Melrose Abbey, under the title of Great Cavers, around the year 1358 (L. de Melros. ii, 429). However, there was much dispute over the patronage, which was of particular importance to the abbot and convent of Melrose following the destruction of their abbey by the English, and in 1402 Pope Benedict XIII re-affirmed their rights to *'Magna Caveris'* and allowed them to annex the revenues of the parish church to a value not exceeding £100 sterling (Pap.L.Scot. Ben.XIII, 100). The hillside position of both village and church may have assisted defence during raids and incursions.

The important town of **Hawick** lies to the west of Cavers, in the foot of the valley at the confluence of the Teviot and the Slitrig Water. When it was created a burgh of barony in June 1511 (granted to Douglas of Drumlanrig), it was a village of only 110 houses. Hawick has since grown to be the largest of the Border burghs, and has always been a place of significance in Border affairs (Pryde 1965; Tranter 1987). The earliest explicit mention of the provision of special troops to assist a Scottish Border official in his administrative duties was in 1560, when Lord Borthwick, Keeper of Liddesdale, was allocated men to assist him when he held justice courts in the town (Rae 1966, 86).

Although Hawick boasts no major castle during the period of the Troubles, there is a Norman motte, which underlies the strategic significance of the area,

Fig. 114. Hawick, St Mary's church standing in an elevated position above the town (after Lang and Lang 1914).

and a defensible tower-house in the centre of the town (now forming the core of the museum at the south end of High Street). A short distance to the south-west, over the Slitrig Water, St Mary's church stands high above the surrounding streets and wynds on a rounded knoll; the composition forms a prominent focus (Figure 114). The present building dates from two periods: the tower, a lone survivor of a complete rebuilding in 1764, and the body which was reconstructed in 1880 following a major fire. The predecessor to the eighteenth-century structure was dedicated in 1214 by Adam, Bishop of Caithness. Fragments of architectural moulding from this period survive, and include fourteenth-century capitals enriched with foliate ornamentation (these are now in the Wilton House Museum). Apart from the few surviving carved stones, very little is known of the medieval construction except for insights gained through documentary sources. An account of the demolition of the old church remarked that the tower was so strong and well built that it defied the efforts of the workmen to take it down by the usual method of dismantling from the top down; eventually, it had to be undermined from the foundation. Another reference is to one John Elliot who was imprisoned in a lower apartment of the tower in 1612, and who was discovered 'deid in the irnes' next morning (Robson 1893, 17). Although the building today bears no resemblance to that in use during the medieval Border disturbances, its siting, high above the town, and references to the strength of its tower and use as a prison, strongly suggest that the church was designed for use as a safe retreat.

When the English entered Hawick in 1570, they found that the townsfolk had unthatched their roofs and then set fire to the thatch, escaping under cover of the smoke; nonetheless the whole town was apparently burnt, with the exception of Drumlanrig castle, and the flames were quenched with some difficulty (Tough 1928, 215; Sharp 1975, 235). There is no mention of the fate which befell the church.

Wilton, on the north bank of the Teviot, was once a separate village but has been effectively merged into the municipality of Hawick. Wilton had its own church, set high above the river and overlooking the valley. It still stood in 1893, although this, like its counterpart in the town below, was an eighteenth-century rebuilding, dating from 1762. Nothing now remains except a few *ex situ* grave-markers.

The hamlet of **Roberton**, beside the Bothwick Water to the west of Hawick, has a plain church dating from 1863; an earlier kirk of 1659 once stood a little to the north (Robson 1893, 97). This seventeenth-century building was designed to supersede the chapel at Hassendean, and tradition has it that the folk of this village, angered at the removal of their bell for transportation to Roberton, recaptured it and threw it into the Teviot at Hornshole, two miles below Hawick (TSA xxviii, 297–8). The site of the medieval church lies between Borthwickbrae and the river, where all that now remains is the graveyard. Another chapel also once existed to the east, near the Newmill Burn, but there are no indications of its site.

From Roberton, the road passes west into Selkirkshire, and into more rugged, hilly terrain, largely devoid of habitation except for isolated farmsteads. About eight miles along the road, two such farms huddle together at the foot of Little Bleak Law, at the place known as **Buccleuch**. A mile and a half southward into the hills once stood the church of Buccleuch. Only the foundations of this building survive to mark the position of the church which formerly served the parish of Rankilburn (RCHMS 1957, 35), but which was in ruins by 1566. However, the precise location of this church is just to the south of the Norman castle motte at Phenzhopehaugh, itself in a position of clear strategic significance, well hidden from the valley to the north, surrounded by hills, but with sufficient room for a clear defensible space. It is quite possible that this early settlement provided a focus for later development, but the history and archaeology of its small church are obscure.

The castle at Branxholme, once the principal stronghold of the Scotts of Buccleuch, guards the main approaches to the south-west of Hawick. This was a large and extensive stronghold, originally dating from the fifteenth century. It was rebuilt in the sixteenth century, and repaired on numerous occasions following English attack, finally being raised in 1570 when the Earl of Sussex largely demolished it with gunpowder. The present building was remodelled by William Burn in 1837 (Lindsay 1986, 95).

South of Branxholme, the upper reaches of Teviotdale are bounded by high, rugged terrain, which provided perfect hiding places and escape routes for the criminal fraternity whose home territory this was during the later medieval period. The last settlement before the Scottish West March lies at **Teviothead**, which, with the nearby hamlets of **Falnash** and **Caerlanrig**, forms a desolate outpost amongst these forbidding, but outstandingly beautiful, hills and glens.

The small kirk of Teviothead, standing at the roadside in the valley, was built in 1855 to replace the small medieval chapel-of-ease to the parish of Cavers. It formerly stood in the old churchyard on the opposite side of the road; a slightly raised mound and a few projecting stones are all that now remain to mark its site. The Reverend Thomas Elliot, Minister of Cavers, wrote in 1794 that there was a chapel-of-ease located for the convenience of the western parts of the parish, and also mentions the chapel of 'Carlenrigg' (OSA, iii, 410–12). Another small chapel also once existed on the west bank of the Teviot, close to Falnash, but this has now completely disappeared.

The size and location of the chapel at Teviothead make it an unlikely candidate for purposes of refuge in the event of an attack. Indeed, the very nature and situation of the valley meant that such attacks, or at least the comings and goings of armed forces, were a regular and accepted part of life, and the hidden valleys and forests probably afforded a more realistic retreat.

This place is, however, famous for one particular event in Border history, which occurred in the summer of 1530 when one John Armstrong, supposed 'Laird of Gilnockie', and leader of a notorious band of reivers, met with King James V of Scotland in the churchyard and was hanged for his crimes. Contemporary sources make little mention of this event but there is general agreement that although Armstrong was a thief and a freebooter, he frequently troubled the English King Henry VIII by his cross-border transgressions, and was therefore a good thing for Scotland. The man James V hanged was probably one John Armstrong of Staplegordon who held land in Langholm for Lord Maxwell, and who had previously been accused of burning Netherby Tower (Cameron 1998, 79). It is unclear where the hanging actually took place, but the story grew in later legend and ballad into a tale of royal deception:

Grant me my life, my liege, my King!
And a brave gift I'll gie to thee –
All between heir and Newcastle town
Sall pay their yeirly rent to thee.

(Marsden 1990, 106)

Armstrong is said to be buried just north-west of the old kirkyard, where a rough stone is reputed to mark the spot. In the churchyard where the deed is said to have actually happened, a memorial stone, erected in 1897, carries the words of the old Border ballad:

> John murdered was at Carlinrigg,
> And all his gallant companie;
> But Scotland's heart was ne'er sae wae,
> To see sae mony brave men die.

To the north-east of Teviothead, in the wild uplands which divide the great valleys of Teviotdale and Liddesdale, three small chapels once existed to serve the scattered population. The first was at **Old Northhouse**, between Inner Hill and Grey Hill, where a few irregular mounds by the roadside mark the site; the last burials took place here in the early years of the nineteenth century (Robson 1893, 96). The second chapel lay on the flat land at the foot of the broad valley by **Priesthaugh**, deep into the hills, but there is now no indication of its site on the ground. Finally, a small chapel once existed at **Cogsmill**, just above Stobbs to the south of Hawick, which has been identified as St Cuthbert's Chapel on Slitrig in the twelfth-century account of Reginald of Durham. According to this account, a great miracle once occurred when, one night, during a terrible storm, all without means of shelter had to seek safe haven within the walls of the (then roofless) chapel; everyone escaped in the morning without harm, though the country around was covered by a thick blanket of snow (Robson 1893, 53).

The road leading due south from Stobbs continues through more wild uplands until, passing by Whitropefoot, it enters Liddesdale, described as 'the cockpit of the Border, and the home of its most predatory clans' (MacDonald Fraser 1989, 39). Liddesdale certainly lived up to its tough reputation, commanding a Warden of its own, known as the 'Keeper'. It was for the most part a lawless haven for any Border reiver, criminal, or refugee seeking to escape justice, and the families who made this area their home, largely the Armstrongs and the Elliots, were more intractable and ruthless than any other Border clan.

There is little that is recognisably both ecclesiastical and medieval in Liddesdale, and what does survive is fragmentary. Religion in this part of the Border during the Troubles was almost non-existent, and what did exist probably did so to serve the dictates of those who effectively commanded this quarter. Although this was true in some part for the whole of the Border by the sixteenth century (Tough 1928; Watson 1974), it was especially true for this dangerous sector where, in 1525, the entire population was excommunicated by the Archbishop of Glasgow, Gavin Dunbar, who also pronounced a Great Curse upon all the Scottish reivers: 'I condemn thaim perpetualie to the deip pit of hell, the remain with Lucifer and all his fallowis, and thair bodeis to the gallowis of the Burrow Mure, first to be hangit, syne revin and ruggit with doggis, swyne, and utheris wyld beists, abhominable to all the warld . . .' (Mac-Donald Fraser 1989, 385). Evidently this had little effect upon the men of Lid-desdale, for only two years later one Simon Armstrong, laird of Whithaugh, commonly called 'Sim the lard', boasted to the Earl of Northumberland that he 'hymself and hys adherents' had laid waste sixty miles of country, and 'laide downe thirty parisshe churches', and that there was 'not oone in the realme of Scotland dar remedy the same' (Armstrong 1883, 94).

If parish churches and hill chapels in this district were ever used as refuges against enemy attack, they were probably of little aid in the face of the lawless culture which prevailed. Nevertheless, churches did exist to serve the small scattered communities and to attempt to exert some cognitive influence upon the inhabitants.

As the Hawick road enters the dale proper, **Hermitage Castle** lies just to the west of the main thoroughfare, strongly situated on a bluff overlooking level ground, above the Hermitage Water. This was the house of the Keeper of Lid-desdale, and the most renowned of the Border fortresses.

The first castle was probably erected here in the middle of the thirteenth century by the de Soules family, and may in part have been the cause of a dis-pute between Scotland and England in 1242 (Simpson 1957). Sometime before 1371 the castle was reconstructed, and the projecting wings were added by degrees (Tabraham 1986b). With the introduction of more sophisticated artil-lery warfare in the sixteenth century, deeply splayed gun-loops were appended, adding to the overall solemnity of the place. It was here, in October 1566, that the Scottish Queen Mary paid a visit to her lover, the Earl of Bothwell, as he lay injured from an encounter with the notorious Border reiver, 'Little Jock' Elliot. It was an astonishing journey made from her court at Jedburgh, to which she returned later the same day; a round trip of forty miles on horseback in harsh and unforgiving terrain, which laid her low with fever for ten days afterwards, and from which she nearly died (Donaldson 1987, 123).

Hermitage castle habitually adorns the pages of contemporary records during the Anglo-Scottish wars, as it frequently changed sides between the two countries. Even when, during the later sixteenth century, it was principally in Scottish hands, it still had to be reclaimed by the king when the Keeper turned to native reiving tactics to supplement his living (Mack 1926).

It is not remarkable that such a lonely and perilous outpost should have its own chapel. What is curious however is that Hermitage Castle chapel lies, not within the strong walls of the contemporary fortress, but some 275 m (902 ft) upstream (Figure 115). The building comprises a single cell, rectangular on plan, measuring 14 m (46 ft) in length by 5.5 m (18 ft) in width, within walls which average 0.9 m (3 ft) in thickness. Although the walls stand only a few courses high, one opening is evident, that of a single south doorway, towards the west end; however, a number of carved window fragments have been exca-vated which indicate a date in the fourteenth century. That security safeguards were taken in the construction of this building is evidenced by the heavy but-

Fig. 115. Hermitage Castle chapel, foundations from the south-west, and showing the castle behind.

tressing, possibly indicating internal stone vaulting (Simpson 1957), whilst the chapel itself is sited within a pronounced bank and ditch enclosure, obviously defensible, and possibly originating in the thirteenth century. It has been conjectured that these earthworks may represent the defences of the earliest castle here, although it is equally possible that they may belong to a smaller fortified homestead and associated settlement (RCHMS 1956, 75). Whatever the origins, it is clear that these earthworks were later used, in part, to encompass the chapel, presumably for similar purposes of protection. This chapel may have continued in use to serve the local population after the new castle was built. The castle, most likely, had its own private chapel within the security of its walls.

From Hermitage the road leads south to the village of Newcastleton, which was created in 1793 by the third Duke of Buccleuch as a weaving community. Two earlier villages once existed either side of the present community: the first at Ettleton, a mile to the south, and the second at Castleton, two miles to the north-east.

Ettleton church formerly stood 70 m (230 ft) above the valley floor, on the east side of Kirk Hill, where only a graveyard and a few architectural fragments, including the head of a small Romanesque window, now remain. Its site commands a fine view both north and south along the glen, and although no evidence of the structure survives, the position of this church must have been regarded as secure, though it was built in this spot well before the principal Troubles began.

At the foot of the track leading up to the church is the Millholm Cross, set up in memory of a laird of Mangerton, traditionally said to have been murdered in Hermitage Castle (Mack 1926, 135), although this story is without authentication. Mangerton Tower, a little to the south-east, was once the chief stronghold of the Armstrongs, but has now been reduced to its lowest few courses. West of here, the bleak expanse of the Tarras Moss marked the boundary between the Scottish Middle and West Marches (*see* page 324).

North of Newcastleton, where the Hermitage and Liddel Waters meet, a road leads north-east, towards the Larriston Fells. Along this road, and high above the river, a graveyard marks the site of St Martin's church at **Castleton**, mentioned in the foundation charter granted by David I to Jedburgh Abbey. The position, whilst not as impressive as nearby Ettleton, is nonetheless markedly strategic, and immediately beyond the graveyard, on the summit of a bluff, are the earthwork remains of Liddle Castle, a Norman stronghold of the de Soules family, who also founded nearby Hermitage. Edward I visited Castleton in May 1296 and spent the night; he came again in 1298.

In 1600 the kirk of Castleton was described as 'waste', and apparently paid no duty, but it must have been repaired, for in January 1649, the English army, commanded by Colonels Bright and Pride, lay at the kirk for several nights on their return to England. During this time they broke and burnt the communion tables and seats of the kirk and all the books were taken and burnt (Armstrong 1883, 89–93). Ironically, one of its last functions was thus to act as a refuge for 'enemy' soldiers. A new church was erected in the same spot in 1777, but only eighteen years later it was in a very poor state (OSA, iii, 391), and evidently did not survive for long.

The road past Castleton continues along the Liddel Water to the hamlet of Saughtree, where a plain church of 1872 stands close to the junction of the routes to Hobkirk and Kielder. Along the narrower track towards the east (and the English border), the road passes by Myredykes, just beyond the present forest plantation. Here began the Wheel Causeway, an important medieval Border thoroughfare, now much damaged and difficult to trace over its full length to Southdean.

It is along the line of this ancient trackway that the site of the remotest church in Liddesdale (and for that matter one of the loneliest on the whole Border) is to be found. **Wheel** village and church formerly existed just to the east of the Causeway, a little above a mile north of Myredykes, but the only evidence today is found in a forest clearing where vague, indiscernible earthworks mark the spot. In 1914 the church was excavated and found to comprise a two-cell plan of nave and chancel, with an overall length of 17.4 m (57 ft) by an average of 6.4 m (21 ft) in width (Alison 1917). A number of carved stone fragments were also discovered, one of which, the head of a small window with bold, characteristically twelfth-century, ornament, is now preserved in the Wilton House museum at Hawick.

Wheel village and church are located prominently high above the valley of the Liddel, and face the bleak Peel Fell, necessitating a steep climb from all directions but the north. It was undoubtedly a defensible location, testified by the fact that Edward I, riding through Scotland from Jedburgh to Castleton, chose to stay here on the night of 24 May 1296, and again on his return three nights later (Watson 1914).

By the year 1600, Wheel, like Castleton, was described as 'waste', and valued at only £10 though the kirk is marked with unusual prominence (as it lay within Scotland) on Christopher Saxton's map of Northumberland, drawn some twenty-four years earlier. The church still appears on Joan Blaeu's map of 1648 (part of his *Theatrum Orbis Terrarum*, but probably originating from Timothy Pont's earlier manuscripts (Stone 1989)), though by this time it was in decay. In 1795 there were still many gravestones in the churchyard, and the building itself was considered to have been of 'excellent workmanship' (OSA, iii, 393), though by 1914 only the outlines of the foundations were still discernible.

SELKIRK AND THE ETTRICK FOREST

The Ettrick Forest is a remote upland region which is largely devoid of villages and towns, and historically it formed a secure sanctuary for raiding bands and lawbreakers. Owing to the nature of the terrain, it was an area which armies found difficult to penetrate. The district is also renowned for its folklore and ballads, many of which have appeared in important literary works of later periods – Scott, Hogg, North, and Wordsworth all played their part – but which were born of an oral tradition whose raw material was often based, in part or whole, upon actual historical events.

There is a marked paucity of medieval churches in the former county of Selkirkshire, and it lacks abbeys, priories, and even hospitals, except the short-lived foundation of Selkirk Abbey, which flourished between c. 1113 and c. 1128 (Gilbert 1985). However, much of the county was held by the abbeys of Melrose and Kelso, and apart from the interests of the bishops of Glasgow at Ashkirk (formerly in the county of Roxburghshire), no other foundations appear to have had holdings in this district (RCHMS 1957).

On the edge of the forest, midway between Hawick and Selkirk, the village of **Ashkirk** sits astride the main road and the Ale Water. The parish church lies half a mile south-west at Woll, an outlying hamlet, which spreads northwards from the valley of the Ale some 50 m (164 ft) up a steep bank. The parish church perches a quarter of the way up this ridge and occupies a commanding position, overlooking the valley below.

The present church was rebuilt in 1790 (OSA, iii, 327), but an aisle, projecting from the west end of the south side, was evidently added later. The interior contains oak panelling said to have been brought from Minto old church after its demolition.

Ashkirk formerly served as a retreat for the bishops of Glasgow, and they had a palace here which partially survived until the eighteenth century. Whilst, no doubt, this palace contained its own elements of defence, the siting of the parish church, high on the edge of a steep bluff, suggests that security may also have been a consideration in this building.

North from Ashkirk, the road leads to **Selkirk**, once the county town and a royal burgh possibly created by David I (Gilbert 1985), or later by Alexander III (Pryde 1965). Whatever the date of its elevation in status, Selkirk was clearly an important centre for trade, local government, and defence, and from the early twelfth century it had a castle which occupied the best natural defences by Haining Loch. The forest around the town was a royal hunting reserve, established by David I.

The centre of the burgh has no natural defensible features capable of supporting a stronghold, and in times of trouble the townsfolk no doubt either used the royal castle or fled into the surrounding forest. Raiding certainly took place, as in 1418 the town was burnt by Sir Robert Umfraville, Governor of Berwick, and strict measures were taken in the fifteenth century to maintain the 'heid roomes' (back walls) and ditches round about, for defensive purposes (Simpson and Stevenson 1980c). By the time of the reign of James V, the burgh of Selkirk was described as 'often burned, harried, and destroyed', and was granted the right to have 'walls and water-ditches' (Dickinson and Duncan 1977, 291). The site of the medieval church is, however, elevated on a high slope in the town centre, and in this it has similarities with Hawick, although nothing now remains of this building and the ruins on the site represent a church of 1748, much altered and repaired in 1829, and finally deserted for a new kirk in 1863.

The ruins of **Lindean** parish church lie a mile and a half north of Selkirk, on the eastern hillside above the Ettrick Water. The remains comprise a rectangular cell, 17 m (56 ft) in length by 5.2 m (17 ft) in width, with walls sunk below the turf to a depth of 1 m. The stone is unmortared, loose rubble, and the building is devoid of all features except a doorway on the south side, and a heavily-weathered seventeenth-century monument to the Kerr family on the north. The church is set into the hillside and, although open to the east, it is in a sheltered spot, above the valley and main road.

Lindean is important as the probable site of Selkirk Abbey, founded by David I *c.* 1120 for the monks of the reformed Benedictine Order of Tiron, known as *Tironensians*. It is known that these monks had been in the county since 1113 when thirteen were invited over from France by the king (Gilbert 1985). Only fifteen years later, the monastery was transferred to Kelso and the site probably reverted to parish status; it continued to serve the village which had grown up around the monastic site until *c.* 1586. Although the location and construction of the abbey – it was almost certainly built of wood – were in no way defensible, nevertheless the place must have been considered to be safe by the French monks who were bestowed with considerable gifts of land and other benefits by the Crown, and who were sited in a place which must have borne more than a passing resemblance to their Mother House of Tiron in the Forest of Perche, near Chartres.

Further to the north, the town of **Galashiels** lies at the junction of the rivers Tweed and Gala, in the same valley as the more easterly Melrose. In the medieval period this town was no more than a small village and only grew in size and prosperity from the late eighteenth century onwards. It was however created a burgh of barony in 1599, when it was granted to Pringle of Galashiels (Pryde 1965) whose former home still survives as Old Gala House, built in 1583 as a minor fortified residence by Andrew Hoppringill, 8th Laird of Gala, to replace an earlier tower.

The parish centre appears to have remained at Lindean until 1617 when a new parish church was constructed in Galashiels, on the edge of a steep embankment overlooking the valley to the north. Of this building there are now no traces above ground, although jougs and a bell have been preserved at Gala Old House. The churchyard however still survives, and in one corner stands the burial aisle of the Scotts of Gala, built in 1636 – dated by a stone panel in the wall – but modified in the nineteenth century, probably around 1813 when the old church was pulled down (RCHMS 1957, 31). The chapel which must have existed here in medieval times was most likely in this vicinity, as the position affords protection from the possibility of flooding, offers excellent views, and is close to the main road from the east. To the west of Galashiels, a chapel once stood at **Torwoodlee**, of which nothing now remains except an oblong burial aisle of post-Reformation date.

Along the valleys of the Ettrick and Yarrow, to the west of Selkirk, a scattering of small farming communities were served by a series of small churches and chapels. **Ettrick** kirk, tucked away deep in the hills beyond Buccleuch, was rebuilt in 1824 on an earlier site. Its position is on the side of Craig Hill, just above a minor road which dwindles into the high hills beyond: in the graveyard lies buried James Hogg, the Border poet better known as 'The Ettrick Shepherd'. To the north, **Yarrow** kirk sits comfortably in the middle of the tiny valley settlement, a building of 1640 with many subsequent alterations the most dramatic of which occurred in 1922 following a serious fire. The kirk was built on a new site in the seventeenth century when it replaced the earlier remote church of St Mary of the Lowes.

The medieval parish church of Yarrow formerly lay on the hillside 60 metres above St Mary's Loch on its north side. Today the site is still marked by the graveyard where, in the north-west corner, a low mound of earth and rubble stone indicates where the church once stood. St Mary's Chapel was recorded in 1292 when it was known as 'The Forest Kirk', and later as **St Mary of the**

Lowes. Its location is highly significant, for it lay in the former royal hunting reserve of Selkirk Forest (William the Lion had a hunting lodge here (Owen 1997)), and it was from the safe cover of this forest that William Wallace made his headquarters before joining Andrew Murray in 1297 to win the battle of Stirling Bridge (Paterson 1996; Watson 1998). Wallace became guardian of the realm sometime between late 1297 and the spring of the following year and it has been conjectured that the 'forest kirk' was the place where he was made guardian. Much of this interpretation hinges on a fifteenth-century account of the event (Gilbert 1985, 169), although it is perhaps significant that in 1298, Edward I made his own, personal, presentation of a priest to St Mary's.

In 1557, St Mary of the Lowes was attacked and plundered by a party of Scotts led by Lady Buccleuch during a feud against the Cranstoun family (Spence 1994). Just why the church was singled out and destroyed is not recorded, but given its position on the hillside, it may have been used by the Cranstouns as a bolt-hole. A similar event took place at Lochmaben, in the Scottish West March, where the Johnstones burnt the church after the Maxwells had taken refuge there (*see* page 336)

One event, said to have taken place at this lonely hill chapel, is preserved in Border ballad and legend. Immortalised by Sir Walter Scott, the *Douglas Tragedy* is a powerful tale of jealously and misfortune (Reed 1991), ending in the death of both hero and heroine who were enshrined thus:

> Lord William was buried in St Marie's Kirk,
>   Lady Marg'ret in Mary's quire;
> Out o' the lady's grave grew a bonny red rose,
>   And out o' the knight's a brier.

A small subsidiary chapel once existed at **Henderland**, a mile west of St Mary's loch, and just above the Meggat Water. This is likely to be the 'Kirk of Enderland' recorded in the *Records of the Presbytery of Peebles* as 'altogedder down and equall wt ye erd' in 1603 (RCHMS 1957, 34). The chapel was not large, measuring only 12.5 m (41 ft) from east to west and 7.3 m (24 ft) in width, and was located on top of a natural hillock overlooking the hamlet. Further south, alongside St Mary's Loch, is the site of **Rodono** chapel. Its dimensions were roughly half those of Henderland, and it was clearly a simple chapel-of-ease.

PEEBLESSHIRE

The former county of Peebles lay in the north-west quarter of the Scottish West March, and was the most remote of the Border regions. The area comprised the entire basin of the upper Tweed above Thornylee, to the west of Galashiels, and in shape resembled an irregular triangle, bounded on all sides by hills.

Although comparatively isolated from the main stretch of the Border, this corner of the Scottish West March contained valuable commodities which did not escape the attentions of enemy action. During the twelfth century an extensive area of the county was designated as royal forest, preserved as exclusive hunting ground for the king and subject to separate forest law (Gilbert 1979). At the start of the Wars of Independence this forest was utilised as a safe base by the Scots from which to launch attacks on the English. Its value was such that Edward I made a deliberate military manoeuvre to capture it in 1301 when he rode his army through Selkirk and Peebles (Gilbert 1985). There was also territorial advantage in this region, as at its northern margin it lay less than twelve miles from the Firth of Forth and, once through the Moorfoot Hills, there was an open road to Edinburgh.

There was only one monastic foundation in the county, that of the Cross Kirk in Peebles town, and the only other religious house was the Hospital of St Leonard at Eshiels, two miles east of Peebles; of the latter there is no trace, although the buildings appear to have survived until the early seventeenth century (RCHMS 1967, ii, 211). However, considerable portions of land were held by the Cistercian monastery of Newbattle in Lothian and by the Bishopric of Glasgow, mainly as a result of royal gifts. Despite the lack of monastic houses, there was no shortage of churches and chapels, many designed to serve small upland communities and settlements in the narrow valleys which criss-cross this coarse terrain.

Along the valley of the Tweed, the road passes through the small village of Walkerburn, and leads to **Innerleithen** at the junction of the Quair Water. No medieval church survives here and the present parish kirk dates from 1867 and 1889, although it occupies the site of a much earlier building as testified by a fragment of pre-Conquest cross discovered during the demolition of its predecessor.

To the south of Innerleithen, Traquair House is positioned by the side of the road and at a bend in the river. Originally a tower-house, and still retaining a fifteenth-century core, the present building is largely the result of alterations made in c. 1640 and 1695. The house was of significant importance as a favourite residence of early Scottish kings. The present **Traquair** parish church is located just over a mile to the south, and in its present form is a rebuilding which dates from 1778. The mound on which it sits no doubt represents the foundations of the earlier building, dedicated to St Bride, and in existence by 1170.

West of Innerleithen, the route narrows as the bulk of the Cardrona Forest dominates the hillside. At the western edge of this forest, and reachable only by crossing the river at Innerleithen or Peebles, is the hamlet of **Kailzie** with its ruined church standing on the hillside at Kirkburn, high above the minor road below. The walls are of grey rubble stone, roughly coursed and now capped with concrete, nowhere standing no more than 2 m (6 ft 7 in.) in height. The building was converted into three burial enclosures, probably in 1724, but utilised a structure which was erected in 1614 (RCHMS 1967, ii, 197). The original church, which may have been situated on this site, comes on record during the twelfth century, when it passed into the possession of Kelso Abbey (Gunn 1910).

The royal burgh of **Peebles** was created by King David I *c.* 1152–3, when he assigned a rent to the castle chapel. The position of the burgh and its adjacent royal castle, occupied a defensible position at the junction of the Tweed and the Eddleston Water. Although the town never achieved much political importance, and its castle was destroyed sometime during the fourteenth century, it nevertheless attracted its share of spoliation from invading English armies. In consequence, Peebles developed its own perimeter defences, prior to the sixteenth century, consisting of 'heid dykes' and gateways. By 1574 it had a stone-built town wall, parts of which still survive (RCHMS 1967, ii, 277).

The present parish church, built in 1885–7 by William Young, replaces a predecessor of 1783 and occupies the site of the royal castle at the west end of High Street. However there are also two medieval churches of significance in Peebles, both lying outside the burgh defences, but both evidently having security provisions of their own.

Cross Kirk sits on the north bank of the Eddleston Water, in an area of Peebles known as the 'old town', and which has been known as such since at least the late fifteenth century. The building takes its name from the discovery, in 1261, of a magnificent cross and an inscribed stone bearing the words *'locus sancti Nicolai episcopi'* – the place of Saint Nicholas the Bishop. An urn containing human remains, discovered at the same time, is now thought to be a Bronze Age burial, but the associations may have been confused at the time of unearthing, and the place became a shrine, with the burial cist being preserved under the south wall. In 1540 a yearly feast was established to commemorate the discovery of the Holy Cross of Peebles.

Although the Cross Kirk began its life as a simple aisleless church, in 1474 its status was raised to that of a friary of the Trinitarians, and subsequently a cloister and domestic buildings were erected on the north side. At about this time, a west tower was added to the church, evidently intended for both defensible and residential purposes. In 1548–9 the buildings were attacked and burnt by an English army, although the walls were repaired soon afterwards (RMS, iv, 3037).

The church remained as the centre of parish worship until 1783, when the new building was erected on Castle Hill. After this time, the walls were heavily robbed, and much of the body of the church, along with most of the conventual buildings, disappeared. What remains principally consists of the thirteenth-century side walls of the nave, the north wall of the chancel and part of the sacristy, and the late fifteenth-century west tower. The remainder of the upstanding fabric includes a seventeenth-century blocking wall at the east end of the nave, and the post-Reformation Erskine and March aisles to the south and north of the nave respectively. Although the plan of the conventual buildings remains visible, the site has been robbed so heavily that there is little to see above ground.

Owing to the fragmentary remains of the buildings, it is difficult to discern what, if any, security measures were implemented in the body of the site. The

Fig. 116. Peebles Cross Kirk, showing the defensible west tower.

side walls of the nave, where they survive, are approximately 1.0 m (3 ft) in thickness and there is no evidence of window openings near to the ground. On a small portion of the surviving nave south wall, the cill of a blocked window is 3.1 m (10 ft) above floor level.

It is however the west tower which carries the hallmarks of defence, and was clearly constructed with that purpose in mind (Figure 116). Rising in height to just over 15 m (50 ft), it has five storeys, and although now much ruined, the interior plan may still be distinguished clearly. The whole is constructed of rubble stone with sandstone quoins, the east wall having been formed from the original thirteenth-century west gable of the nave; the average thickness of the walls varies from the base at 1.45 m (4 ft 9 in.) to the upper parts at 1.2 m (4 ft). The ground floor is tunnel-vaulted in stone on a north–south axis, and there is no visible access to the upper levels; presumably this would have been a wooden ladder or stair positioned in the nave. On the first floor, a spiral staircase rises in the south-west angle to allow access to all other floors. On the second floor is a fireplace in the north wall and, to the east, what appears to have been a garderobe. There is evidence of further fireplaces on the third

Fig. 117. Peebles Cross Kirk, interior of west tower.

and fourth floors, along with seats and cupboards throughout the upper chambers (Figure 117). There is a paucity of fenestration in the tower, which has no windows on the ground floor, and a scattering of diminutive openings at higher levels. Nowhere could entry be gained through any of these apertures. Towards the top of the tower, the construction is without the sandstone quoins seen below. This has been interpreted (RCHMS 1967, ii, 209) as a rebuilding, possibly after the English attack of 1548–9. A drawing, made by Hutton in 1796, indicates that there was formerly a corbelled parapet at the head of the tower (NLS: MS 30.5.17, 50).

Undoubtedly this tower was constructed for residential purposes, and may have been used by an official watching over the relics (Fawcett 1994a, 91). However, the general nature of construction, including the former parapet, the paucity of openings, the lack of easy entry to the first floor, and the stone vaulting below, indicates that the intention was to provide a safe retreat which could

Fig. 118. Peebles St Andrew's, the restored tower of the medieval church.

withstand minor assault. Moreover, there was ample everyday accommodation supplied in the claustral range, of far greater comfort than could be found within the confines of the tower.

On the western edge of Peebles is the church of **St Andrews**, which occupies a spacious area to the north of the river and the Biggar road (Figure 118). It lies only a short distance from Neidpath castle, an L-plan tower-house above the Tweed, formerly the domain of the clan Fraser, although the present building was erected by Sir William Hay early in the fifteenth century (Tranter 1962, 124–5).

A church at Peebles is recorded in the early twelfth century, and it is noted that the church of St Andrew was dedicated by Jocelin, Bishop of Glasgow, *c.* 1185; later references to the site describe the founding of an altar to St Mary around 1427, and in 1543 the establishment was elevated to collegiate status (Gunn 1910). However, the same English raid of 1548–9 which ravaged the

Cross Kirk, imparted even more serious damage to St Andrews, so much in fact that in 1560 the parishioners moved to Cross Kirk and left the old church vacant, complaining that their church had been 'brint and distroyit be Yngland XII yeris syne or thairby' (Spence 1994, 157). The site proved attractive to a party of parliamentarian forces during Civil War, as they used the building as a shelter and stable for their horses whilst besieging the nearby Neidpath Castle.

Over the years, St Andrew's church has been plundered for building stone, and little now remains except the tower and a small section of the north nave aisle wall. The west tower was heavily restored in 1883 by George Henderson, funded by Dr William Chambers (buried nearby), who took away the vaulted interior floors and added a section to the roof and parapet (Strang 1994); an interior spiral stair was added at this time, but no major rebuilding of the walls took place. As evidence of the latter, the character of the extant masonry is decidedly medieval, and a difference may be observed between the lower and upper portions, indicating a rebuilding or later phase during the medieval period; the roof-line of the original nave remains intact on the east gable.

The fact that the tower survived the English destruction of the sixteenth century, Cromwell's troops a hundred years later, and the activities of the pillaging townsfolk, is a testimony to its obvious strength. Constructed of whinstone rubble with yellow sandstone quoins, the walls average 1.15 m (3 ft 9 in.) in thickness, and the elevations have a minimum of original openings (the belfry windows, doors, and sandstone dressings belong to the nineteenth century restoration).

The tower of St Andrew's was probably built, or at least intended, for a similar purpose to that of the nearby Cross Kirk. Its general strength, former vaulted floors, and lack of easy access to the upper levels, indicates a defensible intent, and it may have been the target of the attack by the English in 1548–9 precisely for this reason – to prevent its further use as a form of military stronghold.

The village of **Eddleston** lies four miles due north of Peebles, along the Edinburgh road, and has a nineteenth-century church positioned high on the east bank of the valley. Although the village was largely a new foundation around 1785, there was a much earlier settlement here, and the church appears on record in the twelfth century. In 1796 the building was described as being above 200 years old and some of the pews bore the date 1600. Of this church the only survival is the bell, of Flemish origin, dated 1507.

To the south of Peebles the land rises to form the bleak uplands of the Hundleshope, Glenrath, and Blackhouse Heights, and along the narrow valley of the Manor Water, just to the west of this upland tract, are three fortified tower-houses at Castlehill, Posso, and Kirkhope, and the nineteenth-century church at **Kirkton Manor**. Of the towers there is little remaining except at Castlehill where the ruined fortalice of the Lowis family stands on a rocky knoll. Of the predecessor to the present church of 1874, there is only a small fragment of rubble wall at the east end, standing just 0.6m (2ft) in height. Even this poor fragment may date only from 1697, as there have been a succession of churches in this locality (RCHMS 1967, ii, 201). There is no indication of defence at this site.

Beyond Peebles, the River Tweed emerges from the deep valley to the south-west, swinging away from the narrower pass of the Lyne Water. Here, near the junction of the two rivers, and overlooked by the Iron Age fort of Hamildean Hill, the church of **Lyne** perches on a conspicuous knoll, surrounded by a scattering of farms which make up the settlement of Hallyne. The present building appears to date from the middle of the seventeenth century (Hay 1984), and was comprehensively restored in 1888 (RCHMS 1967, ii, 199). Fragments of the earlier church have been found in the walls, including the medieval font. However, a church is recorded here from the reign of William the Lion when it was subordinate to the parish church at Stobo, and it only became independent around the year 1320. The parish records reveal that, in 1597, the Presbytery found that 'they have not a kirk, but walls', and by 1600 the parish church was 'found altogether fallen to the ground' (Gunn 1910, 144). The reason for the pronounced siting of the building is not clear, but it may have been connected

Fig. 119. Stobo, showing the Norman west tower.

more with the early mission of the church, and its positioning in a locally revered place, than with later considerations for security.

Two miles south of Lyne, along the broad, wooded valley of the Tweed, the Norman church of **Stobo** sits, tucked into the foot of Tarcreish Hill, on a prominently high ridge of land (Figure 119). On the opposite side of the river is Easter Dawyck farmhouse, built on the site of a pele tower using masonry reclaimed from its ruins.

The church features periodically amongst ecclesiastical records of the twelfth and thirteenth centuries when it was confirmed that it belonged to the See of Glasgow, and to the successors of Kentigern by Pope Alexander III in 1174 (Gunn 1910). Early tradition relates that St Kentigern founded a chapel here in the sixth century, and it was widely believed that the north chapel, which was largely rebuilt on old foundations in 1928–9, represented the remains of St Kentigern's original pre-Conquest cell. In reality, this portion of the building was probably a fifteenth-century chantry chapel, and was originally barrel-vaulted, although the existing vault belongs to the period of reconstruction (RCHMS 1967, ii, 213). Although in a poor state during the early sixteenth century, when it was variously described as 'not water-tight', and 'ruinous', the building has largely survived with its medieval core intact, despite a major restoration in 1863 by the architect John Lessels.

This locality was apparently of some importance as, like Ashkirk in Selkirkshire, there was a palace of the bishops of Glasgow, built on land belonging to the church during the thirteenth century. The priests also enjoyed a measure of comfort and protection as they had a handsome dwelling in the 'Drygait of Glasgow', with thick walls and a spiral stair (Seymour and Randall 1989).

Stobo church has a twelfth-century nave and chancel, a west tower probably of the same period, a north chapel, and a south porch (Figure 120). The Norman work is revealed by the south doorway, and by windows in the north walls of the nave and chancel. The window in the nave, immediately opposite the entrance, was once a doorway; a bolt-hole or draw-bar slot (now concealed) was discovered in 1863. The tower's fabric is mainly obscured by harling and plaster, although the arch through to the nave appears to be round-headed and may be contemporary with the Norman fabric elsewhere. It is recorded that, in 1657–8 and again in 1765, major repairs and alterations took place to the tower as it had fallen into disrepair; these modifications have obscured much of the medieval character.

Despite the drastic restorations, enough evidence remains to reconstruct the conjectural form of the medieval building. The tower's upper levels, which are now reached by a modern exterior staircase and doorway, were formerly reached by a nineteenth-century interior wooden stair on the south side, but the original method of access must have been by wooden ladder (MacGibbon and Ross 1896–7, i, 332). The tower has a minimum of openings and several blocked windows. In the chancel, a small round-headed window, of unknown date, may have lit an upper chamber but any evidence for this was thoroughly

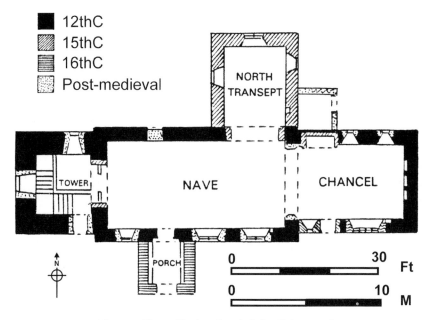

Fig. 120. Plan of Stobo church (after Salter 1994).

effaced in 1863 when the Romanesque chancel-arch was removed and this portion of the building was re-ordered. However, apart from the formerly vaulted
north chapel and the possibility of the chancel also having been vaulted, the
most significant indication of defensible adaptation lies in the narrowing of
the tower-arch to a single doorway, perhaps during the fifteenth or sixteenth
century, which may have served to prevent easy ingress in the same manner
as, for example, Kirkwhelpington and Hartburn in the English Middle March.
There is a also an apparent gun-loop in the head of the window at first-floor
level in the south wall of the tower, but this may be *ex situ* (RCHMS 1967, ii,
213) and would be of little practical use in its current position.

A short distance to the south-west of Stobo, Dawyck House, built between
1832 and 1837 by William Burn, occupies the site of an earlier dwelling, at one
time the property of the Naesmyth family who established a formal garden
here in 1691. Today the landscaped area comprises 24 hectares (60 acres) of
ground rising along the northern slope of Scrape Hill and includes the chapel,
rebuilt by Burn in 1837 on the site of a medieval building.

Dawyck was formerly a chapel dependent upon Stobo, although it became
an independent parish following the Reformation until 1742 when it was suppressed (RCHMS 1967, ii, 195). Records indicate that the church had been in
bad condition for many years prior to its suppression: in 1597 it was found to
be ruinous, in 1600 'somewhat ruinous', in 1624 the parson was charged with
repairing the choir and the parish with mending the remainder, including the

kirkyard dykes, and by 1740 the church was 'long ruinous, and nothing done' (Gunn 1910, 157–60). Throughout these records there is prominent mention of a 'bell-house', which may be a reference to a former tower. Part of the old walls were still standing when Burn demolished them to clear the way for his new building.

Although no remains exist of the fabric of the earlier chapel (a late medieval font does survive, and the bell is dated 1642, re-cast 1791), the most remarkable feature is its location – approximately 100 m (330 ft) above the valley and house, set onto a small natural platform in the hillside. The medieval church was evidently located here to serve the former village of Wester Dawyck and its mill. However, the location, so high above the valley floor, suggests that its builders were circumspect with regard to the vulnerability of the flatter haughlands below.

If the builders of the church at Dawyck chose the high ground for reasons of safety, then their near neighbours to the west at **Drumelzier** paid little heed to this line of thinking (although this foundation may be much earlier). The little church is situated close to the road within the valley, and offers nothing by way of security, except that immediately to the east the land falls, almost vertically, into the stream below. Possibly a retreat to the well fortified Tinnis Castle, which overlooked the village to the south, was the local strategy in times of trouble.

The early ecclesiastical history of Drumelzier is obscure, although the present building may occupy the site of the chapel of St Cuthbert, mentioned in 1291 as having been bestowed upon the monks of Melrose by Sir Simon Fraser (Gunn 1910, 121). It is difficult to interpret the present fabric, as much is obscured by harling, although it is clear that the greater part of the simple rectangular building belongs to the period of the major restoration of 1872. One or two earlier features survive, including a thirteenth-century lancet window in the south wall, a tunnel-vaulted seventeenth-century burial vault with a piscina, and a small seventeenth- or eighteenth-century bell cote.

The burial vault is of some interest as the inscription above the doorway – 'Hic Iacet Honorablis Vir Iacobvs Tvedy De Drvmelzier' – indicates that this is the resting place of the notorious Border laird, James Tweedie, who was killed in single combat with the laird of Dawyck on 29 July 1612.

To the west of Drumelzier the Tweed swings sharply to the south, and here the road was guarded by two tower-houses: Drumelzier Castle on the east side, and the tower of Wreay to the west; both belonged to the locally revered Tweedie family.

Further west, the narrow valley of the Holms Water runs into the high hill country for four miles before it meets the slopes of Leishfoot Hill and Culter Fell, which mark the boundary of the Scottish Middle March. A little over a mile down this valley is the tiny hamlet of **Glenholm** with its ruined medieval church nestling amongst later farm buildings.

The earliest records of Glenholm church are from the thirteenth century, when it was dedicated to St Cuthbert. However, the present remains are too incomplete to determine a date, and only a section of the south-east corner of the chancel survives in order to support a monument to the Reverend Simon Kellie, who died in 1748; this was restored in 1889. The extent of the original ground plan can be estimated from the appearance of earthworks which probably represent the foundations of the walls; these measure: lengthwise east to west, 15.5 m (51 ft) by, north to south, 7 m (23 ft).

In the main valley there is only one major church between here and Moffat (in the Scottish West March) some twenty-two miles to the south; the remainder of the upper reaches of the Tweed pass through rugged terrain, largely devoid of settlements and having only ever contained a scattering of isolated farmsteads. This church is at Tweedsmuir, where the Talla Burn meets the Tweed.

Simply because a route existed which enabled military forces to move eastwards through the harsh hill country, some security precautions would be expected at the head of this valley. However, apart from the early walled enclosure castle of Oliver, and the fourteenth-century tower-house at Hawkshaw, there are no major castles or fortifications, and almost nothing remains of these two castles to determine their form and effectiveness.

A church is said to have existed at **Kingledores**, between Stanhope and Tweedsmuir, where there was reputedly a cell of a hermit named Crispin, but of this there are no remains. A kirk and graveyard are also said to have existed two miles to the south and which now lie under the waters of the Fruid Reservoir.

Tweedsmuir kirk was constructed in 1648. From a drawing made in 1790 it was evidently a simple single-celled building which may have had a thatched roof. In 1874-5 the seventeenth-century building was replaced by the present structure, designed by John Lessels, but erected on the same site as its predecessor, a high mound, mistakenly taken for a motte, but in fact a natural feature which provided protection from the flooding of the river below.

North of Drumelzier lies the village of **Broughton**, its present church, close to the road at Calzeat, dates from 1803-4 by Thomas Brown (Strang 1994). The earlier building is located along a narrow lane to the north-west of the main village, and has a single intact east gable, probably of 1617 or 1726 when rebuildings took place, and rubble side walls, possibly also of post-Reformation date, which stand to approximately 4 m (13 ft) in height. A church is recorded on this site from the twelfth century, but no remains of this building are now extant.

One interesting aspect of Broughton old kirk is the cell of St Llolan. This tunnel-vaulted cell, of uncertain date, was largely rebuilt in 1926-7 in the mistaken belief that it represented the cell of St Llolan, a seventh-century bishop, to whom the church was traditionally dedicated.

In the hill country to the west of Broughton, two routes lead to the town of Biggar, the northerly follows the broad valley of the Biggar Water and the narrower road skirts around Goseland Hill, above the Kilbucho Burn. It is from the latter route that a winding track leads south below White Hill and on to the ruined church at **Kilbucho**.

Kilbucho church is well hidden below the line of the hill and close by a small burn. The remains comprise the east and west gable walls, standing almost to full height, and the more ruined side walls which survive to around 2 m (6 ft 7 in.). This building was abandoned around 1810 when the parish was amalgamated with Broughton and Glenholm. In plan the church is a simple, single-celled, rectangular building which may have had two north doorways. The present remains may be entirely post-Reformation, but in the absence of any architectural detailing this must be conjectural. The church is said to have been dedicated to St Bega, an Anglo-Saxon saint and disciple of St Hilda, but written records only begin in the thirteenth century. The form of the medieval building has been lost due to post-Reformation rebuilding.

The town of **Biggar** lies just beyond the boundary of the March, in the historic county of Lanarkshire. However, although beyond the immediate dangers which attended life in the Borders, Biggar lay in a vulnerable and strategically important position between the Clyde valley and the road to Edinburgh. Indeed, it lay directly in the path of potential enemy troops moving from the Scottish West March north of Lockerbie. Although largely spared from the raiding activities of the Border reivers, riders from Liddesdale plundered the town after the administration of the frontier broke down, following the collapse of Bothwell's ambitious bid for supremacy in 1567 (MacDonald Fraser 1989, 294).

Although there was a church here from at least the twelfth century, the present collegiate foundation of St Nicholas was created in 1545–6 by Malcom, Lord Fleming, the High Chancellor of Scotland (MacGibbon and Ross 1896–7, iii, 343). The purpose was to provide for various clergy and officials, a hospital, and a grammar school which was also a song school for the choir.

In common with other collegiate churches (e.g. Dunglass), the plan is cruciform and aisleless. There is a strong, squat, central tower, the upper levels of which are reached from a spiral stair in the north-east angle. The nave however may have been retained from the earlier building, as a sketch by Grose in 1789 shows this portion of the church to be much simpler, indeed without significant openings, suggesting an older survival (Fawcett 1994a, 181). A considerable amount of restoration took place during the nineteenth century, especially between 1869–71 when David Bryce undertook a major remodelling of the nave and constructed a new belfry in the tower.

Outwardly, the church has simple, debased Gothic architecture, with windows set well above ground level, although in 1789 the nave may have been virtually windowless. The tower is furnished with a first-floor chamber which contains a fireplace, and was evidently intended for habitation. This device may well have been a priest's or sacristans' room, but given the expenditure and patronage on the foundation, it seems highly unlikely that this was intended for permanent occupation; it is more likely that the room was utilised as a secure refuge in the event of unrest. This theory is reinforced by the presence of gun-loops and crenellations in the tower parapet which, despite much

Fig. 121. Biggar, gun-loop and crenel in the tower parapet.

alteration to the tower during Bryce's restoration, appear to have survived unaltered (Figure 121). The gun-loops are offset from the centre, one in each side of
the parapet between crenels, and thus provided good overall coverage of the
approaches to the building (Figure 122).

Just north-east of Biggar, and within the boundary of the Scottish Middle
March, the little village of **Skirling** clusters around its church, perched enig-
matically on top of a sharp knoll. The present building dates from 1720,
though it was significantly altered in 1891. The site may have been in continuous occupation since the late thirteenth century. An earthen bank surrounding the building probably derives from the levelling of the site, but may also
have served to provide a semi-secure enclosure on top of the steep bluff, some
9 m to 12 m (30 ft to 40 ft) above the surrounding land. Such defensible enclosures around churches are known from earlier periods, where they were constructed in response to particular situations of military activity, for example
at Merrington, County Durham in 1144 (Kelland 1982, 95) and Southwell, Nottinghamshire in 1142 (Cathcart King 1983, 382). Alternatively, this building
may occupy the site simply in an attempt to form a focal point, or else as a
characteristic of a foundation to St Michael (Morris 1989, 52–56); a similar situation is also found at Linton in Roxburghshire.

Five miles north-east of Skirling, the scattered settlement of **Kirkurd** has a
church of 1766, erected by John Carmichael on a new site half a mile west of its
predecessor. Of the earlier church, only a rough, barrel-vaulted structure now

Fig. 122. Biggar, exterior of tower showing crenellation and gun-loops.

survives in the grounds of Castlecraig, and this is likely to be a burial aisle of post-Reformation date, probably constructed from the ruins of the medieval church.

Three miles north-east of Kirkurd, near Bordlands, the old and new parish churches of **Newlands** lie within half a mile of each other. Here, the new church, constructed in 1838 by James Currie, sits at the side of the road, leaving the considerable remains of its yellow sandstone forerunner at the foot of Whiteside Hill, a little way to the south.

The old kirk dates from the early sixteenth century, as demonstrated by the east and west windows and the south-west doorway, although a church is first recorded here during the fourteenth century (Pap.L.Scot. Ben.XIII. 72, 78). In plan, the building is a simple rectangle, virtually intact apart from the roof, with all four walls standing to over 3 m (10 ft) in height and with the two gables entire. To this single-celled plan has been added the early seventeenth-century

Murray Aisle to the west, and a post-1838 burial aisle to the north. Considerable alterations to the fabric were made during the eighteenth and early nineteenth centuries, and most traces of late medieval work have been effaced.

The north-west extremity of the Scottish Middle March extends high into the Pentland Hills around Mount Maw and Byrehope Mount, below which lies the small town of **West Linton**. Although a church is known to have been here since the twelfth century (Gunn 1910; RCHMS 1967, ii, 217), the present building dates entirely from 1781–4, with the addition of a spire in 1871. The earlier church lay just to the north of the current site and was found to contain several medieval carved stones at its demolition.

Beyond West Linton, the road sweeps northwards through Carlops, out of the Middle March and on to Edinburgh, fifteen miles away.

Map 6: Principal defensible churches in the English West March

✝ Church

✠ Monastic site

♦ Subsidiary chapel

Annan Building no longer extant or rebuilt

▬·▬·▬ Anglo–Scottish Border

0   10 Miles

0   10   20 Kilometres

Pencaitland

Grantshouse

Whiteadder

Fala

Preston

Duns

SCOTTISH EAST MARCH

Lauder

Greenlaw

Gordon

Coldstream

Biggar   Skirling

Tweed

Walkerburn

Earlston

Birgham

Innerleithen

Clovenfords

GALASHIELS

Melrose

Kelso

Coulter

Lamington

Yarrow

Selkirk

St Boswells

Maxton

Eckford

Town

Tweedsmuir

Cappercleuch

Ashkirk

SCOTTISH MIDDLE MARCH

Crailing

Yetholm

Crawford

Etterick Water

Jedburgh

Denholm

Hawick

Kirkton

Bonchester Bridge

Chesters

Newmill

White Esk

Teviot

Teviothead

Catcleugh

C H E V I O T   H I L L S

Moffat

Beattock

Rede

Newton

ENGLISH MIDDLE MARCH

St Ann's

Johnstonebridge

Newcastleton

N Tyne

Falstone

Parkgate

Annan

SCOTTISH WEST MARCH

Black Esk

Bellingham

Nith

Lochmaben

Langholm

MARCH

Lockerbie

Torthorwald

Collin

Roadhead

DUMFRIES

Ecclefechan

Eaglesfield

Lanercost Priory ✠

Annan

Gretna

Smithfield

Irthing

New Abbey

Bowness

Scaleby ✝

Brampton

Haltwhistle

Harper Town

Kirkbean

P Carlisle ✝

Burgh by Sands

Carlisle

Wetheral Priory ✠

S Tyne

Caulkerbush

Holme

Newton ✝

Arlosh

CARLISLE

Carnwhinton

Cultram

Abbey

Abbey

Town

Carlisle

Friary

Crogan

Alston

Beckfoot

Wigton ✝

Red Dial

High Hesket

S O L W A Y   F I R T H

Crosby

Ellen

Caldbeck ✝

Maryport

Boltongate ✝

Great Salkeld ✝

Melmerby ✝

Dearham ✝

Caldew

Brigham ✝

Cockermouth

Greystoke ✝

Edenhall ✝

Workington

Bassenthwaite

Penrith ✝

Temple

Harrington

Crosswaite ✝

Derwent

Pooley ✝ Barton

Distington

Water

Keswick

Bridge

5

THE ENGLISH WEST MARCH

Where the rivers Eden and Esk flow out into the Solway Firth lies Rockcliffe Marsh, an expanse of flat grassland that characterises the coastal edge to the former county of Cumberland. To the west, at Bowness-on-Solway, the sands of Gowkesk Rig to the north shine deceptively, silver and white in the early evening sunlight, and Scotland seems but a stone's throw away, but here the narrowness of the border crossing is illusive, for what may be slight in distance is heavy with penalties for the unwary in the treacherous, shifting mud and sand. The Solway sweeps on downwards past Morricambe until the mud and dune belts give way to sand south of Silloth, and the flat coastal marshes diminish.

South of the River Derwent the huge bulk of the Cumbrian Mountains acted as a natural barrier against most Scottish incursions further into England (except for early raids such as the one in 1322 which probably caused the prior to construct a gatehouse at Cartmel), although the extent of the English West March included the whole of the former counties of Cumberland and Westmorland. The towns of Cockermouth and Penrith lay on the fringes of Cumberland and defined its lower edge as its boundary ran up to the Durham and Northumberland border near Alston, on the margin of the lonely, upland moor of Gilderdale Forest.

Although technically the former county of Westmorland and the south-west portion of Cumberland lay within the March, they have largely been excluded from this work as they are considered to have been too far from the frontier to have warranted the necessity for commonplace ecclesiastical defensive measures, although examples are to be found (there were Scottish raids in 1315 and 1316 which reached as far as Furness (McKisack 1959, 40)). By the sixteenth century the area was not thought to be vulnerable, its inhabitants never having been called to general service by the Warden (Tough 1928, 16).

The eastern boundary of the March was formed by the Northumberland border, which followed the edge of the Pennines upwards into the foothills of the Cheviots. This eastern edge was characterised by bleak fell country as it ran through the inhospitable hills and moors of Renwick, Knaresdale, Geltsdale, and Tindale, before it met the River Irthing at Gilsland. This point was one of the most strategically significant places on the English Border. Known as the 'Gilsland Gap', a pass, about four miles in length, opens south-eastwards along the line of the Tipalt Burn, which provided a route into the southern part of the English Middle March, and which eventually led to Newcastle (*see* chapter 3). The area was very heavily defended by castles as far west as Naworth, near Brampton, where Ranulph of Dacre first received a licence to crenellate in 1335 (Cathcart King 1983, 89). Apart from the castles, a few scattered settlements lay around the valley of the Irthing but the perimeter line of the March struck northwards into the empty moorland wastes, until it eventually met the Scottish border on Caplestone Fell.

The boundary between the English and Scottish West Marches was the most disputed area of the frontier. At its eastern and western ends it was fairly straightforward; to the east it ran from Caplestone Fell and followed the Kershope Burn towards the Liddle Water. However, where the Liddle flows into the Esk, instead of following it down to the Solway as might be expected, the present border line runs due west along the earthwork known as 'Scot's Dike' until it meets the River Sark; from here all is logical again as it follows the Sark down to Gretna and out into the channel of the Esk just north of Rockcliffe Marsh. Behind this apparent discrepancy in the shape of the frontier lies a story of violence and unrest. This small parcel of land, which measured only four miles wide by twelve miles long, was known as the 'Debateable Land', a wild, lawless tract which belonged by dispute to neither nation or both, as circumstances dictated. The land played host to the worst of the Border villains, which proved a constant embarrassment to both England and Scotland. Finally, in 1552, the dispute was settled by the agreement of a formal border line which included the 'Scot's Dike' earthwork and the placing of the town of Canonbie firmly on the northern side (Mack 1926).

Although the English West March was bounded by hills and mountains on all three landward sides, the lower ground in the centre, and the coastal reaches, supported many small villages and farms which exploited the fertile lands of the small river valleys. This pattern of settlement was established by the twelfth century, before the start of the principal Border Troubles, and many of these villages evidently had, or were acquiring, stone-built churches by this period: Gilcrux, Ireby, Isel, Kirkbampton, Kirkbride, and Upper Denton are amongst the surviving examples. The churches of Brigham and Dearham have towers of the twelfth century which are decidedly defensible in form (although these towers were adapted at a later period), but there are few other towers of this era.

In 1597 a jury of the English West March recorded that the churches of Bewcastle, Stapleton, Arthuret, Lanercost, and Kirklinton were all decayed, some by a space of 'threescore years and more' (CBP, i, 312), indicating that they might have suffered as a result of repeated hostile incursions and the poverty of the troubled parishioners. The move to repair and rebuild was started by Anne Clifford, Countess of Pembroke, in 1655 when she restored St Lawrence's church, Appleby, and so influenced a campaign of rebuilding that slowly spread across the whole of Cumbria (Addison 1982, 171). In the area close to the Border, there are nineteenth-century churches at Walton, Hethersgill, Kirkcambeck, Gilsland, Stapleton, Kirklinton, and Nicholforest, and a building of 1776 at Kirkandrews. A few have traces of their predecessors – a single arch at Kirkcambeck and fragments of twelfth-century arches at Kirklinton. However, all evidence of any defensible traits has long since been destroyed.

Communications throughout the West March were strictly controlled; reference has been made to the Gilsland Gap, and the only other major routes were through the valleys of the rivers Eden and Esk, these being well guarded by the town of Carlisle. However, to the enterprising mind, there were other routes which could be exploited in order to effect illegal entry: over the Solway by boat, through the maze of Burgh Marsh, or by Kershopefoot and across the wild tract of the Bewcastle Fells.

CLOSE TO THE BORDER

Lying in the extreme north-east of the English West March, at its wildest corner, and close to the edge of the 'Debateable Land', is the small village of **Bewcastle**. Established by the Romans, whose six-acre hexagonal fort surrounds the present church and castle, the settlement started out its life as *Fanum Cocidi*, a military outpost just north of Hadrian's Wall.

St Cuthbert's Bewcastle is a comparatively small church, with an aisleless nave, chancel, and west tower. Some of the masonry is of Roman workmanship, and has clearly been robbed from the fort. The earliest portions of the building are the north wall of the nave and the east wall of the chancel which appear to be of *c.* 1200, based on the style of the three lancet windows at the east end, and the heavy, characteristically northern, early thirteenth-century buttresses. The south wall appears to have been restored in the early nineteenth century, when simple lancet windows were inserted. The tower dates from 1792 but probably replaces an earlier structure. Although there is no evidence of defence in the present fabric, it seems unlikely that a medieval church in this dangerous and exposed position would not have had some use as an emergency refuge. The only indication of former security is found in the north wall, part of the surviving thirteenth-century fabric, where there are no windows or doors, merely a robust stretch of unornamented stonework (though equally, this may have been an expedient device against the harsh weather).

Although not in any way related to defence, but illustrating the importance of the site, an exceptionally important pre-Conquest cross stands just to the south of the tower in the churchyard. Standing 4.4 m high above the base, the cross is carved on all sides with sacred figures, animals, birds, foliate decoration, and runic inscriptions. The most likely date of construction is in the first half of the eighth century (Henderson 1988; Smith 1996), although opinion is still divided.

Bewcastle was of some strategic importance to the English West March, and equally to the raiders and reivers of the Scottish West and Middle Marches who used the narrow roads to the north as thoroughfares into England. For this reason, a castle was established here in the fourteenth century, early in the Border wars, to hold a relatively small garrison of fifty horse and fifty foot. The castle, a square structure with a gatehouse and later barbican, was regularly attacked and repaired, and in its later days it was recorded that hardly a room remained 'wherein a man may sit dry' (Watson 1974, 37). However it was not only the Scots who came plundering over the Bewcastle Waste; the Captains of Bewcastle were on occasion equally adventurous as told in the Border Ballad of 'Jamie Telfer of the Fair Dodhead':

It fell about the Martinmas tyde
When our Border steeds get corn and hay
The Captain of Bewcastle hath bound him to ryde
And he's ower to Tividale to drive a prey . . .

(Reed 1991, 105)

In 1593, Lord Scrope, the Warden of the English West March, complained about the behaviour of his Captain at Bewcastle and claimed that he had helped two nefarious thieves to escape, but also accused William Elliot of Larriston, in the Scottish West March, of running 'an open day foray in Tyvedale' driving off over 2,000 nolt, sheep, goats, and horses (Tranter 1987, 200); such incidents amply illustrate the general lawlessness of the area. Even as late as 1632, the incumbent of Bewcastle, William Patrick, was renowned as a freebooter, and was assisted by his curate (Hugill 1939, 41).

No medieval churches have survived in the areas immediately to the west and south of Bewcastle. **Nicholforest** dates from 1867, **Hethersgill** from 1876, and a remnant of an arch at **Kirkcambeck**, reconstructed during the building of the present church in 1885, is all that remains from the earlier church. At **Stapleton**, a new building was erected in 1830 and all traces of the old church were lost. That it was in poor condition is beyond doubt, for Bishop Nicolson, visiting some 128 years earlier, had described it as 'intolerably scandalous . . . the parishioners follow the example of their Parson; and have the Body of the Church in as nasty a pickle as the Quire. The Roof is so miserably Shatter'd and broken, that it cannot be safe sitting under it (considering upon what an Ascent the Church stands) in stormy weather' (Ferguson 1877, 54). Perhaps 300 years of Border unrest had finally taken its toll, and in the relative peace of the seventeenth century the inhabitants were too poor and too few to put the church into a sound state of repair. However, the building was clearly well constructed as a description of 1794 attests: 'The walls are very thick, and the windows were exceedingly small, till they were enlarged about twelve years ago. It has no spire or bells, nor is it dedicated to any saint. The chancel is large in proportion to the church' (Graham 1930, 55). Although there was no tower, and the chancel had evidently been rebuilt at some stage, the thick walls and small

Fig. 123. Lanercost Priory, exterior view from the north-east.

windows of the nave indicate either a Romanesque building, or one which had possibly been made secure.

Seven miles due south of Bewcastle, in the quiet valley of the River Irthing, sits **Lanercost Priory** (Figure 123). Founded *c*. 1169, the priory of Augustinian Canons, probably colonised from Pentney in Norfolk, was given a generous tract of land between the Roman Wall and the Irthing by its benefactor, Robert de Vaux, who acquired the barony of Gilsland about four years previously (Dickinson 1942). Income was derived from further lands given in the nearby parishes of Walton and Farlam, and from the parish churches of those villages, as well as from those in Brampton, Carlatton, and Irthington (Lan.Cart., 1).

The layout of the priory follows the standard Augustinian pattern of an axial church with claustral buildings grouped on the south side. These buildings comprised a cloister with sacristy, vestibule, and chapter house to the east, a warming-house at the south-east corner, the frater and kitchen to the south, and a west range which included the prior's lodgings. In addition, there was a gatehouse to the west of the site, and a vicar's residence in the form of a small defensible tower.

There is little about the siting of Lanercost which is defensible – rather the opposite, for the priory sits on flat land in the foot of the valley, close to the river. It is a normal location for a monastery which included farming amongst its day-to-day activities and which therefore needed flat, fertile land, sheltered from the worst of the weather, and close to a source of fresh water. However, raiding began here right at the start of the Troubles, in 1296, and continued throughout the centuries of unrest. Peter Langtoft, a local poet and Canon of Hexham, was moved to write of the first raid:

> Corbrigge is a toun, thei brent it whan thei cam;
> Tuo hous of religioun, Laynercoste and Hexham,
> Thei chaced the chanons out, their goodes bare away,
> And robbed all about; the bestis tok to prey.

> (Wilson, 1901–5, ii, 157)

During this first raid, which was led by the Earl of Buchan, the Scots set fire to the cloister, and large parts of the claustral buildings were probably destroyed or badly damaged (Chr.Lan., 136). The following year, William Wallace led his army past Lanercost and once again the monastery was raided and partially destroyed. Three years later, with the war well underway, Edward I stayed in the priory on his way to the seige of Caerlaverock castle in the Scottish West March. He returned again in 1306 once more intending to use Lanercost as a stop-over on his journey, but he was taken ill and was forced to remain over the winter until the following March (Moorman 1952). Five years later, King Robert I stayed here during one of his forays over the Border; in the intervening period the priory had gained the churches of Mitford and Carlatton, given by Edward I on account of the damage caused by the Scots and which reflected his obvious gratitude for the prior's help during his illness (Lan.Cart., 248). The use of the priory in this way, as a safe lodging for royal retinues, indicates that the buildings were considered to be secure.

The next major event in the history of the priory was in 1346, when Lanercost was seriously damaged and completely ransacked by the invading army of King David II (Chr.Lan., 332). Against such a formidable attack, any structural defensible measures proved to be of little use, and the buildings were entered and burnt. In 1384 it was again sacked and never fully recovered financially; in 1409 it was the subject of an archbishop's appeal due to its poverty (Robinson 1982, 75). However, the priory was rebuilt after each of these episodes, and elements of security were included, although the almost constant rebuildings took their toll financially on the canons. By the sixteenth century their income had fallen to below £80 per year, mainly due to the necessity to sell off land and assets to pay for damage caused by the raiding.

The buildings at Lanercost today are largely intact, and the west part of the church is still used for worship. Therefore a good idea may be gained of the structure and layout of the site when it was in monastic use.

The church itself has no outwardly defensible features, although the narrow thirteenth-century lancet windows are all placed well above ground level and would not have afforded easy access into the building. The west and central north doorways have evidence of former draw-bar slots. The west end has

Fig. 124. Lanercost Priory, musket-ball damage to the stonework of the west front.

triple lancets, placed very high in the gable above the main doorway, and likewise the east lancets in the sanctuary are well above the ground. To the north, a minimum of windows punctuate the aisle wall with one further opening to the west. There is a strong central tower, now ruined, capped by crenellations, and having only tiny slit windows beneath the parapet. However, none of this is particularly unusual for a monastic church of the thirteenth century, and architectural fashion was mainly responsible for the form of the building. Yet it is interesting to note that, as styles changed during the next two centuries, there was no attempt to introduce larger, lighter windows into the church or tower. Although cost may have been a prime consideration, the more easily defended nature of the narrow, high openings may also have been a factor in the retention of the earlier design, a feature seen at other Border churches such as Brinkburn, Coldingham, and Norham. At least one incident may have prompted the use of the church as a refuge, as damage, apparently caused by musket-shot, is clearly visible in the west front (Figure 124).

Fig. 125. Lanercost Priory, the prior's lodgings in the west range.

In the design of the claustral buildings some regard is clearly given to defence. Although the main utilitarian areas have a standard form, the prior's lodgings and vicar's residence take the form of strong towers. In the case of the prior's lodgings, it is difficult to appreciate the extent of the original scheme, as this building was considerably modified by the Dacre family after the Dissolution in the sixteenth century (Moorman 1967). The tower, which projects from the end of the west range, was probably first constructed in the late thirteenth century, but appears to have been heavily modified in the sixteenth century, and has typically Elizabethan style windows with stone mullions and transoms (Figure 125). Access to the upper floors was by spiral staircase, arranged from ground to first floor in the north-west corner and from first to second floor in the north-east corner, to prevent easy passage for any assailant; however, when first built, the access to the upper floors was probably only from an external stair on the east side of the building.

Fig. 126. Lanercost Priory, 'King Edward's Tower'.

Opposite the west range, at its northern end, is a small defensible tower belonging to an earlier period in the priory's history (Figure 126). Despite being modified in later centuries, the tower, called 'King Edward's Tower', appears to date from the thirteenth century as evidenced by the dog-tooth moulding below the battlements, and was clearly constructed as a fortified adjunct to the priory proper. Its early function remains uncertain although it most probably served as a defensible residence for the prior before the construction of the larger tower in the west range, and it may have also functioned as a guest-house for the monastery's more important visitors.

The small town of Brampton lies a short way down the valley of the River Irthing to the south-west of Lanercost. The present church of St Martin, in the centre of the town, was built between 1874 and 1878, by the Arts and Crafts architect Philip Webb. However, one mile to the west, along a narrow track, is **Brampton Old Church**, overlooking the land to the west from its elevated position above the River Irthing. The church stands in the corner of a Roman fort, and no doubt the stone used in its construction was obtained from the garrison buildings. In its present state, the structure has only a twelfth-century chancel with a nineteenth-century extension to the east; all the rest has long since vanished. The little building is remarkably austere with its solemn red and grey sandstone walls and remarkably few openings; there are just two tiny windows in the north wall, one in the south wall, and one high window in the gable of the east end. These openings are all over 2 m (6 ft 7 in.) above ground level and on average measure only 1 m (3 ft 3 in.) high by 0.25 m (10 in.) wide. The defensible nature of this church is clear enough: in its elevated position, its construction within the confines of the earlier fort, and the singular lack of openings within its walls. However, all this is of the twelfth century, largely before the Border Troubles, and quite in keeping with the style of the period. Yet, although the church continued to be used throughout the medieval period and beyond, no enlargement of the windows was attempted. Perhaps, as at nearby Lanercost, this was a precautionary measure to enable the building to be used as a safe refuge, such as the times in 1318 and 1384 when the town was laid waste (Robinson 1982). Bishop Nicolson described the church in 1704 as 'in a Slovenly pickle; dark, black and ill-seated' (Ferguson 1877, 142).

One church which survived Victorian rebuilding, but only by its ruination to make way for a new church nearby, is at **Upper Denton**. The building is a small two-celled structure, probably containing some pre-Conquest fabric in the east and north walls of the nave. It was restored in 1881. The church is illustrated in a fourteenth-century marginal note in the Lanercost Cartulary (Lan.Cart., 4), which shows a simple, two-celled building, with a large window in the chancel and a narrow single light in the nave.

To the west of Brampton, St Kentigern's church at **Irthington** retains its medieval core with twelfth-century aisle arcades and a thirteenth-century chancel and arch. However, the rest was rebuilt between 1849 and 1853 when the building was refenestrated; the north-west tower was added in 1897. There is no indication in the present fabric of any defensible features. In the church is a watercolour painting by the Reverend John Hancock, vicar at the time of the major restoration. The painting shows the church in 1842, before alterations began, and reveals it to have a been a plain rectangle, possibly with very narrow aisles (cf: Elsdon, English Middle March), and with eighteenth-century style 'domestic' windows on the south – except for two narrow round-headed windows at the east end. In 1703, Bishop Nicolson commented that the choir was 'so vilely out of Repair in the Roof that 'tis hazardous comeing in it' (Ferguson 1877, 52).

Four miles to the north-west of Irthington, the village of **Scaleby** possesses a medieval church which has largely escaped the ravages of the nineteenth-century wave of rebuilding (apart from its chancel), and which contains good evidence for defence.

All Saints church, Scaleby, is essentially a thirteenth-century building, with

Fig. 127. Scaleby, exterior of the defensible west tower.

a simple plan comprising an aisleless nave with a south porch, chancel, and west tower. The original chancel was replaced during the Victorian restoration, probably in 1861, and no medieval work now remains. However, the nave retains its early form, with lancet windows, including two which are placed in the west wall to either side of the tower, well above floor level, at a height of 2.4 m (7 ft 10 in.) to the cills. The retention of these narrow openings throughout the medieval period would certainly have prevented access other than through the main doorways, the southern of which has been secured with a heavy lock. Yet the nave walls are not unusually thick at 0.8 m (2 ft 7 in.); indeed the nineteenth-century chancel walls are of a comparable thickness. However, as usual in medieval defensible structures, it is the tower that contains the greatest evidence for means of security.

The tower of Scaleby church appears to be, like the nave, of thirteenth-century date, except the uppermost level which dates from 1828 (Figure 127). This

Fig. 128. Scaleby, doorway into the tower from the west.

later work is clearly visible on the exterior, where the red sandstone abruptly changes hue above the second level windows (except on the east where medieval and post-medieval work intermix over the nave roof). However, careful examination of the style of construction, and in particular the windows – which appear to be of a functional, late medieval design – implies a date within the fifteenth century (Kelland 1982, 207), which would be more in keeping with the tower's use as a defensible building during the period of the Troubles.

From the exterior the tower appears very simple, with single narrow windows in each accessible face on the first and second floors. On the ground floor, these windows are 1.9 m (6 ft 3 in.) to the lower cills, and are only 0.17 m (7 in.) in width, making access through them impossible. Entry from inside the church was strictly controlled: there is no tower-arch but simply a round-headed doorway, opening straight through the 1 m (3 ft 3 in.) thick wall (Figure 128). Although the present wooden door is modern, there is clear evidence in the form of slots – probably to house two separate draw-bars – and hinge supports, that a much more substantial portal once guarded this entrance. Inside, the tower is square on plan and is 4.75 m (15 ft 7 in.) high to the first floor which has only ever been reached by ladder – further evidence of security. Mortices in the east and west walls above the entrance within this level are of unclear purpose. The whole structure has the appearance of solidity and strength, emphasised by the use of large sandstone blocks. The first floor is similar to the ground in construction, and its fenestration echoes that below. In the east wall, at the south-east corner, a doorway opens through the wall to emerge, plainly visible, in the nave; its purpose is unclear. This portal has a shallow draw-bar slot, showing that it was intended to be secured from within the tower, and it is possible that it was originally intended as a secure upper entrance (cf. Newburn, English Middle March). Above, at second-floor level, is another aperture formed through the centre of the wall. The purpose of high-level doorways such as this remains a puzzle, and was perhaps related to liturgical practice (Bond 1908; Taylor 1978, 829; Morris 1983, 3), but upper doorways are also found which may indicate former use of the nave roof space (Parsons 1979). Here at Scaleby the opening through the centre of the east wall at high level may also have served as a window from the tower to give a clear view into the nave (Graham 1921).

The village of Longtown, only three miles south of the Border, has no medieval church within its bounds, having been newly founded as a planned village in the late eighteenth century by Dr Robert Graham (Pevsner 1967, 158), although a 'Longtown' was known in this area from 1584 (Bulman and Frith, 1987). The settlement is, however, served by the church at Arthuret, some three-quarters of a mile further south.

The exterior fabric of **Arthuret** church is entirely post-medieval in date. Rebuilding started around 1609 and was perhaps not completed until the latter half of the seventeenth century (Bulman 1966), however the core may retain elements of the earlier structure. The reconstruction was almost certainly required due to the maltreatment inflicted by its siting – within, or just outside, the 'Debateable Land' – where conflict and violence were an even greater everyday occurrence than for other parts of the Border. The violence started at an early date, with a devastating raid in the spring of 1296 by John Comyn on his way to attack Carlisle (Barrow 1988). In 1302 and 1319 the church was totally destroyed by the Scots (Graham 1928). In 1597 a jury of the West March found that the church had been decayed for more than sixty years and that the patron was unknown. Finally, in 1606, King James VI and I wrote to the Archbishop of Canterbury to highlight the condition of Arthuret parish and church, and stated that he had granted a licence for a general collection for the rebuilding of the said church (Bulman and Frith 1987, 3–4).

Although most of the present fabric is of the seventeenth century, it is clear that the church was constructed on the foundations of the earlier building, and some medieval work may remain in the core of the south wall and south side of the tower. The siting was significant – above the steep bank of the Esk's flood plain with excellent views northward into Scotland – but nevertheless the church lay on the vulnerable route between the Border and Carlisle.

To the north-west of Arthuret is the Solway Moss. Between the church and the Moss, early on a cold November morning in 1542, Sir Thomas Wharton, Lord Warden of the English West March, led his few English light horsemen in a seemingly impossible action against an invading Scottish army which outnumbered them by four to one. Incredibly, and mainly due to gross disorganisation on the part of the Scots, Wharton's men, picking at their flanks, managed to rout the more numerous northerners and succeeded in trapping them between the Esk ford and the 'muckle black moss' of the swamp behind. Around 1,200 Scots were taken prisoner including Lord Maxwell, Warden of the Scottish West March, and many were drowned in the river or lost in the marsh (McIntire 1941).

The church at **Kirkandrews-on-Esk** was known in the Middle Ages as the 'Chapel of Salom', and was probably served by the monks of Canonbie Priory, as at that time the place was in Scotland and lay within the 'Debateable Land' (Graham 1931). The present building was erected in 1776 leaving no trace of its antecedent.

THE CITY OF CARLISLE

Carlisle has been described as a city 'born under Mars on the highway of war' (Mee 1937, 48). It is the only very large settlement (aside from the town of Berwick) either in England or Scotland which is placed close to the Border. As such it formed a focal point for warlike and political activity of all kinds, reaching well back beyond the start of the principal Anglo-Scottish wars. In the tenth and eleventh centuries, Carlisle was a Scottish town until, in 1092, William II of England captured the city from King Malcom III of Scotland, rebuilt it, and fortified it with a castle. As a result of this action the English frontier was advanced to the Tweed-Cheviot line, and, despite attempts to win back the captured land by the Scots, it was held until David I's violent campaign of the 1130s wrested it back. However, Carlisle was too important to be left alone by either side; it was the gateway to Scotland for the English, and in July 1157 the young King Malcom IV acceded both the town and the northern lands of England to his stronger neighbour, King Henry II. Sixteen years later, the Scots attacked the city again, led by King William the Lion who specifically ordered his troops not to attack the church (Owen 1997, 48), a hint that the building may have been useful for defence; William certainly had no such qualms when his troops attacked Warkworth, slaughtering those who had taken refuge inside the church (*see* page 153).

Carlisle was an important frontier defence, with a strong castle and walls enclosing nearly 18 hectares (45 acres). The city was protected in front by the

River Eden, above which it rose fully 18 m (59 ft), and on its flanks by the tributaries Petterill and Caldew. Within the walls the castle stood on the highest ground, and the precinct of the abbey and cathedral occupied almost a quarter of the entire area. The constant danger from Scottish raids is amply illustrated by the official regulations in the sixteenth century where: 'no Scot was to live within the city; nor to be seen walking therein after watchbell rang at night, save in the company of a freeman; no apprentices were to be admitted, coming from north of Blackford or the Irthing. Watchmen were to guard the walls day and night, gates to be shut before dark, and chains to be drawn tight between the city and the Eden bridges' (Tranter 1987, 194).

A mid-sixteenth-century map of the city, now preserved in the British Library (McCarthy 1993, 72), depicts the castle at the north end, the cathedral and abbey buildings in the centre, and only one other church, just south of the abbey, presumably St Cuthbert's Within, the principal parish church of Carlisle. This last church which was completely rebuilt in 1778, is depicted as a simple rectangular building, with a south porch; there is no tower (only a west bellcote), and no obvious defensible features. Apart from the cathedral there are no pre-nineteenth-century churches in Carlisle today, although in the medieval period there was also the chapel of St Alban (with a bell tower), two friaries – Dominican and Franciscan (the latter also having a separate bell tower), and to the south of the city the hospital of St Nicholas (Summerson 1993, ii, 590). Grey Friars (the Franciscans) is of some interest in the defence of the city, for in an inventory of goods made in 1534, it was noted that there was ordnance and a number of military items including: 41 salletts, 64 archer salletts, 180 beavers, 16 complete bodies of harness, 6 backs for bodies, 180 breasts, 52 pair splints, 10 pair leg harness, 2 sarks of mail, and 3 halberds' (Jones 1981, 161). It was quite clear that the king had commandeered buildings in the friary for the purpose of storing armaments. In an earlier episode of the city's history, Edward Balliol, having barely escaped from Annan with his life (*see* page 330), lodged in the Franciscan friary during Christmas of 1332 (Chr.Lan, 275).

The cathedral has its origins during the early years of Henry I's reign, when, in 1122, keen to introduce a stabilising but controllable element into Carlisle, he invited Augustinian Canons to convert an earlier ecclesiastical foundation into a monastic house (Offler 1965, 178). In 1133, Henry created the See of Carlisle, appointing Adelulf as its first bishop. This was an important political move, as the town had previously been dependent on the ministrations of the Scottish Bishop of Glasgow, and the king was keen to form a clear national partition.

The cathedral, or former abbey church, had a nave with side aisles, a central tower, north and south transepts, and a choir, also with side aisles. Belonging to the twelfth century are the first two bays of the nave, the crossing, and the south transept. A fire in 1292 caused considerable damage, and resulted in the rebuilding of part of the choir. In 1380 the tower was blown down in a great storm which also caused considerable damage to the north transept; the

Fig. 129. Carlisle Cathedral, turret above the tower roof.

rebuilding of tower and north transept was completed in the early fifteenth century, under Bishop Strickland. During the Civil War, in 1644–6, the western 30 m (100 ft) of the nave were destroyed by General Leslie in order to build barracks, and to repair the castle for the parliamentary forces; the cathedral thus unwittingly played a major part in the re-fortification of the town, albeit to its physical detriment (Perriam 1987).

There is little evidence of security within the church itself. The tower was easily defensible in the event of attack, but is little different to any other major church tower of its period. However, the uppermost turret, which dates from around 1419 and has a separate stair, may have been used as a watch and signal tower to warn the town of impending attack by the Scots; lighted beacons were safer if located above the flat leads of the tower roof (Figure 129). It seems probable that the bells would also have been used for this purpose. The bells (probably both town and church bells) were apparently used to rouse the sleeping town when the Scots rescued 'Kinmont Willie' from the castle in 1596 (Will Armstrong was a notorious reiver who had been captured by Scrope, the English Warden, in defiance of a truce agreement):

> We scarce had won the Staneshaw-bank
> When a' the Carlisle bells were rung

And a thousand men on horse and foot
Cam wi' the keen Lord Scroope along.

(Marsden 1990, 175)

Closer examination of the church does suggest that elements of defence were included at the design stages, particularly in the twelfth-century fabric: buttresses are of substantial construction, most windows are positioned well above ground-level, and the outer wall of the south transept is almost 2.5 m (8 ft) in thickness. In the fourteenth-century southern arches of the chancel clerestory are several regular mortice holes, perhaps designed to support a screen or barrier. It has been suggested (Henry Stapleton, *personal communication*) that such a device may have been inserted to prevent missiles, fired from without the city wall, on the vulnerable south side, from reaching the interior of the cathedral. There is evidence to show that such missiles were used – and with effect: in 1383 the Scots, on making their way home, shot fire over the city walls setting one of the streets alight (Summerson 1992, 158). Any elements of defence were, however, of little use in stopping an armed mob who entered the cathedral in 1385 in support of the prior, who had been threatened with excommunication by the bishop over a judicial dispute (Wilson 1901–5, ii, 134).

It is in the claustral buildings to the former abbey that the greatest indications of security are found. In addition to the perimeter wall, three separate buildings existed which were capable of playing a defensible role: the frater, the gatehouse, and the prior's lodging. The first of these, the refectory, formed part of the south range of the cloister, and is still in an almost perfect state of preservation. It was built in the early fourteenth century, though its upper stage was remodelled by Prior Gondibour *c.* 1500. The large perpendicular windows in the west and south walls are nineteenth-century, but the openings which they exploit, and which no doubt contained earlier windows, all have their cills at a considerable height above ground level in order to light only the first floor; the north wall still retains its small, fourteenth-century, two-light windows. The ground floor of this building is an early fourteenth-century undercroft to the former refectory above, and is stone rib-vaulted throughout. Although lacking specific features of security, the general design of this building, with its fireproof ground-floor chamber and secure upper floors and later parapet, could have been utilised for defence.

The gatehouse lies to the north-west of the cathedral and was built in 1527 by Prior Slee, as an inscription over the arch testifies: '*Orate pro anima Christopheri Slee: qui primus hoc opus fieri incipit* A.D. MDXXVII'. The passageway through the gatehouse is divided into two parts, one for pedestrian use and the other for carriages; both are tunnel-vaulted and the main archways are triple-chamfered. The upper floor has a single three-light window on the inner side, lighting the first-floor room. Gatehouses were generally intended to be defensible, and Carlisle's is no exception (Figure 130). The original wooden gates have

Fig. 130. Carlisle Cathedral, Prior Slee's gateway from outside the precinct.

staples on their interior faces to support a large draw-bar, and the masonry of
the side walls bears evidence of former locks and bolts.

   Finally, the most clearly defensible structure (though perhaps only nomi-
nally so) is the former prior's lodgings, which takes the form of a strong tower
(Figure 131). The tower lies to the south of the church, and was constructed *c.*
1510–1520 by Prior Simon Stenhouse. The basement level is tunnel-vaulted with
five substantial transverse arches, and was originally windowless. Access to the
upper floors is by a narrow, partly circular, staircase within the thickness of
the wall, which added considerably to the security arrangements. Once past
the functional defensible area however, the first floor opens out into a comfortable room with two oriel windows on the north and south sides, and a fine
ceiling with moulded beams and painted decoration, an inscription declaring
that: 'Simon Stenhus sette thys roofe and scallope here'.

Fig. 131. Carlisle, the prior's lodgings.

The Chronicle of Lanercost relates that in 1315 the cathedral was attacked and valiantly defended whilst sheltering the king. Within the space of a year, from July 1316, the English West March was attacked twice, but the priory buildings appear to have been unscathed, perhaps due in part to the earlier, spirited defence. However, a letter from Archbishop Melton in 1318 granted an indulgence to the cathedral which had been burnt by the Scots (Hexham Memorials, XLIV). It is possible that the building attacked in 1315 may not have been the cathedral, as the reference in the Chronicle is to the Church of the Holy Trinity, a dedication which the priory church did not assume until 1541. In fact another medieval church, with such a dedication, probably existed in the vicinity of Bridge Street, to the west of Caldew Bridge, although no remains now survive above ground (Perriam 1979). It was perhaps in this church rather than the cathedral that the king placed himself for safety during the Scottish siege.

Fig. 132. Wetheral Priory gatehouse from the exterior.

The incumbents of the priory and cathedral appear to have been reluctant to take part in the general defence of the city, as they are recorded as not willing to participate in the watch. However in 1430 it was agreed that the prior should provide a 'watcheman for to wake on the towne wall, as the mannere is ilk a nygh at his awen coste' (Summerson 1993, ii, 430).

That the building was secure is not in doubt, and even long after the end of the main Anglo-Scottish hostilities this feature was exploited. In 1745, following the suppression of the Jacobite rising, some 300 to 400 rebel prisoners were held captive inside the cathedral.

The main reason that Carlisle cathedral did not need to have greater outward physical protection lies in the fact that it is sited within a walled city in the shadow of a powerful castle. The castle had its own chapel, a church in miniature, within formidable defences. Probably part of a continuous range, the chapel was located within the inner ward, to the north or east of the keep

(McCarthy *et al* 1990), but there are now no traces surviving above ground. Also, there may have been a room allocated as a second chapel within the keep, but considerable alterations to the upper floors have obscured the original purpose of many chambers (Watson and Bradley 1937).

Five miles to the east of Carlisle stand the remains of **Wetheral** Priory. The remnants of the former Benedictine Priory, founded *c.* 1106 by Ranulph de Meschines (Knowles and Hadcock 1971), are located on the west bank of the River Eden. They consist of the intact gatehouse, with fragments of medieval walls in the adjacent farmyard (probably in the area of the former claustral buildings).

The gatehouse of the priory is an imposing structure. It is fashioned out of red sandstone, with a single tunnel-vaulted arch beneath, a vaulted ground-floor chamber on the south side, two floors above, and terminates in a crenellated parapet; the whole dates from the fifteenth century (Figure 132). The upper floors are reached by a narrow spiral stairway in a turret on the north side. The cusped windows, two- light on the front and single light elsewhere, are sufficiently embellished to be fashionable for the day whilst remaining small enough to permit a sound level of defence.

The parish church of Wetheral, a short distance north of the priory, is a complex building belonging to many periods. The core is undoubtedly medieval – the nave arcades are of the thirteenth century – but later modifications, including the tower of 1790, the Howard mausoleum of 1791, and the rebuilding of most of the chancel in 1872, have largely obliterated the form of the medieval structure.

At **Warwick Bridge**, a mile and a half to the north-east of Wetheral, is the church of St Leonard. Although now having no evidence for security or defence (it was largely rebuilt in 1870), the building has a remarkable Norman apse, ornamented on the exterior by a series of pilaster strips each defining a deep recess. The interior arch mouldings are very similar in style to those found in Carlisle Cathedral and as such date to around 1130. The church also once extended further west, the author Thomas Pennant who visited in 1772 thought by as much as 21 ft (6.4 m) further, and there may have been a Norman tower as he described a 'rounded arch, now filled-up' (Graham 1913, 90).

THE SOLWAY FRINGE

The land to the west of Carlisle, bordering the Solway Firth, was particularly vulnerable to surprise raids by sea, and by the perilous crossing places over the sand and mud, known as 'waths'. Although the treacherous nature of the Solway's tides were well known, the inhabitants of the coastal reaches of both West Marches (Scottish and English) understood these waters better than anyone else, and they knew well how to exploit them to their advantage (Blake

1982). Although the Solway presented no significant barrier for the determined men on either side of the Border, it was nevertheless treated with great respect. Of this treacherous tidal estuary, Sir Walter Scott was moved to write: 'He who sleeps on Solway bed, wakes up in the next world.'

Despite the easy access from Scotland, the coastal plains of the English West March do not seem to have suffered as much from raiding as might be expected (MacDonald Fraser 1989, 40). Probably the proximity of Carlisle, with its permanent garrison, helped to curb impromptu Scots forays into this rich area.

The main route westward from Carlisle roughly follows the course of Hadrian's Wall, towards its ultimate termination at Bowness-on-Solway; the Romans clearly considered the estuary an insufficient barrier to enemies from the north. The tiny isolated church at **Grinsdale**, perched above, and in an elbow of the River Eden, was rebuilt in 1740. It has no features pertaining to defence. A fourteenth-century illustration (Lan.Cart., 93) indicates that the medieval building was a simple two-celled structure.

Two miles to the north-west, with the Roman wall actually running through its graveyard, the church of St Mary, **Beaumont**, sits on top of a steep mound in the centre of the village. This mound actually gives the place its name: *Beaumund* (in 1292), meaning 'beautiful hill' (Ekwall 1960, 33). It affords fine views to the north, south, and east, and forms a natural strong-point, which was undoubtedly exploited by the inhabitants as the village lay close to three waths over the Solway, bringing attendant danger (McIntire 1939, 154). The church itself is not defensible, except, perhaps, by virtue of its elevated position. There is no tower, nor would there be room to construct one on the mound. The building has a nave and chancel under one roof, with a west bellcote and a south porch. There is some twelfth-century work, notably the south doorway, which may be a re-used archway (Pevsner 1967, 65), and the east wall with its interior blind arcading and three tiny windows. Re-used Roman stone can be found throughout. The major restorations of 1872 and 1888 considerably altered the interior of the church and were responsible for the style of the present window openings, except those at the east end. Much of the evidence for the building's medieval form has been lost.

St Michael's church, **Burgh-by-Sands**, one mile to the west of Beaumont, is built within the site of the Roman fort of *Aballava*, a frontier post on Hadrian's Wall. Long after the fort had fallen into disuse its stones were used to build a new defence in the shape of one of the most significant defensible churches in the Border region. Lying within the same dangerous area as Beaumont, close to the Solway waths, the need for security was unquestionable. However, the scale on which this is provided at Burgh is comparable with any tower or fortalice built for private use.

The building consists of a nave with north aisle, chancel, west tower, and the remains of another tower east of the chancel (Figure 133). The earliest work is Norman, as evidenced by the *ex situ* north doorway with its characteristic

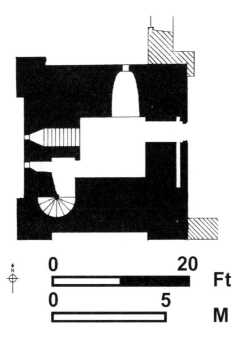

Fig. 133. Burgh-by-Sands, plan of the tower (after Curwen 1913b).

beakhead decoration (though the upper part has been renewed). The body of the nave and chancel has core fabric of thirteenth-century date, with lancet windows and stiff-leaf capitals in the north arcade, although the south wall of the nave was rebuilt in the eighteenth century, when an aisle on this side of the building was removed. Its two towers were added in the fourteenth century. The date and purpose of a blocked doorway in the west wall of the north aisle is unclear. In common with most other churches, there was a major restoration of the building in the nineteenth century (1880–1).

The broad bulky west tower displays a severely defensible form, and ranks alongside the bleakest tower-houses in its display of sombre puissance; it is built like a castle keep (Figure 134). At the angles there are massive buttresses which run up to the top of the first floor, ending where they slope back to form the belfry stage. The lower walls are constructed in heavy ashlar blocks of red, grey, and yellow sandstone, much taken from the Roman station nearby. However, the upper stage lacks the diversity of colour, and is clearly a later modification and a different style of construction. The belfry windows too are obviously post-medieval, being simple round-headed openings, fashioned straight through the wall; they are probably of the eighteenth century, although the restored crenellations on the parapet may echo the earlier work which they supplanted.

At ground-floor level the windows reflect the martial nature of the tower.

Fig. 134. Burgh-by-Sands, exterior of the fortified west tower.

The west is positioned 2.4 m (7 ft 10 in.) high and appears on the exterior merely as a narrow slit, 0.12 m (5 in.) wide, whilst on the north there is a single gun-loop, 0.16 m (6 in.) in diameter (Figure 135). There are no exterior door-ways into the tower, and the gun-loop is positioned so as to defend the prin-cipal entrance to the church through the north doorway of the nave, and would also have protected the former west doorway into the aisle. This form of defence is likely to be a later medieval modification, after firearms came into fashion. Inside, the only way into the tower at ground level is through a heavily defended doorway in the west wall (Figure 136). There is no arch, but instead a substantial iron 'yat', or gate, closes off the pointed opening which leads through the 1.9 m (6 ft 3 in.) thick wall into the lower chamber of the tower; evidence of Roman masonry, robbed from the fort, is conspicuous in the walls, with its characteristically heavy tooling. The yat originally may have had oak planking attached (as at Great Salkeld), and there are two iron staples on the

Fig. 135. Burgh-by-Sands, gun-loop in the north wall of the west tower.

central part of the gate for a draw-bar, with a corresponding deep slot within
the reveal. In addition to this method of closure there are supplementary iron
bolts above and below, which are still in use as a method of securing the gate.
Inside the basement chamber the deeply splayed openings of the west window
and north gun-loop can be seen, and it is apparent that the west opening could
also be used for artillery defence, as its inner reveal takes the form of a stepped
cill, similar to a form found in castle architecture. These external walls are
thicker still, an imposing 2.2 m (7 ft 3 in.), proof against any conventional form
of attack. The roof of the ground-floor chamber is stone tunnel-vaulted, 2.9 m
(9 ft 6 in.) high in the centre (Figure 137). Access to the upper floors is via a
spiral staircase, set within the thickness of the wall, at the south-west corner.

The upper floors of the tower have been considerably modified from their
original form. The first floor is devoid of any features except two splayed windows in the west and south walls, and a small lancet window, opening through

Fig. 136. Burgh-by-Sands, yat closing off the entrance to the west tower from the nave.

the east wall, which gives a view into the nave of the church. Above this floor, the spiral stairway continues up to the roof and passes a now defunct doorway which once led onto a second floor, long since vanished.

The building of Burgh church tower may be dated with reasonable confidence to the mid-fourteenth century, as it was the subject of a commission of enquiry, dated 15 July 1360, by the Bishop of Carlisle, relating to the collapse of several arches in the church whilst building operations were in progress (Grainger and Collingwood 1929).

At the east end of the building a second tower is represented now only by the ground floor (Figure 138), the upper levels having been destroyed when this portion of the church was converted to a schoolroom sometime between 1703 and 1747 (Perriam and Robinson 1998). In the year 1703, Bishop Nicolson described the two towers at Burgh as follows: 'The bells hang in a good square

Fig. 137. Burgh-by-Sands, stone tunnel vaulting to the ground-floor chamber of the west tower.

steeple at the west end, and there has been another in the east. But this is now half broken down. A small charge would turn it into a school house which they want' (Ferguson 1877, 14).

The east tower is 6.75 m (22 ft) in length and is constructed of larger blocks of red and yellow sandstone than the body of the church; the thickness of the walls averages 1.1 m (3 ft 7 in.). There is too little of this tower surviving to provide an indication of its original purpose, but the upper floors may have contained evidence for living accommodation, for example in the form of a fireplace and perhaps a garderobe (cf. Newton Arlosh). However, there can be little doubt that a tower in this position could only have been for defensible purposes, given the nature of the western structure. The difference in the use between the two towers lay in the customary distinction in the division of the church, east and west, between clergy and lay folk (Kelland 1982, 192).

Fig. 138. Burgh-by-Sands, exterior view of the ground floor of the former east tower.

Like most of the villages in the vicinity of Carlisle, Burgh suffered from frequent Scottish raids during the fourteenth century, especially in the middle years when the fortified manor-house was destroyed (Storey 1955), but each time the parish appears to have recovered quickly from these devastations (Summerson 1992).

A fourteenth-century marginal illustration of the church appears in the *Lanercost Cartulary* (Lan.Cart., 37), which shows a tall nave with windows positioned very high, a blank west tower and a short chancel, also with high windows. Indeed, the present north windows, all lancets, are 2.3 m (7 ft 7 in.) to the cills above the floor internally.

Burgh-by-Sands is famous for one major historical event. It was here in 1307 that King Edward I died (Chr.Lan., 182). After months of illness at Carlisle and Lanercost Priory, Edward had set forward, once more intent on challenging the Scots, only to meet his demise whilst encamped with his army just north of the village on Burgh Marsh. Today a monument marks the site where Edward's dream of a conquered Scotland expired; the square pillar, 6 m (20 ft) high, was first erected in 1685, but was rebuilt in 1803 and restored in 1876.

At the westernmost end of Hadrian's wall lies the tiny village of **Bowness-on-Solway**, the *Maia* of the Roman military machine. St Michael's church, predictably built largely of Roman stones, sits on a rise in the south-east corner of the old fort. Despite the severe restoration of 1891, when the interior arches to the chancel and north transept were altered, and many of the windows modified, the building still retains an element of thirteenth-century austerity. The earliest work is in fact a century earlier, shown by the late Norman north and south doorways to the nave, and a single twelfth-century window in the north wall of the chancel. However, it is the massive thirteenth-century buttresses, appearing like rough-hewn, natural rock reinforcements, which give the church its solid and robust appearance.

When John Leland visited Bowness in 1539 he found 'a lytle poore steple as a fortelet for a brunt' (Leland, v, fo.69). Writing as he was, in the thick of the Border skirmishes of the sixteenth century, what he saw may have been the adaptation of the church for use as a fortification, though his words imply that it was not in a good state of repair. Christopher Dacre's survey of 1580 implies that the tower was connected with the rectory, although the church and rectory may have been either juxtaposed or physically united. Dacre commented that 'This house or towre belonge to ye psonadge . . . a place of small receipt and yet very necessarie for defence of yt pte of the border, ptly decayed . . . wth a plattforme for ordnance . . . upon ye same towre' (Perriam and Robinson 1998, 60). There was evidently a turret or small tower either attached to the church, or within the vicinity of the churchyard, with a gun platform, although all evidence of this was destroyed around 1860 (Curwen 1913b, 255; Cathcart King 1983, 92).

It is known from local accounts that the church did suffer at the hands of the Scots, and at a surprisingly late date. In 1626 (twenty-three years after the Union) the Scots raided Bowness church and stole the bells. Unfortunately for them, they were seen and chased by boat across the Solway, where, in order to escape, the Scots threw their plunder overboard into the water in the place now called 'Bell Dub' or 'Bell Pool'. A little while later, in order to set matters right, the men of Bowness raided the Scottish churches of Dornock and Middlebie and stole their bells. The plundered bells are still kept within the church, Dornock's dating from 1611 and the larger, from Middlebie, dated 1616.

From Bowness, the Eden widens out into the estuary and the gap between England and Scotland increases. The coastline turns to the south, fringed by Bowness Common and the tiny villages of Cardurnock and Anthorn. Across the River Wampool lies **Kirkbride**, its church, dedicated to St Bride, is located on a steep rise to the north of the village. The fabric dates largely from the twelfth century, shown by the Norman doorways, chancel-arch, and north chancel window. There is no evidence of security, except perhaps for the building's position, high above the road and river.

To the south-east of Kirkbride, in the cluster of little farms and villages around the valley of the Wampool, there are no churches which, in their present state, may be considered to have been defensible, which is surprising given the vulnerable location of these flat and fertile lands. The only substantial medieval church is at **Aikton**, where the little Norman two-celled building, now much restored, stands on high ground, away from the village.

Two miles south-west of Kirkbride, between the Morricambe Sands and the low marshlands of Wedholme, the village of **Newton Arlosh** boasts one of the best examples of true ecclesiastical fortification in the country. It was built in 1304 by the monks of Holme Cultram Abbey to preside over the new town which they founded at the same time. The church, dedicated to St John the Baptist, is a very serious piece of defensible architecture, and, like the English West March churches of Burgh-by-Sands and Great Salkeld, it outwardly displays a castle-like concern for security.

The village was founded in 1304 after Skinburness, the principal market town of the area, some four and a half miles to the west, had been destroyed by the sea during a furious storm three years earlier. This town had clearly been important as it had a small port which was used by the army of Edward I during his campaigns against Scotland. The appropriator, Holme Cultram Priory, sought and was granted a licence by the Bishop of Carlisle to found a new church (Mon.Ang., v, 595–6) at Arlosk, which later became 'Newton' Arlosh. In the licence, the bishop makes mention of the '*hostiles invasiones et depredationes Scottorum*' and remarks that the church would also be 'for the safety of souls' (Curwen 1913a, 114); with this in mind, the prior of Holme Cultram set about the construction of a fortified church (Goodman 1989), presumably for the personal protection of the incumbent priest. The simple and austere architecture reveals little about the actual date of construction, although Kelland (1982, 200) considers that it was not built before 1393 when the earlier grant was confirmed. This confirmation, although making no reference to permission to fortify or crenellate, does acknowledge that the licence to build the church was granted in 'consideration of their [the villagers] exposure to depredations by the Scots and their consequent impoverishment' and that the construction was for the 'territory of Arlosk for inhabitants within their borders' (CPR, 16 Richard II: 1391–6, Pt iii ,m.14). Evidently the measures of security taken were successful, as in 1573 it was reported that the church tower 'hath ever been a notable safeguard and defence . . . as well for all the tenants on the east side of the River Waver' (Keeling 1975, 176). However, by 1580 the building had fallen into disrepair – the door stood open and sheep were inside (Curwen 1913a, 119). Prior to the restoration in 1844 the upper part of the tower had virtually disappeared.

The church originally had an aisleless nave and a west tower. However, in 1844, the north wall of the nave was largely removed and an extension was built, projecting northwards to provide more space for worship, and which was further enlarged in 1894 (Figure 139). This extension is still in use today, so that the congregation have the core of the fourteenth-century building beside them. The nave proper has a single south doorway at its west end, adjacent to the tower; it is remarkably narrow – only 0.79 m (2 ft 7 in.) in width, clearly for reasons of security. Apart from the doorway, there are only two other open-

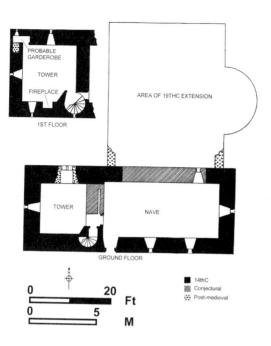

Fig. 139. Plan of Newton Arlosh showing the conjectural form of the east tower wall with draw-bar slot, and the first floor of the tower (after Curwen 1913a).

ings in the south wall of the nave: tiny rectangular windows, 2.2 m (7 ft 3 in.) above ground level and 0.28 m (11 in.) in width, which have evidence of former shuttering or barring within the reveals. In the east wall there is only a single original window of similar character and height above the ground (those at high level having been added subsequently). The walls of the nave are 1.1 m (3 ft 7 in.) in thickness, unquestionably designed for defence, and are constructed of coursed, brown, rubble stone (Figure 140).

It is, however, the tower of Newton Arlosh which carries the most obvious hallmarks of a defensible arrangement. Rising over 1.2 m (4 ft) thick walls, the two storeys have only narrow rectangular windows, one in each face, with no belfry openings in the normal sense. The top of the tower has a parapet with heavy merlons forming a crenellated ring; this was entirely restored in 1844, but one complete medieval merlon appears to have survived at the north-east angle. On the south side a small projecting turret carries a chimney flue from a fireplace on the first floor; the superficial appearance of machicolation is a fanciful creation, made at the time of the restoration.

The tower is constructed with better quality workmanship than the nave, and employs larger blocks of stone, laid in more regular courses. The junction

Fig. 140. Newton Arlosh, exterior from the south-east.

between nave and tower can be seen easily on the south side, just to the west
of the doorway, although the lower six courses appear to run together congruously. Despite the junction, the character of the fabric is very similar and a
fourteenth-century date for both nave and tower seems probable. The change is
most likely due to different phases of building within the same period of time.

Internally, the defensible nature of the tower is continued; the ground floor
has a tunnel-vaulted chamber, 2.5 m (8 ft) high, now made into two compart-
ments. As in other cases of tunnel vaulting, this is seen as a measure of protection against fire, and for the prevention of easy ingress. The east wall was
removed in the nineteenth-century restoration.

Access to the upper floors of the tower may once have been by way of a high-
level doorway, still clearly visible from the nave, which could only have been
reached from a wooden ladder (Figure 141). This doorway, although only tiny
in comparison to modern openings, has nevertheless been enlarged at some
stage in the past, prior to the restoration of the current stairway in 1844 (Kelland 1982, 201). Curwen (1913a, 120) conjecturally thought this opening was in
the form of a window to give a view into the nave; he also depicts the east wall
of the tower as it may have been before it was removed, showing a deep draw-
bar slot in a wall which was of comparable thickness with the exterior walls
(see Figure 139). In a sectional drawing published in 1813 (Lysons and Lysons,
1806–22, iv), the stair is shown, opening within the thickness of the east tower

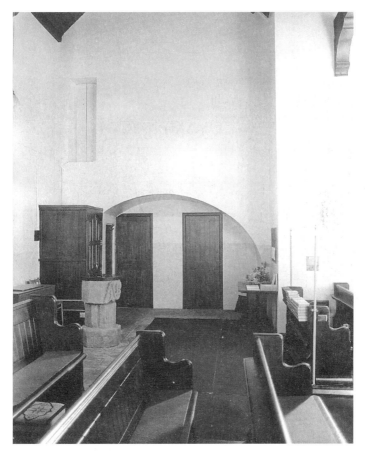

Fig. 141. Newton Arlosh, east face of the tower showing vaulting of the ground floor and the high-level opening.

wall, thus indicating that it was not an entirely new addition made at the time of the 1844 restoration. The upper opening may therefore be either an interior first-floor entrance doorway of the form seen at Penrith, and possibly Scaleby, or, as Curwen thought, a viewpoint into the nave.

The first floor is 4 m (13 ft) square on plan, has a fireplace in the south wall, and is flagged with small stone slabs covering the tunnel vault below. The three exterior walls each have a small, deeply-splayed, window, that in the south wall was offset to accommodate the fireplace (Figure 142). In the thickness of the north-west angle is a tiny chamber leading off the main room, measuring 1.23 m long by 0.61 m wide (4 ft by 2 ft) and in height only 1.4 m (4 ft 7 ins.); although there is no archaeological evidence to suggest a former purpose for this chamber, it seems likely that it served as a garderobe. A plan of 1816 by

Fig. 142. Newton Arlosh, first-floor chamber of the tower showing stair and fireplace.

Lysons (Lysons and Lysons, ibid.) shows this chamber as being 'L' shaped with an irregular hole in the west wall, supporting the theory of a garderobe; part of this area later collapsed and was subject to reconstruction in 1844 which has destroyed all exterior and much interior evidence (Kelland 1982, 202). With a fireplace and probable garderobe, this level of the tower was clearly intended to provide regular accommodation, perhaps for the resident priest or canon.

The second floor has been considerably modified during the period of restoration. Its present wooden floor is of no great age and has clearly been raised above the original level, and the whole spiral stairway from first to second floor is now much restored. There are three splayed windows corresponding to those in the chamber below, with the addition of a small light at the head of the stair in the south-east corner. There are no bells at this level; indeed the chamber shows no evidence of ever having served for this purpose, but this has been largely rebuilt. The present bell dates from 1843 and is housed on the roof of the tower, from where there are excellent views in all directions, particularly to the north across the Solway.

The mother church, which appropriated Newton Arlosh, lies three miles south-west at Abbeytown. The parish church of today is in fact the nave, rent of its aisles, of **Holme Cultram** Abbey, founded as a Cistercian House and

Fig. 143. Holme Cultram Abbey, exterior view.

colonised from Melrose in 1150 by Henry, son of King David I of Scotland (Knowles and Hadcock 1971). In the period of foundation there was relative peace on the Border, and the red sandstone of which the abbey is constructed was brought over the Solway from Scotland. The area was also subject to a brief period of Scottish rule, from 1136 to 1157.

The original abbey occupied ten acres (4 hectares) of land after its completion around 1200. It had a church 78 m (256 ft) in length, with a nave of nine bays, a central tower over 30 m (100 ft) high, and claustral buildings ranged around the south and west sides. After the Reformation, decay and neglect set in and in January 1600 the central tower fell, bringing with it much of the chancel and part of the nave roof. Repairs were undertaken, but four years later a disastrous fire destroyed the new work and much of the remainder of the building. It is recorded that the whole church was burnt with the exception of the south side of the 'low church' which was stone-vaulted (Holden 1990, 264). The implications are, perhaps, that such stone vaulting was previously more widespread in the building but had been destroyed when the tower collapsed. In 1703, Bishop Nicolson, on visiting the abbey, ordered its restoration; the nave was reduced to six bays, and the side aisles were removed. Further restorations were undertaken in 1883 and in 1913. All that remains today of the abbey is the reduced nave, including the twelfth-century west doorway, and the west porch built by Abbot Chamber in 1507 (Figure 143). Above the porch is an upper chamber, access to which is by a spiral stair.

The defensible nature of this building is, not surprisingly, unclear. The con-siderable reduction in size and the serious alterations which have occurred have left only the shell of the main church, bereft of its tower, chancel, and side aisles. Nevertheless, the principal west doors have previously been secured by two separate draw-bars, the blocked mortices for which are plainly visible in the reveals.

Historical records point to a very troubled past, with major Scots raids occurring as early as 1216, after which Henry III granted to the monks the privi-lege of keeping bows and arrows to defend themselves (Curwen 1913b, 241). The raids continued in the years following the death of Edward I, especially in 1315–16 (Wilson, 1901–5, ii). One of the worst episodes appears to have been in 1319 when Robert the Bruce attacked and devastated the abbey, despite the fact that his father, Robert, Earl of Carrick, was buried there (Chr.Lan., 237; Grainger and Collingwood 1929). After this last raid, the value of the abbey was estimated at only one-fifth of its worth in 1291, and many of the monks sought refuge in other monasteries. The vigour of the Scottish raids may in part have been due to the prominence of Holme Cultram during this period; it had many dependent churches and much land, and was also regarded as a secure venue for meetings, as in September 1299 Edward I required the whole chancery to meet at the abbey (Powicke 1962, 702). In August 1385, a force of Scots and French crossed the Solway and forced the abbot to pay £200 in return for not destroying the abbey (Summerson 1992). More raids followed, some allayed by paying ransom money, but most taking their toll on the fabric and people. During the Pilgrimage of Grace, at the time of the Reformation, the abbot of Holme Cultram, Thomas Carter, was charged with high treason for resisting the royal commissioners and for causing 'his tennandes, a gaynes ther wyll, to muster afor hym in the kyrke' (Hexham Memorials, CII). The problem of Scottish raiding was so great that at the Reformation in 1538, the inhabitants of Abbeytown petitioned the Chancellor, Thomas Cromwell, for the 'preservation and standynge of the Church . . . whiche is not onlye unto us our parish Churche . . . but also a great ayde, socor, and defence for us agenst our neghbours the Scots' (Curwen 1913b; Holden 1990, 264). The petition was allowed and thus the building survived, albeit without the financial resources for its upkeep.

Towards the coast, at Wolsty, the abbey had a manor-house which in 1348 was the subject of a formal licence to crenellate (CPR, 22 Edward III: 1348–50, Pt iii, m.29). This may have been used as a safe-house for the prior, or for the security of books and charters. Only earthworks now remain to mark the site which was evidently a strong moated enclosure (Cathcart King 1983, 91).

The large village of **Wigton** sits close to the main Carlisle to Cockermouth road to the east of Abbeytown. The present church was built in 1788, copying St Cuthbert's Carlisle of ten years earlier. However, the medieval building which this replaced was evidently a strongly defensible church of the fourteenth century, which proved extremely difficult to demolish in 1788, despite being considered dangerous (Perriam and Robinson 1998). On 18 March 1374 it was recorded 'that without the King's licence, parcel of the said church is crenellated for defence' (CCR, 48 Edward III: 1374–77. m.27). It is almost certain that the 'parcel' referred to was the west tower which had been constructed, in all probability, post-1328 after the building was damaged by the Scots (Longley 1983). Bishop Nicolson, visiting in 1703, noted the 'square steeple' and also observed that the interior was 'melancholy and gloomy' (Collingwood 1928), a possible reference to small narrow windows in the body of the church which may have had defensible overtones. Wigton, like Newton Arlosh and Burgh-by-Sands, was also owned and maintained by the monks of Holm Cultram.

To the south and west of Abbeytown there are very few ecclesiastical buildings from the medieval period. Apart from the small restored church at **Bromfield**, all the west coast villages have long since had their early churches replaced by fashionable Victorian structures. The popular coastal resorts of **Silloth** and **Allonby** have buildings of 1871 and 1845 respectively; at the latter settlement, the first church was apparently only built as late as 1744. However, close to the small village of Beckfoot lies the site of the Roman fort of *Bibra*, another in a chain of fortifications which highlight the vulnerability of this coastline in the past. It would be surprising if, a thousand years later, the people of medieval Cumberland had not taken similar precautions against their enemies from the north. However, even the larger village of **Aspatria** has succumbed to the Victorian love of rebuilding. Its church of 1846–8, by the architects Travis and Mangnall, displays a mixture of neo-Norman and Early English, and only retains a vestige of the earlier building in the form of a Norman arch, now part of the vestry doorway.

The next major coastal town down from Allonby is **Maryport**. Like the villages to the north, this town too has no church earlier than the mid-Victorian era. St Mary's started out life as a chapel-of-ease in 1760, was rebuilt in 1847, and again rebuilt, except for the west tower, in 1890–2. Yet despite the radical alterations, introduced by Humphrey Senhouse in 1748, to develop the town as a coal port (McCord and Thompson 1998), there still remain vestiges of earlier settlement, and the customary defences – the Roman fort of *Alauna* to the north, a Norman motte at the south end of the town, and a medieval pele tower at Netherhall.

At the mouth of the River Derwent is the large town of **Workington**. The earliest surviving church, St Michael's, dates from 1770 (largely rebuilt in 1887–90), although it retains some vestiges from its medieval predecessor: a Norman arch and capital, and a fifteenth-century font.

THE VALLEYS OF THE ELLEN AND DERWENT

The small coastal village of **Crosscanonby** lies north-east of Maryport, and stands on the 30 m (100 ft) contour above the sands which mark the shoreline.

Fig. 144. Dearham, exterior of the tower from the south-west.

The tiny church of St John the Evangelist has a nave, chancel, and a south porch. Although looking rather incongruous, with its 1930s dormer windows on the north side, the building nevertheless has a robust appearance. There are very few windows earlier than the seventeenth or eighteenth centuries and the east windows are Victorian; a single round-headed opening in the south wall of the chancel probably dates from the twelfth century and is 2.15 m (7 ft) above ground level to the cill. The walls of the building measure only 0.85 m (2 ft 9 in.) in average thickness, although at the west end there are substantial thirteenth-century angle buttresses, similar to those found on other Border churches (e.g., Bowness-on-Solway). Despite the building's solid aspect there are no obvious defensible features.

A mile and a half to the south of Crosscanonby lies the village of **Dearham**. The church of St Mungo is situated at the top of a steep bank where the land falls away sharply on the east and north sides; this provided both a defensible

Fig. 145. Dearham, showing the tunnel-vaulted ceiling in the lower stage of the tower.

position and a prominent viewpoint over the surrounding land. The building comprises nave with south porch and north aisle, the last rebuilt in 1882, chancel, and west tower. The earliest fabric dates from the twelfth century, witnessed by the south nave doorway and chancel windows, along with the impressive font, complete with spirals, scrolls, and dragons. Earlier work, in the form of carved fragments, also exists; however, this is *ex situ* and bears no relationship to the present building. There is evidence of late twelfth- or early thirteenth-century work in the arch between the nave and tower, and the tower may therefore have been the last phase of the building to be completed.

It is in the tower at Dearham that evidence of defensible use of the building is found (Figure 144). Beyond the wide tower-arch, the ground floor is tunnel-vaulted in stone, the maximum height being 4.0 m (13 ft) above ground level in the centre, with springing points for the vaulting on the north and south sides (Figure 145). At some point, this wide arch had been reduced to a strongly-barred doorway and was only opened out in 1882 (Scott 1899, 32; Salter 1998). This device was clearly intended to prevent easy entry to the tower and is a defensible measure seen in other Border churches (e.g., Hartburn and Kirkwhelpington, in the English Middle March). The two-light west window is probably fourteenth century, in a wall which is 1.3 m (4 ft 3 in.) in thickness. In the south-west angle is a doorway giving access to the anticlockwise spiral stair. The doorway appears unusually crude, being formed out of heavy, roughly chamfered stones, running up to a simple point. Both the first and second floors of the tower are similar in arrangement: both measure 4.7 m (15 ft 5 in.) square, have doorways off the stairway which have evidence for small doors fixed in the rebates, and have diminutive, rectangular, single-splayed windows in the west and south walls. The windows do not appear to be contemporary with the fabric of the tower, and may be later widenings of smaller openings. The topmost stage now has no floor, and houses the bells, hung in a modern wooden frame; the belfry openings are formed of two ogee-headed lights. On the east side of the tower roof is, unusually, a further bellcote, now empty, perhaps indicating that the second floor was adapted for a use other than for housing bells. The whole parapet is surrounded by sturdy crenellations, and the view from this position is excellent, particularly to the north and east.

Three miles upriver from Dearham, the tiny church at **Gilcrux** stands on top of a slight bank at the north end of the village. It has a twelfth-century core with later alterations of the thirteenth and fourteenth centuries, and has no obvious signs of security measures. The church was damaged during the Anglo-Scottish wars in the fourteenth century, and the value of the building declined rapidly from £2 6s. 8d. in 1291 to only 10s. in 1318, almost certainly due to damage and loss caused by raiding.

Of the medieval church at **Bridekirk**, to the south of Gilcrux, only the eastern portion of the chancel now remains. It is clear however that it was important, as attested by the magnificent twelfth-century font, now in the Victorian successor to the medieval church, built by Cory and Ferguson between 1868 and 1870. Nikolaus Pevsner described this font as 'one of the liveliest pieces of Norman sculpture in the county' (Pevsner 1967, 78), and it is undoubtedly so, with dragons, birds, allegorical figures, and even the mason who wrought it.

To the south, the villages of **Great Broughton** and **Little Broughton** share a Victorian church. From here, the River Derwent meanders to the west until at **Camerton** it forms a wide loop, within which sits St Peter's church, totally isolated from the village. The building has undergone many changes since its medieval origin; added to a fourteenth-century core there is a small west tower of 1855, and all the windows in the church have been replaced during the same period. Although its position is well defended by the river on three sides, it lies at the bottom of a steep bank – hardly an ideal location for a secure refuge, and the thickness of the medieval walls averages only 0.65 m (2 ft 2 in.). There is a stark reminder of the troubled fifteenth and sixteenth centuries in the form of an effigy to 'Black Tom of the North', or 'Black' Tom Curwen. Curwen was a notorious Border reiver who frequently joined forces with his kinsfolk in Workington to mount raids into the Scottish borderland, and to venture piratical exploits in the Irish Sea. He died shortly after 1500 and is buried at Shap Abbey, although being Lord of the Manor of Camerton, he merited a grand monument in this church.

Fig. 146. Brigham, exterior of the tower from the south-west.

Twenty-two miles south of the Solway, the important medieval town of **Cockermouth** stood guard over the principal routes to the east. The ruins of its castle dominate the south bank of the Derwent, whilst the town itself extends southwards, straddling the river Cocker. By the late medieval period the town had become the administrative centre of regional justice, like its counterpart Alnwick in the English Middle March (McCord and Thompson 1998). The present church of All Saints was rebuilt in 1852 and replaced an eighteenth-century building, itself a rebuilding following the destruction of the medieval church by fire.

To the east of Cockermouth, the last river crossing before Workington lies between Great Broughton and Brigham. Here, in the church of St Bridget at **Brigham**, is an example of a defensible west tower with a highly unusual adaptation (Figure 146). The building, which stands on a slight rise overlooking the river, has a typical layout of nave with north and south aisles, south porch,

Fig. 147. Brigham, the tower stairway looking down from the first-floor chamber.

chancel, and west tower. There is evidence of twelfth-century work in the blocked doorway to the north aisle, the small window over the south arcade, and the square abaci on the round aisle piers; the zig-zag style plasterwork of more recent date echoes the building's Norman origins. The west tower was probably built only a little later, around 1200; even the belfry openings are no later than the early thirteenth century, although a fourteenth-century west window has been inserted.

The secure nature of the tower begins with the ground floor which has walls 1.15 m (3 ft 9 in.) thick, and has a tunnel-vaulted ceiling 5.5 m (18 ft) high to the centre. A west doorway has been constructed at some stage, though this is now blocked with rubble stone on the interior and better quality ashlar on the exterior. From the ground floor, a remarkable stairway, set into the thickness of the west wall, ascends to the next level. The stairway starts in the south-west angle, turns to the north, and leads to a series of extremely steep, straight steps, composed of a variety of stone risers, some evidently taken from an earlier spiral stair which had a newel post; the whole is only 0.6 m (2 ft) wide, and is so steep that it requires both hands and feet to climb (Figure 147). It is unclear whether this stair was deliberately constructed in this manner or whether it was made by an unskilled builder. However, it would undoubtedly assist greatly in the defence of the tower, as only one person would be required to prevent entry to the upper stages by guarding the top of the stairway. As the rest of the tower is constructed soundly, the notion that a poorly skilled mason would be allowed to devise the stairway seems unlikely. The first floor has only tiny windows, barely lighting the interior, on the west, south, and north sides. The east wall has a small doorway 1.3 m (4 ft 3 in.) high which gave access above the tower-arch, perhaps to a west gallery or floor (cf. Scaleby). The upper levels of the tower, reached by modern ladders, were considerably restored by William Butterfield between 1864 and 1876.

The body of the church presents no outward features of defence, although it is to be noted that the chancel and south aisle windows are all over 2 m (6 ft 7 in.) in height above ground level.

South of Brigham the great mass of the Cumbrian Mountains rises to the east, leaving a narrow corridor of land between here and the coast. Only the little church at **Dean**, three and a half miles south of the Derwent, remains largely intact from the medieval period, but there is no evidence of security or defence either in the site or the fabric.

To the north-east, the Derwent flows through Cockermouth and into the large expanse of Bassenthwaite Lake, which has a little medieval church on the eastern shore, under the shadow of Skiddaw. **Bassenthwaite** appears entirely undefensible. It was given to Jedburgh Abbey at the beginning of the twelfth century and still retains its plain Norman chancel-arch. A drastic restoration in 1873 has effaced much medieval detail (Swift 1966).

The town of Keswick formed an important barrier to incursions through the Derwent Valley. Commanding the approach to the town is the village of **Great Crosthwaite** and its church dedicated to St Kentigern. The building is large and dates mainly from the fifteenth and sixteenth centuries, with the exception of the north chapel which is a century earlier. It is the tower however which appears most striking (Figure 148). Built quite late in the medieval period, and perhaps not completed until the 1550s, it is of very solid and imposing construction. The large perpendicular west window is placed extraordinarily high above ground level, 4 m (13 ft) on the exterior, perhaps deliberately to exclude any possibility of using this as a means of ingress; there are no other windows at this level. Within the south-west angle of the tower is a doorway to a spiral stair which leads to the belfry. It once also led to an intermediate floor at about 5 m (16 ft 5 in.) above the ground, shown by a blocked doorway at this height, although such a floor would have cut across both the west window and the tower-arch, and there is no visible evidence of a former chamber within the tower walls. The stair is built unusually steep and presents some difficulty

Fig. 148. Great Crosthwaite, exterior view of the west tower.

in its ascent; this too may have been a deliberate trait, designed to impede
any would-be assailants (Figure 149). Standing 17 m (56 ft) to the parapet, the
tower commands exceptionally good views in all directions. At the south-west
corner, above the stair, is a projecting turret, very similar to that on Carlisle
Cathedral, which may have served to support a beacon used for warning of
raids or invasion.

   Within the body of the church, the doorway in the south aisle has a deep
draw-bar slot, evidence of security for this, the main entrance. Prior to 1844 the
porch was described as 'old and crazy, the doors of which were oak, four inches
[0.1 m] thick, studded with iron nails . . . embedded in the old doors were
several musket balls and there were perforations which penetrated the wood so
as to splinter it on the inside' (Wilson 1970, 19). From this description it may
be taken that the south doorway was made intentionally strong, and that on at
least one occasion it had been attacked.

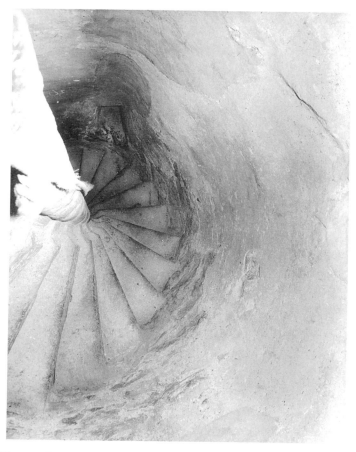

Fig. 149. Great Crosthwaite, the unusually steep spiral stair in the tower.

There are no documented references to any use of the church as a refuge, or as a beacon, although its prominent and high visible situation strongly hints at the latter. The value of the living was reduced by over £20 between 1292 and 1318 owing to the effects of Scottish raiding. In the fourteenth century the living belonged to Fountains Abbey, and there was some dispute over monies owed (Eeles 1974).

Within the parish were six other chapels: that at **Keswick** has entirely disappeared, whilst those at **Borrowdale, Newlands**, and **Wythburn** have been heavily remodelled, and **Thornthwaite**, and **St John in the Vale** have been completely rebuilt.

Just over the administrative county border into Westmorland, the twelfth-century church of **Barton** has an exceptionally strong central tower with a massive stone tunnel vault at ground-floor level. The arches to north and south have been modified, probably in the early fourteenth century when the living was given to the Augustinian priory of Warter near York. High in the west wall is a doorway leading out to a now-vanished floor or gallery above the nave. Although built prior to the main period of the Border Troubles, the builders of this church undoubtedly had security in mind.

ALLERDALE

Torpenhow, seven miles north-east of Cockermouth, has a Norman church, positioned on rising ground to the east of the village. St Michael's church has a nave, aisles, north transept, and a chancel, with a big seventeenth-century bell-cote at the west end and contemporary battlements on the nave. Examination of the exterior reveals two massive western buttresses, tiny west windows, and no original openings at all on the north side of the nave (although there was once a doorway, long since blocked-up). The chancel also has few windows, and the south wall is, unusually, almost completely blank, its twelfth-century openings only 0.22 m (9 in.) wide. Inside, there is evidence of use from the twelfth century onwards, and the walls, despite some variation, average 1 m (3 ft 3 in.) in thickness.

Only the chancel now remains of the old church at **Ireby**, lying isolated in fields to the south of the road between Torpenhow and Ireby village. The building is late Norman in date, and has characteristic splayed windows in the east and north walls; the lower east windows are separated by detached columns with waterleaf capitals. The nave and any associated structures have completely disappeared above ground. Prior to their demolition in 1845–6, the nave and north aisle appear to have been plain low structures, probably with few windows, and the building was without a tower (Swift and Bulman 1965).

Uldale has another isolated church, which lies between Ireby and Uldale villages, and which was established as a church by the thirteenth century. Its lands were devastated by Scottish incursions in the following century (Swift 1959). Although situated on top of a very steep bank above the River Ellen, there is no indication of secure adaptation in the present structure which has been considerably altered in 1730 and again in 1837.

At **Mealsgate** a church of 1896–9 on a new site replaced the earlier building which lay closer to the main Carlisle to Cockermouth road. The old church was demolished in 1935, except for the chancel, which is of the twelfth century. Earlier records show that the church had no tower and was probably a simple two-celled Norman chapel which had expanded in the thirteenth century and gained a south aisle and porch (Swift 1975).

Boltongate lies one and a half miles south-east of Mealsgate. The church has a strong external appearance, and is situated on top of a steep ascent within the village. It has been described as 'one of the architectural sensations of Cumberland' (Pevsner 1967, 70) (Figure 150).

Fig. 150. Boltongate, exterior view.

The building consists of a nave with north and south porches and transepts, and a chancel with north vestry. There is no tower, nor any evidence
that one was ever intended, but a small polygonal turret, carrying a spiral
stair, is located on the north side between the chancel and the nave. The
window tracery is all typically perpendicular in style, of the late fourteenth
or early fifteenth century, and the openings are generally placed high, 1.84 m
(6 ft) above ground level to the cills. When Bishop Nicolson made his visitation in 1703 he found that the five windows in the chancel had each been
half walled-up, perhaps further to restrict access through the lower portions
(although equally this may have been an expediency due to lack of funds
for repairs); the bishop also remarked that there was 'a great rough Heap of
stones at the very Entrance of the Door' (Ferguson 1877, 91–2), conjecturally
this may have been left from a time when it was necessary to barricade the
door.

It is, however, the interior of Boltongate which presents the most secure
image. The roofs of the nave and transepts are constructed in steeply pointed,
stone tunnel vaults (Figure 151). The undersides are formed of ashlar stone
whilst above is rubble masonry with stone roofing slabs laid directly over. The
character is similar to Scottish churches found north of the Border region, e.g.,
Bothwell (Fawcett 1994a), although there are also similarities with the early

Fig. 151. Boltongate, the interior vaulting of the nave.

sixteenth-century Border church of Ladykirk in the Scottish East March. In the transepts the roofs are more properly termed half-tunnels, although their construction and outer roofing style are identical to that of the nave. The most likely reason for this form of architecture was to create a secure and fireproof building. The only windows in these transepts are two small lights in each of the east sides. Towards the base of the roof vault, at approximately 6 m (20 ft) above floor level, is a series of corbels, six on either side of the nave; their purpose is unclear but they may have been to brace the original scaffold construction (Salter 1998), or, less likely, to support a timber upper floor (for which there is no other evidence). At the west end more corbels project to support the bellcote and gable wall.

The small polygonal turret on the north side of the nave contains a spiral stair which leads to a blocked rood-loft doorway, and then to the nave roof

Fig. 152. Caldbeck, exterior from the south-east.

parapet. This narrow parapet walkway is unusual, and may have served simply for purposes of maintenance, although the surrounding wall is surprisingly low, only around 0.30 m (1 ft) high and it may have been reduced in height; there is a single crenel in the centre of the west end. The walls of the church average 0.9 m (3 ft) in thickness, but this would be expected in order to support the weight of the roof vaulting.

Below the church, to the south, is the rectory. Although modified in later periods, it still retains a pele tower attached to it, one of the many vicar's peles built for the personal safety of the clergy (Perriam and Robinson 1998).

Six miles west of Boltongate and thirteen miles south-west of Carlisle, nestling below the northern edge of the mountains, is the village of **Caldbeck**. The church of St Kentigern stands immediately to the south of the river, towards the eastern side of the village, and has a nave with aisles and porch, chancel with south chapel, and a west tower (Figure 152). Although the main body of the building bears little evidence of security considerations, the exception perhaps being the sixteenth-century tunnel-vaulted south porch, the west tower appears more promising. Here there is a problem; quite clearly, there has been a major eighteenth-century restoration of the tower, with all its windows being chamfered, round-headed, and with very clean-cut limestone dressings in contrast to the darker rubble stone of the side walls. These openings appear to be insertions or modifications of earlier openings. Inside the nave, close to the tower on the north side, is an inscription declaring that: 'This steeple was builded in the year 1727'. However, detailed examination indicates that this tower has a core fabric of medieval date, and the year 1727 most likely refers to a period of restoration, probably following Bishop Nicolson's comments, twenty-four years earlier, that the slates near the belfry were ready to drop into the church (Ferguson 1877, 95).

Approaching the tower from the nave, there is no proper arch but rather a round-headed doorway, formed through the thickness of the wall. The implications for defensible use of the tower are obvious (e.g., Scaleby, Burgh-by-Sands, and Great Salkeld). Above this doorway is a plain, rectangular, splayed window, which provides a view of the interior of the nave from the first floor of the tower. Inside the tower, which measures 3 m square (9 ft 10 in.), a large stair-turret has been constructed at the north-west angle which is clearly an addition as it lacks any form of bonding with the side walls. A spiral stair leads to the first floor where the east window can be seen to have been altered on its north side, and reveals evidence for former shuttering. Above this level, at a height of approximately 4 m (13 ft), a distinct change in fabric to a yellow sandstone is evident; this clearly marks a phase of rebuilding, perhaps that referred to as being in 1727.

PENRITH AND THE SOUTH-EAST

To the east of the Cumbrian mountain edge, the high land of the Caldbeck, Carrock, and Bowscale Fells falls away to the valleys of the rivers Petteril and Eden, and the region opens up southwards towards Ullswater where there is a scattering of small villages and the larger market town of Penrith.

The Penrith road out of Caldbeck leads past the secluded village of **Skelton**, its parish church tucked away below a shallow ridge. Despite the rebuilding of the nave and chancel, the latter in 1794 and the remainder during the nineteenth century, the tower remains as a solid reminder of the austere, outward show of simplicity which typifies many medieval Border churches.

The tower lacks conclusive architectural dating evidence, but appears to derive from the fourteenth century from its general form of construction. However the east interior wall reveals a complexity of building phases. Red sandstone blocks characterise the exterior, which has a single Victorian window, inserted at ground-floor level, and an altered, square-headed window in the north face on the first floor. The narrow belfry lights are of uncertain date. There is evidence on the first floor for a deeply-splayed window through the west wall, but this would have produced an opening no more than a few centimetres wide on the outer face.

One feature which may be indicative of security is the door to the spiral stairway on the ground floor of the tower. The construction is of double-

Fig. 153. Skelton, iron-studded door to the tower stair.

planked oak with the outer planks set vertically and the inner horizontally; the exterior face is heavily studded, perhaps to resist attack with iron implements (Figure 153).

Three miles to the south of Skelton, the village of **Greystoke** played a significant historical role as home to the Lords of Greystoke who, in the person of William Lord Greystoke, first obtained a licence to crenellate their castle in 1353 (Cathcart King 1983, 86). The family were a powerful influence on this southern reach of the English West March, and their wealth and influence are reflected by the extent of the current park estate which amounts to around 2,430 hectares (6,000 acres).

The church of St Andrew lies on the opposite side of the village to the castle, a short distance west of the River Petteril. The first impression is of the massive west tower, 11 m (36 ft) long and 7 m (23 ft) wide. Neither does the remainder of

Fig. 154. Greystoke, exterior from the south.

the church disappoint in terms of scale and massing; Mee (1937, 96) describes it
as having 'something of cathedral dignity'. Such grand architecture is probably
due to the foundation of a secular college here in 1374 by Ralf Lord Greystoke,
and which was served by three priests and three clerks (Knowles and Hadcock
1971).

The church is without doubt a very major piece of architecture (Figure 154).
Much of it derives from the fifteenth and sixteenth centuries, but there is earlier evidence, from the thirteenth century, in the interior arches and piers. On
the south side is a two-storeyed late medieval vestry, with a battlemented parapet. The tower is problematical. Apparently 'rebuilt' in 1848 (Bulmer 1901) it
certainly shows evidence of significant restoration in the interior layout and
the Victorian windows at first-floor level. However, there are no openings on
the second floor; the date of the belfry lights is not clear and may, in part at
least, be genuine medieval work. The interior west wall of the nave bears the
scar of the former medieval roof line, and this evidence, combined with the
complexity of the fabric, suggests that this wall was not entirely rebuilt in the
nineteenth century. There is no arch connecting nave with tower, but instead
a simple doorway, evidently a Victorian replacement for an earlier opening,
a feature seen widely elsewhere in an unequivocally defensible situation (e.g.,
Burgh-by-Sands and Great Salkeld).

In the absence of documentary and archaeological evidence, it is difficult
to be certain about the secure role of this church, but Border raids were well

known in the area, and despite the protection of the castle there was without doubt a need for a central defensible refuge for the villagers, a function which would be provided ably by this domineering assemblage.

To the north and east of Skelton and Greystoke lie the almost unrecognisable remains of the once great Inglewood Forest which formerly stretched between Penrith and Carlisle (McCord and Thompson 1998). This area was a haven for those seeking refuge when invasion threatened, and whose regular inhabitants were therefore subject to the rules of the Warden for general or particular service (Tough 1928, 16). Lying on the western edge of this area are the churches of **Newton Reigny** and **Plumpton**. The former is a small, heavily restored, medieval building, apparently without any consideration for security, and the latter was built in 1907 by Sir Robert Lorimer, its tower in the moody and reflective style of a Border pele.

A little to the south of Greystoke, close to the foot of a steep escarpment leading down to the Dacre Beck are the church and castle of **Dacre**. The castle first comes on record in 1354 (Cathcart King 1983, 84) and was probably new at this time, when Margaret de Dacre received a licence to have a chapel within the castle (Curwen 1913b, 269). The church has fabric from the twelfth to the fifteenth centuries and has, unfortunately, lost its original tower – the present construction dates from 1810. Judging by the plain round-headed arch, the former tower was probably of Norman date.

The town of **Penrith** was described in Elizabethan times as 'a little town and of indifferent trade, fortified on the West side with a castle' (Tough 1928, 16), and was recorded in the Treaty of 1597 as being at the extremity of the March jurisdiction (Nicholson 1705). Leland, on his journeys during the early sixteenth century, noted that 'in Perith [Penrith] ys one paroche chirch, and a grey freres' (Leland, ix, fo.71).

The church of St Andrew sits squarely in the heart of the town, surrounded by the narrow streets and central market place which typify the larger Border settlements. Most of the medieval church was destroyed when the nave and chancel were rebuilt between 1720–22. Today all that remains of the early structure is the tower (Figure 155).

It is perhaps surprising that the tower of St Andrew's Penrith was retained during the major eighteenth-century rebuilding, as the neo-classical work of that period is of exceptionally high quality and it would seem logical to have extended it to the whole building. As it was, the massive west tower was perhaps considered too strong and difficult (and consequently expensive) to remove, and was therefore superficially treated during the restoration by the insertion of a pedimented doorway, supported by Tuscan columns at the west end. It is recorded that this west entrance was made 'with great difficulty', and that it was considered that the tower had been used as a place of refuge and great strength (Whellan 1860, 603). The medieval structure shows all the usual traits of a defensible church tower: thick walls, small windows, and former high-level access to the spiral stair in the south-west angle. Much of this may

Fig. 155. Penrith, the medieval tower from the south-west.

date from the work carried out following a survey in 1374 when it was reported that the tower was in a bad state of repair (Perriam and Robinson 1998).

That defence became necessary in the town during the period of the Troubles is borne out by the erection of a new castle in the closing years of the fourteenth century. Penrith castle was first licensed in 1397 and received an additional licence for a 'mantlet' or enclosure in 1399 (Cathcart King 1983, 89); it subsequently expanded, became thoroughly machicolated, and in 1470–84 received a new gate by Richard, Duke of Gloucester (later King Richard III). A little to the east of the town, on the south side of the River Eamont, Brougham castle stands as further testimony to the need for security in this area.

William Walleis, who was vicar in Penrith at the turn of the seventeenth century, recorded several attacks by the Scots as late as 1601; on 3 Apri that year he wrote in the parish register 'the Towndyke at the overend of Penreth newly

casten againne by the townesmen for the defence of the towne and invasion of
the Borderers who do threat the same' (Haswell and Jackson 1938).

Penrith also had an Augustinian friary, founded in 1291, which provided
lodgings for Edward I on his visit here in 1300 (Knowles and Hadcock 1971).
It was located in the vicinity of Friargate, but nothing now remains above
ground.

In the undulating country between the rivers Eamont and Eden, just to the
north-east of Penrith, is the church of St Cuthbert at **Edenhall**. It is isolated
from the present village and lies close to the site of the now demolished mansion of the Stapleton and Musgrave families, which included a defensible tower
(Perriam and Robinson 1998).

Trouble reached into this remoter corner of Cumberland as testified by
the raids on Penrith, and witnessed by the conditions imposed by Mary de
Stapilton of Edenhall who, in 1381, following a Scots raid in the previous year,
granted land in Carlisle to one John de Levyngton, with the reservation that 'if
it should happen that a sudden Scottish attack should occur in Cumberland, it
shall be lawful for Mary to enter that messuage and retain it as she did before'
(Summerson 1992, 157).

St Cuthbert's church is constructed of large blocks of red sandstone, and
displays evidence of its Norman origins, although this is represented architecturally only by a single window in the nave; the Victorian plaster chancel-arch
may also be a copy of the original. There are features from all subsequent periods including a fifteenth-century nave roof (repaired in 1774) and a complete
west tower of the same period (Figure 156).

As usual, it is the tower which displays the principal defensible characteristics of the building. Externally it is of striking appearance, with massive
stone buttresses which rise to support a diminutive stone spire, set within a
pronounced battlement. It is, however, in the interior where the evidence lies
for its use as a secure refuge. The ground floor of the tower is reached through
a modern square-headed doorway from the nave. The interior has a tunnel-
vaulted stone ceiling and a dog-legged stone staircase; the latter is a nineteenth-
century insertion. This stair runs alongside the west and north walls and rises
in the thickness of the north wall to give entry onto an oak gallery at the west
end of the nave, erected by the Musgraves in 1834. About two-thirds of the distance up this stairway, at a height of 4.85 m (16 ft) above the floor, a small doorway leads southwards into the first-floor chamber of the tower. The narrowness
of this opening, only 0.5 m (1 ft 8 in.) in width, coupled with its awkward position – it could only be reached by a ladder or stair within the restricted space
below – make this a highly secure arrangement, and clearly intended to deter
easy entry.

The first-floor chamber bears evidence of having served for residential purposes, in all probability as an emergency retreat during periods of unrest. The
room is tiny, measuring 1.8 m (6 ft) north to south and 2.2 m (7 ft 3 in.) east
to west, and can therefore only have accommodated a very small number of

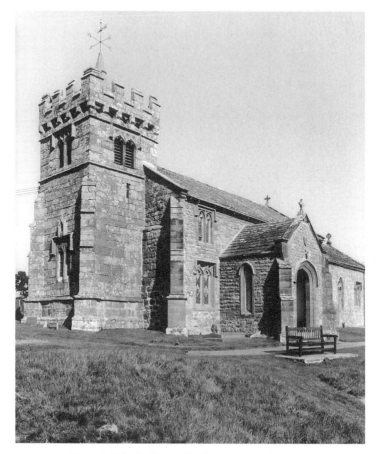

Fig. 156. Edenhall, exterior from the south-west.

people; it was possibly for the exclusive use of the priest. In the south-west angle is a low fireplace with a flue rising into the belfry chamber above. There is a single narrow slit-window in the south wall and two high-quality recesses in the east, probably serving as aumbries for storage purposes, perhaps for church valuables (Figure 157). The north side contains two doorways; the eastern is the entry from the stair below and has a modern plank door; the western opening, containing a much earlier door formed of two vertical planks held together with iron strapwork, leads onto another stairway in the thickness of the wall which extends up to the belfry. The height of the first-floor chamber is only 1.6 m (5 ft 3 in.); the slots for the belfry floor and some medieval timbers are extant in the east and west walls.

The uppermost chamber contains three bells, rehung in 1916, one of which is dated to the fourteenth century, evidently by a local founder, and is inscribed *Sabcti Camp Ana Cuthberti*; this bell is early enough to have been used as part

Fig. 157. Edenhall, aumbries in the east wall of the tower first-floor chamber.

of the general March warning system during the Troubles. In the east wall are two trefoil-headed windows, one still glazed with leaded lights, which allows a view down into the nave. It seems likely that this chamber also served as part of the retreat, with a safe view into the body of the church, an easily defended stairway, and a narrow opening at the base of the spire which leads onto the parapet outside. The purpose of the vertical piercing of the parapet, which has the superficial appearance of machicolation, is unclear, but it may be purely decorative.

Three miles north from Edenhall, along the valley of the River Eden, is another of Cumberland's outstanding examples of fortified ecclesiastical architecture. Ranking in importance alongside Burgh-by-Sands and Newton Arlosh, the church of St Cuthbert at **Great Salkeld** conveys a sturdy impression of security with its crenellated tower and turret, standing 15.9 m (52 ft) to the top of the battlements (Figure 158).

The nave is entered through a twelfth-century doorway with three orders of zigzag and human heads, powerfully sculptured in red sandstone. Many of the interior features of the nave and chancel, along with all the windows, belong to the seventeenth and nineteenth centuries; there was a major restoration in

Fig. 158. Great Salkeld, fortified tower from the south-west.

1866. However the walls of the chancel are constructed from sizable blocks of stone, and the tower, which dates from the late fourteenth century, is largely unaltered (Figure 159).

The stone-vaulted ground floor of the tower is entered through a slightly pointed doorway (restored in 1866) in the west wall of the nave, the level rising by two steps. This entrance is guarded by a heavy iron gate (Figure 160), infilled with wood, of very stout construction, and of similar design to the yat at Burgh-by-Sands. It includes two massive horizontal bolts which can only be operated from the inside of the tower, the slots for which are protected by a strong iron bar. From within the ground-floor chamber the outer walls are pierced by three narrow windows.

The defensible tower of Great Salkeld is more architecturally advanced than its two major Cumbrian counterparts (i.e., Burgh-by-Sands and Newton Arlosh) with its projecting stair-turret and chamfered windows (Kelland 1982,

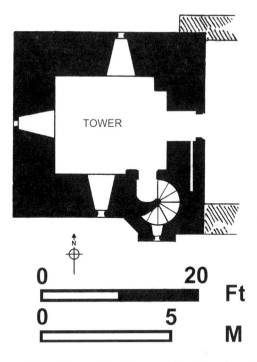

Fig. 159. Plan of Great Salkeld tower (after Curwen 1913b).

196). It is also more spacious, with a tunnel-vaulted basement level below the ground floor which probably served as a storage area, a low internal ledge indicating an original raised wooden floor, and a tiny opening in the 1.74 m (5 ft 9 in.) thick west wall to provide ventilation (Figure 161).

The first floor is reached from the spiral stair in the south-east turret, through a plain square-headed doorway which has rebates to take an internal door. The room is lit by small, chamfered, rectangular openings, centrally placed in each of the exterior walls, except on the north, where the window is offset to accommodate a large fireplace which has, as its lintel, a substantial incised cross-slab. The east wall has a single pointed window, opening out into the nave, which appears to be inserted in the blocking of a much larger opening, perhaps once a doorway. This floor, and the one above which is similar (but which lacks a fireplace and east window), could easily have accommodated a large group of people, and may have served either as a refuge for the village, or as a permanent habitation for the priest in the manner of a pele tower. The stairway continues to the parapet, which has more finely assembled stonework than below. It is recorded that the roof was in a poor state of repair in 1704 and was restored. However, there were instructions to retain it in its 'primitive condition' (Ferguson 1877; Kelland 1982, 198) and the better quality stonework may be attributable to a later medieval addition to the fourteenth-

Fig. 160. Great Salkeld, wood and iron yat closing-off the entrance to the west tower.

century structure. The parapet itself is 2 m (6 ft 7 in.) high with significant merlons and embrasures, and the whole is capped by a small embattled turret above the stair in the south-east corner. This turret may have served a similar function to those found at Carlisle and Crosthwaite, and perhaps housed a beacon.

It is entirely possible that the rectory at Great Salkeld was also defensible, perhaps made so during the later medieval period. The present structure was largely remodelled by Thomas Musgrave, rector in 1674, who was later appointed Dean of Carlisle (Perriam and Robinson 1998).

On the east side of the river Eden, the village of **Little Salkeld** had a church which had disappeared by 1360 (Morris 1989, 332). This is a rare example of an early loss which may have been initiated by the heavy Scottish raiding which took place in the English West March during the first half of the fourteenth century.

Fig. 161. Great Salkeld, the stone-vaulted basement level of the tower.

To the north, a scattering of small villages lies in the shelter of the valley of the River Eden, overshadowed by the high lands of the Gilderdale Forest and the King's Forest of Geltsdale. The majority of the churches in these villages were rebuilt or very heavily restored during the eighteenth and nineteenth centuries: **Kirkland** and **Glassonby** (Addingham) belong to this class, though all have had medieval predecessors. **Armathwaite, High Hesket**, and **Cumwhitton** have been heavily remodelled in the seventeenth and eighteenth centuries, and the former Benedictine nunnery at Armathwaite, ruined by the Scots in 1317–18 (Knowles and Hadcock 1971), has disappeared.

Melmerby church is largely of the fourteenth century, but has a tower which was rebuilt in 1848. At this time much of the medieval detail was effaced, including the north aisle arcade. Further restorations followed, in 1895 and 1928. However, in the north-east corner of the chancel, now used as a vestry, the base of a probable tower has survived (Figure 162). This structure has heavy walls, and its unusual position suggests that it may have been utilised for defence in the same manner as the former east tower at Burgh-by-Sands.

St Oswald's church at **Kirkoswald** was clearly important during the medieval period as Thomas, Lord Dacre, founded a secular college for a provost, five chaplains, and a vicar here *c.* 1523 (Wilson 1901–5, ii; Knowles and Hadcock

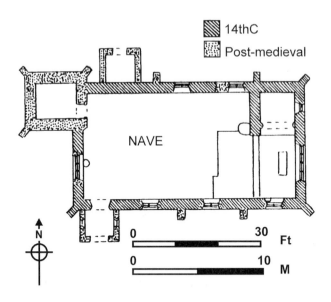

Fig. 162. Plan of Melmerby (after Salter 1998).

1971). This date is borne out by the fabric of the present chancel. The nave is lower, due to the slope of the land, and earlier, presenting evidence from the thirteenth century in the blocked north doorway, and work from the preceding century in the interior south arcade and base of the chancel-arch. There is nothing obviously secure about the building and indeed it is located in a most insecure position, at the foot of a steep ridge. However on top of the hill sits a detached tower serving as a campanile for the church, and although the present structure dates from 1897, itself replacing a wooden tower of 1747 (Pevsner 1967, 149), this represents a much earlier arrangement, as Bishop Nicolson noted in 1704 that the church was 'in such a hole that their Bellfry . . . stands at a distance, on the Top of a neighbouring Hill' (Ferguson 1877, 116–7). The bells may also have served to call out the warning of an invasion or a raid, and prominent towers such as these often acted as lookouts. In 1314 such a warning was certainly needed when the Scots army, returning from their major incursion into North Yorkshire, burnt the town (Chr.Lan., 211).

To the east, the land rises into bleak moorland, broken only by the little villages of **Alston**, **Knarsdale**, and **Garrigill**, and the chapel at **Underbank** (or Kirkhaugh). Their medieval churches are now rebuilt, but they were probably secure from all but the earliest and most concerted of raids, protected by relative inaccessibility amongst the implacable terrain.

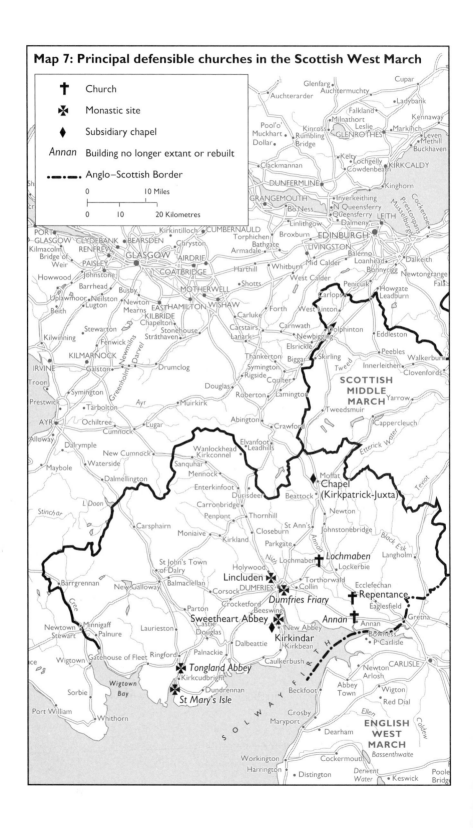

Map 7: Principal defensible churches in the Scottish West March

✝	Church
✠	Monastic site
◆	Subsidiary chapel
Annan	Building no longer extant or rebuilt
▪–▪–▪	Anglo–Scottish Border

0   10 Miles

0   10   20 Kilometres

Glenfarg · Cupar
Auchterarder · Auchtermuchty
Falkland · Ladybank
Pool o' · Milnathort Kennaway
Muckhart · Kinross Leslie Markinch
Dollar · Rumbling GLENROTHES Leven
Bridge Methill
Buckhaven
Clackmannan · Kelty KIRKCALDY
Lochgelly
Cowdenbeath Kinghorn
DUNFERMLINE
GRANGEMOUTH Inverkeithing
Bo'Ness · N Queensferry LEITH
Linlithgow · S Queensferry
Dalmeny
Kirkintilloch · CUMBERNAULD Broxburn EDINBURGH
PORT GLASGOW CLYDEBANK BEARSDEN Torphichen LIVINGSTON
Kilmacolm RENFREW Chryston Bathgate Balerno
Bridge of PAISLEY GLASGOW AIRDRIE Armadale Mid Calder Loanhead Dalkeith
Weir COATBRIDGE Harthill Whitburn Bonnyrigg Newtongrange
Howwood Johnstone West Calder Penicuik Howgate Fala
Barrhead Busby MOTHERWELL Shotts Carlops Leadburn
Uplawmoor Neilston Newton EASTHAMILTON WISHAW West Linton
Beith Lugton Mearns KILBRIDE Forth Dolphinton Eddleston
Stewarton Chapelton Carluke Carnwath Newbigging
Kilwinning Fenwick Stonehouse Carstairs Lanark Peebles
KILMARNOCK Strathaven Elsrickle Innerleithen Walkerburn
IRVINE Galston Thankerton Biggar Skirling Clovenfords
Troon Symington Rigside Symington Coulter SCOTTISH
Prestwick Tarbolton Ayr Muirkirk Douglas Roberton Lamington MIDDLE Yarrow
AYR Ochiltree Lugar Abington MARCH
Alloway Cumnock Crawford Tweedsmuir Cappercleuch
Dalrymple Elvanfoot
New Cumnock Wanlockhead Leadhills Etterick Water
Waterside Kirkconnel
Maybole Dalmellington Sanquhar
Mennock Moffat Teviot
Enterkinfoot ◆ Chapel
L Doon Durisdeer Beattock (Kirkpatrick-Juxta)
Stinchar Carronbridge Newton
Carsphairn Penpont Thornhill Johnstonebridge Black Esk
Moniaive St Ann's Langholm
Kirkland Closeburn
Parkgate ✝ Lochmaben
St John's Town Holywood Lochmaben Lockerbie
of Dalry ✠ Lincluden Torthorwald Ecclefechan
Barrgrennan New Galloway Balmaclellan DUMFRIES ✠ Collin ✝ Repentance
Corsock Dumfries Friary Eaglesfield Gretna
Parton Crocketford Beeswing ✝
Newtown Minnigaff ✠ Sweetheart Abbey ◆ Annan Annan
Stewart Palnure Laurieston Castle New Abbey Bowness
Douglas Kirkindar P Carlisle
Wigtown Gatehouse of Fleet Ringford Palnackie Dalbeattie Kirkbean
Palnure Caulkerbush Newton CARLISLE
✠ Tongland Abbey Arlosh
Kirkcudbright Beckfoot Abbey Wigton
Wigtown Dundrennan Town Red Dial
Sorbie Bay ✠ St Mary's Isle Crosby Ellen
Port William Whithorn Maryport ENGLISH
WEST
S O L W A Y F I R T H Dearham MARCH Bassenthwaite
Workington Cockermouth
Harrington Derwent Poole
Distington Water Keswick Bridge

6

THE SCOTTISH WEST MARCH

The West March of Scotland essentially encompassed the former Counties of Dumfriesshire and Kirkcudbrightshire, and in the later sixteenth century was defined as the Stewartries of Kirkudbright and Annandale, with the sheriffdom of Dumfries (Tough 1928, 21). At times, the Wardens, and indeed the central powers, regarded Wigtownshire, to the west of this area, as also belonging to the March; Robert Lord Maxwell stated in 1533 that 'of lang tyme bypast the scherefdome of Wigton was decernit be the lordis of consell to pertene to the west wardanry' (Rae 1966, 23). However, for the most part the Warden's duties did not extend beyond Dumfriesshire, and Galloway to the west was generally regarded as a separate and somewhat remote district (Brooke 1994; McDonald 1997). To the east the March was defined by the bleak uplands between the valleys of the Esk and the Teviot, and to the north the boundary ran along the high ground of the Lowther Hills. The River Cree marked the eastern edge of the region, whose southern boundary mainly followed the coast along the Solway. For only a few miles, along the rivers Sark, Esk, and the Liddle Water, between Gretna and the Kershope Forest, did the frontier touch English soil, and it was in these few miles that the most disputed area, known as the 'Debateable Land' was located (*see* page 260). The Border presented no great obstacle to crossing from either side, and compared to the alternative route around the Cheviots, the Esk offered a far less serious obstacle than the Tweed as it was easily fordable for most of the time. At low tide on the Solway there were also many crossings such as that from Annan to Bowness, the 'Sandywathe' from Dornock to Drumburgh, and the well-used 'Peat Wath' utilised by Bruce in his devastating raid of 1322, although for the inexperienced such routes could be fraught with danger amongst the treacherous soft sands and pools (McIntire 1939).

The West March was characterised by its rivers and their basins, and in Dumfriesshire it was the valleys of the Nith, Annan, and Esk which formed the principal historic regions. Further west, the Stewartry of Kirkcudbright was generally undulating and hilly except in the west, where the land rose steeply and became mountainous. Like most of the Border region, the population was low and there were few towns, Dumfries having been the only sizable urban area in the March. It was at Dumfries where the Warden lodged, along with his deputy and sheriff, and at Langholm there was a subordinate officer called the Keeper of Annandale. Despite the low population, feuding between neighbouring families was commonplace and this was a particular problem in the Scottish West March for the Warden and his officers.

The area is not noted for its medieval churches, which have survived least well amongst the six Marches, and of the thirty-nine churches which held parochial status in the eastern part of Dumfriesshire before the Reformation, only three now survive with anything like tangible remains (RCHMS 1997). In the March as a whole however, three important exceptions exist: Dundrennan Abbey, Lincluden College, and Sweetheart Abbey. This region is well recognised as being of great religious importance in that it fostered the early Christian church and has a number of exceptionally important sites dating from the fifth to the tenth centuries, the best known being Whithorn, which lies just beyond the West March boundary (Hill 1997), but the evidence for Norman work in standing churches is surprisingly low. Dundrennan has a considerable amount of fabric dating from the middle of the twelfth century, and less tangible indications may be found at Buittle, Dunrod, Southwick, Trailflat, and perhaps Ruthwell. In all, not a great deal has survived from before the Reformation and little remains to determine the extent to which parish churches may have been defensibly adapted, or used as refuges. West of Dumfries, the necessity for such adaptation would in any case be less than on any other part of the Border due to the area's geographical isolation from the principal theatre of Anglo-Scottish conflict, and the simple fact that most raiding and invasions took place in a north–south direction.

David I had a major influence on the region through his act of reconstituting the bishopric of Glasgow, and on history in general by granting considerable portions of land to the Bruce family. It was in the Scottish West March too that the course of history was fashioned: on 10 February 1306, Robert Bruce, the grandson of the original 'Competitor' for the throne of Scotland, murdered John Comyn, his chief rival, in the Greyfriars church at Dumfries. Six weeks later, Bruce was crowned as King of the Scots at Scone, and the war of resistance to the English domination, which Andrew Moray and William Wallace had started in 1297, became a War of Independence, destined to force the two nations into a long and bitter power struggle which was to last 300 years.

ANNAN, ESKDALE, AND THE BORDER

To the east of the little town of Langholm, a narrow road, leading to Newcastleton in the Scottish Middle March, winds precariously across the barren waste of the Tarras Moss (Figure 163). This was the favourite retreat of the Armstrong clan, notorious Border reivers and general troublemakers, who knew the secret paths and tracts and could thus outwit any would-be pursuers. Sir Walter Scott described this place as a 'desolate and horrible marsh', and only those

Fig. 163. The Tarras Moss, Eskdale. The bleak moorland landscape which was a former sanctuary for the lawless Armstrong clan.

who knew the swires (pathways) could safely traverse its perilous tract. Robert Carey wrote in 1601 that the Tarras was 'of that strength, and so surrounded by bogges and marshi ground, with thicke bushes and shrubbes, that they [the Armstrongs] fear no force nor power of England or Scotland' (MacDonald Fraser 1989, 206). Not surprisingly, there were very few habitations in this area, with even fewer churches, and to the north of the Tarras Moss there is only high ground with one good road leading north to Hawick. At a remote spot, below White Hill, some five and a half miles beyond Langholm, once stood a small chapel-of-ease at **Unthank**, in the parish of Ewes, which was abandoned after the Reformation. It was called the 'Overkirk' (Armstrong 1883, 102). The churchyard still exists but the area of the chapel is indicated only by indeterminate earthworks. The parish church of Ewes at **Kirkstyle**, two and a half miles to the south, was rebuilt in 1866–7 on the site of its medieval predecessor.

The northern part of this area was largely devoid of medieval fortifications. There was a tower at Langholm belonging to the Armstrongs and another strong house at Westerhall to the north-west, the property of the Johnstones (Tranter 1965). However in general, despite the accessibility of the area afforded by the major road, which followed the River Esk and the Ewes Water, the local populace appear to have relied on the security of the surrounding maze of hills and forests for safety, rather than devising strong buildings.

Langholm is the principal town in this isolated corner of the West March, sitting where the Ewes and Wauchope Waters meet the River Esk. Although the settlement existed in the medieval period, it did not flourish as a town until it was created a burgh of barony in 1621 (Pryde 1965), and the 'new town' was created later still, in 1778. The present parish church, situated close to the river, dates from 1842, but the remains of the old kirk, the ecclesiastical centre of the now depopulated parish of **Wauchope**, sit below Earshaw Hill and above the Wauchope Water a little to the west of New Langholm. Of this building, only a fragment of the 1m (3ft 3in.) thick south wall has survived, but the site is immediately next to the earthwork remains of an early medieval castle, demonstrating its strategic location. St Bride's chapel, a remoter medieval kirk, once also existed in the parish; it lay three miles to the west, close to Cleuchfoot.

To the north of the town a narrow road leads to **Staplegordon**, a remote and secluded spot, where the site of a church sits above the surrounding countryside. This church appears to have been the most strategically located of those in the former parish of Wauchope (although all are positioned on high or rising ground), as it lay on elevated ground just to the north of Barntalloch castle, a motte site, probably of the twelfth century, which has evidence for the foundations of a later tower. The castle belonged to the Consiborough family and around the year 1153, William de Conisbrough granted the church to Kelso Abbey (Cowan 1967, 8). Such church and motte groupings are seen elsewhere, and a parallel with this arrangement may be seen at Wauchope, and at Buccleuch in the Scottish Middle March. It was to Staplegordon that James V came in July 1530 (Cameron 1998, 79) following the execution of John Armstrong, a local freebooter who was later turned into a Border hero and martyr (*see* page 233). Of the church which the king would have seen, there are no standing remains, but the position can be determined as being approximately central within the churchyard; it was later converted into a mausoleum. At **Bentpath**, two and a half miles to the north-west, the present parish church of Westerkirk dates from 1880–1. The earlier chapel lay a short distance to the east, on the site now occupied by a mausoleum of 1790 by Robert Adam, all of which lies within the original graveyard. The site is positioned on a steep slope high above the River Esk.

To the south of Langholm lay the 'Debateable Land', which embraced the territory between Sark and Esk, and contained a 'motley assortment of broken men who were English or Scottish as they pleased' (Watson 1974, 32). In the extreme south-east corner of this area, hard against the boundary of the Scottish Middle March (whose line follows the Muir Burn) and a short distance to the north-east of **Cauldside**, stand the footings of a small building, orientated east-west, which has the appearance of a small chapel. Possibly a chapel-of-ease in the parish of Canonbie, this little building was located in a position of extreme danger during the period of the Troubles.

Canonbie is situated four miles to the west of the March boundary, and was in a similar position of danger. The town's geographical location made it a disputed point on the Border, and it was not until the Treaty of Norham in 1551 that its ownership by the northern realm was decided (Paterson 1997, 203), despite the declaration nineteen years earlier by the Scottish Lords of Council that Canonbie was 'undowtit propir landis of Scotland' (Cameron 1998, 87). A priory of Augustinian canons, dedicated to St Martin, was founded here in the twelfth century, and it is possible that the gift by Turgot de Rosdale to Jedburgh was that of a parish church, which eventually became a priory (Cowan 1995). The land here is fairly flat and is fertile enough to have supported the small monastic establishment; evidently it was so attractive as to encourage the monks to stay, despite the highly unstable social conditions attendant upon this area. However, despite these conditions, the inhabitants never appear to have been forced out, unlike their contemporaries at Hexham and Newminster in the English Middle March; indeed, regular life appears to have continued largely unabated (Goodman 1989). However, matters did not always run smoothly, as in 1494 the prior complained to the Scottish commissioners at Coldstream that the Charltons, Dodds, and Robsons had taken away 'certain kye, on horse, certain sheep and geit', and had then burnt their sheep and destroyed their goods (Robson 1989, 74). During the next fifty years there are several more complaints of English transgressions (Armstrong 1883). In 1380, the priory was selected as one of the specific Border meeting places where formal accusations of violation of the truce, concluded that same year, could be heard (Neville 1998). During James IV's visit in 1504, the town was selected for the dispensing of justice, and the harsh realities of Border life are made plain in the accounts of expenditure: 'Aug 21. Item, to the man that hangit the theves in Canonby, be the Kingis command . . . xiiijs' (Maxwell 1896, 152).

Of the priory buildings, only a fragment of thirteenth-century architectural detail is now preserved in the churchyard, most having been destroyed following the battle of Solway Moss in 1542, and the remainder before 1620 (Cowan and Easson 1976). In 1610, a charter refers to the place where the cloisters and the garden of the now demolished priory once were (RMS, vii, 290). The present church lies a little to the west of the site of the priory (McDowall 1986), and has replaced the medieval parish church. It was constructed in 1821–2 by William Atkinson of London, for the fifth Duke of Buccleuch who owned the parish in its entirety (Gifford 1996). It is large and imposing, with a heavy, severely battlemented tower, perhaps echoing the sombre, military architecture of this part of the Border (Figure 164). Defensible secular towers abound here – and with good reason. One of the best preserved is Hollows Tower which is positioned on the west bank of the Esk, between Canonbie and Langholm, and which was built originally by the Armstrongs c. 1518. The present tower is largely of a date later in the same century; it was burnt by Dacre in 1528, and has been restored in recent years.

It was in the parish churches of Canonbie and Arthuret (the latter in the English West March) that one Richard Graeme and his collector William Hair

Fig. 164. Canonbie, exterior view of the present church, built in 1821–2.

kept a 'rentall' or account book of those paying blackmail (CBP, ii, 276; Mac-
Donald Fraser 1989). This use of the church implies that the buildings were
considered safe by the very men who were most likely to destroy them. However, in the case of Canonbie it might be argued that strong buildings, capable
of ready defence, would not be tolerated, as they would all too easily fall prey
to the freebooters and outlaws who used the Debateable Land as a refuge from
the legal process.

To the west of Canonbie is **Half Morton**. Its former parish church once
stood next to the Tower of Sark, some distance from the eighteenth-century
building which replaced it. Also in this area were chapels-of-ease situated at
Pingle Bridge and at **Pennershaughs**. At **Carruthers**, now in the parish of
Middlebie, only the churchyard now remains, giving little clue as to the position of the former Norman building. At **Middlebie** itself, the site of the medieval church is now occupied by a building of 1929. None of these sites carry
any defensible implications, and there is no evidence to support or suggest any
such use, although, along with the parish of Wauchope, they once existed to
serve a much larger population than is now apparent (Barrow 1989).

Two miles east of Middlebie, in wooded grounds by the Kirtle Water, a short
distance from Springkell, are the remains of the parish church of **Kirkconnel**.
This served as the centre of the united parish of Kirkpatrick-Fleming after 1609.
The ruined rectangular structure is recognisably of medieval origin, despite

the loss of the east end and considerable seventeenth- and eighteenth-century alterations. These changes included the addition of an upper gallery, or laird's loft, and the possible conversion of the west end to a burial aisle. This western portion of the building has clear evidence of former stone tunnel vaulting, approximately 2.1 m (7 ft) high, and this may be indicative of its medieval form, although it is more likely to relate to a post-Reformation adaptation. A short distance to the north, at the base of Kirkland Hill, is the site of the medieval church of St Connel which, judging from the foundations, was of considerable size, and measured 22.5 m (74 ft) in length by 8.2 m (27 ft) in width; it was appropriated by the canons of Holywood Abbey. At the village of **Kirkpatrick-Fleming**, the church dates largely from 1726–9, 1733, and *c.* 1775, although the walls appear to contain medieval work, possibly utilising re-used material. The nearby former parish of **Irving** (OSA, iv) has no surviving church.

South of Kirkpatrick-Fleming, **Gretna** marks the boundary between Scotland and England, and sits astride the principal route north from Carlisle. The present church was built in 1789–90 but was heavily re-cast in 1909–10, so that all traces of medieval work have long since disappeared. There were two medieval churches by Gretna, the parish church and Redkirk, the latter possibly having been in the independent parish of Rainpatrick, the site of which lies off Redkirk point, a mile and a half to the south-west of the village. The church was lost to coastal erosion in 1675 when it 'fell into the sea' (RCHMS 1997, 246). A map of 1552 depicts both Gretna and Redkirk churches as having west towers (Neilson 1899), and although largely a stylised representation, may reflect the basic architecture of these buildings. Christopher Saxton's map of Westmorland and Cumberland of 1576 also marks these two churches with especial prominence. It was at Gretna parish church that Border truce meetings took place, the venue being called 'Gretnakirk' (Rae 1966). Border truces were also held at the nearby Lochmaben stone, located close to the edge of the Solway, between Gretna and Redkirk point. It was near this place that, in 1449, an English invasion force led by Thomas Percy, the younger son of the Earl of Northumberland, encamped on the bank of the River Sark. The Scottish army, commanded by Hugh Douglas, Earl of Ormond, met with them just to the south of Old Gretna, and in the ensuing battle, now known as the Battle of Sark, routed the English (Neilson 1897; McDowall 1986; Brown 1998).

West along the coast of the Solway estuary, the village of **Dornock** has a church of 1793 just to the north of the site of its medieval predecessor, which was dedicated to St Marjory. A low grass-covered mound represents the site of the early church, and the survival of four small Romanesque capitals in the churchyard may indicate that this building had a Norman tower (RCHMS 1997), although in 1790, three years prior to its rebuilding, the church was described as 'small and inconvenient' (OSA, iv, 95). It was from the medieval church that a bell was stolen in a reprisal raid by the men of Bowness-on-Solway around 1626 (*see* page 287).

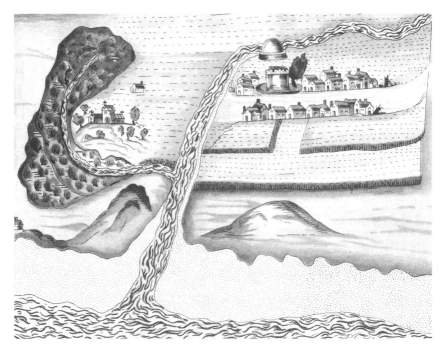

Fig. 165. Map of Annan *c.* 1560 showing the fortified parish church below the motte, and probably the hospital on the west (left) side of the river (after Armstrong 1883).

Annan was a place of some military importance, at least to the invading forces of Edward I who used the town as a base and for the storage of supplies. It was created a burgh belonging to the Bruce Lords of Annandale *c.* 1124, and in 1532 it became a royal burgh, founded by James V (Pryde 1965). It was in the midwinter of 1332 that Edward Balliol, seeking to regain his father's lost Scottish throne, took shelter in Annan, where he was surprised and routed by Archibald Douglas, and forced to flee to England (Chr.Lan., 274–5; Nicholson 1965).

There was a castle here until the seventeenth century which began as a Norman motte, held by the Bruces. Edward I found this castle useful for an invasion base, and in 1299 he was also using the nearby church tower for supplementary safe storage, against the possibility of attack by Robert Bruce (Ewan 1990, 12), despite having burnt the church and its steeple only two years previously when it was in the hands of the Scots (Ridpath 1848). In 1482, a reference to the garrisoning of the castle may refer to the church and its tower (Neilson 1895, 172), especially as it was reportedly only a small garrison, shared with Castlemilk and Bell's Tower (Macdougall 1982, 150). A depiction of the town *c.* 1560 (Figure 165) shows a crenellated tower below the motte which may represent the church steeple (Armstrong 1883).

In 1545, Lord Wharton made an assessment of the military capabilities of the Scottish West March between the Border and Dumfries. He reported to Hertford who wrote in October the same year that there was nothing to be done nearer than Dumfries 'except that he [Wharton] shuld make a rode yn to overthrowe and caste downe a certen chirche and steple called the steple of Annande, whiche is a thinge of litle importaunce and lesse annoyaunce to thenemye' (State Pap. Henry VIII, v(iv), 545). The optimistic view that it was of little importance was justified when, two years later, in September 1547, the church was garrisoned by the Scots under one James Lyone, and was besieged, captured, and destroyed by an English force led by Wharton (Colvin 1963–82, iv(ii), 707). An account of this incident has been preserved:

> . . . and we having in ordenaunce but a facon, a faconette, and foure quarter facons, for that ther is no baterie peice at Carlisle, divised that night how we shulde maik warr agaynst the house on the morowe. At viijth of the clok in the mornying we laid those sex peices to beit the battailling, and appoyntid certane archers and hagbutters to maik warre also until a paveis of tymbre might be drawn to the sidde of the steplee, under which sex pyoners might work to have undermyened the sam; in putting these to effectes, they in the house made sharpe warre, and slewe foure of our men and hurt divers others. And with grett stones from the steple toppe, brooke the paveis after it was sett, and being in that extrymytie, lakking ordenaunce for that purpose, we caused certane pyoners cutt the walle of the east end of the quere, overthuart abone the earthe, and caused the hooll ende to falle, wherwith the roofe and tymbre falling inward, slewe vij Scotesmen. And after that we caused the peices be laid to shoot at the doore of the steplee which was a house hight, and that house hight rampered with earthe, and caused them further to myen . . . And then the captain, about 4 p.m. took down his pensall of defyaunce . . . (CSPS, i, 42).

The following day the successful besiegers 'cutt and raiced down the churche wallis and steplee, and brent the towne, not leving any thing therin unbrent' (CSPS, ibid.). Eighty prisoners, twelve principal hostages, and all the ordnance and munitions in the church tower were taken to Carlisle. The account demonstrates clearly that the whole church, and not just the tower, was used as a fortification by the Scots, some of the defenders being killed inside when the roof of the choir collapsed; the description of shooting at the door of the steeple 'a house hight' may imply that it had no west arch, but was perhaps constructed in the manner of Burgh-by-Sands, or Great Salkeld (Neilson 1896, 269), with a defensible doorway between tower and nave or an upper doorway which gave access to higher levels (cf. Newburn, English Middle March, and Scaleby, English West March).

The troubles continued, for in 1584 it was reported that there had been 'slaughter and outrages done on the poor inhabitants of Annand' (CBP, i, 241). The destruction of the church and wasting of the town in the mid- and later sixteenth century was apparently so thorough that by early the following century Annan was so 'miserablie impoverischeit' that the people were unable to build a new kirk, and permission was granted for the hall and tower of the castle to serve as a church (RCHMS 1920, xlvi). This occurrence is perhaps the greatest irony in any of the Border church histories: the defensible House of God being destroyed in war leading to the fortified secular house becoming the centre of religious worship. The present kirk dates from 1789–90 with a spire added ten years later.

The only other ecclesiastical establishment in the town was a hospital, the record of which appears in a charter of donation to St Bees priory, around the year 1258. Remarkably, despite the severity of the destruction wrought on the town, part of this institution appears to have survived until after the Union, as in 1609 the 'hospital lands' are recorded, although the buildings had probably disappeared (Cowan and Easson 1976). Depicted on the sixteenth-century sketch of the town is a church building, lying on a hill to the west of the river, which has a crenellated central tower (*see* Figure 165); this may represent the hospital, which is generally considered to have been in the region of Howes. It is entirely possible, considering the fortification of nearby Annan church, that this hospital also had defensive precautions.

West of Annan, the parish of **Cummertrees** has no remains of its medieval church; the present building dates from 1777, with Victorian and later alterations. Further west, the tiny village of **Ruthwell** has an intriguing kirk, located north of the present settlement by the side of Thwaite Burn.

On plan, Ruthwell church is a plain rectangle, ostensibly of medieval date with a burial aisle added to the south in the later seventeenth century. The east end was shortened by 9.1 m (30 ft) and the north wall rebuilt to widen the building in 1801–3. A north apse was added in 1886–7 to house the important pre-Conquest cross. The whole structure was further subjected to a remodelling in 1906. However, although the rebuilt walls average 0.7 m (2 ft 4 in.) in thickness, the west gable measures 1.1 m (3 ft 7 in.) and may well represent core medieval fabric, perhaps of the Norman period, although, based on historical description, the original church may have been of pre-Conquest date (Meyvaert 1989). In 1792 the kirk was described as being 'an ancient fabric, perhaps now the most so of any in this part of the country; it is a long building, remarkably narrow' (OSA, iv, 449). Due to the overwhelming number of modifications made to this building in the post-medieval period, it is not possible to speculate on its original form, other than the long and narrow plan. Like its neighbouring villages, Ruthwell was located in a dangerous position, between the Border and Dumfries, and it is reasonable to assume that, on occasions, it may have served as a transitory refuge for the local populace.

To the north of Annan, the graveyard at **Luce**, near Brydekirk, is all that remains of the medieval parish church which was united to Hoddom and Ecclefechan in 1609 (Gifford 1996), whilst nothing remains of the nearby St Bryde's kirk.

Beyond Brydekirk is **Hoddom**. The medieval parish church once stood on the north bank of the River Annan, close to Hoddom Bridge, in an area now marked by a graveyard. The position is unlikely to be in any way connected with defence, but reflects the location of the pre-Conquest monastery which once existed here. Traces of ditches may be seen as cropmarks in the adjacent field, and a building which has been interpreted as a possible baptistery, dating from *c.* 600 and constructed from re-used Roman masonry, was excavated in 1991 (Lowe 1991; Selkirk and Selkirk 1993). Earlier excavations in 1915 and 1952 revealed that the chancel of the medieval church had been added to the nave. The latter, which was found to have incorporated Roman masonry, possibly dates from the early church on this site (RCHMS 1997, 245–7). In 1600 Lord Herries, West March Warden and successor to Sir John Carmichael (though never proclaimed as such) stayed at Hoddom 'to quiet that country' (CBP, ii, 1200). In 1609, Luce, Ecclefechan, and Hoddom were united into a single parish and a new church was built at Hoddomcross. The present ruined building there dates from 1817, although many of the adjacent grave-markers belong to the previous century. The nearby village of **Ecclefechan**, whose name derives from the 'Church of St Fechin' or 'St Vigean', a seventh-century Irish abbot (Darton 1994), may also have hosted an early Christian site (Hill 1997, 13), although no archaeological evidence for this has been found to date. Like Hoddom, the medieval church was abandoned in 1609 in favour of the new church belonging to the united parishes at Hoddomcross, and no visible remains now exist above ground.

A short distance to the west of Hoddom church is Hoddom Castle, a sixteenth-century tower-house belonging to the Maxwells. The almost continuous feud this family had with the Johnstone clan meant that the castle was a major stronghold and focus of military activity entirely internal to the Scottish nation. The upshot was of great benefit to England as Edward Aglionby noted when he wrote to Burghley in 1592, 'They [the Maxwells] have bene in fede with the Johnsons theis many yeres, which is a weakeninge of Scotland and a strength to England' (CBP, i, 743).

One mile south of the castle at Hoddom, Trailtrow Hill rises steeply above the road. On top of the hill are the remains of a church and tower, the latter known as **Repentance Tower** (the word 'Repentance' is inscribed on the door lintel). All that remains of the former church of **Trailtrow** is a mound, the graveyard, and a post-Reformation mausoleum (Figure 166). The structure was demolished in the sixteenth century by John Maxwell, Lord Herries, to provide building material for the repair of the tower. The strategic position of the site is evident, with a view which ranges from the Solway Firth up to the hills which define the northern edge of the Scottish West March. It was precisely because of this vista that Lord Herries rebuilt Repentance Tower primarily as a watch tower, as attested by him in a letter to the king in 1579:

> The wache toure upoun Trailtrow, callit Repentance, mon be mendit of the litill diffaceing the Englische army maid of it; and according to the formar devise, the greit bell and the fyir pan put on it; and ane trew man haiff ane husband land adjacent for the keping of the continuall wache thairupoun' (RPCS, iii, 84).

Fig. 166. Repentance Tower, view from the south showing the tower (left) and the post-medieval mausoleum (right). The gravestones mark the site of the former churchyard belonging to Trailtrow church.

The 'devise' in question was that specified by Border law which required 'the Watch to be keeped on the House-head; and in the Weir the Beaken in the Fire-pan to be keeped, and never faill burning, so long as the Englishmen remain in Scotland; and with ane bell to be on the Head of the Fire-pan, which shall ring whenever the Fray is, or that the Watchman seeing the Thieves disobedient come over the Water of Annand, or thereabout, and knows them to be Enemies (Nicholson 1705, 198).

The appearance of the tower today is largely that of the watch tower Herries repaired, with some later reconstruction and modification. However, it is clear from his correspondence that the tower was already in existence, and used as a watch tower, before the English army damaged it, probably in 1570. The preceptor of Trailtrow, Alexander Menzies, reported in 1562 that the chapel had been destroyed and its lands seized (Robertson 1935). This earlier tower must have been juxtaposed with the church and may even have formed part of it; beacon towers on churches are certainly indicated elsewhere on the Border, for example at Carlisle and Crosthwaite. Within the vicinity of Trailtrow was a medieval 'poor's hospital', which is mentioned in 1455 and again in 1574, although by 1609 it was apparently out of use (Cowan and Easson 1976).

At **Dalton**, a church of 1895 stands below and to the north-west of the medieval building. Of the latter, the ruined shell of a 1704 rebuilding sits atop a steep mound, its foundations and lower courses of the walls, with a splayed plinth, are the only vestiges of the earlier church. Once again, it is only the position of this building which hints at its possible use as a defensible refuge; there are no documentary references to such a use, nor enough surviving medieval fabric to determine its original form, although the walls evidently exceeded 1 m (3 ft 3 in.) in thickness judging by the surviving base. At **Little Dalton**, two miles to the north-west, a smaller church of simple rectangular plan was constructed in the thirteenth century, remodelled in the fifteenth, and abandoned in 1633 (RCHMS 1997, 247). It now stands on high ground as a low ruined shell, and has no obvious defensible traits other than its position and lack of large windows.

LOCHMABEN AND UPPER ANNANDALE

On the north bank of the River Annan, north of Dalton and Kirkwood, are the remains of **St Mungo's** church. Only a portion of the chancel is still extant, and from this section it is clear that most of the upstanding fabric dates from the eighteenth century; a door in the south wall carries the date 1754 on the lintel and the south wall appears to have been rebuilt at this time. Fragments of earlier work may survive in the east and south walls and the whole structure contains much re-used material. The jumble of successive construction phases has obscured the medieval form, although documentary evidence indicates that the church was previously cruciform with very narrow windows; in 1805 the north aisle was demolished and rebuilt (RCHMS 1997).

Lockerbie stands in a significant position astride the principal road leading from the Border to the north, although the development of the town only commenced in the early eighteenth century, and the parish is that of Dryfesdale. The present church dates from 1896–8 which replaced a building of 1858, itself the successor to the first church here, constructed in 1757 when it moved site from Dryfeside (about a mile and a half to the north of the town). The medieval church is said to have been swept away by a flood in 1670 and its replacement so threatened by the same fate that the ecclesiastical centre was moved to safer ground in Lockerbie (OSA, iv, 103). Within the parish were the chapels-of-ease of St Michael's at **Hillside**, and **Little Hutton**, both to the north of Lockerbie town.

Three miles to the east of Lockerbie is the parish church of **Tundergarth**, built by James Barbour in 1900 to replace the late eighteenth-century building which survives as a roofless ruin within the churchyard. To the north are the sites of churches at **Sibbalde** and **Corrie**, and the church at **Hutton** which broke away from Sibbalde and became an independent parish sometime in the thirteenth century. Further to the north-east, the site of the medieval church at **Eskdalemuir** lies three-quarters of a mile south of the new kirk built in 1826.

Lockerbie's neighbour, **Lochmaben**, played a more significant role in medieval Border affairs, primarily as it was the location of a major castle (Macdougall 1982, 150). It was established as a burgh of barony by the Bruce lords of Annandale around 1296. The town passed to the Earl of Moray when Robert Bruce gained the throne of Scotland in 1306, then to the Earl of Douglas in 1409, before finally being subsumed by the Crown as a royal burgh after the forfeiture of Annandale in 1440 (Pryde 1965). It was seldom free of trouble, both from local feuding and from English incursions.

A motte castle existed here in the twelfth century, occupying the ridge between Kirk Loch and Castle Loch, but this was replaced in the fourteenth century by a more substantial stone building, constructed on a highly defensible promontory protruding into Castle Loch. Of this later castle, considerable remains still survive, and comprise inner and outer wards, separated by a ditch, and within the inner ward an entrance and curtain wall; the whole site is defended from the landward side by four ditches and banks, the outer ditch originally being flooded with water from the loch (Cruden 1981). Edward I captured the castle following his victory at Falkirk in 1298, and, although it was briefly regained by the Bruces in 1306, it fell again into English hands the same year, and was still occupied in 1313, making it one of the last strongholds to be garrisoned by English troops before the battle of Bannockburn. After a period of fluctuation in ownership between Scotland and England, the castle was finally taken by Archibald Douglas and George, Earl of March, in February 1384 (Maxwell 1896, 120; Brown 1998), and remained in Scottish hands until Hertford's invasion of 1544–5 when it was besieged and captured. In 1592 after it had been recaptured by Bothwell, Sir John Forster described it as 'the King's Chiefeste streingth one the West Borders of Scotlande' (CBP, i, 750).

The parish kirk of Lochmaben is a large building of 1818–20 on a new site, but close to the old churchyard where the medieval church formerly stood. Once again, the juxtaposition of church and early castle is obvious, and patently arises from the feudal ownership of the twelfth-century estate. There is little documentary material which helps to shed light on the form and construction of the original building, but in 1593 the church was burnt during fighting between the Maxwells and the Johnstons (Fraser 1935) which may be an indication that it was capable of defensible use. In the *Old Statistical Account* a description attests that:

> The church is an old Gothic fabric, dedicated to St Magdalen. In a bloody family feud, between the Maxwells of Nithsdale, and the Johnstons of Annandale, it suffered much. In an engagement between these on a plain called Dryfe Sands, the Maxwells, who were defeated with great slaughter, fled, and took sanctuary in the church of Lochmaben, and were pursued by the Johnstons, who burnt the church to the ground (OSA, iv, 386).

The mound which now represents its site indicates a possible overall length of around 27 m (88 ft), and limited excavation in 1969 indicated a phase of reconstruction early in the medieval period (Wilson 1972). Another reason for the destruction of the church may have been connected to its use for the administration of justice; a Steward Court was supposed to meet in the tolbooth, weekly, but there was no tolbooth, and so it met inside the kirk (Tough 1928, 170). The destruction of the centre of justice by the Johnstons may have been considered legitimate, especially following such a devastating victory which was bound to attract the unwelcome attention of the Warden.

In the tower of the present kirk are two bells, the older of which dates from the early fourteenth century and was said to have been given by Robert Bruce; the second bell is reputed to have been brought from England in a Border raid (RCHMS 1920, 158).

Within the parish of Lochmaben were subordinate chapels at **Rockhall-head**, established by 1223, and near **Hunter House**, the latter dedicated to St Thomas, and whose walls were still standing in 1826 (RCHMS 1997). All traces of these buildings have now disappeared.

Two and a half miles to the north-west of Lochmaben are the ruins of **Trailflat** church, an independent parochial centre until 1650 when it was united with the parish of Tinwald. The building is rectangular on plan and only the west gable stands substantially intact; all other walls do not exceed 0.7 m (2 ft 4 in.) either in height or thickness. Most of the fabric appears to be of late medieval or post-Reformation date, and although built on an elevated site, there are no indications of defensible adaptation.

North of Lochmaben there is a possibility that a small monastic foundation once existed at **Applegarth**, but there is no physical evidence to substantiate this (Reid 1958). The present parish church dates from 1762–3, though on the site of an earlier church. At **Johnstonebridge** a kirk of 1819 stands near the position of its predecessor. A little to the west of Johnstonebridge, on rising ground above the road near Blackacre, stand the ruins of **Garvald** church, the parish having been united with Kirkmichael in 1674. The simple rectangular plan and construction indicate a mainly post-Reformation date, although a jamb of the two-light fifteenth-century east window has survived.

Four miles north-west of Johnstonebridge, in a remote upland location above the Kinnel Water, are the scant remains of **Dumgree** church. Measuring only 12 m (39 ft 4 in.) by 6 m (19 ft 8 in.) in size, this small building has existed here since the late twelfth century when it was granted to the abbey of Kelso (Cowan 1967, 52). Only the foundations now remain within the churchyard, and there are no defensible implications.

At **Wamphray**, three miles north-east of Johnstonebridge, a kirk of 1834 replaced the medieval building, although a re-used carved stone over the tower entrance, of eleventh-century date, attests to the early origin of this church. The site is in an entirely undefensible location but lies in a remote valley and is not easy to locate. Wamphray church played host to a highly unusual episode around the year 1715 when the minister, one Mr Taylor, was deposed from office for his doctrinal beliefs (he had joined the Cameronians, an extremist religious minority). However, the former minister had an exceptionally strong local following, and it was necessary for the Steward Deputy of Annandale to

Fig. 167. Chapel (parish of Kirkpatrick-Juxta), ruins of the church showing a blocked doorway in the east gable.

appear in arms in the church in order to maintain a peaceful assembly (OSA, iv, 534).

The main road from Johnstonebridge leads north through Beattock, where the medieval church of **Kirkpatrick-Juxta**, just to the south of the village, is now represented by a building of 1798–1800, itself replacing a kirk remodelled in 1676 (OSA, iv, 345).

The town of **Moffat** nestles beneath the Lowther Hills and is the last significant settlement in this region of the West March. That the town was regarded as an integral part of the defensive system of the March, despite being twenty-five miles from the Border, is attested by the order of the Earl of Douglas in 1448 that a warning beacon should be burnt on Gallows Hill (Tranter 1987, 180). In 1547, Thomas Wharton, March Warden, established a garrison at Moffat, along with others at Castlemilk and Dumfries (Patterson 1997, 200). The present appearance of the town owes much to its eighteenth-century popularity as a spa resort, although its layout reflects that of the medieval settlement. Of the parish church in High Street only a small portion of the south wall still remains, 0.72 m (2 ft 4 in.) in thickness. The building appears, from the foundation lines, to have been large, measuring approximately 25 m (82 ft) in length by 14.3 m (47 ft) in width. However there is insufficient evidence, both physical and documentary, to determine its original form.

Standing on high ground, just to the west of the town, is a subsidiary chapel of Kirkpatrick-Juxta at **Chapel**. The remains of the east and west gables still stand, and date the building to the thirteenth century; a window in the west gable has contained a triple light which has been reconstructed. The east gable, which is 1.5 m (5 ft) in thickness, may represent the surviving wall of a tower, through which was a narrow doorway 0.9 m (3 ft) in width and 2.9 m (9 ft 6 in.) high, now blocked but clearly visible (Figure 167). Beyond the east wall is a nineteenth-century cottage which has effaced further evidence for the building in this position. A map of 1590 showing defensive sites in the West Marches depicts a tower here (Hyslop and Hyslop 1912, 320), and it may have been that such a tower formed part of the ecclesiastical building, similar to those seen closer to the Border (for example, an east tower was constructed at Burgh-by-Sands). The structure may also have belonged to a medieval hospital on this site (RCHMS 1997, 252).

DUMFRIES AND NITHSDALE

Nithsdale, the last of the Scottish West March dales, had a scattered population of tiny villages and isolated farms, and now contains the lowest density of surviving medieval churches in the Border region. Close to the mouth of the Nith estuary, and guarding the approach to Dumfries from the south, stand the remains of Caerlaverock Castle, the latest in a series of fortified structures in this area. Completed by the closing years of the thirteenth century, the castle occupied lands formerly rented to the monks of Holme Cultram Abbey in the English West March (Gifford 1996). This powerful structure was constructed on a triangular outcrop of rock amidst marshy ground, and its plan, dictated by its position, is that of a triangular castle of enclosure. It was besieged by Edward I in 1300 as part of the English king's attempt to suppress the region, and remained in English hands until 1312. Amidst the complexities of the multitude of rebuilding and remodelling, which took place between the fourteenth and the seventeenth centuries (O'Neil 1952), there was doubtless a private chapel. This was certainly of some significance to the Maxwell family during their occupation in the first half of the seventeenth century, for as a staunch Catholic family they became the focus of military aggression, culminating in a thirteen-week siege during 1640 when the castle was taken by the Covenanting forces (Paterson 1998).

On the eastern approach to Dumfries, the villages of **Mousewald**, **Torthorwald**, and **Tinwald** once had medieval churches, but these have now been entirely replaced, at the first in the nineteenth century and at the others a century earlier. The kirk at Mousewald occupies a high position within the village and may have originally been built in the thirteenth century when the parish formed part of the barony of Torthorwald. In the village of Torthorwald the plain T-plan church, rebuilt in 1730 and again in 1782, stands near to the ruins of the medieval tower-house belonging to the Kirkpatrick family.

Dumfries is the principal urban centre of the March. It was created a burgh by William the Lion in 1186 (Pryde 1965), and had a royal castle also built at the same time (Owen 1997, 125). The town lay in a position of considerable military significance: to the west it was defended by the River Nith, and to the south-east and east, between the lower Annan and the Nith, were dangerous mosses, especially the Lochar Moss, leaving only the road to Lochmaben or an approach by sea, as practicable for invading forces. On making his assessment of the area in 1545, Lord Wharton thought that 'the passages to Dunfreys are so strait that . . . it [is] too dangerous for a warden's raid' (L. & P. Henry VIII, xx(ii), 572). The castle was regarded as an essential acquisition during the early years of the Wars of Independence, and having passed between the Bruces and the English between 1286 and the mid-fourteenth century, it was finally raised by David II sometime before 1357 as a condition of his release from captivity (RCHMS 1920); its site is now at the present Castledykes Park. Dumfries was attacked and burnt by the English on several occasions during the fifteenth and sixteenth centuries, despite its strong natural defences.

The parish church was dedicated to St Michael and appears to have been in existence by the late twelfth century; it survived until 1745 when it was demolished and rebuilt (OSA, iv, 129). During the 1880s, the foundations of the medieval church were uncovered during repairs, and evidence from this work, combined with eighteenth-century written accounts, indicate that there was a nave of four bays with a north and south aisle, a chancel, and a 'thick, short tower' at the west end, the room within which was known as the 'Session' or 'Session House' (Barbour 1888, 44). This description, added to the fact that money was raised to improve the appearance of the steeple, suggest that the tower was a bulky, low structure, certainly without elegance, and which may possibly have been designed originally for security, rather than primarily as a bell tower or architectural statement; though it should also be noted that the walls were felt to be 'insufficient' for additions to be made. Early documents also mention the chapel of St Thomas, which was located on Chapel Hill, between High Street and Queensberry Street (McDowall 1986). The next ecclesiastical establishment in the town appears to have been the Convent of the Greyfriars (Franciscans), founded c. 1265 by Devorgilla, the wife of John Balliol.

It was in the church of the Greyfriars Convent, on a cold February day in 1306, that the course of Scottish history was irrevocably forged. Robert Bruce, fearing that John Comyn (the younger, Guardian of Scotland) would make an attempt on the throne of Scotland (indeed, he was a major obstacle to Bruce's ambitions (Young 1997; Watson 1998)), asked him to attend a meeting in the church on 10 February. What actually transpired in conversation that day will never be known for certain, but it is probable that mutual charges of treachery were made, and in the bitter argument which ensued, Bruce struck Comyn with a dagger and his men attacked him with swords (Barrow 1988; Young 1997). He was left for dead in the church, close to the high altar, but may have lived for a little while longer before being finished-off by Bruce's followers (Maxwell 1896; McNamee 1997). That such a meeting took place in the church implies that it was regarded as neutral territory, and it seems likely that violence was not pre-meditated. However, the lessons of history have taught well that Border churches were never an entirely safe haven, nor was sanctuary respected where warfare or affairs-of-state were concerned.

Although the murder of Comyn was by far the most significant event in the history of the Greyfriars' Convent, the buildings also played host to other noteworthy occurrences during the Troubles. Edward I stayed here several times during his visits to south-west Scotland, and in 1547 the English threatened to destroy the conventual buildings. In the last episode, the Warden and two friars were summoned to Carlisle to receive instructions on the surrender of the friary, an indication that the buildings had been secured against the invading troops; from contemporary accounts, the friary was evidently walled (Barbour 1911). No trace of the medieval building now remains above ground, although limited excavations in 1901 revealed some foundations and drains, and many human remains (Lennox 1903).

Despite the medieval churches of Dumfries having survived several destructive raids by the English, especially during the sixteenth century, not a vestige of these now remains above ground. However, about a mile to the north, one church did survive, and still exists today, although now much ruined. This is the collegiate church, with associated claustral buildings, of **Lincluden**, located in a loop of the Cluden Water close to its junction with the River Nith. Although technically in the parish of Terregles in the Stewartry of Kirkudbright, geographically the area now forms part of the suburbs of Dumfries and therefore it is logical to discuss this building here.

Lincluden started out as a Benedictine nunnery, founded in the mid-twelfth century probably by Uchtred the son of Fergus, Lord of Galloway (Barbour 1884). In 1389, Archibald Douglas ('the Grim') petitioned the Pope to suppress the house. On 7 May that year, the Pope granted the suppression and commissioned the Bishop of Glasgow to erect a collegiate church for a provost, eight priests, and twenty-four bedesmen in its place (Cowan and Easson 1976). Douglas was clearly endeavouring to save himself money in his display of piety by remodelling an existing foundation, a common practice at that period. At the same time he acquired considerable possessions by the arrangement. His justification for the suppression was to portray the nunnery as having fallen into ruin, with local 'very evil men' using the house as a fortress (Brown 1998, 192). Although Douglas doubtless exaggerated in order to achieve his wishes, there is more than likely a strong element of truth in his statement. The nun-

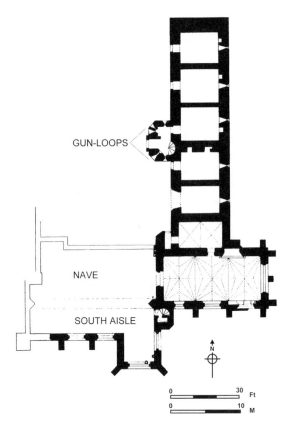

Fig. 168. Plan of Lincluden college showing position of gun-loops to defend the stair-turret in the domestic range (after MacGibbon and Ross 1896–7).

nery was founded in an easily defensible spot, protected by the river on three sides and open only to the west. The place had earlier been chosen as the site for a Norman motte and bailey castle, the landscaped remains of which lie to the south-east of the church, whose re-use by feuding families or outlaws would have been a real possibility. That Lincluden was thought capable of resistance is confirmed by the report of an English agent in the later sixteenth century who commented that: 'The towne of Dumfreiss is subjett to two lytill motes, one called the Beakin hill . . . the other at th' east gate, where upoune the lytill chapell standetht hard by the towne . . . in case of fortification, yt might for that qwarter of the towne be made a moute or bulwork' (Armstrong 1883, cx).

The plan of the recast college utilised the existing church, to the north of which were added a range of domestic buildings which abutted the sacristy. Of the church itself only the choir, south transept, and the exterior wall of the south aisle have survived, but the position of the nave is clear (Figure 168). The choir was rebuilt, sometime shortly after 1450, to accommodate the canons' altars, and also to house the tomb of the Princess Margaret, widow of the fourth Earl of Douglas and daughter of King Robert III, who had augmented the original foundation in 1429 (RMS, ii, 133). The mason commissioned for this prestigious work was evidently John Morow, who was employed at Melrose Abbey during the same period (Fawcett 1994a). The roof of the choir was constructed with stone tierceron vaulting with a plainer barrel vault above, the springers for which are still clearly visible. The purpose of the upper vault was to support a roof of stone slabs, probably in order to create a fireproof structure and also to provide a secure high-level space which may have been utilised as a treasury, or as a safe refuge; it was lit by a square window in the east gable (MacGibbon and Ross 1896–7, ii, 393; Cruden 1986, 178–9; Fawcett 1994a, 47). A similar chamber may also have existed over the vault of the south transept. Comparable secure upper-floor arrangements existed at Brinkburn and Tynemouth Priories in the English Middle March, and a slightly later parallel is to be found outwith the Borders in the St Mirrin's Aisle at Paisley Abbey.

Although Douglas had blamed the corruption of the nunnery on the 'very evil men' who had fortified the buildings on the site, he, or at least his successors, wasted no time in doing precisely the same thing for his new foundation. North of the sacristy, which abuts the choir, lies the domestic range. On the ground floor are five storerooms; all are tunnel-vaulted, with narrow rectangular lights opening eastwards, each formerly barred. This is perhaps unsurprising as these rooms contained the main provisions for the college, though many of the upper windows, where they survive, also have evidence of barring. The most unequivocal indication of defence however is to be found in the projecting octagonal stair-turret in the centre of the block on the west side, which gave entry to the upper floors, and which contains four gun-loops which would provide covering-fire on all approaches to the entrance (Figure 169). This turret was probably constructed by William Stewart, Provost of Lincluden in the early 1530s. At the same time the north end of the range was extended by the addition of a third storey to form a plain tower, whose gables were formerly crowstepped (Barbour 1884). The strong tower (Figure 170), with its minimal fenestration and defensible stair-entrance, was undoubtedly a very necessary precaution for the secular residents of the college, who included the Earls of Douglas in their capacity as Wardens of the Scottish West March. The foundations of a further domestic range and a staircase were uncovered in 1882 when excavations were carried out at the north-west angle of the nave (RCHMS 1914).

The buildings of the college were plainly regarded as secure, as in December 1448 they provided the setting for a great court held to revise the Border laws and to fix sites for warning beacons around the countryside (McDowall 1986). In 1460, following the defeat of the Lancastrian forces at Northampton, Queen Margaret of England and her son Edward, Prince of Wales, fled to Lincluden for safety, where a treaty was hastily concluded with the Scottish

Fig. 169. Lincluden, gun-loops in the lower portion of the stair-turret.

Queen Regent, Mary of Gueldres (Paterson 1997, 89). The domestic range continued in use as a residence until the second half of the seventeenth century
(Stell 1986).

Three miles north-west of Dumfries, above the west bank of the Nith, is
Holywood. Now no more than a small cluster of modern houses and earlier
farms, this was formerly the site of Holywood Abbey, or Dercongal, founded
before 1225 and for most of its existence belonging to the Premonstratensian
order (Cowan and Easson 1976). Much of the history of this foundation is
obscure, but it may have been founded in the twelfth century by John de Kirkconnel, and provided men for the augmentation of Maxwell's troops during
the Border wars (Aitken 1889). In 1372, Archibald Douglas founded a poor's
hospital within the monastic enclosure, later annexed to the collegiate church
at Lincluden (Black 1891; Cowan and Easson 1976). There is no mention of
this monastery being used in a defensive role or having to be secured against
raiding, but such precautions would doubtless have been made. The present
church, built in 1779, occupies the site of the abbey and incorporates masonry
from it in its walls (Martin 1897).

At nearby **Kirkton** the present Kirkmahoe parish church was rebuilt on the
site of its predecessor in 1822–3. A slight mound nearby contains much stonework and may represent the position of the medieval building, which was dedi-

Fig. 170. Lincluden, defensible tower in the domestic range.

cated to St Quintin. The *Old Statistical Account* of 1790–1 recorded that the church was 'an old one', but had 'been for some time in good condition' (OSA, iv, 296).

A little to the north of Holywood and Kirkton, the villages of **Dunscore** and **Dalswinton** now have nineteenth-century churches. Dunscore's medieval church was demolished in 1649, and lay in the lower end of the parish (OSA, iv, 143). Its replacement was a T-plan kirk in the position which is now occupied by its successor of 1823 (Gifford 1996). The site of a church at Farthingwell is recorded by the Ordnance Survey (RCHMS 1920, 59). At Dalswinton, the present ecclesiastical structure is that of a mission church, built in 1881, replacing a now vanished chapel-of-ease in the parish of Kirkmahoe.

Five miles north of Dunscore, at **Closeburn**, the ruins of the old parish church of 1741, extended in 1779, stand juxtaposed with its successor of 1878, by James Barbour. Of the medieval building there are no structural remains above ground, and only the bell of 1606, a Norman beak-head, and a fragment of a pre-Conquest cross-shaft, exist from the earlier church. Within the parish were two medieval chapels-of-ease, at **Nether Mains**, and **Kirkpatrick**; in addition, the former medieval church at **Dalgarnock** was united with Closeburn parish in 1697. Of these buildings, only the site at Dalgarnock now has visible evidence for the position of the church, lying on a flat haugh close to the junction of the Nith and Cample Water. The building has been approximately 19 m (62 ft) in length by 9.3 m (30 ft 6 in.) in width, but only a low mound now survives to mark its position. In the churchyard is a poignant monument of 1925 to the 'Nithsdale Martyrs', who were, of course, Covenanters.

The town of Thornhill was established as late as 1664, and replaced the earlier parish centre of **Morton**. Of the medieval church nothing survives, and only a fragment of its successor of 1781 now remains in the former Manse Road church. Two and a half miles north-east of Thornhill, in a strongly defensible position above a small loch, are the substantial ruins of the fourteenth-century Morton Castle, probably founded in the twelfth century, and forming part of a range of fortifications along the valley of the Nith. A similar distance to the north-west of the town are the remains of Tibbers Castle, also largely of fourteenth-century date. To the west are the sites of medieval churches at **Penpont**, **Tynron**, **St Connel's**, and the fragmentary remains of the remote church at **Glencairn** (at Kirkland). At Glencairn only the east and west gables are extant, with evidence of a thirteenth-century date based on the windows in the west gable; the walls average 1.15 m (3 ft 9 in.) in thickness.

Further north, the Cumnock to Dumfries road runs into much higher land as it skirts below the Lowther Hills, still following the valley of the Nith. Along the higher route towards Glasgow, where the road divides at Carronbridge, the small village of **Durisdeer** is located below the steep slopes of Scaw'd Law. Here, a surprisingly large eighteenth-century kirk dominates the later houses and cottages. A medieval church on this site was demolished in 1716 and was replaced by the present cruciform building, completed by 1729 (Gifford 1996). It is a remarkable structure, having a T-plan, with a large south transept, and with its west end fashioned into a two-storey session house and retiring rooms for the Duke of Queensberry, with a plain bell tower above (MacKechnie 1985). Adjoining the north of the kirk, and formerly attached to its medieval predecessor, is the Queensberry Aisle, a mausoleum for the first Duke, built between 1695 and 1708.

Three miles north-west of Durisdeer, positioned high above the valley of the Nith, and not easily accessible, are the remains of the little church of **Kirkbride**. This medieval parish was divided between Durisdeer and Sanquhar in 1727 when the population fell too low for the parish to be viable (TSA, xii, 246). The church is situated in a lonely spot, now well away from roads and habitation, with the exception of a nearby farm. The ruins are those of a rectangular building, 15.2 m (49 ft 10 in.) in length by 4.5 m (14 ft 9 in.) in width, and from the north side of the chancel projects a small sacristy. From the surviving architectural features – three small windows and a doorway in the south wall, and an arch between the sacristy and the chancel – the building appears to date entirely from the early sixteenth century. The surrounding churchyard is defined by a steep bank reaching 2 m (6 ft 7 in.) on the north side, and the whole site appears to have been built on a platform cut out of the hillside, which may be indicative of an early foundation (Thomas 1971).

Beyond Durisdeer and Kirkbride is the small town of **Sanquhar**, which forms the gateway into Dumfriesshire from the north-west. It had been created a burgh of barony by 1335 when the five burgages, described by the English sheriff of Dumfries, were reported as being 'waste'; in 1484 the burgh was re-created and was granted to the Crichton family in whose feudal tenure it lay until being made a royal burgh in 1598 (Pryde 1965). The town had a castle, the property of the Crichtons, the ruins of which lie at the south-east end of the settlement, and comprise an inner and outer courtyard, with a strong southern tower and two ranges of internal buildings, mostly of fourteenth- and fifteenth-century date.

The parish church of St Bride lies at the opposite end of the town, and was rebuilt in 1822–4 by James Thomson of Dumfries; the chancel was added in 1931. The old church, which lay to the east of the present building, was demolished around the same time, but its foundations were excavated in 1895 when a building measuring 29.3 m (96 ft) in length by 9.3 m (30 ft 6 in.) in width was revealed (RCHMS 1920). The excavations, made by the Marquis of Bute, also revealed that the choir, probably a fifteenth-century addition to an earlier nave, had in all likelihood been stone-vaulted, and that there was a small tower 3 m (10 ft) square at the west end (M'Millan 1930). By 1792 however, the building had fallen into disrepair as a contemporary account describes: 'The church is remarkable for nothing but its antiquity, size, and disproportion – it is in a most ruinous condition . . . From some stones of Gothic architecture in its walls, it appears to be of remote antiquity. It is certain that it was a place of worship, in the times of Popery, as the choir is still entire' (OSA, iv, 476). A further description relates that the church was 'a considerable and large fabrick, consisting of a spacious church and stately quire' (MacGibbon and Ross 1896–7, iii, 435–6). Although these descriptions provide insufficient information on which to base the character of the medieval church, its position on the key northern route to Ayr and the coast, combined with its elevation in the fifteenth century to the status as a prebend in Glasgow cathedral, would afford the rector and patron a good opportunity to ensure that it was a lavish affair. The probable stone roof to the new choir may have been an expression both of status and fireproof security, and it is conceivable that the tower provided for the priest the safety which the castle afforded the patron.

Beyond Sanquhar the large village of **Kirkconnel** lies close to the March boundary, its kirk dating from 1729. The ruins of the medieval church lie a short distance to the north of the present village on a plateau at the base of Kirkland Hill. They have largely been reconstructed from excavations made in 1926; an early thirteenth-century date seems probable for the plain rectangular structure which had a simple subdivision between nave and chancel. Its remote location echoes that of its neighbour, Kirkbride, lower down the valley.

THE STEWARTRY

The Scottish West March was not limited in its westward extent to the Stewartry of Kirkudbright, whose boundaries correspond with the former county of the same name, but also included parts of Wigtownshire, although some areas of this most westerly region were generally outwith the Wardens' duties (Tough 1928; Rae 1966). However, Wigtownshire was so far from the land border with England that many of the defensible traits found in churches further east were unnecessary. The title 'Stewartry' results from the administration of the district by a steward on behalf of the Crown following the forfeiture of the Douglases in 1455 (Brown 1998). Although analogous to a Sheriffdom, the Stewart (administrator) had wider powers, akin to a lord of regality, in the determination of criminal matters. On the east, the area is bounded by the River Nith, and to the west by the River Cree. The valley of the Urr in the centre formed the eastern boundary of the medieval diocese of Galloway.

A short distance to the west of Dumfries is the village of **Terregles**. The body of the kirk was rebuilt in 1814 but the earlier chancel, which dates from 1583–5, was retained. The chancel's neat, rubble-built walls were erected on the instruction of Agnes, Lady Herries; its octagonal east end was designed as a burial vault, to be walled-off from the remainder of the building. The living was held by the nuns of Lincluden and subsequently by the collegiate church which succeeded it. There are no defensible implications within the present structure.

To the north-west of Terregles, and about four and a half miles from Dumfries, is the parish church of **Irongray** in the parish of Kirkpatrick-Irongray, which was rebuilt in 1803 on the site of its medieval predecessor. A little to the west, at Hallhill, is a monument, erected in 1851, marking the graves of two Covenanters, Edward Gordon and Alexander McCubbine, who were hung nearby. The inscription, recording the turbulent events of the seventeenth century, carries an emotive message which echoes the earlier history of Border churches and religion:

As Lagg and blood[y] Bruce comman'd
We were hung up by
Hellish hand
And thus their furio
Us rage to stay
We dy'd near Kirk
of Iron Gray;
Here now in peace

Sweet rest we take
Once murder'd for
Religeon's sake

Five miles south of Dumfries, just to the west of the Nith estuary, lies New Abbey. Here, nestling in a sheltered spot between the road and the river known as the New Abbey Pow, stand the substantial remains of **Sweetheart Abbey**, founded in 1273 by Devorgilla, the mother of John Balliol, King of Scotland (Cowan and Easson 1976). The name 'Sweetheart' is said to derive from the embalmed heart of Devorgilla's husband, another John Balliol, which was buried with the foundress on her death in 1289 (Cruden 1986). The abbey was Cistercian and was dependent on the abbey of Dundrennan, also in the Stewartry.

The first Abbot, John, swore fealty to Edward I in 1279, and in 1300 Edward stayed here on returning from his invasion of Galloway (Chinnock 1901). Despite the allegiance sworn to the English king, the Abbot petitioned Edward II in 1307 for damages caused by his father's Welsh soldiers whilst staying in Dumfries (Richardson 1951). In 1381 or thereabouts the monastery was struck by lightning, causing much damage, and as a result the church at Buittle was granted to the abbey (McKerlie, v, 1879). However, despite its vulnerable position, close to the Solway estuary, Sweetheart does not appear to have been the deliberate target of any major English attack. In the fourteenth century the patron of the monastery was Archibald, third Earl of Douglas, who had re-founded Lincluden, and in whom the monks no doubt saw a powerful, defending figurehead. Following the Reformation, in common with most other Border abbeys, the buildings were used to house the parish kirk, until a purpose-built structure was erected on the south side of the cloister in 1731. In 1877 this was demolished and the present village church was built.

The plan of the monastic buildings closely follows the usual Cistercian form, with a cruciform church to the north, a central cloister, and a gate to the lay brothers' west range. The general design of the church, especially in the detail of the piers and windows, illustrates that Scottish masons understood developments south of the border and were adapting to current architectural fashion (Fawcett 1990, 169). To the east and south lay the administrative, domestic, and ancillary buildings, none of which remains in enough detail to reveal any defensible traits. However, security may have been a consideration during the design of the thirteenth-century church tower, as its substantial crenellations and decidedly secular aspect show (Fenwick 1978). Access to its upper stages was only possible along inter-mural passages, reached from a spiral stair in the north-west angle of the north transept. During the subsequent two centuries, a crowstep-gabled upper storey was added to the tower, pairs of large windows within which imply a possible use for accommodation (Figure 171).

The main doorway leading into the cloister, and the west and north entrances to the church itself, all have draw-bar slots showing that their portals

Fig. 171. Sweetheart Abbey, showing the central tower.

were capable of being secured. The slot within the north entrance to the cloister is particularly deep. Within the claustral buildings, a narrow windowless
chamber was located between the chapter house and the parlour, which may
have served as a treasury for the safe storage of the abbey's valuables.

One further defensive measure was taken and which has in part survived.
The whole precinct, some 12.1 hectares (30 acres) in extent, was surrounded to
the north, west, and east by a massive stone wall, up to 3.7 m (12 ft) in height
with an average thickness of 1.2 m (4 ft). The wall is constructed of large gran-
ite boulders, possibly cleared from the site of the church at the time of its
construction (Figure 172). There were two gateways through this wall, to the
west and to the south-east. Although there is no evidence of a wall to the south
of the site, work in 1877 uncovered a ditch, probably originally filled by water
from the Pow Burn (RCHMS 1914; Richardson 1951). Such defensible walls are

Fig. 172. Sweetheart Abbey, part of the precinct wall to the north- west of the church.

found elsewhere in Scotland, for example at Crossraguel, Coupar Angus, Pittenweem, and St Andrews (Fawcett 1994a, 124).

A little over half a mile to the north-east of the abbey stand the ruins of the Abbot's Tower. The structure is positioned on the edge of an extent of marshy ground, making this a very secure place for retreat. It was built as an L-plan tower-house in the sixteenth century, and was possibly the fortified personal residence of Abbot John Broun.

To the south of New Abbey, Loch Kindar lies directly beneath the shadow of Criffel which dominates the area for many miles around. On a small island within the loch, at a distance of about 61 m (200 ft) from the shore, are the ruins of **Kirkindar** church. The building is a plain rectangle, built of rough boulders, with walls averaging 0.6 m (2 ft) in thickness. At some stage, probably during the early nineteenth century, the building was adapted for domestic use at its west end (RCHMS 1914). This kirk may have been the parish church of Kinderloch (Richardson 1951) and may have existed prior to the foundation of New Abbey. The present building has no ecclesiastical features, and although it is generally acknowledged to have been a church, may have been substantially altered in the past two centuries. The position however is without doubt defensible, and, lying so close to the Solway and the mouth of the Nith, its builders may have used the loch as a ready means of security. There is some evidence of a former causeway which would have given restricted access to the island by foot.

Along the coast around the base of Criffel, the village of **Kirkbean** has no trace of its medieval church. At **Southwick** are the fragmentary remains of a small twelfth- or thirteenth-century church. No medieval fabric has survived above ground at **Colvend**, a church which also had a subordinate chapel at **Fairgirth**, which belonged to Lincluden.

At this point the coastline is broken by Rough Firth and Auchencairn Bay, forcing the road to sweep inland, and at the point where it joins the main thoroughfare to Dumfries is Dalbeattie. This settlement is a planned village, constructed from 1781 onwards, and its present churches all date from the nineteenth century.

A short distance to the south-west of Dalbeattie is the parish of **Buittle**, whose church was granted to Sweetheart Abbey in the late fourteenth century. Today the ruins lie to the south of the present kirk, built in the early nineteenth century by Walter Newall. Although roofless, the old church is otherwise intact, and has a nave with slightly higher and wider chancel separated by an arch. From the two small windows in the north wall of the nave, this section of the building would appear to date from the twelfth century, whilst the chancel, of a different phase of construction, probably dates from the thirteenth century, characterised by the three lancet windows in the east gable wall. There have been a considerable number of post-Reformation alterations to the church, including the rebuilding of the west gable and part of the south wall of the chancel, and the insertion of a doorway beneath the medieval east windows. There are no features which are characteristic of defence.

In the south of the parish is **Orchardton Tower** (Figure 173), a fifteenth-century house probably belonging to Alexander Cairns, Provost of Lincluden, but completed by John Cairns around 1456 (Tranter 1965). Uniquely in Scotland, for a free-standing defensible tower, it is of circular form (Gifford 1996). On the first floor, above the tunnel-vaulted lower room, is a fireplace and a trefoil-headed aumbry, the latter having a piscina worked in on the cill, indicating that part of this floor was used as a private chapel.

To the north-east of Dalbeattie, the parish church at **Kirkgunzeon** was rebuilt in 1790 and extended in 1869. Its predecessor was clearly of some interest as the *Old Statistical Account*, written in 1791, describes it as 'almost in a state of ruin . . . the roof, which is of a peculiar construction, is said to have been formed at Holmcultram in Cumberland, and brought hither when the parish of Kirkgunzeon belonged to the Abbey' (OSA, v, 221–2). All evidence of this church and its unusual roof has long since been destroyed. Nearby is Drumcoltran, an L-plan tower-house built in the sixteenth century for the Maxwell family.

The villages to the north of Kirkgunzeon have little by way of surviving medieval ecclesiastical architecture. At **Haugh of Urr**, the present parish church of 1914–15 has replaced a Victorian kirk and sits on the site of the early building. There are several possible chapel sites elsewhere in the parish, and the remains of a small chapel at the **Glen of Spottes**. The churches of **Kirk-**

Fig. 173. Orchardton Tower, exterior view.

patrick Durham to the north and **Balmaghie** to the west both have post-Reformation buildings; Balmaghie was described in 1793, the year before it was rebuilt, as 'almost ruinous' (OSA, v, 32).

At **Crossmichael** the greater part of the church dates from *c.* 1750, but a small round tower, 8.5 m (28 ft) in diameter, on the south side, is apparently earlier and has a small round-headed window, now blocked, approximately 5 m (16 ft 6 in.) above the later doorway. The date of this tower is unclear, but may be early seventeenth-century (Gifford 1996), the date of the bell being 1611. Further to the north, **Parton** has the ruins of its late medieval church adjacent to the present building of 1832. The walls stand to a height of approximately 2 m (6 ft 7 in.) but have been modified to form a burial-aisle, leaving the design of the medieval building unclear.

Castle Douglas, like Dalbeattie, is an example of a late eighteenth-century planned village which has expanded into a small town, and there are no pre-Victorian churches. The name derives from the tower-house of the Douglas family, the ruins of which are positioned on an island in the River Dee. Threave Castle was almost certainly first constructed by Archibald, third Earl of Douglas in the third quarter of the fourteenth century, and was occupied until 1640. During the fifteenth century it was furnished with artillery fortification (Tabraham and Good 1981), and in 1455 it held out for three months against King James II (McGladdery 1990, 155).

At **Kelton**, a short distance south-west of Castle Douglas, there is only a fragment of the old parish church, south-east of its Victorian replacement, but this had been rebuilt in 1743 and extended in 1783 (OSA, v, 165). Kelton is made up of three united parishes, and there were also medieval churches at **Kirkcormack** and **Gelston**. Only at the former are there any visible remains, but the walls are virtually reduced to the foundations. A fourth church also existed in the parish at **Kirkmirran**; excavations in 1985 revealed the plain rectangular foundations lying 12.2 m (40 ft) above the Doach Burn (Crowe 1986). From the evidence found, it appears that this building was used between the thirteenth and the sixteenth centuries.

The village of **Tongland** sits above the Dee, close to its junction with the Tarff Water. It is a naturally defensible spot, and there are the remains of a motte castle on the south bank of the river, another nearby at Culdoach, and the whole is overlooked by a small prehistoric hillfort on Bar Hill. It was here in 1218, on a flat holm high above the river, that Alan of Galloway founded Tongland Abbey, a Premonstratensian house, colonised by monks from Cockersand Abbey in Lancashire (Cowan and Easson 1976). Soon after the founding, violence in the form of the insurrection of 1235 resulted in the deaths of the prior and sacrist 'within the church' (Chr.Mel., 62). In 1430, James Herries, prior, repaired the monastery which was 'greatly decayed' and enclosed the precincts with a high wall (OSA, v, 338). This high wall was almost certainly built as a means of protection for the monks, and may have been constructed along the lines of its neighbour at Sweetheart. In 1529 the abbey was reportedly ruinous, although there were still a few monks in residence. Between 1588 and c. 1606, William Melville held the abbey as commendator, when presumably there was sufficient of the structure standing, not only to provide a comfortable lodging, but also a secure one. Certainly there was a tower, as in 1684 it was described as still standing, along with part of the walls (MacGibbon and Ross 1896–7, ii). All that remains today is a single thirteenth-century doorway, lying *ex situ* in the north wall of the ruined eighteenth-century kirk which stands close to its Victorian successor.

Kirkcudbright is the principal town of the Stewartry. Created a royal burgh in or just before 1330 it was granted to Archibald Douglas by David II in 1369, whose family held it until the forfeiture by the Crown in 1455 (Pryde 1965). It was a walled town with a royal castle in existence by 1288, and although it grew to be a prosperous trading centre with a useful harbour, it fell into decline during the eighteenth century. Of the royal castle, only a few earthworks are now visible at Castledykes, close to the river, but excavations in

1911–13 revealed a courtyard castle with double-towered gatehouse surrounded by a moat (Stell 1986).

A Franciscan convent was established in Kirkcudbright around the middle of the fifteenth century, probably by James II, but by the sixteenth century it had decayed. In 1569 it was given by James VI to Thomas MacLellan, who constructed a tower-house in the convent garden and gave the friar's church over to be the new parish church. The present Greyfriars church has little medieval fabric as it was largely rebuilt in 1730 except for the chancel. Of the original parish church, there are no remains and the site is now occupied by the town's cemetery on St Cuthbert's road. On the west side of the river, a separate parish church once stood at **Kirkchrist**, the site of which is now marked by a burial ground in an elevated position over 12 m (40 ft) above the road, overlooking the town. Within this parish was also a nunnery, dedicated to St Evoca, but this had been abandoned and was in ruins by the early fifteenth century (Cowan and Easson 1976). To the south-east of Kirkcudbright, near Low Banks, is the site of **Galtway** church. Further south still, east of Drummore, are the meagre remains of **Dunrod** church, a simple two-celled building, probably of the twelfth century.

Projecting into Kirkcudbright Bay is a narrow-necked isthmus called **St Mary's Isle**. On this strip of land formerly stood the Augustinian Priory of St Maria de Trail, which is first recorded in 1219/20, but whose foundation is unclear (Cowan and Easson 1976). According to the *Old Statistical Account*, the buildings on the site were all removed in the seventeenth century, including (perhaps removed at a slightly later date) two gates defining inner and outer courtyards (OSA, v, 215). The form of these gates, combined with the very confined nature of the site, suggest that elements of defence were probably intentionally incorporated into the monastery. However, no standing remains now survive to determine the extent of such measures.

Four and a half miles south-east of Kirkcudbright, in a secluded valley, stand the substantial ruins of **Dundrennan Abbey**. At the earliest, the monastery may have been founded by King David I, or possibly by Fergus, Lord of Galloway, in 1142, and was colonised, most likely, by Cistercian monks from Rievaulx in Yorkshire (McDowall 1884; MacGibbon and Ross 1896–7, i). A foundation date somewhat later than this, perhaps 1156, has also been postulated (Scott 1988). Fealty was sworn to Edward I at the outbreak of hostilities in 1296, and three years later the convent sought compensation from the English king for £8,000 (Scots) of losses caused by destruction and burning (CDRS, ii, 1123). However, this seems to have been the only major episode in which the abbey buildings themselves suffered during the Troubles, despite reports of English attacks in 1529 (Gifford 1996). Although the abbey had a fairly uneventful history, it is famous for having sheltered Mary, Queen of Scots, after her sixty-mile ride south following defeat at Langside; the following day, 16 May 1568, she crossed the Solway to England and never again returned to Scottish soil (MacKenzie 1957, 171).

The church was built in the second half of the twelfth century and remains largely unaltered apart from the addition of a west porch. The general architecture is characteristic of the Transitional style, although a substantial amount of restoration was carried out in the mid-nineteenth century. The monastery had the usual Cistercian plan of a cruciform church to the north with an attached cloister and associated buildings to the south, but the west range was remodelled in the fourteenth century into storage cellars, following the departure of the lay-brothers (Butler and Given-Wilson 1979). Although there is nothing overtly secure within the remaining buildings, there was an enclosure forming the boundary of the monastery which had a gatehouse at the west end, but none of these structures survives above ground (Tabraham 1981).

That violence, and the consequential need for defence, was a part of everyday life as early as the thirteenth century, is attested by the incised effigy of an abbot, now set into the former north doorway in the west front (Figure 174). The carving displays a small dagger penetrating the cleric in his chest, strongly indicating an assassination; at his feet is a small figure with an abdominal wound, possibly representing the attacker, who was also slain (RCHMS 1914).

Following the Reformation, part of the abbey was used as the parish church until 1742 when it was vacated in favour of the nearby church at **Rerrick**. The ruined north wall of Rerrick church is largely that of the building reconstructed in the eighteenth century, and an inset panel reads 'This church, originally a chapel, was enlarged in 1743, taken down in 1865.' The fabric appears to contain some re-used medieval stonework, and it is clear from the monuments in the graveyard that an earlier building stood on this site.

Beyond Kirkcudbright to the west there are no further churches which could be called defensible, or which have any secure traits in their construction, and any which may have been constructed or adapted with defence in mind have long since disappeared. The need for such adaptation was certainly less, for at this point the land border with England lies some forty-five miles to the east, and there are no significant political or military targets to attract major enemy incursions. Raids did occur in the west, such as that led by Sir Thomas Carlton in 1547 when he laid siege to the town of Kirkcudbright (MacDonald Fraser 1989, 108), but in general the area enjoyed a less troubled time than other regions of the Border.

On the west side of Kirkcudbright Bay, no trace of the parish church at **Borgue** now remains, described in 1793 as 'very much out of repair' (OSA, v, 44), whilst the medieval church of **Senwick** is now little more than a rectangular foundation and only the base of the west wall is clearly discernible. At **Kirkandrews** the medieval church has long since been demolished, the stone being used to construct two burial enclosures in the old churchyard. To the north-west, **Girthon** parish church survives as a roofless shell, the visible remains probably dating from the early seventeenth century, although much of the east gable and eastern end of the south wall appear earlier, and may be part of the pre-Reformation building. Nearby, at **Anwoth**, the fabric of

Fig. 174. Dundrennan Abbey, figure of an unknown abbot with a dagger in his chest and a probable assassin lying mortally wounded at his feet.

the ruined church is also of the seventeenth century; it was built in 1627 and altered in 1710.

Other medieval churches once existed; at **Kirkdale**, where the thirteenth-century foundations of a single-celled rectangle are just visible, and at **Kirkma-breck**, where the east gable and lower parts of the walls still remain, though the structure has been divided into burial enclosures. In the extreme west of the Stewartry, at **Minnigaff**, the rubble-built rectangle of a church, which was reconstructed in the seventeenth century, sits high above the river on a spur of land. Portions of the fabric may be medieval, including a two-light window in the east gable, but the general form of the early building has now been lost. Close by, to the south, a motte castle was constructed on another strategically located spur.

The northern area of the Stewartry was sparsely populated, the main village being **St John's Town of Dalry** where the Gordon Aisle, constructed in 1546, was originally attached as a transeptal chapel to the south side of the medieval church. It is all that remains from the pre-Reformation period. At nearby **Balmaclellan**, no trace of the early church has survived a rebuilding of 1753, but the whole site is overlooked by a small motte. New Galloway, to the west, was founded as a burgh in 1630 and superseded the small parish of **Kells**, whose present church dates from 1822, itself replacing a post-Reformation rebuild of 1745. Finally, in the extreme north of the district, the plain early nineteenth-century church at **Carsphairn** marks the site of its medieval predecessor, described in 1792 as being 'small, but in tolerable repair' (OSA, v, 78).

Beyond here lies the March boundary, considerably removed from England and beyond all the immediate dangers which attended life on the Border. However, although there is little evidence in the north and west of the Stewartry for defensible churches, such use clearly extended beyond the Marches. In 1308, during the most intense years of early Border fighting, St Bride's church in the village of Douglas, Lanarkshire, was the scene of a spirited English defence against a successful attack by James Douglas. The episode was captured in John Barbour's epic fourteenth-century poem 'The Bruce':

> The folk apon the Sonounday
> Held to Saynct Bridis kyrk thar way
> And thai that in the castell war
> Ischyt out bath less and mar
> And went thar palmys for to ber . . .

> On the Sunday the people held their way to St Bride's kirk, and those who were in the castle, great and small (apart from a cook and a porter), issued out and went to carry their palms. James Douglas had knowledge of their approach and of who they were, and sped hastily to the kirk. But before he arrived, one of his men shouted prematurely, 'Douglas! Douglas!' Tom Dickinson, who was nearest to those who came from the castle, who were all inside the chancel, . . . drew his sword and without regard rushed among them here and there . . . Douglas came right to hand and reinforced the assault on them. But they held the chancel very strongly and defended themselves well until a number of their men were killed. But the Douglas bore himself so well that all the men who were with him were inspired by his prowess, while he spared himself no effort but so proved his strength in fighting that by his valour and his courage he helped his men so boldly then that they won the chancel for themselves . . . (Duncan 1997, 206-8).

CONCLUSION

Life on the medieval Anglo-Scottish frontier was harsh. The people were exposed to violent attacks, their livestock and personal goods often stolen, and their crops laid waste. Poorly constructed houses were burnt and lives put at risk. However, despite all the attendant dangers, these people thrived. It was due, in no small part, to the ingenuity of the inhabitants, and to a lesser extent the patronage of the rulers, that successful defensive measures were taken. One of these measures, the integration of military and ecclesiastical architecture, is seen as expedient both in terms of the proximity of church buildings to centres of population, and in the cost-effective adaptations which could be effected with relative ease. However, the poverty of the region, and general lack of financial support from wealthy ecclesiastical patrons, resulted in buildings which, in terms of defensibility, pale in comparison to those found elsewhere in Europe.

Of the 533 sites examined in this book, only ninety-six have been found to have features which are characteristic of defence, above average security, or evidence which relates to defensive or military use. This is due, in part, to the scale of the loss of medieval churches since the sixteenth century. Most buildings have been restored, many extensively. The loss is noticeably greater north of the Border, and many sites now have no standing remains. Of the ninety-six churches which are listed in Appendix A as having been defensible or secure, twenty-nine rely substantially or wholly on documentary accounts of their use for this purpose. If not entirely lost, these buildings have been too modified to enable the archaeological analysis of the upstanding walls. Many sites, both standing and demolished, had no adaptation to defence, but the secure nature of churches now demolished, for which little or no written record has been left, remains unknown. The choice of adapting a church for safety appears, for the most part, to have been left entirely to the personal wishes of the local populace, though sometimes aided by a generous landowner or patron. This has resulted in a hotch-potch distribution of defensible churches across the region, each having its own idiosyncratic style of modification borrowed directly from contemporary military architecture.

Four parish churches and one priory, all built or modified in the fourteenth century, are outstanding in the extent to which defence was provided. Burgh-by-Sands has an immense west tower with thick walls and a protected entry; it formerly also had a strong east tower. Great Salkeld has a similar west tower, though is more complete. Newton Arlosh possesses a strong tower and nave, entry to which was well defended. At Ancroft the west tower is constructed more like a secular refuge, with an external, first-floor entrance, and a deeply vaulted basement. Tynemouth priory was protected by a curtain wall, towers, and a gatehouse which was constructed like a castle. These five sites, plus the former church of Annan, may properly be classed as *ecclesiae incastellatae*, where truly military features are associated with ecclesiastical architecture.

Churches built prior to the outbreak of war in 1296 were probably utilised for defence without recourse to physical change, especially where they were already of robust construction. The internal vaulting at Chirnside, Aldcambus, Thockrington, and Warkworth may have sufficed to create a secure, fireproof refuge. The high windows at Warkworth and at Norham would also assist in preventing unwanted ingress. Some twelfth-century towers, such as that at Barton on the edge of the English West March, already had sufficient features of defence to be used as they stood. Vaulting, and sometimes stone roof tiles, were introduced at a number of sites, undoubtedly to create fireproof chambers: at Dunglass, Ladykirk, Kirknewton, Boltongate, Elsdon, and Bellingham. At two sites, Bedrule and Roxburgh, documentary accounts reveal that the buildings may have been partially underground, as well as being, in the case of the latter, stone vaulted.

Some churches were utilised as strong points in the sixteenth-century Civil War, again without further physical adaptation; examples include Coldingham, Newburn, Newcastle St Andrew, and possibly Eglingham. The churches at Castleton, Cockburnspath, and Peebles St Andrew were also used to shelter troops at this time, and the construction of Berwick-upon-Tweed Holy Trinity was only allowed on condition that the west tower, which could have been used defensibly, was omitted.

The most characteristic of defensible adaptations in Border churches involves the tower, and with few exceptions this was a west tower. Of the sites examined, thirty-five have strong towers, twenty-one of which have stone vaulting to the ceilings of the ground floor. Higher floors were also vaulted at Ladykirk and Peebles St Andrew, and Great Salkeld has a vaulted basement. In some cases, as at Embleton and Newbiggin-by-the-Sea, this vaulting was inserted into an earlier structure. Access to higher levels of these towers was by ladder or spiral stair, the former obviously being more secure, but less convenient for a large body of people. Access by ladder to the first floor of vaulted towers, through an upper doorway, is evident at Ancroft, Edenhall, and Dunglass, and possibly at Greenlaw, Newton Arlosh, Penrith, and Bywell, St Peter (though Bywell is not vaulted). At Newburn and Scaleby there are first-floor doorways in the east wall of the tower, formerly secured by draw-bars; these may have led to galleries or upper floors, although they may equally have served to provide secure access to the upper levels of the tower, by ladder, from within the nave. This may also have been the case at Annan, based on the description of the siege in 1547. This form of defence was borrowed directly from the equivalent arrangement in secular tower-houses. Other towers had spiral stairs or vertical ladders without vaulting. Stairs were often protected by secure doors and doorways such as that at Blanchland which, in addition to a strong lock, had a heavy draw-bar, and the lower stair at Hartburn which was evidently protected by a secondary door or gate to which access was restricted. The offset and change in direction of the stair in the south-east turret at Alnwick St Michael may also be a feature borrowed directly from castle architecture, designed to hinder advancement. The most unusual adaptation of a stairway is found at Brigham, where the angle and construction of the risers, through a narrow space in the thickness of the wall, makes ascent extremely difficult. Also difficult to reach was the chamber over the chancel at Warkworth, where a tiny stair and wall-passage will admit only one person at a time. At Newbiggin-by-the-Sea, the inserted stair, which passes through a stone vault, may also have been defended by a crude form of machicolation. All these forms of access are in contrast to normal church-tower stairs, and appear to have been devised to allow reasonably rapid ascent for the defenders whilst permitting the exclusion of others.

The upper chambers of these secure towers were, on occasion, clearly intended for limited habitation. Fireplaces are extant in the towers of Ladykirk, Biggar, Peebles Cross Kirk, Ancroft, Newton Arlosh, Great Salkeld, and Edenhall. The same feature is also present in the upper chamber sacristy at Hulne Priory, the watch tower at Heiferlaw Tower, the hermitage at Warkworth, and in the room above the south choir aisle at Tynemouth. Garderobes are less frequently found, but, apart from the seventeenth-century example at Greenlaw, three medieval latrines have survived: Newton Arlosh, Peebles Cross Kirk, and in the Prior's Tower on Farne.

Monastic houses were more accustomed to security than parish churches. Nevertheless, above-average precautions appear to have been taken in the Border region. At Dryburgh, the normal west range was excluded in favour of a high wall. At Alnwick Abbey, Carlisle, Sweetheart, Dumfries, and Tongland there were strong precinct walls, and Hulne Priory had both inner and outer walls. Even more businesslike were the perimeter walls of Holy Island and Tynemouth Priory, both crenellated and designed to withstand assault. Gatehouses also appear as defensible buildings at most of the monastic sites. At Alnwick and Wetheral these have survived despite the loss of all other structures. At Tynemouth, the gatehouse effectively became a castle in its own right, and Holme Cultram Abbey had, in addition to its own defences, a separate fortified manor house within the parish at Wolsty.

Evidence for artillery fortification is not prolific, and in only a handful of instances do physical features occur. Burgh-by-Sands has a shot-hole in the lower part of the tower, Lincluden has gun-loops to defend the stair to the domestic range, and Biggar has four similar gun-loops in the parapet of the

tower. At Jedburgh Abbey, excavations have revealed two possible gun platforms, though artillery was an integral part of the defences at Tynemouth. In
three instances, at Alnwick St Michael, Dryburgh Abbey, and Lanercost, the
walls bear witness to handgun exchange in the form of damage caused by
musket balls or shot, and at Dryburgh there is a single gun-loop in the wall
of the commendator's lodgings. At Holy Island, documentary accounts record
the storage of artillery pieces, though these may never have been used.

Other physical features in the walls of churches testify to their former
secure nature. Most commonly encountered are draw-bar slots, used to house
the heavy wooden bar which prevented a door from being opened externally.
This is yet another trait taken directly from military architecture. Some of
these slots are very deep, such as the two at Edlingham which assisted in the
protection of the west and south doorways, that which protected the door
through the blocked tower-arch at Newbiggin-by-the-Sea, and on the outer
entrance to the cloister at Sweetheart. The arrangement on the west tower door
at Bywell St Peter's is exceptional, with three separate draw-bar slots set into
the reveal and a further four notches, probably for locks, besides. A modern
draw-bar is still in use at Morpeth, which makes use of the medieval slots. The
tiny rectangular church at Bassendean has had a draw-bar to defend the door,
which appears to have been the only substantial opening in the original building. More unusual forms of security occur at Tynemouth, Brinkburn, Warkworth, Lincluden and Thockrington in the form of upper chambers, which
were secure above the stone vaulting of their respective chancels, and at Kelso
a small chamber was constructed over the north doorway. A few unique adaptations exist, in particular the narrow passage at the top of the tower stair at
Blanchland, the square-sectioned stairway, added to the tower at Bamburgh,
and the insertion of mullions and transoms to the lower lancet windows of the
chancel at Brinkburn (now removed). Also unique are the earthworks which
surround the ruins of the chapel by Hermitage Castle, though these may be
earlier in origin.

Some churches had purpose-built defensible west towers, where access from
the nave was restricted to a narrow passage or doorway, as at Burgh-by-Sands,
Great Salkeld, Scaleby, and possibly at Chapel (Kirkpatrick-Juxta). This feature
may also be an original defensible measure in the towers of Caldbeck, Chollerton, and Greystoke, although later alterations have effaced some of the evidence. At Edlingham and Bywell St Peter, the later towers were never given an
arch, access being through a narrow doorway, and at Stamfordham the arch
is uncommonly low. This device was borrowed by a small group of Northumbrian churches, one Cumbrian and one Scottish church, each of which has
evidence for the deliberate blocking of the tower-arch at a date subsequent to
its original construction. Three of these buildings lie close together, at Hartburn, Kirkwhelpington, and Bolam. The last has a pre-Conquest tower, and
the blocking was removed in the eighteenth century. Another pre-Conquest
tower, previously blocked but now re-opened, is at Whittingham. The deliber-

ate infilling of the tower-arch at Ingram was removed in the late nineteenth century, and although its former nature is now unclear, the tower is of the type well suited as a defensible refuge. Also amongst this specialised group of churches, Newbiggin-by-the-Sea has a blocked arch, behind which is a stone vault and stair, obviously inserted to make the tower secure. At Dearham in Cumbria, the tower-arch was blocked and had been reduced to a strongly-barred doorway until it was opened out in 1882. Finally, the church at Stobo in the Scottish Middle March has a Norman tower whose arch was deliberately restricted, probably in the fifteenth or sixteenth century.

More problematical are the handful of churches which may have been secure by their position in the landscape. Places of worship are often sited in prominent locations, sometimes reflecting earlier, pre-Christian, traditions, and sometimes for reasons of emphasis. Only one building is situated on an inland island – Kirkindar, and the nature of this site is far from clear. Holy Island, Farne, and Coquet Island all have churches, the location of which provides obvious defence, and Tynemouth and St Mary's Isle (Scottish West March) were situated on headlands which afforded strong, natural security. A few others are positioned on knolls, such as Haydon, Kirkton, Linton, Lyne, and Skirling but these are without any obvious signs of security. Balmaclellan, Buccleuch, Lochmaben, Staplegordon, and Wauchope are closely associated with early castles and are therefore positioned in places of natural strategic significance, although too little remains of the fabric in each case to determine whether the churches themselves were defensible. Lincluden also was positioned next to a Norman motte castle, but here the evidence for defence is unequivocal. Lastly, a small number are located on high ground or atop steep banks, and the reasons for this may be various: protection from flooding, a foundation dedicated to St Michael (whose churches are often in elevated situations in acknowledgement of the Saint's heavenly endeavours), a shift in the position of the medieval village, or for security and physical defence. Churches at Belford (Scottish Middle March), Dearham, Kailzie, Preston, and St Mary of the Lowes are most likely to have been placed on high ground for fear of flooding, but the reasons for the siting of Ashkirk and Crailing are less clear. At Castleton, Dawyck, and Ettleton, the church is positioned high above the valley floor, close to the settlement which it served. At Ellemford, the site of the church is so restricted that, although the main reason for its high location was in all probability to avert the danger of floods, the notion of defensibility may also have played a part. Alone amongst this class of building, Trailtrow (Repentance Tower) appears to have been located on its prominent hilltop probably for reasons of safety from raids.

Historical descriptions provide important evidence for the fortification of churches and for their use as secure refuges. Two Border churches were granted formal licences to crenellate: Tynemouth Priory, and the hospital at Bolton. The terms of the bishop's licence, and later confirmation, to construct a new church at Newton Arlosh suggest that there was an intention to use the building as a refuge. The enigmatic site at Nunraw, on the edge of the Scottish Middle March, was given permission to fortify, and the church of Wigton in Cumberland was recorded as being fortified without licence. The monks of Holy Island tried, without success, to have their fortifications dismantled. The Franciscan friary in Carlisle was requisitioned by the king for the storage of weapons and ammunition, and parts of Roxburgh Friary were pressed into similar use by English troops. Accounts illustrate the benefaction of the Northumberland estate in assisting with the provision of defensible church towers, notably at South Charlton. In other cases, such as at Newton Arlosh and Holme Cultram, contemporary testimony of the parishioners confirms that the buildings were used as safe refuges from Scottish incursions. Most illuminating of all are the descriptions of attacks on churches, especially the sieges of Annan and Kelso, but also minor skirmishes such as the one which took place at Bellingham. There are topographical descriptions and military reports which indicate that churches were used as defensible retreats: Longhoughton was used by the villagers, Lochmaben during a family feud, Hexham by its canons, and Eccles, Coldingham, and Norham were capable of being garrisoned. Finally, there are frequent references to the use of monasteries and, occasionally, parish churches, by royalty and their retinues; the purpose was normally for overnight accommodation or meetings, indicating that these places were considered reasonably secure.

The use of the church as a safe retreat was not always successful. In 1437 James I was assassinated whilst staying at the Dominican Friary in Perth. At Warkworth, during the twelfth century, the townsfolk were massacred and the priests injured during a Scottish raid, and, during the same period, those trying to escape into the church at Belford were captured. None of the recorded church sieges held out for long, Annan fell within the day, and Kelso within two days, although the English troops garrisoned in Coldingham successfully held off the Scottish attackers for two days, finally forcing them to retreat. Perhaps most unlucky of all were the Maxwells who took shelter in the church at Lochmaben which the pursuing Johnstones promptly burnt to the ground.

This analysis of religious structures on the medieval Anglo-Scottish frontier has revealed the extent of the comparatively rare practice of church fortification and defence. The need was triggered by a highly unstable political and cultural situation, brought about by a struggle for power between two puissant nations. Unlike similar struggles elsewhere in Europe, there was little by way of mainstream patronage on this remote northern Border. Although bishops engaged in battle alongside their monarch, they did little to physically strengthen their symbols of power in the towns and countryside – the churches. This was left, for the most part, to the ordinary people and priests who saw in these buildings a logical safe sanctuary from the vicissitudes of medieval frontier life, and who thus set about adapting them, introducing a variety of ingenious and life-saving features.

APPENDIX 1

A principal list of churches and other ecclesiastical establishments on the Anglo-Scottish Border, which have primary evidence for, or strong indications of, defensible adaptation or use, including military use.

P = Parish or collegiate Church
C = Subsidiary chapel
M = Monastic establishment
S = Heavily restored/partially rebuilt

R = Ruin
PtR = Part Ruin
I = Site now incomplete

Buildings in *italics* are no longer extant or have been completely rebuilt after the seventeenth century

Scottish East March

Auldcambus (PR)	Overall construction
Bassendean (PR)	Overall construction
Chirnside (PS)	Documentary; tower
Coldingham Priory (MI)	Documentary (garrisoned)
Dryburgh Abbey (MR)	Commendator's lodgings; perimeter wall; documentary
Dunglass (PR)	Overall construction; documentary
Ellemford (PRI)	?Location
Eccles (M)	Documentary
Ednam (P)	Documentary
Greenlaw (PS)	Tower; documentary
Ladykirk (P)	Tower and overall construction
Nunraw (M)	Documentary
St Abbs, St Ebba's chapel (C)	Position; earthworks (pre-twelfth-century)
Swinton (PS)	Documentary

English East March

Ancroft (P)	Defensible west tower
Bamburgh (P)	Tower and stair
Bamburgh Dominican Friary (MRI)	Overall construction and later adaptation
Belford (PS)	Documentary

Embleton (P)   Tower
Farne (RMI)   Overall construction; documentary; location
Holy Island, St Mary (P)   Features in construction; location
Holy Island, Priory (MR)   Overall construction; documentary; location
Kirknewton (PS)   Overall construction
Lesbury (P)   Tower; documentary
Longhoughton (P)   Documentary
Norham (PS)   Documentary (garrisoned)
South Charlton (P)   Documentary

English Middle March

Alnwick Abbey (MI)   Gatehouse; former precinct wall
Alnwick, St Michael (P)   Tower and turret; musket shot damage
Bellingham (P)   Overall construction; documentary
Blanchland Abbey (MI)   Tower; gatehouse; abbot's lodging
Bolam (P)   Documentary
Bolton Hospital (C)   Documentary (licensed)
Brinkburn Priory (MRI)   Features in construction
Bywell, St Peter (P)   Tower
Chibburn (MCRI)   Overall construction; later perimeter wall and
                                      moat
Coquet Island (MIS)   Overall construction; documentary; location
Edlingham (P)   Tower; features in construction
Eglingham (P)   Tower; documentary
Elsdon (P)   Features in construction
Guyzance (MCRI)   Features in construction; ?position
Hartburn (P)   Tower and restricted arch
Hexham (MI)   Documentary
Hulne Priory (MRI)   Overall construction and perimeter wall
Ingram (P)   Tower; documentary
Kirkwhelpington (P)   Tower and restricted arch
Morpeth (P)   Tower
Newbiggin-by-the-Sea (P)   Tower and restricted arch
Ponteland (P)   Documentary; features in construction
Stamfordham (P)   Tower
Thockrington (P)   Features in construction
Tynemouth Priory (MRI)   Fortified monastery (licensed)
Warkworth (P)   Tower; chamber over chancel
Whittingham (P)   Documentary

Scottish Middle March

Biggar (P)   Tower with shot holes in parapet
Hawick (P)   Documentary
Hermitage Castle chapel (CRI)   Features in construction; earthworks
Jedburgh Abbey (MRI)   Archaeological evidence in excavation;
                                      documentary
Kelso Abbey (MRI)   Overall construction; documentary

Melrose Abbey (MRI)	Commendator's lodgings; features in construction
Peebles, St Andrew (PRI)	Tower
Peebles, Cross Kirk (MRI)	Tower
Roxburgh (P)	Documentary
Roxburgh (burgh) Friary (M)	Documentary (adapted for military use)
St Mary of the Lowes (P)	Documentary; ?location
Stobo (P)	Tower; features in overall construction

English West March

Barton (P)	Tower (twelfth-century)
Boltongate (P)	Overall construction
Brigham (P)	Tower; restricted stair
Burgh-by-Sands (P)	Fortified west tower and former east tower
Caldbeck (PS)	Tower
Carlisle Franciscan Friary (M)	Documentary (ordnance store)
Carlisle Cathedral (MI)	Claustral buildings; perimeter wall; gatehouse
Dearham (P)	Tower; documentary
Edenhall (P)	Tower
Great Crosthwaite (P)	Tower; documentary
Great Salkeld (P)	Fortified west tower
Greystoke (PS)	Tower
Holme Cultram Abbey (MI)	Documentary; features in construction
Lanercost Priory (MPtR)	Towers in claustral range; musket damage to church; features in construction
Melmerby (PS)	Possible former east tower
Newton Arlosh (P)	Defensible west tower and overall construction
Penrith (PS)	Tower
Scaleby (P)	Tower
Wetheral Priory (MRI)	Gatehouse
Wigton (P)	Documentary (fortified without licence)

Scottish West March

Annan (P)	Documentary (garrisoned)
Chapel (Kirkpatrick-Juxta) (CRI)	Features in construction; documentary
Dumfries, Franciscan Friary (M)	Documentary
Kirkindar (?CRI)	Location
Lincluden (MRI)	Tower and defensible stair; features in construction; documentary
Lochmaben (P)	Documentary
Repentance (Trailtrow) (PRI)	Location; later strong tower on site
St Mary's Isle (M)	Documentary and position
Sweetheart Abbey (MRI)	Tower; features in construction; perimeter wall
Tongland (M)	Documentary (former perimeter wall)

APPENDIX 2

DRAMATIS PERSONAE

Adelulf of Nostell First Bishop of Carlisle 1133–55.

Albany, Robert, Duke of Scottish regent 1406–20 during captivity of James I; d. 1420.

Albany, Murdoch, Duke of Scottish regent 1420–4 during captivity of James I; son of Robert, Duke of Albany.

Balliol, John King of Scots 1292–1296/1304.

Bek, Anthony Bishop of Durham 1283–1311.

Blac(k)adder, Robert Bishop of Glasgow; Archbishop of Glasgow 1492–1508

Bothwell, James Hepburn, Earl of Lieutenant of the Scottish Marches; Keeper of Liddesdale; husband of Mary Queen of Scots; d. 1578.

Bowes, Sir Robert Keeper of Tynedale 1545; Warden of the English Middle March 1545–7; Master of the Rolls 1552; undertook surveys of the Border in 1542 and 1550.

Bruce, Robert Earl of Carrick 7th Lord of Annandale, King of Scotland 1306–29.

Bruce, Robert Earl of Carrick 6th Lord of Annandale, father of Robert I King of Scots; d. 1304.

Bruce, Robert of Annandale 5th Lord of Annandale and claimant to the Scottish throne; d. 1295.

Burghley, William Cecil, Lord principal advisor to Queen Elizabeth I; d. 1598.

Bury, Richard de Bishop of Durham 1333–45.

Carey, Sir Robert youngest son of Henry Carey (1st Baron Hunston); Warden of the English East March 1597–8; Warden of the English Middle March 1598–1603.

Carey, Sir John second son of Henry Carey (1st Baron Hunston); Warden of the English East March 1601–3.

Carmichael, Sir John Keeper of Liddesdale; Warden of the Scottish West March 1588–92 and 1599–1600; murdered 1600.

Cecil, Sir Robert Queen Elizabeth I's Secretary of State 1596–1603; created Earl of Salisbury 1605.

Comyn, Sir John son of Sir John Comyn, claimant to the Scottish throne; killed by Robert Bruce in 1306.

Dacre, Lord Thomas — Baron of Gilsland; Warden General 1511–25.

Dacre, William — 3rd Baron of Gilsland; Warden of the English West March 1558–63.

Dacre, Sir Christopher — Keeper of Redesdale 1515; brother of Thomas Dacre.

Douglas, Archibald 'the Grim' — 3rd Earl of Douglas; Lord of Galloway; d. 1400.

Dunbar, Gavin — Archbishop of Glasgow 1525–47.

Eure, Sir Ralph — Keeper of Tynedale 1543; Warden of the English Middle March 1544; killed at Ancrum Moor 1545.

Eure, Sir Ralph, 3rd Lord — Warden of the English Middle March 1595–8.

Fantosme, Jordan — chronicler; probably a clerk at Winchester during the reign of Henry II.

Fenwick, Sir Ralph — Keeper of Tynedale 1514–25 and 1528–35.

Forster, Sir John — Warden of the English Middle March 1560–87 and 1588–95; d. 1602.

Fox, Richard — Bishop of Exeter 1487–92; of Bath and Wells 1492–4; of Durham 1494–1501; of Winchester 1501–28; Keeper of the Privy Seal 1487.

Gilpin, Bernard — rector of Houghton-le-Spring, Co. Durham in the mid-sixteenth century; reformer; known as 'The Apostle of the North', he volunteered to preach widely in Northumberland.

Hatfield, Thomas — Bishop of Durham 1345–81.

Heron, Sir John — Keeper of Tynedale 1525–7.

Hertford, Edward Seymour, Earl of — Lord Admiral of England 1542; 1st Duke of Somerset, Treasurer and Protector of England 1547; Earl Marshal 1547.

Home, Sir Alexander, 6th Baron — Warden of the Scottish East March 1600–3 and then Lieutenant and Justiciar over all three Scottish Marches.

Home, Sir Patrick — Earl of Marchmount; conspirator in the Rye House Plot to kidnap Charles II in 1684.

Hunsdon, Henry Carey, 1st Baron — Warden of the English East March 1568–96; Warden of the English Middle March 1587–8.

Johnstone, Sir James — Warden of the Scottish West March 1600–3.

Ker(r), Sir Walter of Cessford — Warden of the Scottish Middle March 1558–69.

Ker(r), William of Cessford — Warden of the Scottish Middle March 1585–1600.

Ker(r), Sir Robert of Cessford — Warden of the Scottish Middle March 1600–3.

Ker(r), Sir Thomas of Ferniehirst — Warden of the Scottish Middle March 1584–5.

Ker(r), William of Cessford — Warden of the Scottish Middle March 1573–84.

Kirkham, Walter of — Bishop of Durham 1249–60.

Kirkby, John — Bishop of Carlisle 1332–52.

Lamberton, William — Archdeacon of Glasgow; Bishop of St Andrews 1297–1328.

Leland, John — Keeper of the king's libraries; undertook several journeys of investigation around England between 1534 and 1543.

Leslie, Sir Alexander — Earl of Leven; Scottish commander-in-chief 1650.

March, Patrick Earl of — claimant to Scottish throne; keeper of Berwick, 1298; Warden of Scottish East March 1298–9.

Maxwell, John, Earl of Morton	8th Lord Maxwell; Warden of the Scottish West March 1585–6; slain at Dryfe Sands in 1593.
Maxwell, Sir John of Terregles	4th Baron Herries from 1566; Warden of the Scottish West March 1557–68.
Pilkington, James	Bishop of Durham 1561–77.
Scrope, Henry, 9th Baron of Bolton	Warden of the English West March 1563–92.
Scrope, Thomas, 10th Baron of Bolton	Warden of the English West March 1593–1603.
Skirlaw, Walter	Bishop of Lichfield 1386; of Bath and Wells 1386–8; of Durham 1388–1405; Keeper of the Privy Seal 1382–6.
Somerset, 1st Duke of	see Hertford.
Strickland, William	Bishop of Carlisle 1400–20.
Surrey, Thomas Howard, Earl of	Lord Admiral of England 1513–25; Earl Marshal of England 1533; later Duke of Norfolk; d. 1554.
Umfraville, Gilbert de	Earl of Angus; Lord of Redesdale and Coquetdale in the English Middle March; d. 1307.
Wharton, Lord Thomas	Vice Warden and later Warden of the English West March 1541; Lord Deputy General of the English Marches 1553; established the 'watch' system of guarding the English frontier during the 1550s.
Widdrington, Sir John	Keeper of Redesdale 1537–40 and Vice Warden of the English Middle March.
William 'the Lion'	William I King of Scotland 1165–1214.
Wishart, Robert	Bishop of Glasgow 1271–1316; strong supporter of Scotland's independence; d. 1316.

MONARCHS

England		*Scotland*	
1066 – 1087	William I	1057 – 1093	Malcom III
1087 – 1100	William II	1093 – 1094	Donald Bane
1100 – 1135	Henry I	1094	Duncan II
1135 – 1154	Stephen	1094 – 1097	Donald Bane
1141	Matilda	1097 – 1106	Edgar
1154 – 1189	Henry II	1106 – 1124	Alexander I
1189 – 1199	Richard I	1124 – 1153	David I
1199 – 1216	John	1153 – 1165	Malcom IV
1216 – 1272	Henry III	1165 – 1214	William I
1272 – 1307	Edward I	1214 – 1249	Alexander II
1307 – 1327	Edward II	1249 – 1286	Alexander III
1327 – 1377	Edward III	1286 – 1290	Margaret
1377 – 1399	Richard II	1290 – 1292	(Interregnum)
1399 – 1413	Henry IV	1292 – 1296	John Balliol
1413 – 1422	Henry V	1296 – 1306	(Interregnum)
1422 – 1461	Henry VI	1306 – 1329	Robert I
1461 – 1483	Edward IV	1329 – 1371	David II
1483	Edward V	1371 – 1390	Robert II
1483 – 1485	Richard III	1390 – 1406	Robert III

1485 – 1509	Henry VII	1406 – 1437	James I
1509 – 1547	Henry VIII	1437 – 1460	James II
1547 – 1553	Edward VI	1460 – 1488	James III
1553 – 1558	Mary I	1488 – 1513	James IV
1558 – 1603	Elizabeth I	1513 – 1542	James V
1603 – 1625	James I	1542 – 1560	(Mary of Guise – as regent)
1625 – 1649	Charles I	1561 – 1567	Mary (in Scotland)
1649 – 1660	(Interregnum)	1567 – 1587	Mary (in England)
1660 – 1685	Charles II	1567 – 1587	James VI (and regents)
1685 – 1688	James II	1587 – 1603	James VI (in Scotland)

APPENDIX 3

GLOSSARY OF TERMS

(Scot.) denotes a term or meaning exclusively used in Scotland
(Eng.) denotes a term or meaning used exclusively in England
(vb) verb

Abacus a flat slab forming the top of a capital

Advowson the right of appointing a priest to a parish or other ecclesiastical *benefice*

Aik oak (Scot.)

Airns irons; shackles (Scot.)

Aisle the space alongside the nave, chancel, or transept of a church, separated from it by columns or piers; a separate chamber used for private burial (Scot.)

Altar the Holy Table, consecrated for the celebration of the Eucharist

Anchorite hermit; religious recluse

Appropriation the formal transfer to a monastic house of the tithes and other endowments of a parish church

Apse semicircular or polygonal extension, usually to the east end of the chancel or transepts

Arcade a series of arches supported by piers or columns

Ashlar square-edged stonework with even faces

Aumbry a recess or cupboard

Bailie a magistrate; a chief executive officer in a barony (Scot.)

Bailey an open space or court within a castle

Barbican tower, wall, or outwork defending the entrance to a castle, town, or at the head of a bridge

Barmkin an enclosing wall, normally for purposes of defence, or the space between a tower and outer wall in a castle

Barrel vault see *Tunnel vault*

Barony the tenure of a baron (Eng.); basic unit of local government in medieval Scotland (Scot.)

Bartizan a corbelled, overhanging turret

Basinet a form of metal head-dress used in armour

Bastion a projecting chamber from the outer face of a wall to enable defence

Bastle a defensible farmhouse, usually of two storeys

Batter slight inward inclination of a wall from its base upwards, normally built to add strength to the structure

Battery a work designed as a position for a group of guns

Battlement fortified parapet, usually crenellated

Beaver the lower face-guard of a helmet

Belfry stage of a tower where bells are hung, usually the uppermost

Bellcote a small gabled housing for bells, often on the west wall of a church

without a tower, but also found on
parapets and on the east gable of the
nave

Benefice an ecclesiastical living;
property attached to a church office

Bigged built

Bigging the act of building

Bill a formal complaint

Black mail protection money

Blind – arcading; – tracery; architectural
detail applied as a decorative motif,
usually to the surface of walls

Blockhouse a one-storeyed building with
gun-loops used as a fort

Bole-hole a small window or peep-hole
through the wall of a building (Scot.)

Bombard a medieval siege gun; an
artillery piece

Bracket a corbel or support projecting
from a wall

Brattice a temporary breastwork or
parapet, used during a seige or
conflict

Brent burnt

Bretasche see *Brattice*

Broken men men without responsibility
to the head of a clan or family

Bruiking possessing

Burgage tenure of land on a yearly rent

Burgh town having trading privileges.
Burghs of regality were founded by
the monarch, burghs of barony were
created by local barons to whom
trade duty was paid

Butt-joint a straight masonry joint
which lacks keying or overlaps

Buttress a vertical projection from a wall
face or angle designed to stabilise it

Cap-house small chamber at the head of
a stair or within a parapet

Capital the head of a column

Caput the head-place of a *barony*; the
dwelling of a feudal overlord

Castellated battlemented

Chamfer a surface formed by cutting
away a square edge, usually at an
angle of forty-five degrees

Chancel the eastern compartment of a
church or chapel, normally set apart
for the use of the clergy in the
performance of the liturgy

Chapel-of-ease a chapel subordinate to
a parish church, founded for the ease

of those living at some distance

Chapter house room in which the
brethren of a monastery met to
conduct business

Choir often used to described the
chancel, but more correctly that
area where services are sung which
may include the crossing or eastern
portion of the nave

Cill the lowermost member of a door
or window

Claustral associated with the cloister
of a monastery; the buildings, other
than the church, in an abbey or
priory

Clerestory the uppermost storey of
the body of the church, pierced by
windows

Commendator an official who held
the revenues of an abbey when
no abbot was appointed but who
was commissioned by secular
recommendation

Convent a religious community;
the buildings in which a body of
religious live

Conventicle religious ceremony practised
by the *Covenanters*

Conventual monastic or religious
community buildings other than the
church

Corbel a projecting block of stone or
timber to support something above

Cornice a moulded ledge or decorative
moulding at high level

Course an individual horizontal layer of
stones or bricks in a wall

Covenanters bodies of Presbyterians in
Scotland who bound themselves by
oath to maintain their religion

Crenel gap in a parapet wall to allow
the projection of missiles, normally
divided either side by *merlons*

Crenellation a battlemented parapet
having *crenels*

Crossing the central space formed by
the junction of nave, chancel, and
transepts

Crow-steps squared stones set like steps
on a gable for decorative purposes

Crypt subterranean room

Culverin a large medieval artillery piece;
a battering gun

Cupola   a small dome crowning a roof or turret

Curate   a clergyman who has charge of a parish; an assistant or unbeneficed clergyman

Curtal   a medieval field gun

Dado   the finishing of the lower part of a wall, often with panelling

Debateable Land   small areas of land on the Anglo-Scottish border the ownership of which was the subject of dispute between England and Scotland, especially part of Liddesdale around Canonbie which was a notoriously lawless area

Demesne   land attached to a particular ownership; an estate

Ding   smash; break

Diocese   a territorial unit of administration governed by a bishop

Dissolution   the abolishment of the medieval monastic system by Henry VIII

Dorter   dormitory in a monastery

Draw-bar   heavy, usually wooden, bar used to secure a door from the inside by crossing it, the bar being located in wall slots to either side

Dyke   a wall of stone or turf (Scot.); a ditch (Eng.)

Early English   period of *Gothic* architecture broadly covering the period 1200–1280

Embattled   having *battlements*

Embrasure   a small splayed opening in a wall or *battlement*

Enceinte   the line of the wall encircling a fortress

Escheator   a bailiff

Eucharist   the Holy Communion, or Sacrament of the Lord's Supper; the central ceremony of the mass

Face-alternate quoins which are laid on the face of the stone in the same courses as the main fabric of the structure

Facon   see *falcon*

Falcon   a medieval artillery gun

Falconet   a small *falcon*

Fattie   faulty

Fealty   a feudal tenant's fidelity to a lord or acknowledgement of this allegiance

Fenestration   the arrangement and form of windows

Feu-ferme   land or property subject to a perpetual lease at a fixed annual rent (Scot.)

Flow   bog; marsh

Foil   a common *Gothic* architectural ornament in which a number of arcs are divided by cusps, often used in *tracery*. A trefoil has three cusps, a quatrefoil four, and so on.

Foray   a raid

Fortalice   a small fortress, usually a defensible tower with or without a *barmkin*

Fosse   ditch

Frater   refectory in a monastery

Fray   alarm; conflict

Freebooter   lawless adventurer; *reiver*

Furniture   military equipment

Gae doon   to be executed (Scot.)

Gait   road; track; way

Gallery   a passage, walkway, or upper balcony

Gang   go (Scot.)

Garderobe   a medieval latrine, the chamber for which was often formed in the thickness of a wall or in a small turret

Gargoyle   a water spout, normally projecting from a tower or parapet

Gauntlet   a protective glove used in armour

Gear   movable goods

Gonne   gun

Gothic   the period of architecture characterised by the pointed arch

Grange   a farm or barn belonging to a monastery, often situated on outlying parts of its estates

Grippit   captured

Gun-loop   a hole in a masonry wall or parapet from which firearms could be discharged

Hack   a medieval hand-gun, a variant of a *hackbut*

Hackbut   early form of handgun

Hagbut   see *hackbut*

Hagioscope   a squint cut through a wall providing a view of the altar

Halberd   a combined spear and battle-axe

Harling   render, wet dash, or

roughcasting, thrown against a rubble wall to help protect against the weather (Scot.)

Hau(l)d hold, to (vb); tower; fortress

Hauberk a coat of mail

Haudins holdings, i.e. *pele towers* and strong houses

Haugh low lying, level ground by a stream or river

Heritor proprietor; one who inherits property

Hoarding a wooden gallery, protected by boarding in front, which projected from the surface of a wall or parapet to enable defenders to protect the foot of the wall

Hobelar a small, sure-footed horse, well suited to rough, hilly terrain

Holm see *haugh*

Hot trod the lawful pursuit of thieves or *reivers* to recover stolen property

Howk to dig

Ilk ain every one (Scot.)

Impost the horizontal moulding at the springing point of an arch

Ingate a road or track crossing the border between two countries

Insight gear household goods

Ja(c)k a stout leather jacket

Jamb a vertical side of an opening; a wing or extension (Scot.)

Jetty the projection of an upper storey beyond the one below

Jougs a hinged iron collar or shackle used to chain lawbreakers to the wall of a building, often a church (Scot.)

Keep the principal tower of a castle

Kirk church

Kye cows; cattle

Lancet a slender pointed-arched window, often found singly but also occurring in groups

Lantern a small *turret* with windows all around

Lavabo trough with running water in a monastery for purposes of washing hands before a meal

Lavatorium washing place in a monastery

Light a window, or compartment within a window

Linn a pool; a small waterfall

Lintel a horizontal beam or stone

bridging an opening

Long-and-short quoins of alternately tall and flat, slab-like proportions, characteristic of Anglo-Saxon workmanship

Low-side window a window set lower than the others in a chancel side wall

Lucarne small gabled opening in roof or spire; a spire *light*

Machicolation a series of vertical openings, usually under a projecting parapet, through which objects may be dropped

Mail rent; levy

March a large administrative zone in the Border region, governed by a *Warden*

March days meetings of opposite Wardens or their deputies for the administration of law and justice on the Anglo-Scottish frontier

Mark unit of medieval currency (not a coin); in Scotland the merk was a unit of value equalling two-thirds of £1 Scots, i.e. 13s. 4d. Scots.

Mass ceremony of the *Eucharist*

Merk see *Mark*

Mickle much; great (Scot.)

Mirk(e) dark

Megalithic large stones; *quoins* of roughly hewn, large proportions, sometimes characterising Anglo-Saxon construction

Merlon upright stone on a battlement providing shelter from incoming projectiles

Mony many

Mortice socket in timber or stone

Moss boggy moorland

Mosstrooper mid- to late seventeenth-century *freebooter* or thief, the successor to the medieval *reiver*

Mote see *motte*

Motte a mound forming the focal point of many Norman earthwork castles

Muckle see *mickle*

Mullion a vertical member within a window opening

Murage tolls charged by the authorities of a town to pay for its defences

Murder hole a single opening through which objects may be dropped; see *machicolation*

Nave the body of a church to the west of the chancel or crossing

Newel central post in a spiral or circular staircase

Niche recess in a wall, smaller than an *aumbry*

Night stair access into the body of a monastic church from the dormitory used by monks for night offices

Nolt cattle

Octopartite describing a *vault*, where a bay is divided into eight parts

Ogee a double curve motif used in decoration

Onsett attack

Open-day foray raid

Oratory a private chapel

Outriding men *reivers*; thieves; raiders

Owsen oxen

Parapet wall at the edge of a roof

Paveis a large shield

Peel see *Pele tower*

Pele tower a defensible stone tower, normally associated with secular use

Pend an open-ended passage through a building, at ground level

Pensall flag or pennant

Perpendicular historical division of English *Gothic* architecture covering the period from the mid-fourteenth century to *c.* 1530

Petronel an early form of pistol

Pick pitch

Pile see *Pele tower*

Pioneer member of an infantry group of soldiers

Piscina basin with drain for washing Mass or Communion vessels, normally found in the thickness of the wall adjacent to an altar

Plinth a projecting course or courses at the foot of a wall

Poneis punish

Portcullis a gate which rises and descends in vertical grooves, designed to prevent entry through a portal or passageway

Postern small gateway at the back of a building

Pow a ditch or stream which has been diverted for drainage purposes (Scot.)

Preceptory a community of the Knights Templars, often used to describe the associated buildings

Prelate high-ranking ecclesiastical officer such as a bishop

Presbyter an ecclesiastical administrative overseer, appointed by the bishop

Presbytery the sanctuary or eastern part of the chancel beyond the choir

Pulpit a raised platform from which sermons are preached

Pulpitum a stone screen between nave and chancel

Putlog hole in a wall designed to receive a wooden scaffold member during construction, alteration, or repair of a building

Quadripartite a form of *vault* in which ribs divide each bay into four sections

Quadrant vault A quarter section of a *tunnel vault*, also known as quarter vaults

Quatrefoil see *Foil*

Quey heifer

Quhilk which

Quoins dressed stones at the corner of a building

Rampart a stone or earthen wall surrounding a fortification

Rank riders raiders; *reivers*; thieves

Reeve an official supervising a landowner's estate

Regality unit of local government in which the lord enjoyed certain exemptions from royal authority

Reif robbery; raid

Reiver raider; thief; rustler

Refectory dining hall

Reformation the overthrow of Papal power by Henry VIII; see *Dissolution*

Rental rental book or rent roll; check-list of rents due

Reredos a screen or panel, behind and above the altar

Resett to receive or harbour stolen goods

Respond a half-column in a wall end, normally to terminate an arcade

Reveal the inward plane of a *jamb* between the edge of an external wall and the frame of a door or window

Riser the vertical face of a step

Rode raid

Romanesque the architectural style

which prevailed largely in the eleventh and twelfth centuries, often called Norman in Britain

Rood loft a small gallery on top of a rood screen, used in pre-Reformation liturgy

Rood screen wooden screen dividing the nave from the chancel

Ryde raid

Sacrament House cupboard in a side wall of the chancel used for the reservation of the sacrament

Sacristy the room in a church or monastery for the storage of sacred vessels

Saiffing securing

Saker a small *culverin*; a medieval artillery piece

Sallett a light helmet with an outward-curving rear part

Sark a shirt

Sawfie an allowance for expenses, equal in value to the damage incurred

Searchers officials who visited the *watch* at intervals to ensure that they were still on duty

Sedilia seats for priests, normally set into the wall on the south side of the chancel

Serpentine a medieval field gun

Setters an official responsible for posting the *watch*

Shot-hole see *gun-loop*

Sic such

Side-alternate quoins laid such that each quoin-stone is the height of two or more courses of the main fabric, each set on its longer edge

Sike see *Syke*

Sill see *Cill*

Slype a passageway, especially in a monastery

Soffit the underside of an arch

Spandrel the space between adjacent arches

Spire a tall pyramidal or conical structure rising from a tower

Splint a simple plate defence for the arms, worn by infantry

Squinch an arch built diagonally across the angle between two walls to support a structure such as a spire

Spiral stair a circular or winding stair

Splay a *chamfer*, often describing a window opening

Spoil despoil; damage; goods taken by force; plunder

Steeple the tower of church including a spire if present

Stirk(e) a bullock or heifer between the ages of one and two years

Stoire goods; stock

Stot a young ox

Stown stolen

String course a projecting horizontal band of masonry running around a building, usually for decorative purposes

Swire a hill path used by reivers; a border crossing-point; a slope

Syke a ditch; trench; drainage channel; marshy hollow

Teind see *tithe* (Scot.)

Theek thatch

Tithe a tax, payable to the rector, one tenth of the annual produce of land or labour

Tower-house defensible or fortified medieval house with principal rooms on the first floor and above

Trace plan of a fortified place and its angles of fire

Tracery ornamental intersecting work usually within a window, screen, or panel

Transept a crossing arm of a church, normally projecting between the nave and the chancel

Transitional period of architecture between *Romanesque* and *Early English*

Transom a horizontal member within a window opening

Tread the horizontal part of a step

Trefoil see *Foil*

Trews see *March days*

Triforium the middle storey of the body of the church, above the arcade

Trod pursuit; see *Hot trod*

Troubles a period of Anglo-Scottish Border history from approximately 1296 to 1603, which, by the sixteenth century, was referred to as 'troublesome tymes'

Trow believe; understand

Truce days see *March days*

Tunnel vault a continuous stone arch forming a ceiling to a chamber or passage, unbroken in its length by cross vaults

Turret a small tower, usually attached to a building or rising from the top of a principal tower

Tympanum the area between the lintel of a doorway and the arch above it

Undercroft a vaulted room, often underground and used for storage in a monastery

Union the Union of the Crowns of England and Scotland in 1603 under a single monarch, James VI (of Scotland) and I (of England)

Upweir defend

Valentine a royal warrant for arrest

Vallum a rampart, usually one built for defensible purposes

Vault ceiling, usually of stone, formed like arches or in a single arch (see *Tunnel vault*)

Vawmure earthen fore-wall or bank, used as a defensible outwork

Visitation a periodic inspection by a diocesan official

Voussoirs the wedge-shaped stones forming an arch

Ward a day *watch*

Warden the administrator for a region of the Border, usually a *March*

Warming house room in a monastery where a communal fire was kept burning during the winter months

Watch watchmen or the watches which they kept against raids, especially at night

Watch-house a small detached building in a churchyard, used by watchmen to deter body-snatching in the nineteenth century

Wath path crossing the sand and mud of an estuary (especially the Solway)

Wawis walls

Wear guard

Weir war

Westwork the western end of a church with associated towers and superstructure, more complex in form than a simple west tower or gable

Wynd street; lane

Yat see *Yet* (this spelling tends to be Eng.)

Yet(t) gate, often in the form of an iron grille (Scot.)

BIBLIOGRAPHY

Abbreviations

CWAAS   Cumberland and Westmorland Antiquarian and Archaeological
             Society
NS   New Series
PSAS   *Proceedings of the Society of Antiquaries of Scotland*
TAASDN   *Transactions of the Architectural and Archaeological Society of Durham
             and Northumberland*
TCWAAS   *Transactions of the Cumberland and Westmorland Antiquarian and
             Archaeological Society*
TDGNHAS   *Transactions and Journal of Proceedings of the Dumfriesshire and Galloway
             Natural History and Antiquarian Society*

Note: Volume numbers and page references for the *Old Statistical Account* (OSA) are
taken from the new edition of 1978–9. This edition contains a cross-reference to the
original published *Account.*

Addison, Sir W., 1982, *Local Styles of the English Parish Church.* London: Batsford.
Addleshaw, G.W.O., 1951, *Blanchland: A Short History.* Sunderland: Privately Printed.
Aitken, J.C., 1889, 'Some Notes on the Abbey of Holywood and the Welshes of
   Colliestoun and Craigenputtock', TDGNHAS. **6**, 110–127.
ALC, edited by Hannay, R.K., 1932, *Acts of the Lords of Council in Public Affairs
   1501–1554, Selections from Acta Dominorum Concilii.* Edinburgh: H.M. General
   Register House.
Alison, J.P., 1917, 'Recent Excavations at the Wheel Kirk', *Transactions of the Hawick
   Archaeological Society 1917*, 12.
Allan, A., 1897, *A History of Channelkirk Church.* Channelkirk: n.pub.
Allan, R., and Candlish, I. (eds), 1988, *The Scottish Borderland – the Place and the People.*
   Kelso: The Border Country Life Association.
Allen, R., n.d., *St Cuthbert's Church, Bellingham, Northumberland.* Hexham: Peter
   Robson.
Anghel, G., 1982, 'Typologie des Eglises Fortifiees de Roumanie', *Chateau Gaillard,*
   9–10, 13–27.
Armstrong, R.B., 1883, *The History of Liddesdale, Eskdale, Ewesdale, Wauchopedale, and
   the Debateable Land.* Edinburgh: David Douglas.
ASC, *The Anglo-Saxon Chronicle,* translated by G.N.Garmonsway, 1972. London: Dent.
Audouy, M., Dix, B., and Parsons, D., 1995, 'The Tower of All Saints' Church, Earls'
   Barton, Northamptonshire: its Construction and Context', *Archaeological Journal,*
   152, 73–94.

Baldwin, J.R., 1985, *Exploring Scotland's Heritage – Lothian and the Borders*. Edinburgh: HMSO.

Barbour, J., 1884, 'Notes on Lincluden Abbey', TDGNHAS. **4**, 18–34.

Barbour, J., 1888, 'The Old Church of Dumfries', TDGNHAS. **6**, 42–51.

Barbour, J., 1911, 'The Greyfriars Convent of Dumfries and its Environs', TDGNHAS. N.S., **XXIII**, 18–35.

Barnes Injunctions, edited by James Raine, 1850, *The Injunctions and other Ecclesiastical Proceedings of Richard Barnes, Bishop of Durham from 1575 to 1587*. Surtees Society Volume 22, Durham: Surtees Society.

Barrett, R.G., and Watson, L., n.d., *Church of the Holy Cross Haltwhistle*. Haltwhistle: n.pub.

Barrett, R.G., Boddington, A., Ryder, P., Moat, N., 1990, *Bywell St Andrew, Northumberland*. Revised edition. London: Redundant Churches Fund.

Barrow, G., 1989, 'Frontier and Settlement: Which Influenced Which? England and Scotland, 1100–1300', in: Bartlett, R., and Mackay, A. (eds), *Medieval Frontier Societies*, 3–21. Oxford: Oxford University Press.

Barrow, G.W.S., 1962, 'The Scottish Clergy in the War of Independence', *The Scottish Historical Review*, **XLI**, 1–22.

Barrow, G.W.S., 1974, 'A Note on Falstone', *Archaeologia Aeliana*, 5th Series, **II**, 149–52.

Barrow, G.W.S., 1988, *Robert Bruce and The Community of The Realm of Scotland*. 3rd edn, Edinburgh: Edinburgh University Press.

Barrow, G.W.S., 1992, *Scotland and its Neighbours in the Middle Ages*. London: Hambledon Press.

Baskerville, G., 1937, *English Monks and the Suppression of the Monasteries*. London: Jonathan Cape.

Bates, C.J., 1891, *The Border Holds of Northumberland*. Vol. 1. Newcastle-upon-Tyne: Society of Antiquaries of Newcastle-upon-Tyne.

Bates, C.J., 1895, *The History of Northumberland*. London: Elliot Stock.

Bateson, E., 1893, *A History of Northumberland: Volume I. The Parish of Bamburgh with the Chapelry of Belford*. Newcastle-upon-Tyne: Andrew Reid.

Bateson, E., 1895, *A History of Northumberland: Volume II. The Parishes of Embleton, Ellingham, Howick, Long Houghton, and Lesbury*. Newcastle-upon-Tyne: Andrew Reid.

BBH, edited by James Raine, 1865, *The Black Book of Hexham (Rentale Prioris et Conventus de Hextildeshame)*. Surtees Society Volume 46, Durham: Surtees Society.

Bede, *Historia Ecclesiastica Gentis Anglorum*, edited by Plummer, C., 1896. Oxford: Oxford University Press.

Billings, R.W., 1845–52, *The Baronial and Ecclesiastical Antiquities of Scotland*. 4 vols, Edinburgh: n.pub. / Blackwood.

Binnie, G.A.C., 1995, *The Churches and Graveyards of Berwickshire*. Ladykirk: Binnie.

Black, G.F., 1891, 'Holywood Abbey', TDGNHAS. **7**, 126–9.

BM.HARL.MS. No. 1757. 1544, British Museum, Harleian MS. *1757, Damages done to the Scots by the inroads of the English, and the Scottish Borders under English assurance, from 9th September 1543 to 29th June 1544*.

Boardman, S., 1996, *The Early Stewart Kings: Robert II and Robert III 1371–1406*. East Linton: Tuckwell Press.

Bond, F., 1908, *Screens and Galleries in English Churches*. London: Henry Frowde.

Bonde, S., 1994, *Fortress-Churches of Languedoc*. Cambridge: Cambridge University Press.

Briggs, G.W.D., 1982, 'The Church of St Andrew Bolam', *Archaeologia Aeliana*, 5th Series, **X**, 125–41.

Briggs, G.W.D., 1998, *An Architectural Account of the Church of St Bartholomew Newbiggin-by-the-Sea*. Newbiggin: Newbiggin PCC.

Brooke, D., 1994, *Wild Men and Holy Places: St Ninian, Whithorn, and the Medieval Realm of Galloway.* Edinburgh: Canongate.

Brooke, C.J., 1996, The Application of High Resolution Photographic Remote Sensing and Digital Image Processing in the Archaeological Examination of Historic Buildings, in: Donoghue, N.M., and Zong, Y. (eds), *Remote Sensing Science and Industry, Proceedings of the 22nd Annual Conference of the Remote Sensing Society*, 667–75. Nottingham: The Remote Sensing Society.

Brown, J.M., 1977, *Scottish Society in the Fifteenth Century.* London: Edward Arnold

Brown, M., 1994, *James I.* Edinburgh: Canongate.

Brown, M., 1998, *The Black Douglases.* East Linton: Tuckwell.

Brown, R.A., 1976, *English Castles.* 2nd edn, London: Batsford.

Bulman, C.G., 1966, 'The Parish and Church of St Michael, Arthuret', TCWAAS. N.S., **LXVI**, 179–89.

Bulman, C.G., and Frith, R.E., 1987, *Arthuret Church and Parish.* 2nd edn, Longtown: n.pub.

Bulmer, T.F., 1901, *History, Topography and Directory of Cumberland.* 2nd edn, Preston: Bulmer.

Butler, L., and Given-Wilson, C., 1979, *Medieval Monasteries of Great Britain.* London: Michael Joseph.

Caldwell, D.H., 1981, Royal Patronage of Arms and Armour Making in Fifteenth and Sixteenth-Century Scotland, in: Caldwell, D.H. (ed.), *Scottish Weapons and Fortifications 1100–1800.* Edinburgh: John Donald. 73–93.

Cambridge, E., and Williams, A., 1995, 'Hexham Abbey: A Review of Recent Work and its Implications', *Archaeologia Aeliana.* 5th Series, **XXIII**, 51–138.

Cameron, J., 1998, *James V The Personal Rule 1528–1542.* East Linton: Tuckwell.

Cathcart King, D.J., 1983, *Castellarium Anglicanum.* 2 vols, New York: Kraus.

CBP, edited by Joseph Bain. 1894–96, *Calendar of Letters and Papers Relating to the Affairs of the Borders of England and Scotland* (Vol i 1560–1594; Vol ii 1595–1603). 2 vols, Edinburgh: HMSO.

CCR, edited by W.H. Stevenson, *et al.*, 1902–, *Calendar of Close Rolls.* 61 vols, London: HMSO.

CDRS, edited by Joseph Bain, 1881–8, *Calendar of Documents Relating to Scotland.* 4 vols, Edinburgh: HM General Register House.

Charleton, R.J., 1885, *Newcastle Town: An Account of its Rise and Progress: Its Struggles and Triumphs: and its Ending.* London: Walter Scott.

Charlton, B., 1986, *The Story of Redesdale.* Hexham: Northumberland County Council.

Child, F.J. (ed.), 1882–98, *The English and Scottish Popular Ballads.* 5 vols, Boston: Houghton Mifflin.

Chinnock, E.J., 1901, 'Edward I at Sweetheart Abbey', TDGNHAS. **XVII**, 172–4.

Chr.Lan., *The Chronicle of Lanercost 1272–1346*, edited by Sir H. Maxwell, 1913. Glasgow: James Maclehose and Sons.

Chr.Mel., *The Chronicle of Melrose.* Facsimile reprint of Joseph Stevenson's translation, 1991. Lampeter: Llanerch Press.

Clark, Sir G., 1956, *The Later Stuarts 1660–1714.* 2nd edn, Oxford: The Clarendon Press.

Collier, C., and Stewart, L.A., 1986, *Wooler and Glendale: A Brief History. Vol I – Wooler.* Wooler: Glendale Local History Society.

Collier, C., and Stewart, L.A., 1987, *Wooler and Glendale: A Brief History. Vol II – Glendale.* Wooler: Glendale Local History Society.

Collingwood, W.G., 1928, 'Wigton Old Church', TCWAAS, N.S., **XXVIII**, 96–102.

Colvin, H.M. (ed.), 1963–82, *The History of the King's Works.* 6 vols, London: HMSO.

Conzen, M.R.G., 1969, *Alnwick, Northumberland.* London: Institute of British Geographers.

Coulson, C., 1982, 'Hierarchism in Conventual Crenellation: An Essay in the Sociology and Metaphysics of Medieval Fortification', *Medieval Archaeology*, **26**, 69–100.

Cowan, I.B., 1967, The Parishes of Medieval Scotland. *Scottish Record Society*, Old Series, xciii. Edinburgh: Scottish Record Society.

Cowan, I.B., 1995, *The Medieval Church in Scotland*, edited by Kirk, J. Edinburgh: Scottish Academic Press.

Cowan, I.B., and Easson, D.E., 1976, *Medieval Religious Houses Scotland*. 2nd edn, London: Longman.

Cox, J.C., and Ford, C.B., 1947, *Parish Churches of England*. 5th edn, London: Batsford.

CPR, edited by J.G. Black, *et al.*, 1901–, *Calendar of Patent Rolls*. 74 vols, London: HMSO.

Craster, H.H.E., 1907, *A History of Northumberland. Volume VIII. The Parish of Tynemouth*. Newcastle: Andrew Reid.

Craster, H.H.E., 1909, *A History of Northumberland. Volume IX. The Parochial Chapelries of Earsdon and Horton*. Newcastle: Andrew Reid.

Craster, H.H.E., 1914, *A History of Northumberland. Volume X. The Parish of Corbridge*. Newcastle: Andrew Reid.

Crossman, W., 1890–1, 'The Recent Excavations at Holy Island Priory', *Berwickshire Naturalists Club, History*, **XIII**, 225–40.

Crowe, C., 1986, 'An Excavation at Kirkmirran, Dalbeattie, 1985', TDGNHAS, 3rd Series, **LXI**, 55–62.

Cruden, S., 1981, *The Scottish Castle*. 3rd edn, Edinburgh: Spurbooks.

Cruden, S., 1986, *Scottish Medieval Churches*. Edinburgh: John Donald.

CSP, edited by Joseph Bain, *et al.*, 1898–1969, *Calendar of State Papers Relating to Scotland and Mary Queen of Scots 1547–1603*. 13 vols, Edinburgh: H.M. General Register House.

CSPS, edited by Thorpe, M.J., 1858, *Calendar of The State Papers Relating to Scotland* [1509–1603]. 2 vols, London: Longman.

CTRS, edited by Sir J. Balfour Paul, 1877–1978, *Compota Thesaurariorum Regum Scotorum*. 13 vols, Edinburgh: H.M. General Register House.

Curwen, J.F., 1913a, 'The Fortified Church of St John the Baptist, Newton Arlosh', TCWAAS, **XIII**, 113–21.

Curwen, J.F., 1913b, *Castles and Fortified Towers of Cumberland, Westmorland, and Lancashire North-of-the-Sands*. CWAAS, Extra Series, Vol. XIII.

Darton, M., 1994, *The Dictionary of Place Names in Scotland*. Orpington: Eric Dobby.

Davis, J.G., 1968, *The Secular Use of Church Buildings*. London: SCM Press.

Dent, J., and McDonald, R., 1998, *Christian Heritage in the Borders*. Melrose: Scottish Borders Council.

Dickinson, J.C., 1942, 'A Note on the Foundation of Lanercost Priory', TCWAAS. N.S., **XLII**, 183–87.

Dickinson, W.C., and Duncan, A.A.M., 1977, *Scotland from the Earliest Times to 1603*. 3rd edn, Oxford: Oxford University Press.

Dixon, D.D., 1895, *Whittingham Vale*. Newcastle: Robert Redpath.

Dixon, D.D., 1903, *Upper Coquetdale*. Newcastle: Robert Redpath.

Dobie, W., 1891, 'Notes on Ladykirk Parish Church', *Proc. Berwickshire Naturalist Club 1890–1*, 369–78.

Dobson, B., 1992, The Church of Durham and the Scottish Borders 1378–88, in: Goodman, A., and Tuck, A. (eds), *War and Border Societies in the Middle Ages*, 124–54. London: Routledge.

Dobson, R.B., 1967, 'The Last English Monks on Scottish Soil', *The Scottish Historical Review*, **XLVI**, 1–25.

Dodds, J., 1999, *Bastions and Belligerents: Medieval Strongholds in Northumberland.* Newcastle-upon-Tyne Keepdate.

Donaldson, G., 1987, *Scotland, the Making of a Kingdom: James V-James VII.* The Edinburgh History of Scotland, Volume III. Edinburgh: Mercat Press.

Donnelly, A.F., 1988, *An Account of the Parishes of Hartburn, Meldon, and Netherwitton in the Diocese of Newcastle and in the County of Northumberland.* Hartburn: Hartburn PCC.

Duffy, C., 1979, *Siege Warfare, The Fortress in the Early Modern World 1494–1660.* London: Routledge.

Duke, J.A., 1937, *History of the Church of Scotland to the Reformation.* Edinburgh: Oliver and Boyd.

Dunbar, J.G., 1996, 'The Emergence of the Reformed Church in Scotland', in: Blair, J., and Pyrah, C. (eds), *Church Archaeology: Research Directions for the Future*, 127–34. York: Council for British Archaeology.

Duncan, A.A.M. (ed.), 1997, *The Bruce*, by John Barbour. Edinburgh: Canongate.

Durham Depositions, 1845, *Depositions and Other Ecclesiastical Proceedings from the Courts of Durham, Extending from 1311 to the Reign of Elizabeth.* Surtees Society Volume 21, Durham: Surtees Society.

Eeles, F.C., 1974, *The Parish Church of St Kentigern Crosthwaite.* 2nd edn, Kendal: Titus Wilson & Son.

Ekwall, E., 1960, *The Concise Oxford Dictionary of English Place-Names.* 4th edn, Oxford: Clarendon Press.

Evans, R., 1987, *Ferniehirst Castle.* Kelso: Ferniehirst Press.

Ewan, E., 1990, *Townlife in Fourteenth-Century Scotland.* Edinburgh: Edinburgh University Press.

Fairclough, G., 1983, 'Fortified Houses and Castles', in: Clack, P., and Ivy, J. (eds), *The Borders*, 81–99. Durham: CBA Group 3.

Fantosme. *Chronicle of the War Between the English and the Scots in 1173 and 1174*, by Jordan Fantosme. Edited by Francisque Michel, 1834. Surtees Society Volume 11, London: Surtees Society.

Fawcett, R., 1985, *Scottish Medieval Churches.* Edinburgh: HMSO.

Fawcett, R., 1990, 'Ecclesiastical Architecture in the Second Half of the Thirteenth Century', in: Reid, N. (ed.), *Scotland in the Reign of Alexander III*, 148–80. Edinburgh: John Donald.

Fawcett, R., 1994a, *The Architectural History of Scotland: Scottish Architecture from the Accession of the Stewarts to the Reformation 1371–1560.* Edinburgh: Edinburgh University Press.

Fawcett, R., 1994b, *Scottish Abbeys and Priories.* London: Batsford.

Fawcett, R., 1996, 'The Archaeology of the Scottish Church in the Later Middle Ages', in: Blair, J., and Pyrah, C. (eds), *Church Archaeology Research Directions for the Future.* CBA Research Report 104, 85–102. York: Council for British Archaeology.

Fenwick, H., 1978, *Scotland's Abbeys and Cathedrals.* London: Hale.

Ferguson, J., 1890, 'Notices of Remains of Pre-Reformation Churches, &c in Berwickshire', *Proceedings of the Berwickshire Naturalist Club 1890–1*, 86–188.

Ferguson, R.S., 1877, *Miscellany Accounts of the Diocese of Carlisle with the Terriers by William Nicolson, Late Bishop of Carlisle.* CWAAS, Extra Series, Vol. I. Carlisle: CWAAS.

Fisher, E.A., 1969, *Anglo-Saxon Towers.* Newton Abbot: David and Charles.

Forster, B., Robson, B., and Deadman, J., 1993, *Ripon Cathedral: It's History and Architecture.* York: William Sessions.

Fraser, C.M., 1968, *The Northumberland Lay Subsidy Roll of 1296.* Society of Antiquaries of Newcastle-upon-Tyne, Record Series No. 1. Newcastle: Society of Antiquaries.

Fraser, R., 1935, 'The Story of Lochmaben Kirk', TDGNHAS 3rd Series, **XIX**, 296–311.

Fraser, Sir W., 1894, *The Annandale Family Book of the Johnstones Earls and Marquises of Annandale*. 2 vols, Edinburgh: n.pub.

Froissart, Sir John, *Chronicles of England, France, Spain, and Adjoining Countries*. Translated from French editions by Thomas Johnes, 1839. 2 vols, London: William Smith.

Frontier I, by Sir Robert Bowes & Sir Ralf Elleker 1541–2, *A View and Survey Along the Borders of the East and Middle Marches of England of all Castles, Towers, Barmkins and Fortresses*. Cotton MS. Caligula B.vii. f.636 printed in Hodgson, J., 1828, 171–242. Newcastle: J.Hodgson.

Frontier II, by Sir Robert Bowes, 1550, *The Book of the State of the Frontiers and Marches betwixt England and Scotland*, Cotton MS. Titus F.13., printed in Hodgson, J., 1828, 171–248. Newcastle: J.Hodgson.

Gem, R., 1986, 'Lincoln Minster: Ecclesia Pulchra, Ecclesia Fortis', in: *Medieval Art and Architecture at Lincoln Cathedral*, Transactions of the British Archaeological Association Conference 1982, 9–28.

Gibson, R., 1905, *An Old Berwickshire Town: History of the town and parish of Greenlaw, from the earliest times to the present day*. Edinburgh: Oliver and Boyd.

Gifford, J., 1992, *The Buildings of Scotland: Highland and Islands*. London: Penguin.

Gifford, J., 1996, *The Buildings of Scotland: Dumfries and Galloway*. London: Penguin.

Gilbert, J.M., 1979, *Hunting and Hunting Reserves in Medieval Scotland*. Edinburgh: John Donald.

Gilbert, J.M., 1985, *Flower of the Forest*. Selkirk: Selkirk Common Good Fund.

Gill, H., 1913, 'Autumn Excursion', *Transactions of the Thoroton Society*, **17**, 36–49.

Goodman, A., 1989, 'Religion and Warfare in the Anglo-Scottish Marches', in: Bartlett, R., and Mackay, A. (eds), *Medieval Frontier Societies*, 245–66. Oxford: Oxford University Press.

Goodman, A., and Tuck, A. (eds), 1992, *War and Border Society in the Middle Ages*. London: Routledge.

Gordon, L., 1985, *Berwick-Upon-Tweed and the East March*. Chichester: Phillimore.

Graham, A,, 1949, 'An Old Road in the Lammermuirs', *PSAS*, **83**, 198–206.

Graham, F., 1987, *Northumbrian Castles: The Coast*. Rothbury: Butler.

Graham, F., 1988, *Famous Northern Battles*. Rothbury: Butler.

Graham, F., 1988b, *Hexham and Corbridge A Short History and Guide*. Thropton: Butler.

Graham, F., 1994, *Alnwick A Short History and Guide*. Thropton: Butler.

Graham, R., 1929, 'An Ecclesiastical Tenth for National Defence in 1298', *English Ecclesiastical Studies 1929*, 317–18.

Graham, T.H.B., 1913, 'The Parish of Warwick', TCWAAS, **XIII**, 87–112.

Graham, T.H.B., 1921, 'Scaleby', TCWAAS, N.S., **XXI**, 139–51.

Graham, T.H.B., 1928, 'Arthuret, Kirklinton and Kirkoswald', TCWAAS. N.S., **XXVIII**, 41–58.

Graham, T.H.B., 1930, 'The Parish of Stapleton', TCWAAS, N.S., **XXX**, 55–67.

Graham, T.H.B., 1931, 'The Two Kirkandrews', TCWAAS, N.S., **XXXI**, 21–28.

Grainger, F., and Collingwood, W.G., 1929, *The Register and Records of Holm Cultram*. CWAAS. Record Series, Vol. VII. Kendal: CWAAS.

Grainger, J.D., 1997, *Cromwell Against the Scots: The Last Anglo Scottish War, 1650–1652*. East Linton: Tuckwell.

Grant, A., 1984, *Independence and Nationhood: Scotland 1306–1469*. Edinburgh: Edinburgh University Press.

Grigson, G., (ed.), 1975, *The Penguin Book of Ballads*. Harmondsworth: Penguin.

Gunn, C.B., 1910, *The Ministry of the Presbytery of Peebles*. Peebles: Allan Smyth Neidpath Press.

Hadcock, R.N., 1936, 'Tynemouth Priory', *Archaeologia Aeliana*. 4th Series, **XIII**, 122–38.

Hamilton Papers, edited by Joseph Bain, 1890-2, *The Hamilton Papers*. 2 vols, Edinburgh: H.M. General Register House.

Harbottle, B., and Cowper, R.A.S., 1963, 'An Excavation at Memmerkirk, Northumberland', *Archaeologia Aeliana*, 4th Series, **XLI**, 45-63.

Harbottle, B., and Newman, T., 1977, 'Excavation and Survey in North Tynedale, 1973-1975', *Archaeologia Aeliana*, 5th Series, **V**, 121-54.

Haswell, J.F., and Jackson, C.S., 1938, *The Registers of St Andrew's Parish Church, Penrith. Volume I 1556-1604*. Parish Registers, CWAAS, Vol. 26.

Hay, G., 1984, 'Scottish Renaissance Architecture', in: Breeze, D., *Studies in Scottish Antiquity*, 196-231. Edinburgh: John Donald.

Hearnshaw, F.J.C., 1924, *Newcastle-Upon-Tyne*. London: Sheldon Press.

Henderson, I., 1988, 'The Arts of Late Celtic Britain (AD 600-900)', in B. Ford (ed.), *The Cambridge Guide to the Arts in Britain: Prehistoric, Roman, and Early Medieval*. Vol. 1, 206-19. Cambridge: Cambridge University Press.

Heslop, R., 1986, *Blackfriars*. Newcastle-upon-Tyne: Newcastle-upon-Tyne City Libraries.

Hexham Annals, edited by James Raine, 1863, *The Priory of Hexham, its Chroniclers, Endowments, and Annals*. Vol I. Surtees Society Volume 44, v-cxxx. Durham: Surtees Society.

Hexham Charters, edited by James Raine, 1865, Charters and Other Documents, in: *The Priory of Hexham, its Title Deeds, Black Book, etc., Vol II*, Surtees Society Volume 46, 83-169. Durham: Surtees Society.

Hexham Memorials, edited by James Raine, 1863, *The Priory of Hexham, its Chroniclers, Endowments, and Annals*. Vol I. Appendix: Memorials of Hexham Priory. Surtees Society Volume 44, i-clxviii. Durham: Surtees Society.

Hickes, J.C., n.d., *The History and Development of Lesbury and Alnmouth*. Alnwick: Alnwick Gazette.

Hill, P., 1997, *Whithorn and St Ninian*. Stroud: Sutton.

Hinds, A.B., 1896, *A History of Northumberland. Volume III. Hexhamshire: Part I*. Newcastle: Andrew Reid.

Hodges, C.C., 1893, 'Pre-Conquest Churches of Northumbria', *Reliquary*, N.S., **7**, 65-85.

Hodgson Hinde, J., 1858, *A History of Northumberland*, Part I. Newcastle-upon-Tyne: Society of Antiquaries of Newcastle-Upon-Tyne.

Hodgson, J., 1820, *A History of Northumberland*, Part III, Vol. I. Newcastle-upon-Tyne: John Hodgson.

Hodgson, J., 1827, *A History of Northumberland*, Part II, Vol. I. Newcastle-upon-Tyne: John Hodgson.

Hodgson, J., 1828, *A History of Northumberland*, Part III, Vol. II. Newcastle-upon-Tyne: John Hodgson.

Hodgson, J., 1832, *A History of Northumberland*, Part II, Vol. II. Newcastle-upon-Tyne: John Hodgson.

Hodgson, J., 1835, *A History of Northumberland*, Part III, Vol. III. Newcastle-upon-Tyne: John Hodgson.

Hodgson, J., 1840, *A History of Northumberland*, Part II, Vol. III. Newcastle-upon-Tyne: John Hodgson.

Hodgson, J.C., 1897, *A History of Northumberland: Volume IV. Hexhamshire Part II and the Parish of Chollerton, the Chapelry of Kirkheaton, the Parish of Thockrington*. Newcastle-Upon-Tyne: Andrew Reid.

Hodgson, J.C., 1899, *A History of Northumberland. Volume V. The Parish of Warkworth, The Parish of Shilbottle, The Chapelry or Extra-Parochial Place of Brainshaugh*. Newcastle: Andrew Reid.

Hodgson, J.C., 1902, *A History of Northumberland. Volume VI. The Parish of Bywell St*

Peter, The Parish of Bywell St Andrew with Blanchland, The Chapelry or Parish of Slaley. Newcastle: Andrew Reid.

Hodgson, J.C., 1904, *A History of Northumberland: Volume VII. The Parish of Edlingham, The Parish of Felton, The Chapelry or Parish of Brinkburn.* Newcastle-Upon-Tyne: Andrew Reid.

Hogg, O.F.G., 1968, *Clubs to Cannon, Warfare and Weapons before the Introduction of Gunpowder.* London: Gerald Duckworth & Co.

Holden, J., 1990, 'The Fate of Monastic Churches in Cumbria: A Consideration of the Position At Law', in: Loades, J. (ed.), *Monastic Studies, The Continuity of Tradition*, 255–66. Bangor: Headstart History.

Honeyman, H.L., and Hunter Blair, H., 1990, *Warkworth Castle and Hermitage.* 3rd edn, London: English Heritage.

Hope Dodds, M., 1926, *A History of Northumberland. Volume XII. The Parishes of Ovingham, Stamfordham, and Ponteland.* Newcastle: Andrew Reid.

Hughes, Q., 1991, *Military Architecture.* 2nd edn, Liphook: Beaufort.

Hugill, R., 1939, *Borderland Castles and Peles.* London: Burrow and Co. Ltd.

Hyslop, J., and Hyslop, R., 1912, *Langholm as it was: A History of Langholm and Eskdale from the Earliest Times.* Sunderland: Hills.

Johnson, S., 1984, *Belsay Hall, Castle, and Gardens.* London: English Heritage.

Jones B.C., n.d. *St Michael's Church Burgh by Sands.* Burgh-by-Sands: n.pub.

Jones, B.C., 1981, 'The Grey Friars, Carlisle', TCWAAS, N.S., **LXXXI**, 160–2.

Jones, G.P., 1969, 'King James I and the Western Border', TCWAAS. N.S., **LXIX**, 129–51.

Keeling, S.M., 1975, *Church and Religion in the Anglo-Scottish Border Counties, 1534–72.* PhD. Thesis, University of Durham.

Kelland, C.H., 1982, *Ecclesiae Incastellatae: A Documentary and Architectural Study of the Concept of 'Fortified Churches' in England and Wales.* M.Phil. Thesis, 2 vols, University College, University of London.

Kightly, C., 1979, *Strongholds of the Realm.* London: Thames and Hudson.

Knowles, D., 1959, *The Religious Orders in England, III: The Tudor Age.* Cambridge: Cambridge University Press.

Knowles, D., and Hadcock, R.N., 1971, *Medieval Religious Houses England and Wales.* 2nd edn, London: Longman.

Knowles, W.H., 1896, 'Church of St John the Baptist, Edlingham, Northumberland', *TAASDN*, **V**, 37–48.

Knowles, W.H., 1910, 'The Priory Church of St Mary and St Oswin, Tynemouth, Northumberland', *Archaeological Journal*, **LXVII**, 1–50.

L. & P. Henry VIII, edited by J.S. Brewer, *et al*, 1862–1932, *Letters and Papers, Foreign and Domestic of the Reign of Henry VIII.* 21 vols, London: HMSO.

L.de Melros, edited by Cosmo Innes, 1837, *Liber Sancte Marie de Melros: Munimenta Vetustiora Monasterii Cisterciensis de Melros.* 2 parts, Edinburgh: Bannatyne Club.

Laing, L., and Laing, J., 1979, *Anglo-Saxon England.* London: Routledge & Kegan Paul.

Lamont-Brown, R., 1988, *The Life and Times of Berwick-upon-Tweed.* Edinburgh: John Donald.

Lan.Cart., 1997, *The Lanercost Cartulary*, edited by Todd, J.M., Surtees Society Vol. 203, Gateshead: Surtees Society.

Lang A., and Lang J., 1913, *Highways and Byways in the Border.* London: MacMillan and Co. Ltd.

Lang, L.R., 1972, 'Medieval Pottery from Coldingham Priory, Berwickshire', *PSAS*, **104**, 242–47.

Lang, T., 1957, *The Queen's Scotland: The Border Counties.* London: Hodder and Stoughton.

Leland. John Leland, 1535–43, *The Itinerary*. Leland's Itinerary in England and Wales, edited by Cohen, J.M., 1964. 5 vols, Carbondale: Southern Illinois University Press.

Lemasson, A., and Hanotaux, G., 1938, *Les Eglises Fortifiees de la Thierache*. Vervins: Societie Archaeologique de Vervins.

Lennox, J., 1903, 'Excavations on the Site of the Monastery of Dumfries', TDGNHAS, **XVII**, 254–6.

Let.Nor.Reg., edited by James Raine, 1873, *Historical Papers and Letters from the Northern Registers*. London: Longman & Co., & Trubner & Co.

Lewis, J., and Ewart, G., 1995, *Jedburgh Abbey: the Archaeology and Architecture of a Border Abbey*. Society of Antiquaries of Scotland Monograph Series No. 10. Edinburgh: Society of Antiquaries of Scotland.

Lewis, S., 1846, *A Topographical Dictionary of Scotland*. 2 vols, London: S Lewis & Co.

Liber de Dryburgh, edited by Spottiswoode, J., 1847, *Liber S. Marie de Dryburgh: Registrum Cartarum Abbacie Premonstratensis de Dryburgh*. Edinburgh: Bannatyne Club.

Lindsay, M., 1986, *The Castles of Scotland*. London: Constable.

Lomas, R., 1992, *North-East England in the Middle Ages*. Edinburgh: John Donald.

Lomas, R., 1996a, *County of Conflict: Northumberland from Conquest to Civil War*. East Linton: Tuckwell.

Lomas, R., 1996b, 'The Impact of Border Warfare: The Scots and South Tweedside *c.* 1290 – *c.* 1520', *The Scottish Historical Review*, **LXXV**, 143–67.

Lomas, R., 1999, *A Power in the Land: The Percys*. East Linton: Tuckwell.

Longley, K.M., 1983, 'The Scottish Incursions of 1327: A Glimpse of the Aftermath (Wigton Church Accounts, 1328–9)', TCWAAS, N.S., **LXXXIII**, 63–72.

Lowe, C.E., 1991, 'New light on the Anglian "Minster" at Hoddam', TDGNHAS, 3rd Ser., **66**, 11–35.

Lynch, M., 1992, *Scotland A New History*. 2nd edn, London: Pimlico.

Lysons, D., and Lysons, S., 1806–22, *Magna Britannia: Being a Concise Topographical Account of the Several Counties of Great Britain*. 6 vols, London: T.Cadell and W.Davies.

M'Millan, W.W., 1930, 'The Church of Sanquhar', TDGNHAS, 3rd Series, **XVI**, 87–101.

MacDonald Fraser, G., 1989, *The Steel Bonnets*. London: Collins Harvill.

Macdougall, N., 1982, *James III: A Political Study*. Edinburgh: John Donald.

Macdougall, N., 1997, *James IV*. East Linton: Tuckwell.

MacEwen, A.R., 1913, *A History of the Church in Scotland*. 2 vols, London: Hodder and Stoughton.

MacGibbon, D., and Ross, T., 1887–92, *The Castellated and Domestic Architecture of Scotland*. 5 vols, Edinburgh: David Douglas.

MacGibbon, D., and Ross, T., 1896–7, *The Ecclesiastical Architecture of Scotland*. 3 vols, Edinburgh: David Douglas.

MacIvor, I., 1981, 'Artillery and Major Places of Strength in the Lothians and East Border, 1513–1542', in: Caldwell, D.H. (ed.), *Scottish Weapons and Fortifications 1100–1800*, 94–152. Edinburgh: John Donald.

Mack, J.L., 1926, *The Border Line*. Edinburgh: Oliver and Boyd.

MacKechnie, A., 1985, 'Durisdeer Church', PSAS, **115**, 429–42.

MacKenzie, A.M., 1957, *The Scotland of Queen Mary and the Religious Wars 1513–1638*. Edinburgh: Oliver & Boyd.

Mackie, A.O., and Robson, M.J.H., n.d., *The Parish of Linton*. Linton: n.pub.

Mackie, J.D., 1978, *A History of Scotland*. 2nd edn, Harmondsworth: Penguin.

Marsden, J., 1990, *The Illustrated Border Ballads*. London: Macmillan.

Martin, J.W., 1897, 'Ruins and Stones of Holywood Abbey', TDGNHAS, **13**, 67–70.

Maxwell, Sir H., 1896, *A History of Dumfries and Galloway.* Edinburgh: William Blackwood & Sons.

McCarthy, M., 1993, *Carlisle History and Guide.* Stroud: Alan Sutton.

McCarthy, M.R., Summerson, H.R.T., and Annis, R.G. 1990, *Carlisle Castle, A survey and documentary history.* English Heritage Archaeological Report No. 18. London: Historic Buildings & Monuments Commission.

McCord, N., and Thompson, R., 1998, *The Northern Counties from AD 1000.* London: Longman.

McDonald, R.A., 1997, *The Kingdom of the Isles: Scotland's Western Seaboard c.1100 – c.1336.* East Linton: Tuckwell.

McDowall, W., 1986, *History of Dumfries.* 4th edn, Dumfries: T.C.Farries.

McDowall, W.M., 1884, 'The Founder of Lincluden Abbey and his Relatives', TDGNHAS, **4**, 10–12.

McGladdery, C., 1990, *James II.* Edinburgh: John Donald.

McGuiness, P., 1986, *An Outline History of Woodhorn.* Ashington: Wansbeck District Council.

McIntire, W.T., 1939, 'The Fords of the Solway', TCWAAS, N.S., **XXXIX**, 152–70.

McIntire, W.T., 1941, 'Solway Moss', TCWAAS, N.S., **XLI**, 5–9.

McKerlie, P.H., 1870–9, *History of the Lands and their Owners in Galloway with a Historical Sketch of the District.* 5 vols, Edinburgh: Paterson.

McKisack, M., 1959, *The Fourteenth Century 1307–1399.* Oxford: Oxford University Press.

McNamee, C., 1997, *The Wars of the Bruces: Scotland, England and Ireland 1306–1328.* East Linton: Tuckwell Press.

McNamee, C.J., 1990, 'William Wallace's Invasion of Northern England in 1297', *Northern History,* **XXVI**, 40–58.

McWilliam, C., 1978, *The Buildings of Scotland: Lothian.* Harmondsworth: Penguin.

Mee, A., 1937, *The Lake Counties: Cumberland and Westmorland* [King's England Series]. London: Hodder and Stoughton.

Meyvaert, P., 1989, 'A New Perspective on the Ruthwell Cross: Ecclesia and Vita Monastica', in: Cassidy, B. (ed.), *The Ruthwell Cross,* Papers from the Colloquium Sponsored by the Index of Christian Art Princeton University 8 December 1989, 95–166. Princeton: Princeton University.

Miket, R., 1974, 'Excavations at Kirkhill, West Hepple, 1972', *Archaeologica Aeliana,* 5th Ser., **II**, 153–87.

Miller, E., 1960, *War in the North: The Anglo-Scottish Wars of the Middle Ages.* Hull: University of Hull.

Mitchison, R., 1970, *A History of Scotland.* London: Methuen.

Moffat, A., 1985, *Kelsae, A History of Kelso from the Earliest Times.* Edinburgh: Mainstream.

Moffat, B., 1988, 'Medieval Documentation of Soutra', in: Moffat, B., and Fulton, J. (eds) 1988, 47–68.

Moffat, B., and Fulton, J., (eds) 1988, *Sharp Practice 2: The Second Report on Researches into the Medieval Hospital at Soutra, Lothian Region, Scotland.* Edinburgh: SHARP.

Mon.Ang., *Monasticon Anglicanum,* by Sir William Dugdale. New edition, edited by Caley, J., Ellis, H., and Bandinel, B., 1817–30. 6 vols, London: Harding, Harding, and Lepard.

Moorman, J.R.H., 1952, 'Edward I at Lanercost Priory', *English Historical Review,* **LXVII**, 161–74.

Moorman, J.R.H., 1967, *Lanercost Priory.* 2nd edn, Brampton: John Moorman.

Morris, C. (ed.), 1984, *The Illustrated Journeys of Celia Fiennes c.1682 – c.1712.* London: MacDonald & Co.

Morris, R., 1989, *Churches in the Landscape.* London: J.M. Dent.

Morris, R.K., 1983, *The Church in British Archaeology*. CBA Research Report No. 47. London: The Council for British Archaeology.

Moulins, C., 1857, 'Esnandes et Beaumont-de-Perigord, Analyses Comparatives de Deux Eglises Fortifiees du XIV Siecle', *Bulletin Monumental*, **23**, 17–51.

Murray, P.J., 1995, 'The Lay Administration of Church Lands in the Fifteenth and Sixteenth Centuries', *The Scottish Historical Review*, **LXXIV**, 26–44.

Neilson, G., 1895, 'Old Annan', TDGNHAS, **II**, 152–81.

Neilson, G., 1896, 'Churches as Forts', *The Antiquary*, **32**, 265–70.

Neilson, G., 1897, 'The Battle of Sark', TDGNHAS, **13**, 122–131.

Neilson, G., 1899, 'Annals of the Solway until AD 1307', *Transactions of the Glasgow Archaeological Society*, N.S., **3**, 245–308.

Neville, C.J., 1998, *Violence, Custom and Law: The Anglo-Scottish Border Lands in the Later Middle Ages*. Edinburgh: Edinburgh University Press.

Newminster Chart., *Chartularium Abbathiae de Novo Monasterio. The Newminster Cartulary*, edited by James Raine, 1878. Surtees Society Volume 66, Durham: Surtees Society.

Nicholson, R., 1961, 'The Seige of Berwick, 1333', *Scottish Historical Review*, **XL**, 19–42.

Nicholson, R., 1965, *Edward III and the Scots: The Formative Years of a Military Career 1327–1335*. Oxford: Oxford University Press.

Nicholson, W. (ed.), 1705, *Leges Marchiarum, or, Border Laws*. London: Timothy Goodwin.

NLS, National Library of Scotland, Manuscripts Collection (Hutton Collection).

Nor.Est.Acc., edited by James, M.E., 1948, *Estate Accounts of the Earls of Northumberland 1562–1637*. Surtees Society Volume 143, Durham: Surtees Society.

Nor.Pet., edited by Fraser, C.M., 1966, *Ancient Petitions Relating to Northumberland*. Surtees Society Volume 176, Durham: Surtees Society.

O'Neil, B.H., St J., 1952, *Caerlaverock Castle*. Edinburgh: HMSO.

Offler, H.S., 1965, 'A Note on the Early History of the Priory of Carlisle', TCWAAS, N.S., **LXV**, 176–81.

Oman, C., 1979, 'Security in English Churches, AD 1000–1548', *Archaeological Journal*, **136**, 90–98.

OSA, edited by Sir John Sinclair, 1978–9, *The Statistical Account of Scotland 1791–1799 (The Old Statistical Account)*. 20 vols, East Ardsley: EP Publishing Ltd.

Owen, D.D.R., 1997, *William the Lion: Kingship and Culture 1143–1214*. East Linton: Tuckwell.

Page, W., 1893, *The Chartulary of Brinkburn Priory*. Surtees Society Volume 90, Durham: Surtees Society.

Pap.L.Scot. Ben.XIII., edited by McGurk, F., 1976, *Papal Letters to Scotland of Benedict XIII of Avignon 1394–1419*. Edinburgh: Scottish History Society.

Parsons, D., 1962, 'The West Tower at St Andrew's Church, Corbridge', *Archaeologia Aeliana*, 4th Series, **XL**, 171–84.

Parsons, D., 1979, 'Past History and Present Research at All Saints' Church, Brixworth', *Northamptonshire Past Present*, **6**, 61–71.

Paterson, R.C., 1996, *For The Lion: A History of the Scottish Wars of Independence 1296–1357*. Edinburgh: John Donald.

Paterson, R.C., 1997, *My Wound is Deep: A History of the Later Anglo-Scots Wars 1380–1560*. Edinburgh: John Donald.

Paterson, R.C., 1998, *A Land Afflicted: Scotland and the Covenanter Wars 1638–1690*. Edinburgh: John Donald.

Patrick, G., 1903, 'Hulne Priory, Alnwick, Northumberland', *Journal of the British Archaeological Association*. NS., **IX**, 49–58.

Patten, W., 1548, 'Diary', in: Sir J.G. Dalyell, 1798, *Fragments of Scottish History*. Edinburgh: A.Constable.

Perriam, D.R., 1979, 'An Unrecorded Carlisle Church: the Church of the Holy Trinity, Caldewgate', TCWAAS, N.S., **LXXIX**, 51–55.

Perriam, D.R., 1987, 'The Demolition of the Priory of St Mary Carlisle', TCWAAS, Ser.2, **87**, 127–58.

Perriam, D.R., and Robinson, J., 1998, *The Medieval Fortified Buildings of Cumbria*. CWAAS Extra Series, Vol. XXXIX. Kendal: CWAAS.

Pevsner, N., 1957, *The Buildings of England: Northumberland*. 1st edn, Harmondsworth: Penguin.

Pevsner, N., 1967, *The Buildings of England: Cumberland and Westmorland*. Harmondsworth: Penguin.

Pevsner, N., and Metcalf P., 1985, *The Cathedrals of England: Midland, Eastern, & Northern England*. New York: Viking.

Pevsner, N., Grundy, J., McCombie, G., Ryder, P., 1992, *The Buildings of England: Northumberland*. 2nd edn, London: Penguin.

Philips, G., *The Anglo–Scots Wars, 1513–1550, A Military History*. Woodbridge: Boydell Press.

Platt, C., 1990, *The Architecture of Medieval Britain*. New Haven and London: Yale University Press.

Poole, A.L., 1954, *From Domesday Book to Magna Carta 1087–1216*. Oxford: Oxford University Press.

Potter, K.R., (ed.), 1955, *The Historia Novella*, by William of Malmesbury. London: T. Nelson.

Powicke, Sir M., 1962, *The Thirteenth Century*. 2nd edn, Oxford: Oxford University Press.

Prescott, E., 1992, *The English Medieval Hospital 1050–1640*. London: Seaby.

Pride, G.L., 1996, *Dictionary of Scottish Building*. Edinburgh: Rutland Press.

Pryde, G.S., 1965, *The Burghs of Scotland: A Critical List*. London: Oxford University Press.

Rae, T.I., 1966, *The Administration of the Scottish Frontier 1513:1603*. Edinburgh: Edinburgh University Press.

Raine, J. (ed.), 1865, *The Priory of Hexham, its Title Deeds, Black Book, etc. Vol II*. Surtees Society Volume 46, Durham: Surtees Society.

Raine, J.R., 1852, *The History and Antiquities of North Durham*. London: Nichols.

RCHMS, 1914, *List of Ancient and Historical Monuments and Constructions in the County of the Stewartry of Kirkudbright*. Edinburgh: HMSO.

RCHMS, 1915, *Sixth Report and Inventory of Monuments and Constructions in the County of Berwick*. Edinburgh: HMSO.

RCHMS, 1920, *Seventh Report with Inventory of Monuments and Constructions in the County of Dumfries*. Edinburgh: HMSO.

RCHMS, 1956, *An Inventory of the Ancient and Historical Monuments of Roxburghshire*. 2 vols, Edinburgh: HMSO.

RCHMS, 1957, *An Inventory of the Ancient and Historical Monuments of Selkirkshire*. Edinburgh: HMSO.

RCHMS, 1967, *Peeblesshire an Inventory of the Ancient Monuments*. 2 vols, Edinburgh: HMSO

RCHMS, 1997, *Eastern Dumfriesshire an Archaeological Landscape*. Edinburgh: The Stationery Office.

Reed, J., 1991, *The Border Ballads*. 2nd edn, Stocksfield: The Spredden Press.

Reg.Mon.Dunelm., edited by James Raine, 1835, *Reginaldi Monarchi Dunelmensis Libellus de Admiradis Beati Cuthberi Virtutibus*. Surtees Society Volume 1, Durham: Surtees Society.

Reid, R.C., 1958, 'The Monastery at Applegarth', TDGNHAS, 3rd Ser., **35**, 14–19.

Richardson, J.S., 1951, *Sweetheart Abbey*. 2nd edn, Edinburgh: HMSO.

Richardson, J.S., and Wood, M., 1948, *Dryburgh Abbey*. 2nd edn, Edinburgh: HMSO.
Richardson, J.S., and Wood, M., 1949, *Melrose Abbey*. 2nd edn, Edinburgh: HMSO.
Ridpath, G., 1848, *The Border History of England and Scotland*. Berwick: Philip Ridpath.
RMS, edited by J.M. Thomson, *et al.*, 1984, *Registrum Magni Sigilli Regum Scotorum*. 11 vols, Edinburgh: Clark Constable.
Robertson, A., 1935, 'Repentance Tower', TDGNHAS, 3rd Series, **XIX**, 162–8.
Robinson, J., 1982, 'Notes on Brampton Old Church', TCWAAS, N.S., **LXXXII**, 73–89.
Robson, J., 1893, *The Churches and Churchyards of Teviotdale*. Hawick: W. Morrison & Co. Ltd.
Robson, J., 1896, *The Churches and Churchyards of Berwickshire*. Kelso: J. & J.H. Rutherford.
Robson, R., 1989, *The Rise and Fall of the English Highland Clans: Tudor Responses to a Mediaeval Problem*. Edinburgh: John Donald.
Rowland, T.H., 1991, *Waters of Tyne*. Warkworth: Sandhill.
Rowland, T.H., 1994, *Medieval Castles, Towers, Peles, and Bastles of Northumberland*. Warkworth: Sandhill.
RPCS, edited by John Hill Burton, *et al.* 1877–1898, *The Register of the Privy Council of Scotland: 1545–1625*. 14 vols, Edinburgh: H.M. General Register House.
RRS, edited by Duncan, A.A.M., 1988, *Regesta Regum Scottorum. Volume V, The Acts of Robert I*. Edinburgh: Edinburgh University Press.
RRS, edited by Webster, B., 1982, *Regesta Regum Scottorum. Volume VI, The Acts of David II*. Edinburgh: Edinburgh University Press.
RSRS, edited by Burnett, G., 1878–1908, *Rotuli Scaccarii Regum Scotorum*. 23 vols, Edinburgh: H.M. General Register House.
Rushton, S., 1996, 'Recent Work at Low Chibburn', *Archaeology in Northumberland 1995–1996*, 6–7. Morpeth: Northumberland County Council.
Ryder, P.F., 1996a, *Bastle Houses in the Northern Pennines*. Alston: North Pennines Heritage Trust.
Ryder, P.F., 1996b, 'Puzzling Evidence at Elsdon', *Archaeology in Northumberland 1995–1996*, 38–39. Morpeth: Northumberland County Council.
Ryder, P.F., 1999, 'Lesbury, St Mary', *Church Archaeology*, **3**, 54–5.
Salter, M., 1994, *The Old Parish Churches of Scotland*. Malvern: Folly Publications.
Salter, M., 1997a, *The Old Parish Churches of Northumberland*. Malvern: Folly Publications.
Salter, M., 1997b, *The Castles and Tower Houses of Northumberland*. Malvern: Folly Publications.
Salter, M., 1998, *The Old Parish Churches of Cumbria*. Malvern: Folly Publications.
Sanderson, M.H.B., 1982, *Scottish Rural Society in the 16th Century*. Edinburgh: John Donald.
Saunders, A., 1993, *Tynemouth Priory and Castle*. London: English Heritage.
Scott, D., 1899, *Bygone Cumberland and Westmorland*. London: William Andrews.
Scott, J.G., 1988, 'The Origins of Dundrennan and Soulseat Abbeys', TDGNHAS, 3rd Series, **LXIII**, 35–44.
Scott, W., 1815, *The Border Antiquities of England and Scotland*. 2 vols, London: T. Davison.
Scott, W.W., 1993, The March Laws Reconsidered, in: Grant, A., and Stringer, K.J. (eds), *Medieval Scotland: Crown Lordship and Community*, Essays presented to G.W.S. Barrow, 114–130. Edinburgh: Edinburgh University Press.
Scott-Moncrieff, G., 1964, *The Border Abbeys*. Edinburgh: HMSO.
Selkirk, A., and Selkirk, W. (eds) 1993, 'Hoddom', *Current Archaeology*, **135**, 88–92.
Seymour, C., and Randall, J., 1989, *Stobo Kirk: A Guide to the Building and its History*. Selkirk: Walter Thompson.

Sharp, Sir C., 1975, *The Rising in the North the 1569 Rebellion* [reprint of Sir Cuthbert Sharp's *Memorials of the Earls of Northumberland and Westmorland*, 1840]. Durham: Shotton.

Simpson, A.T., and Stevenson, S., 1980a, *Historic Kelso: the archaeological implications of development*. Glasgow: University of Glasgow Dept. of Archaeology.

Simpson, A.T., and Stevenson, S., 1980b, *Historic Lauder: the archaeological implications of development*. Glasgow: University of Glasgow Dept. of Archaeology.

Simpson, A.T., and Stevenson, S., 1980c, *Historic Selkirk: the archaeological implications of development*. Glasgow: University of Glasgow Dept. of Archaeology.

Simpson, A.T., and Stevenson, S., 1981, *Historic Duns: the archaeological implications of development*. Glasgow: University of Glasgow Dept. of Archaeology.

Simpson, W.D., 1939, 'Coldingham Priory: A Famous Border Monastery', *TAASDN*, **IX**, pt.1, 69–86.

Simpson, W.D., 1954, *Craigmillar Castle*, Edinburgh. Edinburgh: HMSO.

Simpson, W.D., 1957, *Hermitage Castle*. Edinburgh: HMSO.

Smailes, A.E., 1968, *North England*. 2nd edn, London: Thomas Nelson.

Smith, I., 1996, 'The Origins and Development of Christianity in North Britain and Southern Pictland', in: Blair, J., and Pyrah, C. (eds), *Church Archaeology Research Directions for the Future*. CBA Research Report 104, 19–37. York: Council for British Archaeology.

Spence, A., 1992–4, *Discovering the Borders*. 2 vols, Edinburgh: John Donald.

St John Hope, W.H., 1887, 'On the Premonstratensian Abbey of St Mary at Alnwick, Northumberland', *Archaeological Journal*, **XLIV**, 337–46.

St John Hope, W.H., 1890, 'On the Whitefriars or Carmelites of Hulne, Northumberland', *Archaeological Journal*, **XLVII**, 105–29.

State Pap. Henry VIII, The Record Commission, 1830–52, *State Papers Published under the Authority of His Majesty's Commission, King Henry VIII*. 11 vols, London: G. Eyre and A. Strahan.

Stell, G., 1977, 'Architecture: the changing needs of society', in: Brown, J.M. (ed.), *Scottish Society in the Fifteenth Century*, 153–83. London: Edward Arnold.

Stell, G., 1981, 'Late Medieval Defences in Scotland', in: Caldwell, D.H. (ed.), *Scottish Weapons and Fortifications 1100–1800*, 21–54. Edinburgh: John Donald.

Stell, G., 1986, *Exploring Scotland's Heritage: Dumfries and Galloway*. Edinburgh: HMSO.

Stell, G., 1991, 'Destruction and Damage: a reassessment of the historical and architectural evidence', in: Macdougall, N. (ed.), *Scotland and War*, 24–35. Edinburgh: John Donald.

Stone, J.C., 1989, *The Pont Manuscript Maps of Scotland, Sixteenth Century Origins of a Blaeu Atlas*. Tring: Map Collector Publications Ltd.

Stones, E.L.G., and Simpson, G.G., 1978, *Edward I and the Throne of Scotland 1290–1296*. 2 vols, Oxford: Oxford University Press.

Storey, R.L., 1955, 'The Manor of Burgh-by-Sands', TCWAAS, N.S., **LIV**, 119–30.

Storey, R.L., 1956, *The Register of Thomas Langley, Bishop of Durham, 1406–1437*. Surtees Society Volume 166, Durham: Surtees Society.

Strang, C.A., 1994, *Borders and Berwick: An Illustrated Architectural Guide to the Scottish Borders and Tweed Valley*. Edinburgh: The Rutland Press.

Summerson, H., 1992, 'Responses to War: Carlisle and the West March in the later fourteenth century', in: Goodman, A., and Tuck, A. (eds), *War and Border Societies in the Middle Ages*, 155–77. London: Routledge.

Summerson, H., 1993, *Medieval Carlisle: the City and the Border from the Late Eleventh to the Mid-Sixteenth Century*. CWAAS, Extra Series, Vol. XXV. 2 vols, Kendal: CWAAS.

Swift, F.B., 1959, 'Uldale Church', TCWAAS, N.S., **LIX**, 51–64.

Swift, F.B., 1966, 'The Oldest Parish Registers of Bassenthwaite', TCWAAS, N.S., **LXVI**, 276-92.

Swift, F.B., 1975, 'The Old Church of Allhallows', TCWAAS, N.S., **LXXV**, 119-31.

Swift, F.B., and Bulman, C.G., 1965, 'Ireby Church', TCWAAS, N.S., **LXV**, 222-39.

Tabraham, C., 1972, 'Excavations at Kelso Abbey, Roxburghshire', *PSAS*, **104**, 248-51.

Tabraham, C., 1981, *Dundrennan Abbey*. Edinburgh: HMSO.

Tabraham, C., 1985, *Smailholm Tower*. Edinburgh: HMSO.

Tabraham, C., 1986a, *Jedburgh Abbey*. Edinburgh: HMSO.

Tabraham, C., 1986b, *Scottish Castles and Fortifications*. Edinburgh: HMSO.

Tabraham, C.J., and Good, G.L., 1981, 'The Artillery Fortification at Threave Castle, Galloway', in: Caldwell, D.H. (ed.), *Scottish Weapons and Fortifications 1100-1800*, 55-72. Edinburgh: John Donald.

Taylor, G.N., n.d., *The Story of Elsdon*. 2nd edn, Elsdon: St Cuthbert's Church.

Taylor, H.M., 1978, *Anglo-Saxon Architecture*. Vol. 3, Cambridge: Cambridge University Press.

Taylor, H.M., and Taylor, J., 1965, *Anglo-Saxon Architecture*. 2 vols, Cambridge: Cambridge University Press.

Taylor, W.T., 1959, *Hexham Abbey*. Hexham: Abbey Press.

Terry, C.S., 1899, *The Life and Campaigns of Alexander Leslie, First Earl of Leven*. London: Longman, Green.

Thomas, C., 1971, *The Early Christian Archaeology of North Britain*. London: Oxford University Press.

Thompson, A.H., 1949, *Lindisfarne Priory*. London: HMSO.

Thomson, T.D., 1972, *Coldingham Priory*. Berwick-on-Tweed: How and Blackhall.

Tomlinson, W.W., 1888, *Comprehensive Guide to the County of Northumberland*. Newcastle-on-Tyne: Walter Scott.

Tough, D.L.W., 1928, *The Last Years of a Frontier*. Oxford: Oxford University Press.

Toy, S., 1939, *Castles: A Short History of Fortifications from 1600 B.C. to A.D. 1600*. London: Heinemann.

Tracy, C., 1992, 'The St Albans Abbey Watching Chamber: A Re-assessment', *Journal of the British Archaeological Association*, **CXLV**, 104-11.

Tranter, N., 1962, *The Fortified House in Scotland: Volume 1 South-East Scotland*. Edinburgh: Oliver and Boyd.

Tranter, N., 1965, *The Fortified House in Scotland: Volume 3 South-West Scotland*. Edinburgh: Oliver and Boyd.

Tranter, N., 1987, *The Illustrated Portrait of the Border Country*. 2nd edn, London: Hale.

Traquair, P., 1998, *Freedom's Sword: Scotland's Wars of Independence*. London: Harper Collins.

TSA, edited by Strawhorn, J., Boyd, W., *et al.* 1951-92, *The Third Statistical Account of Scotland*. 33 vols, Edinburgh: Scottish Academic Press.

Tuck, A., 1979, *Border Warfare*. London: HMSO.

Turner, R. (ed.), 1996, *Discovery and Excavation in Scotland 1996*. Edinburgh: Council for Scottish Archaeology.

Tyson, C., 1992, 'The Battle of Otterburn: When and where was it fought?', in: Goodman, A., and Tuck, A. (eds) *War and Border Societies in the Middle Ages*, 65-93. London: Routledge.

Vickers, K.H., 1922, *A History of Northumberland: Volume XI. The Parishes of Carham, Branxton, Kirknewton, Wooler, and Ford*. Newcastle: Andrew Reid & Co. Ltd.

Wallis, John., 1769, *The Natural History and Antiquities of Northumberland*. 2 vols, London: W. and W. Strahan.

Ward Davis, C.D., 1991, *The Great Parish of Simonburn*. Simonburn: St Mungo's Church Council.

Watson, F., 1998, *Under the Hammer: Edward I and Scotland 1286–1307*. East Linton: Tuckwell.

Watson, G., 1914, 'Wheel Kirk, Liddesdale', *Transactions of the Hawick Archaeological Society 1914*, 20–22.

Watson, G., 1921, 'Bell-Kirk: A Border Chapel', *Transactions of the Hawick Archaeological Society 1921*, 18–20.

Watson, G., 1974, *The Border Reivers*. London: Hale.

Watson, G.P.H., and Bradley, G., 1937, *Carlisle Castle*. London: HMSO.

Whellan, W., 1860, *The History and Topography of the Counties of Cumberland and Westmorland: . . .* Pontefract: W.Whellan & Co.; Whittaker & Co.

White, J.T., 1973, *The Scottish Border and Northumberland*. London: Eyre Methuen.

White, R., 1859, 'The Battle of Flodden', *Archaeologia Aeliana*. N.S., **3**, 232–3.

Wilfrid, *The Life of Bishop Wilfrid*, edited by Colgrave, B., 1927. Cambridge: The University Press.

Willis-Fear, M.J.W., 1965, *Blackfriars: It's Past and Future*. 2nd edn, Newcastle-upon-Tyne: City and County of Newcastle-upon-Tyne.

Wilson, F.R., 1870, *An Architectural Survey of the Churches in the Archdeaconry of Lindisfarne*. Newcastle: M. and M.W. Lambert.

Wilson, J., 1901–5, *A History of the County of Cumberland*, The Victoria History of the Counties of England Series. 2 vols, London: Constable.

Wilson, J., 1972, 'Two Finds from Lochmaben Old Church Yard', TDGNHAS, 3rd Ser., **49**, 119–20.

Wilson, T., 1970, *History of Crosthwaite Church*, Keswick. Revised by J.W. Kaye. 2nd edn, Keswick: G.W.McKane and Sons.

Wood, G.O., 1987, 'The Norman Church at Minto', *Transactions of the Hawick Archaeological Society 1987*, 9–32.

Wright, A.B., 1823, *An Essay Towards a History of Hexham*. Alnwick: W. Davison.

Yeoman, P., 1995, *Medieval Scotland*. London: Batsford.

Young, A., 1997, *Robert the Bruce's Rivals: The Comyns, 1212–1314*. East Linton: Tuckwell.

INDEX

County names follow those of the historic county divisions, prior to modern local government reorganization

Berwks.= Berwickshire
Cumb. = Cumberland
Dumf. = Dumfriesshire
Kirkud. = Kirkudbrightshire

Northd. = Northumberland
Peebl. = Peeblesshire
Roxb. = Roxburghshire
Selk. = Selkirkshire